Virginia Woolf Writing the World:

Selected Papers from the Twenty-fourth Annual International Conference on Virginia Woolf

VIRGINIA WOOLF WRITING THE WORLD:

Selected Papers from the Twenty-fourth Annual International Conference on Virginia Woolf

EDITED BY

PAMELA L. CAUGHIE AND DIANA L. SWANSON

CLEMSON UNIVERSITY PRESS

Works produced at Clemson University by the Center for Electronic and Digital Publishing (CEDP), including *The South Carolina Review* and its themed series "Virginia Woolf International," "Ireland in the Arts and Humanities," and "James Dickey Revisited," may be found at our website: http://www.clemson.edu/cedp/press. Contact the director at 864-656-5399 for information.

Published by Clemson University Digital Press at the Center for Electronic and Digital Publishing, Clemson University, Clemson, South Carolina.

Produced with the Adobe Creative Suite CS6 and Microsoft Word. This book is set in Adobe Garamond Pro and was printed by CPI Group (UK) Ltd, Croydon, CR0 4YY

Editorial Assistants: Karen Stewart, Tenesia Head, and Charis Chapman.

Front cover art adapted from a design by Ginny Sykes.

Table of Contents

v

ANIMAL AND NATURAL WORLDS

WRITING AND WORLDMAKING

Introduction

by Pamela L. Caughie and Diana L. Swanson

In early June, 2014, over 230 students, professors, independent scholars, and common readers from around the world came together in Chicago for the 24th Annual International Conference on Virginia Woolf. Chicago, an international hub, was an ideal location for a conference entitled "Woolf Writing the World"; two years earlier, in 2012, Chicago set a visitation record, hosting over 46 million visitors from around the world (Wikipedia). These figures may dwarf our own, but the conference created its own international hub. On a world map displayed in the conference lounge, using pins (with points!), conference participants reported coming from eighteen countries, listed below (see Fig. 1).

Argentina	Japan	South Korea
Australia	Mexico	Sweden
Brazil	The Netherland	Taiwan
Canada	Norway	Taiwan
Colombia	Poland	United Kingdom
France	Qatar	United States

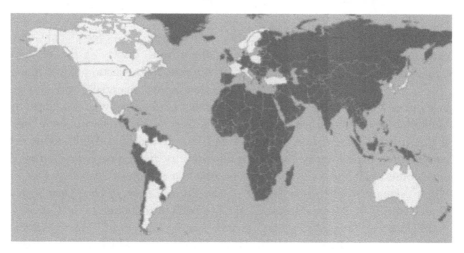

Figure 1: Countries from which participants traveled to the 2014 Woolf conference (shaded in light gray). Travel Map Generator (http://www.29travels.com/travelmap/index.php)

Co-sponsored by Loyola University Chicago and Northern Illinois University, Woolf Writing the World took place on Loyola's beautiful lakeshore campus in a meticulously restored art deco skyscraper, The Mundelein Center, built by nuns during the Great Depression, a history memorialized by Prudence Moylan, Professor Emerita of Loyola, at the opening reception. The Sisters of Charity of the Blessed Virgin Mary (BVMs), in response to a call by Cardinal George Mundelein for a Catholic women's college in Chicago, raised the funds to build the iconic skyscraper in 1929, the first self-contained skyscraper college for women. Rejecting the Cardinal's wish for a building in the classical style, the nuns chose the art deco design, with its striking main entrance flanked by two guardian angels, Uriel and Jophiel (see Fig. 2). A fitting setting for a Virginia Woolf conference, The Mundelein Center allowed us to experience a woman's college from the *inside*.

Figure 2: The Mundelein Center, Loyola University Chicago

The conference officially began on June 4th with a Bloomsbury Exhibit at The Newberry Library, an internationally recognized independent humanities research library located in the heart of Chicago's Gold Coast. The exhibit, displaying the Newberry's extensive collection of Woolf and Bloomsbury materials, was curated by modernist scholar and Newberry staff member Liesl Olson, who was joined by Mark Hussey, Distinguished Professor of English at Pace University in New York, at the opening presentation. As Olson and Hussey provided details about the materials on display, many connecting Bloomsbury and Chicago, we borrowed one another's cell phones to snap pictures of a first edition of *The Voyage Out*; of Woolf's signature on the title page of a first-edition *A Room of One's Own* or in a limited edition of "Street Haunting"; of Clive Bell's introduction to the *Catalog of An Exhibition of Original Drawings by Pablo Picasso, 1923*; or of Katherine Mansfield's desk blotter. That evening The Poetry Foundation—which publishes *Poetry* magazine, founded by Harriet Monroe in 1912—welcomed participants to its auditorium for "Off the Shelf: A Woolf-Inspired Poetry Reading" by Canadian poet Sina Queyras, author of *Unleashed* and *Lemon Hound*, among other collections. Other special events over the next four days included a lunchtime presentation of *The Glass Inward*, an fascinating multi-media performance inspired by *Orlando* and created by Anna Henson, a visual and performance artist formerly of DePaul University and now living in New York; an enchanting performance of Woolf's story "A Mark on the Wall" by Adrianne Krstansky (Brandeis University) and Abigail Killeen (Bowdoin College) that brought Woolf's story to life and demonstrated how we can come to know Woolf's writings through our bodies as well as our minds; guided tours of The Art Institute of Chicago's Modern Wing by Paula Wisotzki, Fine Arts professor at Loyola University Chicago, who introduced us to its many treasures, the well-known and the obscure, such as *Exquisite Corpse* (1928), a drawing made in pen, pencils and crayons by Man Ray, Joan Miró, Yves Tanguy, and Max Morise in the form of the parlor game played in *The Years* (http://www.artic.edu/aic/collections/artwork/119117?search_no=2&index=3); and a brilliant, uproarious performance of Sarah Ruhl's *Orlando* directed by Ann Shanahan of Loyola's Department of Fine and Performing Arts (see Fig. 3). Performances were followed by talkbacks with Professor Shanahan, co-host Diana Swanson (Northern Illinois University), Jaime Hovey (DePaul University), Anna Henson, and the student actors from Loyola. Christine Froula enthused afterwards, "with its magical flow of bodies and voices, Sarah Ruhl's *Orlando* seems to me especially enhanced when young actors perform it." These special events allowed us to move through the city, across the campus, and into the community as well as to virtually travel the world through the conference presentations.

Figure 3: *Orlando* (credit: Julia Eberhardt, Photographer and Designer)

Fifty-eight panels with 181 papers, seven seminars, and three keynotes made up the bulk of the conference. Twenty-seven papers and two of the three keynotes are included here. Mark Hussey organized the first keynote event, an inspiring and thought-provoking roundtable on Woolf and Violence, and a most fitting opening as we observed that month the 100th anniversary of the start of the Great War. Presenting to a standing-room-only audience in a hall overlooking Lake Michigan, Hussey and his co-presenters—Sarah Cole, Ashley Foster, Christine Froula, and Jean Mills—made us all confront the ethical and political implications not just of Woolf's writings but of our own writing and teaching on Woolf. Maud Ellmann (University of Chicago) presented the second keynote address with a highly engaging lecture on how war—specifically World War II—resonates in the fiction of Virginia Woolf and Sylvia Townsend Warner. Ellmann's lecture took an atmospheric perspective, focusing on what their fiction tells us about "*war in the air*, where words and weapons, wireless and weather coincide." Tuzyline Jita Allan (Baruch College, CUNY) gave the final, provocative keynote address, "The Voyage In, Out, and Beyond: Virginia Woolf and Postcolonialism," in which she revisited the impact of postcolonial criticism on Woolf studies and feminist criticism more generally. Arguing that postcolonial Woolf criticism is an unfinished project, Allan challenged us to accept the responsibility of unearthing "Woolf's racial knowledge that lies in her historical subtexts," a challenge that demands we confront our "knowledge deficit" of the black Atlantic. Unfortunately, Professor Allan was unable to contribute to this volume.

Although themes of war and peace prevailed at the conference given its commemorative year, panel and paper topics ranged widely, from the perennially interesting (trauma, feminism, nature, cinema, Bloomsbury homosexuality) to emerging critical concerns (animal studies, ecology, queer studies, object oriented ontology) to the delightfully quirky (with panels entitled "Propaganda, Codebreakers, and Spies," "Ghosts and Hauntings," and "Horses, Donkeys, and Dogs, Oh My!"). Given the conference theme, many papers placed Woolf in the context of European, African, Asian, and Middle Eastern writers, histories, and classrooms. Panel presentations took us to Brazil, Canada, France, Greece, India, Qatar, Sweden, Taiwan as well as the US and the UK. We sat in various classrooms, literally, of course, but also figuratively—a feminist theory classroom in the Middle East, a community college classroom, a composition classroom, a global citizenship classroom—and learned about teaching Woolf in these contexts. We investigated various kinds of worlds created by Woolf: natural worlds and animal worlds; worlds of forests and flowers, butterflies and moths; ethical and philosophical worlds; homosexual and queer worlds; and the world of two world wars. Between sessions, as we moved through the spaces of that 1930 architectural feat of the Mundelein skyscraper, we heard the constant buzz of conversation, outbursts of laughter, and the din of camaraderie that are the signs of a successful party. Had there been curtains hanging, we would have beaten them back!

The diversity of participants and topics at this conference made us wonder how far Woolf's reach extends. To get a sense of where Woolf scholarship is being read across the globe, we ran a search of one scholar's (and by no means the most well-known or well-published Woolf scholar) publications on Woolf that are available on her university's eCommons. In one 30-day period, her work was downloaded 297 times in 51 countries across six continents. The countries are listed below:

Algeria	Indonesia	Norway
Australia	Iran	Pakistan
Bangladesh	Ireland	Portugal
Brazil	Israel	Romania
Canada	Italy	Russian Federation
China	Jamaica	Rwanda
Croatia	Japan	Saudi Arabia
Cyprus	Jordan	Slovakia
Czech Republic	Kenya	Slovenia
Egypt	Lebanon	South Korea
France	Luxemburg	Spain
Georgia	Malta	Sweden
Germany	Mauritania	Turkey
Hong Kong	Mexico	Ukraine
Hungary	Morocco	United Kingdom
Iceland	Nepal	United States
India	The Netherlands	Zambia

The next month brought 386 downloads of her Woolf scholarship. And in a year's time, between March 2014 and March 2015, she had well over 3,000 downloads in 78 countries (see Fig. 4). We cite these examples as evidence of the continued, and it seems growing, interest in Virginia Woolf around the world. Our conference title, "Woolf writing the world," might also have been phrased "the world reading, and writing, Woolf."

Figure 4: Map of eCommons downloads: the darker the shading, the higher the number of downloads (credit: Margaret Heller)

The conference theme, Writing the World, was motivated by our desire to see what kinds of answers people—scholars, teachers, students, common readers, artists—would have to the question of whether and how Woolf still matters in the world. We, two white American women scholars of English literature, believe that Woolf still matters—we spend and have spent much of our scholarly and teacherly time and energy with Woolf in one way or another. But did other people from around the world, from different social and geographical locations and from different generations, believe that Woolf matters, that Woolf speaks to them or to their students or to questions that resonate deeply today around the globe? The answers we received from Canada, the UK, the US, from Turkey, Taiwan, and Qatar, were many and insightful. You will find some of them here in this book.

Several major themes run through the papers people presented about how Woolf matters in the world today: violence, war, and the quest for peace; Woolf as a world writer; Woolf's writing of animal and natural worlds; and how writing itself is world-making. Laced throughout these papers are messages about how Woolf's writing is a rich resource for thinking, feeling, writing about, and acting upon urgent questions of meaning, community, and justice.

Most striking to us are the connections that appear again and again through-out these papers. So much of the received wisdom and scholarly consensus about everything from modernism to globalization emphasizes breaks and gaps, con-flicts and irresolvable—even incommensurable—differences. As Erica Gene Delsandro points out, for example, the common narrative of modernism is that of "generation gaps" between the Victorians and the modernists (such as Woolf) and between the modernists and the "Younger Generation" (such as Auden and Isherwood). But Delsandro sees important continuities between Woolf and Ish-erwood, shared values about war and peace, and some similar literary strategies. And over and over again, writers in this volume (and speakers at the conference) reveal continuities and connections between generations, between the social and political landscapes in Woolf's day and in ours, and they find Woolf's writings making connections across classes, genders, nations, and the arts and sciences.

This is to say, the connections are there despite the differences threading through them. Throughout her writing life, Woolf continued to ring changes on central questions of war and peace, imperialism and community, human and nonhuman nature, and the power of art, and her writing continues to inform and inspire diverse critical and creative work.

As Mark Hussey says in his introduction to the keynote roundtable on Woolf and violence, "it is a long time since it has been possible to think of Woolf in isolation from her contemporaries or as a voice disconnected from the political currents of her time" (2). He, Sarah Cole, J. Ashley Foster, Christine Froula, and Jean Mills approach Woolf's connections to "political currents" from a fruitful diversity of perspectives—pedagogy, literary form, modernism's pacifist history, the long history of Western cultural traditions, and social activism. They find that war and violence are constantly at hand and relevant, and that Woolf's writing and praxis continue to inform the search to delineate sources of violence and to form peace-making practices and movements. As Ashley Foster writes, "fighting for Woolf is a 'habit,' something cultivated and taught, and therefore can be either socially encouraged or sublimated" (8). All five of these scholars connect not only Woolf but also modernism to pacifism and situate Woolf's interest in violence, war, and peace-making in material historical contexts. In various ways, they each answer "yes" to Mark Hussey's question "Does Woolf's "thinking is my fighting" (*D5* 285) really make a difference now?"

Judith Allen and Charles Andrews, in different ways, assert Woolf's relevance to current political controversies regarding government surveillance, propaganda, justifications of war, and peace activism. Paula Maggio argues both sides in the debate about whether or not Woolf should be considered pacifist or feminist, undermining the division between the "sides." Christine Haskill demonstrates connections between the "sex war" and the Great War and shows that Woolf's arguments in *Three Guineas* draw upon rather than deny late-19th-century New Woman feminism. David Deutsch and Ann Martin connect culture and industry, respectively, to Woolf's writings on war and peace, enriching our understanding of Woolf's engagement with contemporary developments in both music and manufacturing. Eleanor McNees shows that Woolf's early drafts of *The Years*, prior to Woolf's heavy editing, weave connections as well as reveal distinctions among the social classes in their responses to World War I. Many of these threads are lost when Woolf deletes a big "chunk" from the novel. Finally, in her keynote lecture, Maud Ellmann connects the now-canonical Woolf with the non-canonical Sylvia Townsend Warner, tracing the themes of war (in the air) and news (on the air) in their public and private writing during the Spanish Civil War and World War II. Warner, unlike Woolf, supported the use of war against fascism; however, both "Woolf and Warner," Ellmann notes, "remind us of the atmosphere of war—an atmosphere in which the thunder and lightning of the bombing raids can scarcely be distinguished from the weather" (77).

Ever-present questions about war, violence, and feminism thread their ways through the essays about Woolf as/and "World Writer(s)." Erin Amann Holliday-Karre's approach to the question of whether and how Woolf matters in the world today is pedagogical; she offers an account of her experience teaching *Three Guineas* to women students in Qatar. Holliday-Karre contrasts Woolf's feminism with that of the International Women's Alliance (IWA), which embarked on a world-wide campaign in the 1930s and whose liberal humanist feminism led to an all-too-common insistence on the oppression of Middle Eastern women. Resisting such a claim, her students from various Middle-Eastern cultures connect with but also question Woolf's ideas about feminism as regards education, religion, and the sociopolitical significance of clothing. David J. Fine discusses teaching in the Global Citizenship Program at Lehigh University in Pennsylvania, using *Three Guineas* to unsettle his students and challenge them to more rigorously interrogate their own privileges. Both Holliday-Karre and Fine critique intellectual and political "fads" and Western truisms about "feminism," "globalization," and "global citizenship."

Taking a different approach to Woolf as a world writer, Matthew Beeber and Alan Chih-chien Hsieh engage closely with Woolf's fiction to demonstrate Woolf's own "global" engagement. Beeber offers an analysis of *Orlando* as a knowing satire of Orientalism that challenges academic and popular views of Constantinople/the Ottoman Empire/the East as androgynous and feminized. Hsieh refers to the scenes of reading and of cultural contact in *The Voyage Out* to argue for a "postcolonial Woolf." Responding in part to "the ethical turn/return proposed by the postcolonial scholar Simon Gikandi," Hsieh argues that Rachel is moved by the gaze of the colonial Other and that *The Voyage Out* "registers a planetary love that entails an ethical reading of alterity" (118). Departing from the focus on a single novel in the context of global issues, Shao-Hua Wang analyzes Woolf's influence on another world writer—one of the most famous post-1949 Taiwanese writers, Hsien-yung Pai. Noting that Pai himself attested to the influence of *Mrs. Dalloway* on his "Wandering in the Garden, Waking from a Dream" (1968), Wang traces Woolf's influence on technique and theme in "Wandering in the Garden," showing that the novel's representation of the lived moment was one inspiration for Pai's story.

Susan Stanford Friedman makes a different kind of world connection in her "'Shakespeare's Sister': Woolf in the World before *A Room of One's Own*." Friedman suggests reading Woolf's tropic/iconic theories (a room of one's own, killing the angel in the house, as a woman I have no country, Shakespeare's sister) as travelling through distance and time as "part of a wider, even potentially worldwide discourse for which she remains central, but only as part of the story" (124). Friedman argues for a transnational literary genealogy independent of direct influences. Like Holliday-Karre, Friedman critiques the narrative of knowledge-creation, including that of feminism, that places the West at its center, and as its origin, and the rest of the globe as periphery. Finally, Steven Putzel returns to the topic of war and peace, analyzing Leonard Woolf's rigorous and evolving assessments of the political and ethical matters at stake in Palestine and Israel from WWI onwards. Putzel argues that "the evolution of Woolf's thoughts on Palestine, Zionism, and the State of Israel can help us navigate this international, national, and educational controversy in a broader historical context, and can increase our appreciation for the ways Woolf's essays, letters, Labour Party white papers, and his autobiography helped to 'write the world'" (129). As the essays in the "War and Peace" section do with regard to Virginia's writings, Putzel's essay connects Leonard's writings to political currents today.

The third section extends the connections beyond the human world to animal and natural worlds. As animal studies and ecocriticism have been burgeoning in literary studies in general, Woolf's works are proving fertile ground for such approaches. Elizabeth Hanna Hanson's and Vicki Tromanhauser's essays focus on the significance of animals in Woolf's fiction and nonfiction. Hanson singles out the trope of the donkey and connects it to themes of feminism, class, social justice, art, propaganda, and the writing process. "The donkey has its place in the literary tradition," writes Hanson, "but it can also make us aware of the power relations that have made that tradition possible" (141). Tromanhauser evokes the literary and ideological work of the dog in *Three Guineas*, comparing the sensory and cognitive worlds of dogs and women. Woolf "endows her narrator with canine aptitudes in order better to navigate the fraught terrain of contemporary social life and sniff out its repressive structures" (143). Moving to inanimate nature, Elisa Kay Sparks turns to an aspect of nature generally considered far from the human and cultural, forests. Forests, as Sparks points out, are usually considered wild and thus the opposite of gardens as places of cultivation and civilization. In contrast, Sparks shows that in Woolf's works, "while a few basic patterns for forest associations can be mapped, in many cases forests are endowed with a variety of meanings so diverse as to seem to purposefully dissolve preconceived generalities, a practice of complicating and undercutting dichotomies" (173). Kim Sigouin, Elsa Högberg, Michael Tratner, and Joyce E. Kelley sustain this theme of undercutting dichotomies and blurring categories. Sigouin, for example, argues that in *To the Lighthouse* Woolf's language "erodes sharp distinctions between human and nonhuman nature" (167), arguing that cultural and natural rhythms are constantly at play with each other throughout the novel. In her analysis of "Kew Gardens," Kelley finds that Woolf shows the large in the small, the macrocosm in the microcosm, and connects "the worlds of the seen and the unseen" (161). Högberg brings object-oriented ontology as a form of posthumanism to bear on Woolf's writing of inanimate objects (e.g., teacups, rocks). She argues that the way Woolf imagines an object world independent of human thought or action highlights the objectification and vulnerability of human beings as well as the need for human humility and responsibility. Tratner offers a new reading of *The Waves* in light of early 20th-century neuroscience; Woolf's contemporaries in physiology and psychology were proposing that the body and the mind were not two, but rather one. "Woolf's essays and novels," Tratner suggests, "seek to develop ways of understanding this new vision of the body [as outside civilization] and in particular to counter the type of masculinity being proposed as the only way to control such a body" (158). This type of masculinity, imperial and dominating, is represented by Percival and was promulgated by Mussolini and Hitler.

Thus Tratner, through an analysis based in sciences contemporary to Woolf, brings us back to themes of feminism, war, and justice. The final section of this volume, on "Writing and Worldmaking," begins with an essay that treats feminism in a manner counter to the expected, specifically, the progressive narrative of women's development into self-defined and self-sufficient agents-in-the-world. Anne Cunningham argues that Rachel Vinrace in *The Voyage Out* can be read as an example of "negative feminism," feminism as refusal. Cunningham sees Woolf creating a "modernist aesthetics of failure" and, like the other essays in this final section of the book, discusses how Woolf's writing directs our attention to writing itself. Maayan P. Dauber argues that Woolf creates a modernist form of pathos in *To the Lighthouse*, a pathos which functions to create characters and relations in a world where to know another is impossible. In "The Reconciliations of Poetry in Woolf's *Between the Acts*; or Why It's 'perfectly ridiculous to call it a novel'," Amy Huseby delves into the texture, rhythm, and form of Woolf's prose itself, showing how she developed a new kind of writing—"euphonic prose." Kelle Sills Mullineaux, in "Virginia Woolf, Composition Theorist," demonstrates how Woolf's reflections on the writing process, in her essays and novels, constitute an enabling composition theory that can help students "write without fear" (202). Finally, Madelyn Detloff's essay, "The Precarity of 'Civilization' in Woolf's Creative Worldmaking," returns us to the question with which we began: does Woolf's writing matter in the world today and, if so, how? As Detloff says, "to contemplate how and why an aesthetically complex and intellectually challenging artist such as Woolf still matters today for her artistry is to open up a more fundamental conversation about why and how the life of the mind matters. This pursuit is no less trivial today than it was seventy-three years ago when Woolf, in her last novel, *Between the Acts* (written between 1938 and 1941—some very dark years in European history), depicted a community coming together to rebuild '[c]ivilization […] in ruins […] by human effort' in the course of an ordinary village pageant (BTA 181)" (207).

We will let you read Detloff's answers for yourself. Let us just say that, *au fond*, Detloff's essay, and all the essays in this book, reconfirm the creative power of writing, and Woolf's writing in particular, to make and re-make meaning and community. Woolf's writing does matter to how violence and peace-making continue around the world today; how literature circulates globally; how, at least in the "First World," we continue to struggle to redefine our relationship to other animals and to the "environment"; and how writing powerfully worlds and re-worlds us.

Acknowledgments

In the years of preparation that go into organizing a conference as large as the annual conference on Virginia Woolf, one accrues many debts of gratitude. Special thanks go to the institutions that provided the funding for the event: the Colleges of Arts and Sciences, the departments of English, and the women's studies, gender studies and LGBT studies programs at Loyola University Chicago and Northern Illinois University. The *Orlando* performance was made possible by a grant from the Illinois Humanities Council (IHC) and the generous support of Loyola's Department of Fine and Performing Arts, Gannon Center for Women and Leadership, and Room(s) Theatre. For the conference logo and striking artwork that graces the cover of this book, we are grateful to Chicago artist Ginny Sykes and her assistant, Ruby Barnes. For the Vanessa Bell-inspired drawings that decorated the conference program, some of which also adorn this book, thanks go to Robyn Byrd. For the conference website creation and maintenance, we thank Katie Faber of Northern Illinois University. We gratefully acknowledge the Conference Committee who helped select the exciting papers and workshops for this conference: Kristin Czarnecki (Georgetown College), Beth Daugherty (Otterbein University), Jeanne Dubino (Appalachian State University), Christine Froula (Northwestern University), Ann Martin (University of Saskatchewan), and Vara Neverow (Southern Connecticut State University). Special thanks to our smart, responsible, creative, and dedicated Graduate Assistants who handled so many emails, spreadsheets, phone calls, Dropbox files, meetings, and even tastings, and provided not only help with various tasks but also creative advice and counsel: Sarah Polan and Katie Dyson (Loyola University Chicago) and Robyn Byrd (Northern Illinois University). For her invaluable assistance on this collection, our heartfelt thanks to our collaborator, Andrea Fryling (Northern Illinois University). And for his guidance, patience, and editorial acumen, we express our deep gratitude to Wayne Chapman.

VIRGINIA WOOLF
STANDARD ABBREVIATIONS
(as established by *Woolf Studies Annual*)

AHH	*A Haunted House*
AROO	*A Room of One's Own*
AWD	*A Writer's Diary*, ed. Leonard Woolf
BP	*Books and Portraits*
BTA	*Between the Acts*
CDB	*The Captain's Death Bed and Other Essays*
CE	*Collected Essays* (ed. Leonard Woolf, 4 vols.: *CE*1, *CE*2, *CE*3, *CE*4)
CR1	*The Common Reader*
CR2	*The Common Reader, Second Series*
CSF	*The Complete Shorter Fiction* (ed. Susan Dick)
D	*The Diary of Virginia Woolf* (5 vols.: D1, D2, D3, D4, D5)
DM	*The Death of the Moth and Other Essays*
E	*The Essays of Virginia Woolf* (ed. Stuart Clarke and Andrew McNeillie, 6 vols.: *E*1, *E*2, *E*3, *E*4, *E*5, *E*6)
F	*Flush*
FR	*Freshwater*
GR	*Granite and Rainbow: Essays*
HPGN	*Hyde Park Gate News* (ed. Gill Lowe)
JR	*Jacob's Room*
JRHD	*Jacob's Room: The Holograph Draft* (ed. Edward L. Bishop)
L	*The Letters of Virginia Woolf* (ed. Nigel Nicolson and Joanne Trautmann, 6 vols.: *L*1, *L*2, *L*3, *L*4, *L*5, *L*6)
M	*The Moment and Other Essays*
MEL	*Melymbrosia*
MOB	*Moments of Being*
MT	*Monday or Tuesday*
MD	*Mrs. Dalloway*
ND	*Night and Day*
O	*Orlando*
PA	*A Passionate Apprentice*
RF	*Roger Fry*
TG	*Three Guineas*
TTL	*To the Lighthouse*
TW	*The Waves*
TY	*The Years*
VO	*The Voyage Out*
WF	*Women and Fiction: The Manuscript Versions of* A Room of One's Own (ed. S. P. Rosenbaum)

War and Peace

ROUNDTABLE: WOOLF AND VIOLENCE

by Mark Hussey, with Sarah Cole, J. Ashley Foster, Christine Froula, and Jean Mills

The reason why it is easy to kill another person must be that one's imagination is too sluggish to conceive what his life means to him—the infinite possibilities of a succession of days which are furled in him, & have already been spent.

Virginia Woolf,
Diary, August 27, 1918

When Diana Swanson and Pamela Caughie first invited me to organize this roundtable, we discussed bringing together some of the contributors to *Virginia Woolf and War*, the 1991 essay collection published in the Syracuse UP series, Studies on Peace and Conflict Resolution. But in the more than two decades since I claimed in that volume that "*all* Woolf's work is deeply concerned with war; that it helps redefine our understanding of the nature of war; and that from her earliest to her final work she sought to explore and make clear the connections between private and public violence, between the domestic and the civic effects of patriarchal society, between male supremacy and the absence of peace, and between ethics and aesthetics" (3), there has been such an abundance of sophisticated work done on violence in its many forms, both in the context of modernist studies and of Woolf scholarship generally, extending and complicating our understanding of violence, conflict, force and aesthetics, that a retrospective look seemed likely to be less valuable than more current reflections. It is a long time since it has been possible to think of Woolf in isolation from her contemporaries or as a voice disconnected from the political currents of her time. *Virginia Woolf and War* played its part in that transformation of Woolf's reception.

The four scholars on this roundtable each have thought deeply about issues of violence, war, peace, conflict, force, and form in the work of Virginia Woolf. In *At The Violet Hour: Modernism and Violence in England and Ireland*, Sarah Cole describes Woolf as "one of the great formalists of violence in the twentieth century" (37), a description that brought home to me the vast change in Woolf's cultural presence effected by the past few decades of scholarship. Ashley Foster's work examines the interrelationships among pacifism, modernism, and war and tries to recuperate the lost threads of modernism's pacifist history. "Stopped at the Border," her *Three Guineas*-inspired reflection on the force of borders encountered with her own body, is a trenchant manifestation of Woolf's continuing urgency as a thinker on twenty-first century questions. Christine Froula's scholarship on modernist writers has consistently made visible the many ways in which those writers were aware of and immersed in a Western literary tradition that has been entangled with violence from its origins. Jean Mills's engagement with Woolf and the classical tradition and how that informs peace studies and pedagogy is deeply informed by the voices of her students, often themselves veterans of wars, foreign and domestic.

In preparing for the roundtable, I suggested a number of questions or topics which the participants were free to take up or not in brief preliminary remarks. What follows is an expanded version of those suggestions.

Violence never is a problem to be studied in some objective or neutral fashion. It brings to the fore most clearly the realization that education and critical pedagogy are by definition forms of political intervention. (Evans, "Inaugural Statement")

How do we enact such intervention in our literature classes? What is the relation of Woolf's writing and thought to peace studies and the pedagogy of non-violence? Mills, for example, reads Jane Ellen Harrison's "Epilogue on the War: Peace with Pacifism" (*Alpha and Omega* 1915) alongside Woolf's *Three Guineas* and sees both helping to "create a vocabulary and a language for discussing peace, which in turn lays an early foundation for the theories and methodologies of global pacifism, peace studies, and peace research" (135).

What are the sources of violence and war?

In Woolf's lifetime, a great deal of attention was given to anthropological explanations of the roots of violence. In "The Daughter's Seduction," Froula describes the unfolding of the Western ethos according to a "hysterical cultural script: the cultural text that dictates to males and females alike the necessity of silencing woman's speech when it threatens the father's power" (623). She discovers that script by placing the violent marriage plot of the *Iliad*—the beginning of our literature's war canon—alongside Freud's accounts of "hysterical" female patients (628–29). Mills, in turn, explains that as "one of the most astute readers of Harrison's research and example, Woolf saw in her work on ancient Greece and later on Russian language and literature, issues of immediate feminist significance for the culture of war, heroism, and death she recognized in her patriarchal and imperialistic present" (6). And Cole, too, has discussed how Harrison promulgated a different view of the Greeks as chthonic, chaotic, bound to strange and violent gods, in contrast to the harmonious Hellenism promoted by nineteenth-century intellectuals (48). Foster begins her letter to a border guard by pointing out the gulf between his actions and "certain philosophical and ethical problems" of which she has no doubt he is unaware ("Stopped" 57).

Cole states that "by the 1930s Woolf had been betrayed by her male modernist peers" (263).

Do modernist studies in a sense continue that betrayal? Mills implies as much: "Despite trends in transnationalism and digital 'one world, we're all connected' technologies in Modernist Studies, much of current scholarship in literary modernism continues to focus on Joyce, Pound, Eliot, and Yeats, 'the men of 1914,' and their male contemporaries" (2). But is it still fruitful to dwell on masculinity when discussing issues of violence, force, and war? Certainly it was for Woolf herself, but where has our conversation about these relations got to? In *Virginia Woolf and War*, I wrote that technology had rendered gender obsolete in terms of war fighting but that the social institution of war is still bound up with notions of valor, manhood, and masculinity. The shadow of the warrior, as Susan Griffin wrote in *A Chorus of Stones*, continues to fall over every boy's upbringing.

Can we (should we?) separate "war" and "violence" as separate categories for discussion? And "violence" and "force"?

Julian Bell—the paradox of whose life is nicely captured in Patricia Laurence's description of him as a "violent pacifist"—criticized the liberalism of the older Bloomsbury generation for not recognizing that force is the basis of all power (Bell 340–41). In Woolf's "A Sketch of the Past," we find the challenging paradox that she discovers the roots of her artistic creativity in moments of violent force: a suicide; a fight with her brother (71–73). Sarah Cole imagines force as "almost a condition of existence, a way of considering the swell of power that surrounds and can demolish the individual, even as, in some cases, it provides a sense of that individual's purpose (to resist, to rebel)—or, as Holocaust survivors tell it, to resist or rebel by the bare fact of remaining human" (24).

Does Woolf's "thinking is my fighting" (D5 285) really make a difference now?

Froula has argued that Bloomsbury did not believe reason could save civilization from violence but that rational institutions could (*Virginia* 331 n20). In *Quack, Quack!* (122), Leonard Woolf notes that Bertrand Russell identifies Kant as the origin of "The Revolt Against Reason" (*Political Quarterly* Jan-March 1935). Recently, Brad Evans has spoken of how, in the "post-9/11 moment," the United States' "war effort has been mobilized and tied to a Kantian-inspired liberal ethics" ("Ten"). What can we learn by juxtaposing Woolf's notions about "outsiderism" to her contemporaries' attitudes toward rational institutions? In "A Sketch of the Past," Woolf wrote that she spent "the morning writing, when I might be walking, running a shop, or learning to do something that will be useful if war comes. I feel that by writing I am doing what is far more necessary than anything else" (73). Do we feel similarly, sitting at our conference panels and roundtables, standing in our classrooms?

≷

The following are edited versions of each participant's opening remarks. My great thanks to Sarah, Ashley, Christine, and Jean.

SARAH COLE

Woolf and violence: this is an expansive topic and one that has emerged in recent years as pivotal to Woolf's career. We now see violence in many registers of Woolf's work: as its ongoing theme and content, one of the great realities with which Woolf was always engaged in her writing; in terms of gender, her feminism being inextricable from her lifelong antagonism to violence; and in the breadth of her politics, as her pacifism has come out of the critical shadows, a credible and important form of political intervention that continues to resonate today. In these and other contexts, violence in Woolf's writing stands out as something both raw and transformative, its relation to the composition and quality of her texts being always one of friction, and of movement. Every one of Woolf's works, really, fiction and non-fiction, can be read for the way violence manifests, changes, compels, and frustrates. And as Mark Hussey's opening list of questions suggests, we are really at the beginning of a critical conversation about how to approach this enormously rich and important topic.

So for today, in the spirit of conversation, I am going to set my lens at the widest setting and think in somewhat synthesizing terms about the place of violence across her works. Specifically, I want to offer a single provocation: that violence in Woolf's writing impedes change; it disrupts and derails the narrative of life, movement, thought. In every way, formally and thematically, small scale and large, violence finds a way to slam on the brakes. I have argued, in my recent book, that violence is deeply absorbed into Woolf's texts, that it drives many of her aesthetic moves, and that it stands as both antagonist and motivating force in her work; so I am not trying to suggest, in saying that violence halts change, that it is somehow outside the frame of narrative or other to its developments. But violence does have a unique power in Woolf's writings; the way it acts on the flesh and the spirit is to create full stops and to challenge the principle of progress. It is always ready to take its place in the passage of time, as the foe of what time can give us, as the ally of how time fails us. Woolf, as we know, was one of the twentieth century's great champions of the human spirit, "Life" in the classic words of "Modern Fiction," and violence as an obstacle is more than local; it is the dark hole into which the whole enterprise of life, ever in motion and elapsing through time, falls. Just think of how fundamental the operations of suspension and interruption are throughout Woolf's works; violence is not the only thing that creates these essential disruptions, but it is a big part of that story. The telling of lives—or even the making of sentences—as broken, interrupted, possibly open to completion or recuperation, is fundamental to Woolf's structures and might be seen as a formal answer to violence's destructive agenda. Let's recall a moment in "Time Passes" when the violence of war acts on both time and life: "Night after night, [...] only gigantic chaos streaked with lightning could have been heard tumbling and tossing, as the winds and waves disported themselves like the amorphous bulks of leviathans whose brows are pierced by no light of reason, and mounted one on top of another, and lunged and plunged in the darkness or the daylight (for night and day, month and year ran shapelessly together) in idiot games, until it seemed as if the universe were battling and tumbling, in brute confusion and wanton lust aimlessly by itself" (*TTL* 134–35). It's so clear here; violence undoes the Enlightenment, sending its signal prospect, civilization, into a tailspin, and it undoes time too.

What *is* the relationship of violence to time? It's such a potent question not just for Woolf, but for anyone who takes up the gauntlet thrown down by history and attempts to write about violence, felt intimately in time and the body, yet often distributed in huge waves, impersonally. For many in the modernist period, violence stops time, but I don't think that's quite it for Woolf. Time is more likely to be arrested, in Woolf's works, by the creation of beauty, memory, and the breath of the eternal than by violence, around which time seems to go rampaging forward, leaving us instead in the warp. It is Lily Briscoe, Mrs. Ramsay, and Clarissa Dalloway who say to time "stand still here." There is perhaps no aspect of time that Woolf did not consider; Bergsonian, Proustian, historical, evolutionary, entropic, circular, all the big narratives or modes of time are expressed in her work, visualized, sounded, felt—and violence is always the spoiler.

One time scheme in particular calls up the raw realities of violence: geological time, or *longue durée*, the scheme of rocks, soil, and the ocean floor and, above all, of the origins of humanity. It is, as Woolf suggests in the person of Lucy Swithin, who dreams and riffs on what she reads in *The Outline of History*, the stuff of the imagination more than of history, and indeed it captured Woolf's, as it did so many of her contemporaries. In one sense, it is not surprising, fifty years after Darwin and right smack in the Freudian moment, that Woolf and her fellow modernists would find the prehistoric to lodge not out at the other end of an evolutionary chain, but right here in our consciousness or hearts of darkness (this may help to account for Woolf's persistent interest in Conrad's novella). But prehistory is also there for Woolf as a kind of container, an imaginative holding space, for a vision of the human story that strips away just about everything and leaves us, like Miss LaTrobe's next play, with the basics, "two figures, half concealed by a rock," or like Isa and Giles at the end of *Between the Acts*, teeth and claws bared to fight like animals, in the starkest of settings: "The house had lost its shelter. It was night before roads were made, or houses. It was the night that dwellers in caves had watched from some high place among rocks" (210, 219). At the beginning, if we can imagine our way back, people seem almost like vessels containing the future, what will come through the centuries and eras. History. And Woolf was always telling and retelling the story of Western history, a story extravagantly marked and punctured by violence, particularly against women. But the point I want to make is less about this marking or puncturing than about how violence seems to keep sending us back, resetting the clock, erasing all the great achievements of humanity, or civilization, to use the term of her era, and returning us, as she puts it in *Three Guineas*, to "an infant crying in the night, the black night that now [in 1938] covers Europe […] a very old cry" (167). *Three Guineas*, especially, shows with great urgency and comprehensiveness how fully violence invokes repetition and return, jolting us out of whatever might be the accomplishment of the present into the deadening cycle of the mulberry tree: round and round in a circular dance of war, weapons, and futility. And the book itself is like that circling, repetitive in both style and lexicon, modeling itself on that which it seeks to overcome.

There is something intensely mutual, is what I am trying to suggest, about the past and violence. The one conjures the other; to recognize, experience, apprehend or even contemplate violence is to be thrust back, to some fantasmatic prehistoric moment when, perhaps, we knew no better; but also to one historical epoch after another, whether it is that of Creon the dictator or of the Victorian home or of bombs ripping apart houses and bodies. To think of violence is to find history, and to write about history is to find violence—or, better, to find the *structure of violence as repetition*, those acts whose inevitability bends and distorts life. To discover that we are all, always already, living between the acts of historical violence is another way of saying that there can be no progress, no change, no improvement.

And yet, the way violence drags us back or stops us in time has its corollary in another repetitive gesture, but this is one of resistance, or of hope. It is not only violence that reshapes history into cycles; the desire for peace is part of that pattern too, what in *Orlando* Woolf describes as a voice answering a voice, or in *Three Guineas*, as the poets eternally dreaming the dream of peace, the dream of freedom, or, in *The Years*, after the all-clear has sounded, the lifting of a glass to a new world. That novel, *The Years*, one whose register is really of survival, finds a way nevertheless to end in the terms not of the retrograde vortex of violence but of the equally eternal fight for harmony, a move that is more willful than descriptive—and also heartbreaking: "The sun had risen," she wrote in 1937 at the end of her novel, "and the sky above the houses wore an air of extraordinary beauty, simplicity and peace" (*TY* 435).

J. ASHLEY FOSTER

In light of recent American military incursions in Afghanistan and Iraq,[1] the outpouring of refugees from Syria,[2] and Russia's recent invasion of Crimea,[3] Mark Hussey's statement that Virginia Woolf's work is "unfolding in contexts that resonate deeply with current cultural questions" ("After Lives" 14) could hardly be more apropos. As Hussey continues in his essay, "Woolf: After Lives," to relate Woolf to philosophers in the lineage of Nietzsche, Kierkegaard, Heidegger, Wittgenstein, Bachelard, Benjamin, Adorno, to name a few, he observes that Woolf's "philosophy" is "grounded in embodied being-in-the-world" (20). This embodied being-in-the world, written in the existentialist language of Heidegger, invites a thinking of being-with, the way in which being-in-the-world is constituted by being-with-others,[4] and how that being-with-others makes ethical claims upon the self. This is especially the case when the lives and bodies of those others are threatened by violence, as unfolded with the advent of total war (where civilians become military targets) during the Spanish Civil War (1936–1939), and as is happening around the globe in our current cultural moment. Woolf's central question of *Three Guineas*, posed during the Spanish Civil War, needs as urgently to be asked today as in 1930s Britain: "How in your opinion are we to prevent war?" (*TG* 5). *Three Guineas*, and its accompanying texts that include Woolf's diaries and reading notebooks, grapples with and anticipates some of the more pertinent philosophical questions that still plague us when thinking about our responses to violence and ways in which we can propose viable pacifist alternatives. It also shows our students that non-military choices exist.

Three Guineas, written in a generic-hybrid epistolary format, epitomizes the modernist projects throughout the 1930s that were consistently undertaken for a variety of pacifist missions, projects that include Pablo Picasso's *Guernica* and the Quaker publication and art exhibition *They Still Draw Pictures*, introduced by Aldous Huxley. The pacifist emphases of these projects have largely been drowned out by the metanarrative that the peace movement was overwhelmed and undermined by the Spanish Civil War. Woolf studies may be the refuge of pacifist thought in modernist studies, but I maintain that Woolf was part of a larger pacifist conversation that should be moved from the periphery to the mainstream of modernist discourses because it offers frameworks for thinking through problems of violence that still plague us. Modernists worked actively within international organizations and peace networks to provide relief work and change the consciousness of the public, for "think[ing] peace into existence" (Woolf, "Thoughts" 243) is, first and foremost, a problem of imagination. If we follow the archival train initiated by *Three Guineas*,[5] and read Woolf's "major documentary project" (Marcus xlv) in conversation with Louis Delaprée's pamphlet *Martyrdom of Madrid*, and the relief work records contained in the Friends House archives in London, a hypertextual[6] pacifist mission unfolds. This mission, as *Three Guineas* shows us, hinges on the idea that using force is a personal choice and not an inevitability, and discloses alternate responses to the violence in Spain. These projects give us methods of war-resistance to share with our students, allowing us to facilitate the pedagogical intervention that Woolf calls for in *Three Guineas*.

At the crux of *Three Guineas'* pacifist argument is a focus on pedagogy, as well as women's role in the workplace and women's ability to effect change due to their outsider status. Woolf traces the influence of education upon men and women's "differing" perspectives. Using the "fact of education" and the "fact of property" as examples, Woolf arrives at the conclusion that "such differences make for very considerable differences in mind and body" (*TG* 22). It is woman's very status of outsider,[7] outsiders who have been historically prohibited from the central systems of power, that saves her from committing the same violent atrocities as her brothers and constitutes the foundations for Woolf's ethical imaginings. Women have not been educated within the same institutionalized systems as men and have therefore not cultivated the fighting "habit": "For though many instincts are held more or less in common by both sexes, to fight has always been the man's habit, not the woman's" (9). *Three Guineas* expresses concern for the idea that if women become educated in the same system as men, if they partake in the same professions, hold political office, and enter the power structure uncritically, women will adopt the same values and forfeit their revolutionary or subversive potential.

What these concerns show is that fighting for Woolf is a "habit," something cultivated and taught, and therefore can be either socially encouraged or sublimated. Sarah Cole argues that there was a "large-scale theorizing of war and violence among 1930s intelligentsia, which circulated around the question of whether war and barbarity are endemic to the human condition" (201), a question which Woolf takes up in her use of French journalist Louis Delaprée's pamphlet *The Martyrdom of Madrid.* The way in which Woolf cites this posthumously collected and translated pamphlet, which was pasted into her reading notebooks,[8] emphasizes the potential for women to become violent. Woolf quotes Delaprée at length in footnote 15 from section III, transcribing the story of a woman, "Amalia," who has killed five men, maybe six, in order to avenge her daughter's death in the Alto de Leon. Here, Woolf shows that though men and women alike may have violent tendencies, their ability to either enact violence or redirect it is informed by prevailing norms and expectations, an "instinct" inculcated through "centuries of tradition and education" (*TG* 127) that can be changed, sublimated, taught, or re-taught. In other words, while the capacity for violence may always already be embedded within us, the use of force is not inevitable. There is a choice; in responding to the letter writer who poses the question with which *Three Guineas* opens, Woolf comments, "You must have argued, men and women, here and now, are able to exert their wills" (8). For example, in "Thoughts on Peace in an Air Raid," Woolf says that, "if we are to compensate the young man for the loss of his glory and of his gun, we must give him access to the creative feelings" (247–248), creative feelings such as the kind involved in making poetry or art. Part of that choice, however, extending this argument and bringing it into the present day, is realizing that we have one.

If we read further into Delaprée and situate his pamphlet, the *Martyrdom of Madrid*, within the activist networks and humanitarian aid during the Spanish Civil War, a discourse of non-military options that support Woolf's pedagogical mission to "use our influence through education to affect the young against war" (*TG* 34) unfolds. Bringing these materials into the classroom, exposing students to alternate possibilities of action and behavior, introduces and helps them to envision pacifist and humanitarian endeavors as an alternative to violence and force.

Though Delaprée's pamphlet is most widely quoted for his violent, gruesome images,[9] his reporting can be read as a powerful testimony against war. Delaprée, who feels "ashamed at being a man, when mankind proves to be capable of such massacres of innocents" (15), strings together fragments, vignettes, and stories of tragedy, blood and death. Delaprée mourns: "But what is the use of abiding any longer on the description of this martyrdom of Madrid, to enumerate the places where bombs have been dropped, to describe these mass murders. Horror itself becomes monotonous" (27). We can tell from the terms "mass murders" and "horror" that Delaprée issues a strong condemnation of war. His language is loaded, and he frames the actions of the fascist army as criminal. He ends the dispatch with the declaration: *"Christ said: Forgive them, for they do not know what they are doing. I think that after the massacre of innocents in Madrid, we must say: Do not forgive them for they know what they are doing"* (28, emphasis original).

In the *Martyrdom of Madrid*, Delaprée tells the story of Amalia in a call-to-action for the English to break the non-intervention clause and support the Spanish republic in non-military ways. Delaprée has joined a group of British parliamentarians who are investigating the situation in Spain, and he writes about his time with their tour in an attempt to support their humanitarian mission by disseminating their message (which is in accord with his own) throughout the foreign presses, while he simultaneously impresses upon the M.P.s the desperation of the civilian conditions.[10] He feels that Amalia serves as "an excellent introducer" to the realities of the war, remarking "they bethought immediately on the means not of putting an end to it, but of saving as many innocents as possible" (36). The parliamentarians, after having visited the front, return to the British embassy and work on a report that is to "appeal to England, without any political intention … to appeal to England to save thousands of women and children" (37), documents Delaprée. During the conversation between Delaprée and the delegates that occurred after the report was made, two versions of fascist pamphlets were dropped from the air—one bribing the people of Madrid with food in exchange for their surrender, the other demanding surrender and threatening destruction. Delaprée recounts his reaction to the bundles: "As you see, I said to my English friends, time has come for working. Otherwise, soon perhaps, before Amalia kills her sixth man—and you know she does quick work—thousands of innocents will perish" (37).

Considering Woolf's quotes within the larger context of Delaprée's message, a hypertextual pacifist mission appears. The traces and transmissions of these pacifist sentiments, and the urgent need to take action before more lives are lost, become clear in reading *Three Guineas*, Woolf's peace pamphlet, next to Delaprée's humanitarian call. Women's status as outsider contains the necessary power to subvert the violent process that is institutionalized and ongoing; however, that power can be lost if women choose to cultivate the fighting habit. It is an urgent intervention that must be made "before Amalia kills her sixth man."

I found the appeal issued by the parliamentarians in the Quaker archives of Spanish Civil War relief work activities, where a newspaper clipping from *The Observer* dated November 29, 1936 stands out. The article, "British M.P.s in Madrid: Fears of 'Unspeakable Horrors,'" issues an appeal: "We urge the need of immediate and large-scale action by neutral powers acting through an international organization. The evacuation and partial maintenance of women, children, and non-combatants are urgent in order to mitigate—it cannot prevent—unspeakable horrors."[11] This article emphasizes the horrific conditions in which the civilians are living, proposing international co-operation to help feed and evacuate the inhabitants and refugees under constant bombardment.

The report that Delaprée references was published as a pamphlet by Lawrence & Wishart in London that documents the six parliamentarians' (F. Seymour Cocks, W. P. Crawford Greene, D. R. Grenfell, Wing-Commander A. W. James, Captain J. R. J. Macnamara, and Wilfred Roberts) visit to Spain. This was a cross-party coalition from the House of Commons who traveled to Spain "with a humanitarian object" (Report 3). Particularly interested in the "condition of the civilian population, of the prisoners, and of the sick and wounded inmates of hospitals" (3), the delegates travel to Spain and witness the attacks on Madrid, the overcrowded prisons, and terror of the civilian populations. After a full assessment of the situation in Spain, this inter-party group adopts a pacifist mission statement: "Our hope is that plans for co-operative action to help those in distress and danger will be adopted, and that the adoption of such plans will stimulate the sense of mutual responsibility and fellowship which is the antithesis of war, and will lead to a more comprehensive and positive plan for safeguarding mankind" (5). In addition to a meeting held by the Republic with Largo Caballero, the Prime Minister at the time, and the Foreign Minister Alverez de Vayo, in order to "put forward propositions with regard to the treatment and safety of prisoners" (8), the coalition calls for gas masks to be sold to the Spanish Republic, and they write a statement condemning the attack on civilian lives. They also try to mastermind a plan for evacuation that involves "at least one thousand Frenchmen and one thousand Britons driving their own cars fully supplied with reserve petrol and ample food organised in columns to come to Madrid to assist evacuation immediately. Suggest Royal Automobile Club and Automobile Association and Society of Friends organize British volunteers" (Delaprée Appendix C, 13).

Their call for help was successful. Though to my knowledge the one thousand French and one thousand Britons driving private cars in a colony of mass evacuations never manifested, Wilfred Roberts and the M.P.s did succeed in creating a coalition of Spanish Relief, which assisted with food, refugee aid, and evacuations, and worked as a conglomerate of existing international organizations. The Society of Friends worked with the new organization, called the National Joint Committee for Spanish Relief,[12] as well as the Save the Children Fund, the British Red Cross, and the Catholic Bishop's Fund, to name a few.[13] These humanitarian efforts helped to sustain and feed refugees and inhabitants throughout Spain for the duration of the war and beyond. Also contained in the Friends House archive is another *Observer* article, dated the end of January, 1937, that announces: "Food for Spanish Refugees: Relief ship sails from London." According to this article, the food, listed as "25,000 tins of condensed milk, 3,000 slabs of chocolate, 600 large bottles of beef extract, 60 cases of corned beef, 1 ton of biscuits, 3 tons of flour, 5 tons of sugar, 1 ton of flaked oats, half ton of butter, and a 3-cwt. barrel of cod liver oil," was provided by the General Relief Fund for Distressed Women and Children in Spain, another organization working co-operatively with the Society of Friends and the other Aid Spain coalitions. This food was to be "distributed in conjunction with agents of the Save the Children Fund, British Red Cross, and the Society of Friends."[14] This archival train, initiated by Woolf's *Three Guineas* reading notebooks, opens up a world of international co-operation and discloses an elaborate network of global citizens working together to alleviate the sad fate of many civilians. It reveals the extensive international networks working to construct a pacifist world mission.

It becomes clear in piecing together the lost histories of Spanish Civil War pacifism that Woolf is one piece of an elaborate discourse. Violence can always call forth more violence, but in the shadow of the ruins and the dust of the ashes, those who responded to the call of the other in the 1930s through their writing, fundraising, and volunteer work offer a different possibility. Traces of these missions are being carried forward today in projects such as *historiesofviolence.com*, where the annual journal *On Violence* edited by Brad Evans calls for us to "demand a politics that is dignified and open to the possibility of non-violent ways of living" ("Inaugural Statement"). In the inaugural issue, Todd May points out that there is a rich history of non-violence, a history that is under-taught and written over: "[A]s the writer Gene Sharp has detailed…nonviolent resistance has a long history. It is not a history that is taught in schools, which, after all, are largely state institutions. It is, for the most part, not a history of political leaders engaged in glorious exploits. Instead it is the expression of people asserting their dignity against the violence that seeks to warp or derange them" (9). Art Works Projects For Human Rights at artworksprojects.org offer digital exhibits and photographic slide shows that issue compelling, modern-day artistic testimonies against war and injustice. Bringing these past and present pacifist missions into the classroom, perhaps we can stage some interventions in the current fatalistic rhetoric and belief that violence and war is inevitable. Perhaps we can carry the work of peace forward, and encourage our students to do the same.

CHRISTINE FROULA

The history of the war is not and never will be written from our point of view.
—*Virginia Woolf,* "The War from the Street" (1919)

Thinking about "War, Peace, and Internationalism" for *The Cambridge Companion to Bloomsbury* reminded me that the "ruined houses and dead bodies" of *Three Guineas* have deeper sources in Woolf's modernist imaginary than the April 1937 bombing of Guernica in the Spanish Civil War (30). On August 6, 1914, just days after war was declared, a German zeppelin bombed the Belgian city of Liège, killing nine civilians (Strachan 211).[15] Artillery bombing killed thousands more, yet with this unprecedented air attack on a European city—"the first attempt in history to strike directly at the will-to-resist of a civilian population in war"—war burst the bounds of the battlefield (Slessor ix-x).[16] If, as Paul Fussell, Mary Favret, and others emphasize, British civilians experienced "war at a distance" from the front, Karen Levenback, Trudi Tate, and others point out that the aerial bombing of civilians shattered the walls of the private house and the private/public divide, bringing the war into the houses, streets, and lives of civilians.[17] The first zeppelin raid on Britain occurred on January 19, 1915, killing four people and injuring sixteen (Poolman 33), but even before the giant German zeppelins floated into British skies, they invaded the civilian imaginary—"the sky of the mind," Woolf calls it in *Between the Acts* (212).[18] H. G. Wells had imagined aerial warfare in 1908, specifically a German air attack on New York; the London *Times* had closely followed Count Ferdinand von Zeppelin's development of the dirigible in the years preceding the war and on August 6, 1914 assessed the danger of air attacks by zeppelins and planes and the strength of Britain's defenses ("The German Airships"). British defense forces became adept at fending off, shooting down in flames, and destroying in their hangars these "huge, surprisingly elusive monsters" (Poolman 6), and only 557 people died in zeppelin attacks on Britain. Still, the strange prospect of a bomb falling from a gigantic invisible balloon shook the deep sense of invincibility that British sea power had secured for centuries. To an American journalist who witnessed the terrible zeppelin raid of September 8, 1915, London suddenly seemed a "night battlefield" in which "[s]even million people ... stand gazing into the sky from the darkened streets"[19] (William G. Shepherd qtd. in Poolman 63).

If, as Woolf declared, "the history of the war is not and never will be written from our point of view," her wartime letters and diaries bespeak not only the psychological presence of the eerily silent zeppelins in the minds of British civilians but a powerful "will-to-resist," manifest, among other ways, in the imaginative assimilation of this unprecedented war technology to familiar forms and representations of catastrophic violence ("The War from the Street" 3).[20] Walking across the Green Park ten days after the first raid on Britain, Virginia and Leonard heard "a terrific explosion" in St. James Street: "people came running out of Clubs; stopped still & gazed about them. But there was no Zeppelin or aeroplane—only, I suppose, a very large tyre burst. But it is really an instinct with me, & most people, I suppose, to turn any sudden noise, or dark object in the sky into an explosion, or a German aeroplane. And it always seems utterly impossible that one should be hurt" (*D1* 32). No zeppelin after all, just a loud explosion, quickly domesticated into an ordinary danger; an everyday event that lays bare the exaggerated "instinct" of fear during the war years, its aftershock felt in the reflexive alarm of *Mrs. Dalloway's* postwar civilians on hearing a motorcar backfire in the street.

After the attack of September 8th left a "crescent scar of fire and ruin" from Euston to Liverpool Street, and Londoners "buzzing with fearful excitement" (Poolman 62, cf. Castle 32–39), Woolf wove zeppelin references and anecdotes into her letters to evoke and make light of this new condition of danger. Three weeks later, Woolf pictures the indomitable Nelly Cecil, wife of Lord Robert Cecil, the British Under-Secretary of State for Foreign Affairs, in terms that presage Clarissa Dalloway's awe of Lady Bexborough: "I rejoiced to hear of you following the zeppelin in a taxi; such it is to have the blue blood of England in one's veins: my literary friends hide in cellars, and never walk at night without looking at the sky" (*L2* 64).[21] She paints other London friends as no less intrepid, coolly assessing fire and ruin while carrying on regardless (as it were). From Asheham, she marvels to Ka Cox, "I am often seriously alarmed when I hear that the zeppelins have been over London, but accounts from Sydney and Nessa prove that you never turn a hair, but merely take a look at them, put the cowards in the cellar, and then walk the streets till you've seen all the fires!" (*L2* 70). Writing to Vanessa in 1916, a year of twenty-three zeppelin raids that killed 293 people and injured 691, Virginia seems almost to recommend the comparatively calm existence of zeppelin-threatened Londoners what with "these raids going on" in Sussex: "We actually had a zeppelin over the house here—in broad daylight. We were away, but the servants say the sound is unmistakable, and were in a panic; Nelly hiding in the wood, and Lottie running to the Woolers, where Mrs Wooler did nothing but dash into her house and out again. But it was so high up that no one saw it. Eleven aeroplanes chased it. I cant help thinking it was really English" (*L2* 112). As if content to let the servants do the panicking for her, Woolf relays their account of a zeppelin "actually" over Asheham (indeed, there was a zeppelin raid that day), which, however, "no one saw"; it was detected instead by its "unmistakable" sound and finally chased off by a phalanx of English planes (cf. Castle 55–60).[22] Then, she undercuts the scene of frantic fear with a wild surmise; Britain, of course, had no dirigibles, though they did have blimps.[23] A few months later she recounts allaying a similar panic at Hogarth House, this time over a nonexistent zeppelin: "we have the Aurora Borealis, which a man in the street took to be zeppelins, so shouted out loud under the servants window. At midnight we heard them carrying their bedding to the kitchen, there to lie on the floor till day—With great difficulty we got them up again, and lectured them on the nature of northern lights" (*L2* 138).[24]

Huge though they were, the zeppelins' uncanny power to reach great heights and hover for hours unseen and unheard made phantom zeppelins difficult to distinguish from those actually—and of course rarely—present. A material correlative of the zeppelin in the sky of the mind could appear in the real sky at any moment; indeed, it might already be floating up there undetected. The civilian will-to-resist thus expressed itself not only as sangfroid in the face of actual risk and destruction but as imaginative combat against phantom zeppelins in the sky of the mind. A cheery letter Virginia wrote to Saxon Sydney-Turner in early February 1917—when Germany had readied for deployment a fleet of new and improved zeppelins—shows everyday awareness of existential risk taking on the chances and colors of ordinary life—doings, hours, moods.[25] After describing a contemporary's patriotic epigrams as firecrackers that fizzle out instead of exploding, Woolf continues: "As to Aeschylus, on the other hand, I've been reading him in French which is better than English; I dont think I have read anything else. Aeschylus however excited my spirits to such an extent that, hearing my husband snore in the night, I woke him to light his torch and look for zeppelins. He then applied the Freud system to my mind, and analysed it down to Clytemnestra and the watch fires, which so pleased him that he forgave me" (*L2* 141). Even in bed at Hogarth House, the Woolfs aren't quite spectators at a safe distance from the war but imaginatively all too near—if not as near as the people of Liège in August 1914 or of Guernica twenty years on, or as they themselves would be during the 1940–1941 Blitz, still, much nearer than Clytemnestra and her watchman to Troy, at least until Agamemnon returns from the war to the retaliatory violence awaiting him at home. But Virginia makes allusive comedy of these phantom zeppelins. Leonard—has he been reading Freud's *On Dreams*?[26]—casts his high-spirited spouse as a modern Clytemnestra and himself as her watchman.[27] Aeschylus's Clytemnestra wields astounding royal power through the beacon fires that flash advance news of the Greek victory from mountaintop to mountaintop; Virginia, who may or may not have heard rumors about the new zeppelins, mobilizes the snoring Leonard to peer into the skies for signs of a modern war that is no more contained by the battlefield than are the effects of Tantalus's violent curse by the house of Atreus. Superimposing Aeschylus's fiery skies upon the skies over Hogarth House, Virginia's amusing anecdote assimilates the technological violence of aerial bombing to the age-old violence that pervades the *Agamemnon* and Western literary history. Prefiguring *Three Guineas*, it aligns the private/public violence staged in Aeschylus's great trilogy with the new, and escalating, private/public violence of modern war.

Virginia's francophone Clytemnestra of 1917 may also have contributed to the charisma emanating from the Clytemnestra of "Mr Bennett and Mrs Brown" (1924). The Greek Clytemnestra Virginia studied with Janet Case is already a brilliant, passionate figure of resistance, a woman with a brain and a heart who "strips naked the unjust bias of men's condemnation" and whose "spirit…has in it the freshness of a new ideal" (Janet Case, "Women in the Plays of Aeschylus"; qtd. in Mills 51–3). It is this touchstone of the will-to-resist with whom, Woolf proposes, modern readers may find themselves in unexpected sympathy after a long, grueling war; and who seeds the ground for *Three Guineas*'s meditation on what counter-strategy, counter-force, or weapons of peace Outsiders might wield, in and beyond the spirit of the outlaw queen, mother, avenger who stands dreaming of peace at the end of the *Agamemnon*.

In the last zeppelin raid on London, on the night of October 19, 1917, a fleet of the new Height-Climbers crossed the Channel and eluded detection. From Hogarth House Virginia reported, "We had Zeppelins over last night. They are said to have destroyed Swan and Edgar at Piccadilly. We only heard the guns at a distance, and never heard the warning at all" (*L2* 189).[28] The diary, seedbed for her fiction, weaves her delayed and mediated experience of this surprise air attack in central London into an ad hoc narrative. That day, she notes on the nineteenth, she met in the street Alix Sargant-Florence, who, a few days earlier, had put in an afternoon of work at the Hogarth Press before deciding that printing was not for her. Virginia describes her character and mood and reports trying in vain to cheer her up:

> She has a kind of independence & lack of concern for appearances which I admire. But as we walked up & down Dover Street she seemed on the verge of rolling up the usual veil of laughter & gossip & revealing her sepulchral despair—poor woman.
> Where are you going now Alix?
> I really dont know.
> Well that sounds dismal! Don't you look forward to say eleven tomorrow morning?
> I merely wish it didn't exist that's all!
> So I left her, hatless, aimless, unattached, wandering in Piccadilly. (*D1* 63)

The next day, Woolf narrates the raid as the denouement of this anecdote: "Happily, or she might say unhappily for Alix she didn't presumably wander in Piccadilly all night, or the great bomb which ploughed up the pavement opposite Swan & Edgar's might have dug her grave. We heard two soft distant but unmistakable shocks about 9:30; then a third which shook the window; then silence. It turns out that a Zeppelin came over, hovered unseen for an hour or two & left. We heard no more of it" (*D1* 63). Charting Alix Sargant-Florence's road-not-taken, this mini-serial with its shadow of chance, its frisson of beware-of-what-you-merely-wish-for annihilation, catches the tension between the actual zeppelin raid and the persistent—and resistant—narrative impulse to net the war's senseless violence into some sort of meaning, however virtual, ironic, or fatalist. With another throw of the dice, the hole in the street—itself a senseless accident, for the zeppelin missed its intended target—might have been Alix's wished-for grave, not to mention Virginia's unwished-for one. That night, indeed, zeppelins dropped several three-hundred kilogram bombs not on the targets they meant to hit (Sheffield, Manchester, Liverpool) but on Piccadilly, Camberwell, and Hither Green, leaving many ruined houses and dead bodies. (Intended for Sheffield, the bomb dropped near Swan & Edgar killed seven and injured eighteen; see Poolman 225; Castle 86–89.)[29] Through the lives of the diarist and her aimless wandering subject, the anecdote writes small the force of mindless chance that ruled the skies that night. The zeppelin that bumbled over Piccadilly and killed seven people there by mistake has in the diarist's mind a phantom counterpart that might have killed Alix or any Londoner—or anyone else, wandering or not—beneath its errant path in the vague direction of Sheffield.

In the spirit of Thomas Hardy, much admired by Woolf, the sad undertones of Alix's talk as heard by the diarist imbue this technologically mediated instance of modern chance with several shades of irony, not unlike the irony Fussell finds everywhere in Great War literature. Actual or phantom, silent and unseen or factitious and unreal, errantly destructive or (a few times) on target, escaping or falling in flames, allusively Aeschylean or purely apparitional: from August 1914 to its ignominious end, the surreal zeppelin seemed a quintessential embodiment of modern war and modern irony. "We invent a vessel to swim beneath the sea and at once it is appropriated to increase the terrors of war. We learn to fly like the birds, and at once flying becomes a new arm of military science, and has little other meaning," wrote British journalist A. G. Gardiner in 1914 (Poolman 1). Woolf's writings track the zeppelin in the sky of the mind from the outbreak of the First World War, when London was aghast with dire predictions ("they talked and talked, and said it was the end of civilisation, and the rest of our lives was worthless" [L2 51]), to the eve of the Second, when Colonel Mayhew mutters "What's history without the Army, eh?" between the acts of La Trobe's avant-garde pageant and a departing voice asks "And what's the channel, come to think of it, if they mean to invade us? The aeroplanes, I didn't like to say it, made one think...." (BTA 157, 199). A century later, as our technologies of violence—scarcely less errant, ever more powerful, spanning the globe—threaten to extinguish all human voices, how do thought and speech express the will-to-resist? If, as Woolf reflected on seeing her brother talking with a German POW in 1918, "The reason why it is easy to kill another person must be that one's imagination is too sluggish to conceive what his life means to him—the infinite possibilities of a succession of days which are furled in him, & have already been spent" (D1 186), how far can thinking and talking, artmaking and teaching, keep this counter-force of imagination alive? (cf. Froula, Virginia Woolf 96).

JEAN MILLS

I'd like to focus on one of the six points Mark has raised in my brief remarks today on Virginia Woolf and Violence: is Woolf's contention that "thinking is my fighting" something we can usefully claim for ourselves today?

Yes.

When Virginia Woolf writes, "thinking is my fighting" or "all I can do is write—fight with the mind," what she's advocating and participating in is a strategy of what is later coined as "positive peace," an emphasis on analyses of the conditions necessary for peace, such as conflict transformation and conflict resolution via mechanisms such as peacebuilding and peacemaking, to which her work attends. Her essays, her novels, her journalism, criticism, her stature as a philosopher and public intellectual, and major voice of the twentieth century participate in this conversation that is crucial to ourselves, to our students, to our children, and to "the millions of bodies yet to be born" ("Thoughts on Peace" 243). It's a conversation Virginia Woolf insisted we continue, inform, and enrich, and it is what has brought us here together at this roundtable, in this hall, at the 24th annual international Woolf conference: Virginia Woolf: Writing the World.

But, you may say…isn't violence everywhere? Isn't war inevitable? These are the opinions of my students, many of whom have first-hand experience of war, either as soldiers, refugees of war, witnesses to war trauma, and/or victims of war; and many others of whom are victims of domestic violence, street violence, or violence in other forms. Violence is everywhere. War is inevitable. This is just how it is. And my answer to them is:

No.

Violence is not everywhere. And, war is not inevitable.

Virginia Woolf asked the very same question as the Battle of Britain raged on in the skies overhead and as she lay there "in the dark […] listening to the zoom of a hornet which may at any moment sting you to death" ("Thoughts on Peace" 243).

"Why not," she asked, "bury the head in the pillow, plug the ears, and cease this futile activity of idea-making?" ("Thoughts on Peace" 244).

And, in "Thoughts on Peace in an Air Raid," she answers that question: "Because there are other tables besides officer tables and conference tables" (244).

Other rooms, besides the war room.

Indeed, the history of resistance to violence, peace history, tells a different story, and Virginia Woolf's work is very much a part of the tale.

Of course, implicit in my students' concern that "this is just how it is" is a belief that nonviolence is meek or ineffective. It is a position which reflects a misunderstanding of the rich tradition of nonviolent resistance. Nonviolent actions have achieved historic gains for African Americans, for women, for farmworkers. Nonviolent methods have undermined dictatorships in Eastern Europe, ended civil war in Liberia, and helped bring an end to Apartheid in South Africa. The power of this discourse is real and has proven to be far more effective as a method of social change than the resort to violence and destruction.

And, once again, Virginia Woolf's work is very much a part of this tapestry of truth we must continue to put forth in our classrooms and in our own personal narratives in our lives. All of her work, but especially, of course, her essays *Three Guineas* and "Thoughts on Peace in an Air Raid," constructs a counter narrative to the myth of war experience, which was given new life with the outbreak of World War I. (See also Atkin; Winter; and Brockington for recent work done in this area.) Virginia Woolf posits a different world view, one that explores the root causes of war, dismantles patriarchy, and revises culture.

Woolf sought alternatives to the patriarchal language of the state and to the imperialism and militarism she saw as responsible for war. She transforms forward a politics of positive peace, which makes of her pacifism a specifically feminist expansion. As she writes, "Every day they tell us that we are a free people, fighting to defend freedom. That is the current that has whirled the young airman up into the sky and keeps him circling there among the clouds. Down here, with a roof to cover us and a gas mask handy, it is our business to puncture gas bags and discover seeds of truth" ("Thoughts on Peace" 244–45). This continues to be our "business," today, in our classrooms, for as Woolf points out, "It is not true that we are free" (245). War makes prisoners of both women and men—"he boxed up in his machine with a gun handy; we lying in the dark with a gas mask handy" ("Thoughts on Peace" 244)

Virginia Woolf sought alternatives to Modernism's war story—the hero's quest—and the language of imperialism and militarism, which she read as a failure, and grappled with issues such as disparities in rights, disparities in institutions, and explored the unfair distribution of wealth, each of which informs conceptions of peace that we now consider part of the formalized discipline of Peace Studies and Research. In *Three Guineas*, she comments on the glorification of war displayed in the uniforms, ribbons, and bows of Britain's heads of state, and famously asks, "What connection is there between the sartorial splendours of the educated man" and the corpses found strewn about a battlefield or landscape devastated by war's destructive force (26)? She explores the use of military dress "to impress the beholder with the majesty of the military office, partly in order through their vanity to induce young men to become soldiers" (*TG* 27). She links the idea of war to the dangers of competition, jealousy, and the fostering of intolerance that the university system often represents, encourages, and funds. She explores the qualities and instincts, psychological, biological, and social that might help reveal the sources of violence and war, making a connection between man's "instincts" and the system of education that produces him.

Virginia Woolf's work offers us much to mine in constructing a critical pedagogy in the classroom, as we acknowledge the importance and relevance of her voice at the peace table. I am recently returned from a colloquium of historians at the German Historical Institute in Paris on "Les Défenseurs de la Paix: The Defense of Peace from 1899 to 1918," during this 100th anniversary year of the outbreak of World War I in 1914. I spoke with others on women's roles and their importance in peace history and the ways in which women like Jane Addams, Madeleine Vernet, Jane Harrison, and, yes, Virginia Woolf demanded in one form or another political engagement, despite attempts to dismiss and undermine their arguments. As historian Sandi E. Cooper pointed out, "Peace activists did not prevent the war. They had feared it, but their analyses were more accurate than those of the men who brought us 1914." Indeed, it is an unreflective culture, which ties masculinity to military prowess, and as Woolf noted in "Thoughts on Peace," we have to find ways to "compensate the young man for the loss of his glory and of his gun" (247–48). She discusses "access to the creative feelings" in order to bring us all out of the prisons created by violence and war (248).

With women's increased participation in the peace movement and nonviolent resistance in all its forms, a different voice emerged, and continues to emerge to this day, for the strategies of peace activism haven't yet been realized, and this is where our work needs to focus. At the end of his life, Gandhi pointed out that the "technique of unconquerable non-violence of the strong has not been discovered as yet" (qtd. in Cortright 212), a position one of the great peacemakers of our own times, the recently deceased Barbara Deming, insisted upon, arguing that, "It has *not* been tried. We have hardly begun to try it. The people who dismiss it…do not understand what it could be" ("On Revolution and Equilibrium" 199). But Virginia Woolf understood and framed the very same possibilities and methods in her work and in the "idea making" of her personal correspondence and diaries, when she wrote "thinking is my fighting," which remains a useful claim for the untested, "in the process of invent[ing]" (Deming 198) methods of positive peace.

Notes

1. For further consideration of the wars in Afghanistan and Iraq, see Brenkman.
2. For more on the Syrian refugee situation, see Onishi and the accompanying series of photographs by Addario.
3   For more on Russia's invasion of Crimea, see Simpson. See also Myers.
4. According to Heidegger in *Being and Time*: "The world is always the one that I share with Others. The world of Dasein is a *with-world* {*Mitwelt*}. Being-in is *Being-with* Others. Their Being-in-themselves within-in-the-world is *Dasein-with* {*Mitdasein*}" (155). As we can see from this passage, Others constitute Dasein's being (Dasein is that being which can contemplate its own being). In other words, "I" is not an isolated ontological entity—the metaphysics of the "I" is a "We"—Others make me who "I" am.
5. Mills underscores the kinetics of reading Woolf and the importance of Woolf's reading notebooks to the construction of her argument, noting: "When she confronts one of the more controversial aspects of her argument, exposing women's complicity in patriarchy and thereby their 'consent' to fascism, she does so by sending us back and forth between endnotes, text, and her notebook archive, which become creatively and politically significant as Woolf's rhetorical structure again challenges so many of our readerly assumptions about what a conventional argument looks like" (138).
6. Anne Fernald's essay, "Woolf and Intertextuality," pulls upon Gérard Genette's framework of intertextuality outlined in *Palimpsests*, itemizing five categories we can employ to think through the references and sources of *Three Guineas*. Fernald describes them as: "1) quotation and plagiarism; 2) paratextuality, or the relation between a major text and its many ancillary texts (including diaries, prior versions, and even publicity material); 3) metatextuality, or commentary by critics and readers; 4) architextuality, or a text's relationship to its genre, and finally 5) hypertextuality, which comprises any relationship between two texts other than commentary" (55–56).
7. Christine Froula, exploring the socially and religiously imposed hierarchical divisions between men and women in "St. Virginia's Epistle to an English Gentleman," unpacks "Woolf's analysis of women's scapegoat role" through the figure of a veiled St. Virginia who "dons the public garb St. Paul mandates for women prophets" (*Virginia* 261). From the perspective of veiled outsider, Woolf is able to critique masculine society, and "to expose the scapegoat mechanism by telling the story of collective violence from the victim's perspective, thereby to advance humanity from tyranny and war toward peace and freedom" (265). Froula shows how Woolf subverts the scapegoating of the veiled woman, instead offering up her difference as a source of power. "She will help to prevent war by remaining an Outsider" (273), writes Froula.
8. A copy of the *Martyrdom of Madrid* was first given to me by Jane Marcus from her personal collection, for which I thank her. Woolf pasted this pamphlet into her third reading notebook, which is housed at the University of Sussex, and listed as item 20 in the index.
9. For further discussion on Delaprée and Woolf, see Marcus, "Introduction"; Laurence, "The Facts and Fugue of War"; Rogers's section "'Dead Bodies and Ruined Houses': Spain, War, and Feminism" in ch. 4; Berman 69–70; Dalgarno; and Foster, "The Weeping Woman." For further discussion on Delaprée as journalist, see Preston 14, 37–8, and 148; and Deacon 23, 62, and 176.
10. It should be noted that the dispatches collected in *The Martyrdom of Madrid* contain several small factual errors in describing the parliamentarians' time in Spain. Delaprée specifies "five" English parliamentarians, when there were in fact six. A few of the names are spelled wrong or recorded inaccurately, and there is question as to the dates. At one point, it appears as though Delaprée started an article and continued to write it over a period of days. However, though the official report presented on Spain by the parliamentarians makes no mention of Amalia, many other points of reference line up among the two accounts and are consistent with the November 29th newspaper appeal from *The Observer*, which leads me to believe that Delaprée captured the spirit, if not all the details, of the events of their visit.
11. "British M.P.s in Madrid: Fears of 'Unspeakable Horrors.'" *The Observer*. 29 November 1936. From Friends House archives, FSC/R/SP/5 News cuttings 1936–1940. My gratitude goes to Lisa McQuillan and the staff of the Library of the Religious Society of Friends at Friends House for their assistance.

12. This was the organization that sponsored the *Spain & Culture* fundraising event at Royal Albert Hall, which Virginia and Leonard Woolf attended. For further reading on Woolf's political activism, see Rogers.

13. The Friends' Spain Committee, a branch of the Friends Service Council which oversees relief and field work, documents the inception, organization, and having joined the National Joint Committee for Spanish Relief in Minute 75 of the Spain Committee meeting records, dated December 22, 1936. FSC/SP/M1.

14. "Food for Spanish Refugees. Relief Ship Sails from London." *The Observer*. January 31, 1937. FSC/R/SP/5 News cuttings 1936–1940.

15. On August 25–6, 1914 a zeppelin bombed Antwerp, killing six civilians. Poolman cites the headline in the British tabloid *Daily Sketch* of 26 August: "ZEPPELIN'S ATTACK ON ANTWERP / SIX SHRAPNEL BOMBS FROM AN AIRSHIP AT NIGHT/ THE KING'S PERIL / TWELVE PEOPLE KILLED AND HOSPITAL DAMAGED" (26). The M class zeppelins deployed in August 1914 were 158 meters (518 feet) long, held 22,500 cubic meters (794,500 cubic feet) of gas, could carry 9,100 kilograms (20,100 pounds), and could reach 84 kilometers per hour (52 mph) (Robinson, *Giants in the Sky* 378).

16. See also Hearne.

17. See Morris, esp. summary tables, 265–79. Castle's *London*, illustrated by Christa Hook, includes invaluable visual materials: maps, period photographs, artworks, postcards, posters, leaflets, cartoons. In Castle's summary, the fifty-one zeppelin raids on Britain were intended "to crush the morale of the British population—particularly that of London—and bring about an end to the war"; they "claimed 557 lives and caused injury to 1,358 men, women and children, with material damage estimated at the time at £1.5 million, with almost £1 million of this inflicted on London. Some 26 raids targeted the capital, but only nine actually reached the central target area. These successful raids killed 181 in the capital and injured 504 people, or 36 per cent of the total casualties" (91). The first raid on London occurred on 31 May/1 June 1915, the last on October 19, 1917. In addition, as Levenback notes, "German aeroplanes raided England twenty-seven times between May 25, 1917 and May 20, 1918, including 17 raids on London"; reports of zeppelin attacks were "censored, and their precise targets...unspecified" (*Virginia Woolf* 122–23).

18. Goss includes three chapters on the Spanish Civil War. Levenback finds "Echoes from the Great War were becoming deafening...as they merged with portents of WWII" in Woolf's 1936 diaries (124); "More and more, distinct echoes, conscious memories, and secondary remembrance from the Great War were blurring her daily experience, her reading, and her writing" (144). See also Tate, 26–7; and McNees.

19. The zeppelin raid on central London of September 8, 1915 caused over half a million pounds of damage—more than half the material damage done by all raids against Britain that year, and the most done by a zeppelin raid during the war.

20. In *Zeppelins and Super-Zeppelins* R. P. Hearne describes the effect on civilian morale: "It is particularly humiliating to have an enemy come over your capital city and hurl bombs upon it. His aim may be very bad, the casualties may be few, but the moral effect is wholly undesirable. When the zeppelins came to London [as they did twelve times], they could have scored a falling technical triumph over us if they had showered us with confetti" (qtd. in Levenback 124).

21. The First Viscount Cecil served as British Under-Secretary of State for Foreign Affairs from June 1915 to January 1919.

22. Twelve zeppelins were launched on August 24–25, 1916; four reached England and one reached London. Flying above low clouds, it dropped thirty-six bombs in ten minutes on southeast London, killing nine people, injuring forty, and causing damage assessed at £130,203 (Cole and Cheesman, 149).

23. See Robinson, *Giants in the Sky*, ch. 5: "The Imitators: British Military Rigids," on the history of Britain's reactive efforts to make dirigibles (or "rigid airships" as the British called them), including the Royal Navy's anxiety on seeing German "successes with zeppelins—exaggerated in the eye of the distant beholder" (153); the Grand Fleet crews' "exaggerated" sense that their movements in the North Sea were "under constant surveillance by Zeppelins" (161); and the program's sad end with the "violent explosion" of rigid airship R 38 on August 23, 1921 (172). Britain did, however, build over 200 Sea Scout and North Sea small pressure airships (blimps) during the war for coastal scouting, mine clearance, and convoy patrol duties and at the war's end led the world in this airship technology. Woolf's idea that "it was really English" may allude to these non-rigid airships deployed along the coast.

24. Light notes other wartime tensions between the "largely pacifist" Woolfs and their servants with their "enthusiastic patriotism," even as they all "s[at] out air-raids on orange boxes...down in the basement kitchen" together (141).

25. In February 1917 third-generation Height Climber zeppelins which could rise to 20,000 feet entered service; in fact, that year's first raid did not occur until March 16–17, when five zeppelins were prevented by strong winds from reaching their targets (see Robinson, *Zeppelin* chap. 16, esp. 216f).

26. *The Library of Leonard and Virginia Woolf* lists Freud's "*On Dreams*. Trans. by M. D. Eder. London: Heinemann, 1914"; it is the only book by Freud published before the end of the war that appears in the catalog (81).

27. *The Library of Leonard and Virginia Woolf* lists "Aeschylus. *Eschyle; traduction nouvelle*. Trans. by Leconte de Lisle. Paris: A. Lemerre, [1889?]. VW—binder" (3). This letter to Sydney-Turner is the only mention of Aeschylus I have found in the letters, diaries, and notebooks of 1917.

28. The zeppelin raids of 1917 did less than 90,000 pounds damage. Nearly half of the airships were destroyed on the return flight.

29. A zeppelin bomb dropped that night on Hither Green (now Nightingale Grove) destroyed three houses, damaged many others, killed five women and nine children, and injured five adults and two children (Lewisham War Memorials, Local History and Archives Center, Lewisham, June 27, 2014).

Archives Consulted

Friends House Archives, Library of the Religious Society of Friends, London.
>   Minutes of the Friends Service Council Spain Committee 1936–1940: FSC/SP/M1.
>   FSC/R/SP/5 News cuttings 1936–40.
Monks House Papers, University of Sussex Special Collections, University of Sussex.
>   B.16 *Three Guineas* [Kirkpatrick A23]. f. 3 volumes containing press cuttings and ms and typed extracts collected or copied by VW, relative to *Three Guineas*.

Works Cited

Addario, Lynsey. "The Historic Scale of Syria's Refugee Crisis." *New York Times*. 16 Oct. 2013. *Art Works Projects for Human Rights*. Web. 28 June 2014.

Atkin, Jonathan. *A War of Individuals: Bloomsbury Attitudes to the Great War*. Manchester, UK: Manchester UP, 2002.

Bell, Julian. "War and Peace: A Letter to E. M. Forster." *Essays, Poems and Letters*. Ed. Quentin Bell. London: Hogarth, 1938. 335–90.

Berman, Jessica. *Modernist Commitments: Ethics, Politics, and Transnational Modernism*. New York: Columbia UP, 2012.

Brenkman, John. *The Cultural Contradictions of Democracy: Political Thought since September 11*. Princeton, NJ: Princeton UP, 2007.

Brockington, Grace. *Above the Battlefield: Modernism and the Peace Movement in Britain, 1900–1918*. New Haven: Yale UP. 2010.

Castle, Ian. *London 1914–17: The Zeppelin Menace*. Long Island City, NY: Osprey Press, 2008.

Cocks, F. Seymour, W.P. Crawford Greene, D.R. Grenfell, A.W. James, J.R.J. Macnamara, Wilfrid Roberts. *Spain: The Visit of an All-Party Group of Member of Parliament to Spain: Report*. London: Lawrence & Wishart, 1936. *Warwick Digital Library*. Web. 9 February 2015.

Cole, Christopher, and E. F. Cheesman. *The Air Defence of Britain 1914–1918*. London: Putnam, 1984.

Cole, Sarah. *At the Violet Hour. Modernism and Violence in England and Ireland*. New York: Oxford UP, 2012.

Cooper, Sandi E. Lecture. "Summary Remarks." Les Defenseurs de la Paix: 1899–1917: Approches actuelles, nouveaux regards. Colloque International. L'Institut Historique Allemand et L'Université Paris-Est, Paris, France. 15–17 January 2014. Web.

Cortright, David. *Peace: A History of Movements and Ideas*. Cambridge: Cambridge UP, 2008.

Dalgarno, Emily. "'Ruined houses and dead bodies': '*Three Guineas*' and the Spanish Civil War." *Virginia Woolf and the Visible World*. Cambridge: Cambridge UP, 2001. 149–78.

Deacon, David. *British News Media and the Spanish Civil War: Tomorrow May be Too Late*. Edinburgh: Edinburgh UP, 2008.

Delaprée, Louis. *The Martyrdom of Madrid: Inedited Witness*. Madrid: 1937, no publisher.

Deming, Barbara. "On Revolution and Equilibrium." *Revolution and Equilibrium*. New York: Grossman, 1971.

Evans, Brad. "Inaugural Statement." *On Violence* 1 (2013–2014): 2–6. *Histories of Violence.com*. Web. 5 February 2015.

——. "Ten Years of Terror." *On Violence*, Special Series: Full Lectures. *Histories of Violence.com*. Web. 5 February 2015.

Favret, Mary A. *War at a Distance: Romanticism and the Making of Modern Wartime*. Princeton, NJ: Princeton UP, 2010.

Fernald, Anne E. "Woolf and Intertextuality." *Virginia Woolf in Context*. Ed. by Bryony Randall and Jane Goldman. Cambridge: Cambridge UP, 2012. 52–64.

"Food for Spanish Refugees. Relief Ship Sails from London." *The Observer*. January 31, 1937. Friends House Archives, Library of the Religious Society of Friends, London. FSC/R/SP/5 News cuttings 1936–1940.

Foster, J. Ashley. "Stopped at the Border: Virginia Woolf and the Criminalization of Dissent in Democratic Societies." *Interdisciplinary/Multidisciplinary Woolf: Selected Papers from the Twenty-Second International Conference on Virginia Woolf*. Ed. Ann Martin and Kathryn Holland. Clemson: Clemson U Digital P, 2013: 57–67.

——. "The Weeping Woman and Virginia Woolf's Call of Conscience: Radical Pacifist Politics in *Three Guineas*." *The Virginia Woolf Bulletin*, No. 44 (September 2013): 11–18.

Froula, Christine. *Virginia Woolf and the Bloomsbury Avant-Garde: War, Civilization, Modernity*. New York: Columbia UP, 2005.

——. "The Daughter's Seduction." *Signs* 11.4 (1986): 621–44.

Fussell, Paul. *The Great War and Modern Memory*. Oxford: Oxford UP, 1975.

"The German Airships. Raiding and Its Effects. Means of Defence." *Times* (London). 6 August 1914: 4. *The Times Digital Archive*. 23 June 2014.

Goss, Hilton P. *Civilian Morale Under Aerial Bombardment, 1914–1939*. 2 vols. Maxwell Air Force Base, AL: Air University Research Studies Institute, 1948.

Griffin, Susan. *A Chorus of Stones: The Private Life of War*. New York: Doubleday, 1992.

Harrison, Jane Ellen. "Epilogue on the War: Peace with Pacifism." *Alpha and Omega*. 1915. New York: AMS Press, 1973.

Hearne, R. P. *Airships in Peace and War*. 2nd ed. London: John Lane, The Bodley Head, 1910.

Heidegger, Martin. *Being and Time*. Trans. John Macquarrie and Edward Robinson. New York: Harper San Francisco, 1962.

Hussey, Mark, ed. *Virginia Woolf and War: Fiction, Reality, and Myth*. Syracuse, NY: Syracuse UP, 1991.

——. "Woolf: After Lives." *Virginia Woolf in Context*. Ed. Bryony Randall and Jane Goldman. New York: Cambridge UP, 2012. 13–27.

Laurence, Patricia. "The Facts and Fugue of War: From *Three Guineas* to *Between the Acts*." Hussey, *Virginia Woolf and War*. 225–45.

——. *Julian Bell, the Violent Pacifist*. London: Cecil Woolf, 2006.

Levenback, Karen L. *Virginia Woolf and the Great War*. Syracuse, NY: Syracuse UP, 1999.

——. "Placing the First 'Enormous Chunk' Deleted from *The Years*," *Virginia Woolf Miscellany* 42 (Spring 1994): 8–9.

The Library of Leonard and Virginia Woolf: A Short-title Catalog. Compiled and edited by Julia King and Laila Miletic-Vejzovic. Foreword by Laila Miletic-Vejzovic. Intro. Diane Gillespie. Pullman, Washington: Washington State UP, 2003.

Light, Alison. *Mrs. Woolf and the Servants*. New York: Fig Tree Press, 2007.

Marcus, Jane. Introduction. *Three Guineas*. By Virginia Woolf. Orlando, FL: Harcourt, 2006. xxxv–lxxii.

May, Todd. "The Dignity of Non-Violence." *On Violence* 1 (2013–2014): 7–12. *Histories of Violence.com*. Web. 28 June 2014.

McNees, Eleanor. "History as Scaffolding: Woolf's Use of *The Times* in *The Years*." *Interdisciplinary/Multidisciplinary Woolf*. Ed. Ann Martin and Kathryn Holland. Clemson, SC: Clemson U Digital P, 2013. 41–49.

Mills, Jean. *Virginia Woolf, Jane Ellen Harrison, and the Spirit of Modernist Classicism*. Columbus: Ohio State UP, 2014.

Morris, Joseph (Captain). *The German Air Raids on Great Britain, 1914–1918*. London: Sampson Low, Marston & Co., Ltd., 1925.

Myers, Steven Lee. "Russia's Move Into Ukraine Said to be Born in Shadows." *New York Times*. 7 March 2014.

Onishi, Norimitsu. "Scattered by War Syrian Family Struggles to Start Over." *New York Times*. 16 October 2013.

Picasso, Pablo. *Guernica*. 1937. Oil on canvas. Musée Nacional Centro de Arte Reina Sofia, Madrid.

Poolman, Kenneth. *Zeppelins Against London*. New York: John Day, 1961.

Preston, Paul. *We Saw Spain Die: Foreign Correspondents in the Spanish Civil War*. New York: Skyhorse Publishing, 2009.

Robinson, Douglas H. *Giants in the Sky: A History of the Rigid Airship*. Seattle: U of Washington P, 1973.

——. *The Zeppelin in Combat: A History of the German Naval Airship Division, 1912–1918*. 3rd ed. Henley-on-Thames, UK: Foulis, 1971.

Rogers, Gayle. *Modernism and the New Spain: Britain, Cosmopolitan Europe, and Literary History*. Oxford: Oxford UP, 2012.

Simpson, John. "Russia's Crimea plan detailed, secret, and successful." *BBC News*. 19 March 2014.

Slessor, John, RAF Marshal. Foreword. *Zeppelins Against London*. By Poolman. ix–x.

Strachan, Hew. *The First World War. Vol. I: To Arms*. Oxford: Oxford UP, 2001.

Tate, Trudi. *Modernism, History and the First World War*. New York: Manchester UP, 1998.

They Still Draw Pictures: Drawings Made by Spanish Children During the Spanish Civil War, circa 1938. USCD Mandeville Special Collections Library digital archive. Standing Digital Exhibit. *Times* (London). *The Times Digital Archive*. 23 June 2014.

Wells, H. G. *The War in the Air: and Particularly How Mr. Bert Smallways Fared While It Lasted*. Illus. A. C. Michael. London: G. Bell, 1908.

Winter, Jay. *Dreams of Peace and Freedom: Utopian Moments in the 20th Century*. New Haven: Yale UP, 2006.

Woolf, Leonard. *Quack, Quack!* London: Hogarth, 1935.

Woolf, Virginia. *Between the Acts*. 1941. San Diego: Harcourt, 1969.

——. *The Diary of Virginia Woolf*. Ed. Anne Olivier Bell. 5 vols. New York: Harcourt Brace, 1977–1984.

——. *The Letters of Virginia Woolf*. Vol. 2. 1912–1922. Ed. Nigel Nicolson and Joanne Trautmann. New York: Harcourt Brace Jovanovich, 1976.

——. "Mr. Bennett and Mrs. Brown." 1924. *The Captain's Death Bed and Other Essays*. New York: Harcourt Brace, 1950.

——. "A Sketch of the Past." *Moments of Being*. Ed. Jeanne Schulkind. 2nd ed. San Diego: Harcourt Brace Jovanovich, 1985.

——. "Thoughts on Peace in an Air Raid." 1940. *The Death of the Moth and Other Essays*. New York: Harcourt, 1942. 243–48.

——. *Three Guineas*. 1938. Annot. and intro. Jane Marcus. Orlando, FL: Harcourt, 2006.

——. *To the Lighthouse*. 1927. San Diego: Harcourt, Inc., 1981.

——. "The War from the Street." *The Essays of Virginia Woolf*. Vol. 3. 1919–1924. Ed. Andrew McNeillie. New York: Harcourt Brace Jovanovich, 1988.

——. *The Years*. 1937. San Diego: Harcourt, 1965.

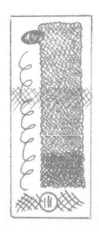

Intersections: Surveillance, Propaganda, and Just War

by Judith Allen

> Governments fear expression of independent thought more than an army.
> Leo Tolstoy, "Christianity and Patriotism" (1894) 532.

> The conscious and intelligent manipulation of the organized habits and opinions of the masses is an important element in democratic society. Those who manipulate this unseen mechanism of society constitute an invisible government which is the true ruling power of our country.
> Edward Bernays, *Propaganda* (1928) 37.

> Sometimes I try to worry out what some of the phrases we're ruled by mean. I doubt whether most people even do that. Liberty, for instance.
> *The Diary of Virginia Woolf*, 13 April 1918, 138.

My first email on the day I presented this paper came from Edward Snowden! Snowden's letter—sent through the *American Civil Liberties Union*—was to celebrate the first anniversary of "the leak." Here are his first words: "Technology has been a liberating force in our lives. It allows us to create and share the experiences that make us human, effortlessly. But in secret, our very own government—one bound by the Constitution and its Bill of Rights—has reverse-engineered something beautiful into a tool of mass surveillance and oppression. The government right now can easily monitor whom you call, whom you associate with, what you read, what you buy, and where you go online, and they do it to all of us, all the time." As I revised this paper, I thought about the Edward Snowdens of our world, the increasing importance of whistleblowers, and their diminishing status. My epigraphs highlight the significance of "independent thought," "invisible government," and the meanings of "those phrases we're ruled by." I re-read them more closely now, as our current world—in all of its contextual complexity—impinges upon them, expanding their meanings.

The concept of "control"—in its multitudinous uses—is resoundingly communicated by the epigraphs I have chosen. Tolstoy's prescient commentary brings to mind the control of dissent, of resistance, and the suppression of free speech—of a free press—that exists today; Edward Bernays, the creator of the field of "public relations," defends "propaganda," with its ability to manipulate people's thoughts and shape "public opinion"; and last, Virginia Woolf expresses her ever-present concern with the politics of language, her thoughts about those who seek to control us, and, crucially, the significance and power of their chosen words and their ease in justifying wars. In her diary entry, she interrogates the power of the word "liberty," leading readers to re-assess words she repeatedly questions twenty years later in her anti-war manifesto, *Three Guineas*. In that 1938 work, her narrators interrogate the gendering of language, focusing on the words "freedom," "influence," "patriotism," and "society," and the extremely different meanings they express and enact for "educated men" and the "daughters of educated men."

As I explore the varied modes of "control," I will delve into "surveillance," "propaganda," and the ever-changing face of "just war theory," terms that involve diverse aspects of control (political, economic, cultural, and social) facing us today. Attempts to decipher what our leaders justify in our name generates questions regarding the manufacturing of consent, the manipulation of public opinion, and the politics of language. These complicated questions will take us back to Virginia Woolf's readings and writings, the varied contexts that influenced them, and will ultimately show how these issues resonate in our current world. Finally, I will show how Tolstoy's prescient commentary testifies to the US government's vilification and punishment of whistleblowers—especially those who have exposed unconstitutional acts of torture and surveillance.

One finds some of the roots of surveillance in Jeremy Betham's eighteenth-century prison structure, the "Panopticon"—appropriated by Michel Foucault for his writings on "power" and "control" through surveillance. Foucault's Panopticon, like the surveillance of personal information by the US National Security Agency (NSA), functions to monitor individuals who are unaware of when they are being watched; just their knowledge of this possibility supposedly transforms their behavior. This type of power and control would be anathema to Woolf, for such an affront to "freedom"—explored so well in *Three Guineas*—would destroy autonomous life. Many investigative journalists—like Jim Risen[1] of the *New York Times*—are being silenced by the US Justice Department and/or arrested and killed by other governments as I write. When Snowden's revelations exposed the surveillance of German Chancellor Angela Merkel's emails and cell-phone calls, they posed important questions about democracy, fascism, and more generally—"security" versus "civil liberties." Many compared the NSA and the government's assault on freedom of the press to the East German Stasi. Interestingly, those in the NSA or involved with Intelligence about the Soviet Union years ago were some of the first to make comparisons to the Stasi.[2]

As early as 1742, the British Postal Service read, censored, and deciphered coded letters from abroad, although other types of surveillance can be traced back much further. During World War I, the British government examined mail, took photographs from airplanes, observed operations from Zeppelins—also used for bombing—and in 1917 trained cryptographers were used for code-breaking. The first half of the 1900s saw the establishment of government surveillance agencies such as the FBI (1908), CIA (1947), and NSA (1952) in the US, and MI5 (1909) and Government Communications Headquarters (GCHQ) (1919) in the UK. Today, with many of these organizations intact and working together, we are subject to increased "surveillance" as we utilize our electronic devices; "fear-mongering" is also easier and faster than ever as audiences are manipulated by governments and their security organizations. Our electronic devices are filled with last summer's photographs of Gaza's "ruined houses and dead bodies," as the almost unanimous US Congressional vote in August, 2014, replenished the financial support to continue the killing (2,200 civilians including 490 children) and destruction. We recall this echoing of gruesome photographs—repeatedly referenced, but intentionally not shown—in Virginia Woolf's *Three Guineas* (10–11). Many in the United States question our own "democracy" when told that our interventions, supported by allies, will "impose democracy" on other—mostly oil-rich—countries. Our country's history of deposing democratically elected leaders whom we cannot control still engenders tremendous skepticism.

The mainstream media's repeated words and phrases, however, especially the term "war on terror," and the word "terrorism" (echoing the language of various leaders), are not questioned by "most people" (*D1* 138). As Tomis Kapitan writes in the *New York Times*: "The powerful rhetoric centered on the word 'terrorism' makes it difficult to speak intelligently about its real sources" because "there is no consensus about the meaning of 'terrorism'." He adds that "the rhetoric of terror has been used by those in power not only to sway public opinion, but to direct attention away from their own acts of terror." A recent example would be the sentence spoken by President Obama: "We tortured some folks."[3] The relaxed tone and the use of the word "folks" seem scripted, but are simultaneously an indication of his sanctioning of his administration's continuation of Bush's unconstitutional acts at Guantanamo. The statement itself is Kafkaesque in its level of nonchalance, as if he were saying: "we had bacon for breakfast"!

After viewing photos of the Bush Administration's torturing of prisoners, the world watched Israel's 2014 assault on Gaza; the media reported Obama's shocked response to the killing of over 2,000 civilians at the same time as they reported his support of "one's right to defend oneself against rockets." Witnessing these barbaric acts and the words permeating our news media today, returns us once again to *Three* Guineas: the newspapers write of "horror and disgust," and assert that this "war [...] is an abomination; a barbarity"(11); they stop short, however, of invoking the ultimate goal in *Three Guineas*: "war must be stopped at whatever cost" (11). And even today, "the control of the Press—the decision what to print, what not to print"—is under corporate control, and still "in the hands of your sex"(*TG* 12), of patriarchy. It is not surprising that statements to stop war—by women and other anti-war activists—"scarcely inflict one scratch" (*TG* 12). The everyday violence in the United States continues, supported by the power of the National Rifle Association (NRA) as the militarization of our local police forces continues, and as the repeated killings of unarmed young Black men (Trayvon Martin, Tamir Rice, and so many more), demonstrate. I often think back to Mark Hussey's 1991 work, *Virginia Woolf and War*, and his aptly titled Introduction, "Living in a War Zone"; sadly, this title still resonates today: "we all—are living in a war zone" (Hussey 13).

Always present within this varied assemblage of declared wars and undeclared conflicts, with their attendant protests and resistance movements, are the government's acts of "surveillance," its hired media "propagandists," and its "Just War" theories. Woolf was certainly aware that "surveillance" and "propaganda" were in full force in Britain in the early 20th century. Walter Lippmann, an established American journalist and propagandist during WWI, is known for his 1922 work, *Public Opinion* (in the Woolf's library), and for his important phrase: "the manufacturing of consent" (158). Many of Lippmann's ideas in *Public Opinion* were very important to Edward Bernays, a nephew of Sigmund Freud, who used them in his later work, *Propaganda* (1928). Noam Chomsky strongly criticized *Public Opinion* because of its undermining of democracy since it called for finding "experts" to decide what the public was too ignorant or too busy to understand. Chomsky appropriated Lippmann's term, "manufacturing consent,"[4] to elaborate on its downside, its damage to the democratic process, and its links with oligarchy. Confronting the propaganda effort, Arthur Ponsonby, a Member of Parliament, a pacifist, and friend of the Woolfs, wrote *Falsehood in Wartime: Propaganda Lies of the First World War* (1928). His book counteracted the thesis of Bernays' work by exposing the lies propagated by both journalists, politicians, and many well-known writers.

Woolf's writings express and enact a different mode of surveillance, as her narrators prompt readers to "see," to observe, to expose, but also to be aware that much is hidden, or re-named in an Orwellian sense. As citizens, as readers, we are urged to doubt, to think critically, to question everything. As her narrator states in *Three Guineas*, explaining why she must read "three dailies, and three weeklies": "I should no more dream, given the conditions of journalism at present, of taking my opinions of pictures, plays, music or books from the newspapers than I would take my opinion of politics from the newspapers. Compare the views, make allowance for the distortions, and then judge for yourself. That is the only way"(*TG* 95–96). The scrutiny of the media that Woolf advocates resonates with Noam Chomsky's recent commentary about Gaza on *Democracy Now*: "It's a shameful moment for U.S. media when it insists on being subservient to the grotesque propaganda agencies of a violent aggressive state."[5]

In his book on WWI, Adam Hochschild notes that "conscription spurred the country's anti-war movement into new life" and, in 1916, 200,000 Britons signed a petition calling for a negotiated peace. Antiwar organizations had their offices raided, their mail opened, and were infiltrated by informers. The United Kingdom was using the "Official Secrets Act," with its 1911 version making it illegal to disclose information without lawful authority.[6] Given the growth of pacifism in 1918, surveillance intensified, and with that came suppression of the National Labour Press which printed the *Tribunal*, an antiwar secret newspaper (Hochschild 324). Speeches by Charlotte Despard, one of many women then involved in the anti-war movement, were prohibited; Despard's organizations, The Women's Peace Crusade and the Women's Freedom League, were carefully watched, as was her mail, but the *Tribunal* newspapers remained hidden.

In the United States, Congress passed The Espionage Act in 1917, the act under which Edward Snowden, if captured, will be charged; Snowden exposed the National Security Agency's unconstitutional eavesdropping on everyone's email and phones, as well as the government's insertion of spyware in foreign orders for computer routers. Snowden, a polarizing figure viewed as a traitor or hero, has been vilified by many governments, including the Obama Administration, and praised by civil rights advocates, Libertarians, and others. He is considered by all to be a "whistleblower," a term created by well-known whistleblower, Ralph Nader, in the 1970s. Although these individuals were later offered protection by the Whistleblower Act (1989)—this law does not apply to Snowden, a government "contractor." Given that whistleblowers[7] are not looked upon with kindness by the US government— clearly reflecting Tolstoy's commentary in my epigraph—one finds ample evidence of severe punishments for speaking out. Given Woolf's feminist politics, she would clearly support voices that uncover abuse and call attention to the exposure of illegalities.

Newspapers were also vehicles of censorship, as well as propaganda machines, and Woolf often complained bitterly about "the damned newspapers" (*L2* 90) of the Northcliffe Press, owned by Lord Alfred Harmsworth, Director of Propaganda in the Lloyd George government. In Woolf's diary of 1918, she states: "the Northcliffe papers do all they can to insist upon the indispensability & delight of war" (*D1* 200). We see this replicated today, as newspapers, owned by various corporations, "spin" things for financial benefit and often cave to government pressures to withhold important news; an egregious example is the *New York Times*, which withheld a story in late 2003 about "warrantless wiretapping" during the lead-up to the Iraq War. Complying with the request of George W. Bush, who was running for re-election at the time, the *New York Times* withheld the story for 15 months. When Edward Snowden released the NSA surveillance information, he chose to exclude the *New York Times* because it allowed the government to dictate what was news.

In *Three Guineas*, Woolf's narrators call for reading several newspapers daily in order "to strip each statement of its money motive, of its power motive, of its advertising motive, of its publicity motive [...] before you make up your mind about which fact of politics to believe" (*TG* 96). Woolf emphasizes the need to be aware of how language is used by those in power—to persuade, and, importantly, to gain market share. Bernays, in order to sell cigarettes to women, had to link an image of a powerful woman with the smoking of a cigarette; his advertizing campaigns for products were so successful that he knew he could easily sell war to the public. Clearly, consent was easily manufactured.

Although I had written about Lippmann and Bernays in greater detail in *Virginia Woolf and the Politics of Language* (2010),[8] I was uncertain about Woolf's familiarity with Bernays's *Propaganda*. Recently I was able to examine a copy of *The Forum* magazine of March, 1929, which includes Woolf's "Women and Fiction," and found a debate titled: "Are We Victims of PROPAGANDA?" Answering affirmatively, Everett Dean Martin, an educator, titled his response "Our Invisible Masters," while Bernays's negative response, "Our Debt to Propaganda," clearly denied any victimhood (*Forum* 146). Martin found that propaganda's "aim was to put something over on people, with or without their knowledge and consent....It is never disinterested information" (142). Martin interestingly quoted Bernays's defense of propaganda: "in its sum total, it is regimenting the public mind every bit as much as an army regiments the bodies of its soldiers....There are invisible rulers who control the destiny of millions" (*Forum* 143). Bernays, like Walter Lippmann, speaks of "experts," of "the intelligent few," of "specialists," as those chosen to make important decisions.

"Just War" theorizing goes back to Cicero, Aquinas, and Augustine, and forward to Barack Obama's Nobel Peace Prize acceptance speech (December 10, 2009).[9] Giving this speech a week after he ordered 30,000 more troops to Afghanistan, Obama used the term "just war" as he justified the actions he had taken in Afghanistan. He failed, however, to mention Pakistan, where the United States was and still is using predator drones in an "undeclared" war. His speech opposed Woolf's "Thoughts on Peace in an Air Raid," which thinks about peace in the context of war; Obama spoke of war in the context of peace, in the exceptionally ironic context of accepting the Nobel Peace Prize (as politically driven as that prize may be)! In the process, he invoked phrases—"phrases we're ruled by"—that were reminiscent of former President George W. Bush. Obama's finding that "the instruments of war do have a role to play in preserving the peace" (Oslo 2009) became one of the "sound bites," along with his chosen quotations linking himself with Martin Luther King, Nelson Mandela, and Gandhi. Obama also spoke of his responsibility for deploying thousands of young Americans for war, noting that "some will kill, and some will be killed." Later in this speech, his justification of force includes his emotional statement that "inaction tears at our conscience and can lead to more costly interventions later"; instilling fear with such threatening statements serves to "manufacture consent."

As Margaret Denike points out, "in the devastation created and exacerbated by the very individuals who stand to personally profit from the new imperial order they impose in its place, [these leaders are consistently] talking the moral talk of 'Operation Infinite Justice' or 'Iraqi Freedom'"(103). Although many who have examined "Just War" theory find the term to be oxymoronic, other explorations focus on varied justifications involving human-rights discourses that "when used together with the pretense of self-defense and preemptive war, do the opposite of what they claim—entrenching the sovereignty of Western imperialist states while eroding the conditions necessary for the recognition of the human rights of others" (Denike 95).

I began this paper with Edward Snowden's comments, and now, in January 2015, he has leaked new information: Britain's GCHQ has intercepted emails from the *Guardian,* the BBC, *The New York Times,* the *Washington Post,* and others, including emails between editors and journalists. The GCHQ, the successor to the famous Bletchley Park code-breakers, has also listed investigative journalists alongside terrorists and hackers (Chester). It is not insignificant that this "leak" followed so closely the killings in the office of French satirical weekly, *Charlie Hebdo,* and the massive marches for freedom of the press in Paris and elsewhere.

As journalist John Pilger asks: "Why do we tolerate the threat of another world war in our name? Why do we allow lies that justify this risk? 'The scale of our indoctrination,' wrote Harold Pinter, is a 'brilliant, even witty, highly successful act of hypnosis', as if the truth 'never happened even while it was happening'."[10] Pinter's invocation of "hypnosis" is indeed very important at this time, as it was when invoked by two pacifists—Leo Tolstoy and Virginia Woolf. Arthur Ponsonby tried to reveal that "war is fought in this fog of falsehood, a great deal of it undiscovered and accepted as truth....Any attempt to doubt or deny even the most fantastic story has to be condemned at once as unpatriotic, if not traitorous" (16). Perhaps avoidance of this "fog of falsehood" has resonances with the firm espousal by Tolstoy and Woolf to refuse to allow oneself to be "hypnotized." In Tolstoy's "Patriotism and Government" he calls for "shaking off the hypnotism of patriotism" (13). Woolf clearly resists "the power of medals, symbols, orders and even, it would seem, decorated ink-pots to hypnotise the human mind [for] it must be our aim not to submit ourselves to such hypnotism" (*TG* 114).[11] Our resident whistleblower, Virginia Woolf, would never succumb!

Notes

1. Jim Risen, charged with refusing to reveal his sources after exposing the government's "warrantless wiretapping," has refused to testify. He recently claimed "Obama the greatest enemy to press freedom in a generation" (Huffington Post, 8/17/2014). Risen was excused from testifying in January 2015.
2. See Washingtonsblog.com, June 30, 2014; whistleblowers Thomas Drake and Bill Binney liken NSA, their former employer, to Stasi and Soviet Spying.
3. White House News conference, August 1, 2014.
4. Noam Chomsky's *Manufacturing Consent* (1988) critiques the media's propaganda, its self-censorship.
5. *Democracy Now,* with Amy Goodman, is a public TV news show with no corporate sponsors. "The Media's Shameful Moment," with Noam Chomsky, aired August 11, 2014. Access online.
6. In 1989, the "Official Secrets Act" was revised and now targets whistleblowers and investigative journalists.
7. Look up each "whistleblower" online: Ronald Ridenhour (1969); Jesselyn Radak (2001); Thomas Drake (2005–11); John Kiriakou (2007).
8. See Allen, Chapter 6, 97–112.

9.   Obama's acceptance speech for the Nobel Peace Prize, December 10, 2009, is online at The White House, Office of the Press Secretary.

10.   See John Pilger, "Break the silence: a world war is beckoning," *johnpilger.com*, 13 May 2014. His film, *The War You Don't See*, which references Edward Bernays, is available online.

11.   The endnote in *Three Guineas* suggests the "decorated ink pot" is "a large silver plaque in the form of a Reich eagle…created by President Hindenburg for scientists and other distinguished civilians" (*TG* 179n19).

Works Cited

Allen, Judith. *Virginia Woolf and the Politics of Language*. Edinburgh: Edinburgh UP, 2010.

Bernays, Edward. 1928. *Propaganda*. Brooklyn, NY: Ig Publishing, 2005.

Chester, Tim. *The Guardian*. 19 January 2015.

Chomsky, Noam and Edward S. Herman. *Manufacturing Consent: The Political Economy of the Mass Media*. New York: Pantheon Books, 1988.

Democracy Now. Public News Radio/TV show with Amy Goodman and Juan Gonzalez.

Denike, Margaret. "The Human Rights of Others: Sovereignty, Legitimacy, and 'Just Causes' for the 'War on Terror'." *Hypatia* 23.2 (2008): 95–121.

The Forum. Ed. Henry Goddard Leach. 81.3 (March 1929): 142–147.

Hochschild, Adam. *To End All Wars: A Story of Loyalty and Rebellion, 1914–1918*. Boston, MA: Houghton Mifflin Harcourt, 2011.

Kapitan, Tomis. "The Reign of Terror." *The New York Times*. 19 October 2014.

Lippmann, Walter. 1922. *Public Opinion*. New York: Simon and Schuster, 1997.

Pilger, John. *johnpilger.com*.

Snowden, Edward. "One Year Later." Message to aclu@aclu.org. 5 June 2014.

Tolstoy, Leo. 1894. "Christianity and Patriotism." *The Kingdom of God and Peace: Essays*. London: Oxford UP, 1936.

——. 1900. "Patriotism and Government." *Anarchy Archives*. Web. 2 June 2004.

Woolf, Virginia. *The Common Reader: First Series*. 1925. Ed. and intro. Andrew McNeillie. San Diego: Harcourt Brace Jovanovich, 1984.

——. *The Death of the Moth and Other Essays*. 1942. New York: Harcourt Brace Jovanovich, 1970.

——. *The Diary of Virginia Woolf*. 5 vols. Ed. Anne Olivier Bell. New York: Harcourt Brace Jovanovich, 1977–84.

——. *A Room of One's Own*. 1929. New York: Harcourt Brace Jovanovich, 1957.

——. *Three Guineas*. 1938. New York: Harcourt Brace Jovanovich, 1966.

MODERNISM AND MEMORIALS:
VIRGINIA WOOLF AND CHRISTOPHER ISHERWOOD

by Erica Gene Delsandro

Scholarly narratives that define modernist fiction traditionally position Victorian Age-born innovators of the novel *against* those with whom they share the realm of literature and letters during the interwar years. On one hand, there are veteran soldiers-cum-authors emerging ten years after the Armistice; on the other hand, there are Younger Generation writers born in the first years of the twentieth century, writing in the wake of war and modernism, too young to have participated in either. Veteran authors occupy a privileged position in this critical discourse: they may or may not be modernist since, as Jay Winter has convincingly argued, their primary impetus is the "aesthetics of direct experience" (2). Consequently, what remains when scholars assess the literary landscape of the interwar years are two seemingly distinct groups of writers, commonly characterized as antagonists: the aging modernists and the thirtysomething Younger Generation writers. Although studies such as *A Shrinking Island* (2004) and *Intermodernism* (2009) do shed new light on this literary interwar landscape, they trend in two directions: they *either* chart modernism's evolution in the 1930s privileging the work of canonical modernists (Jed Esty) *or* create new categories to characterize literature produced by those too young—or too political or too female—to be modernist (Kristin Bluemel). Ultimately, both approaches participate in an antagonistic discourse situating modernist writers in opposition to their Younger Generation counterparts despite the literary-historical reality that both groups are responding to the consequences of the Great War by testing the efficacy of fiction in a postwar world.

My essay complicates the dominant literary-historical narrative by comparing Virginia Woolf's *Jacob's Room* (1922) and *To the Lighthouse* (1927) with Christopher Isherwood's *The Memorial* (1932) in the context of the Great War and the national memorialization in its wake. (Woolf's essay "The Leaning Tower" [1940] will help me tie the threads together.) Such a constellation advocates for a discourse of affiliation highlighting the shared literary sympathies of modernist and Younger Generation writers in a world saturated by memorials both military and masculine.

MODERNISM AS WAR MEMORIAL

One of the most convincing characterizations of modernism is as a response to the Great War. Authors such as Paul Fussell, Jay Winter, Allyson Booth, Trudi Tate, and, very recently, Sarah Cole, are just a few of the many scholars who have contributed to our understanding of the relationship between modernism and war. Vincent Sherry synthesizes this approach: "[b]y the rule of well-established associations, the Great War of 1914–18 locates the moment in which the new sensibility of English—and international—modernism comes fully into existence" (6). Sherry, like other scholars, extends Winter's "aesthetics of direct experience:" not only a framework to understand combatant and veteran narratives but also a framework revealing the impact of total war, for example, on literary intellectuals sensitive to the nuances of political discourse (see Sherry), on women confined to the home front (see Claire Tylee), and on mass culture in general (see Patrick Deer). This brief overview underscores the primary position the Great War has in our construction of modernism. There are other ways to position and examine modernist production in the first half of the twentieth century; however, to borrow from Steven Schroeder, war plays a significant role in how we divide history, these divisions "themselves [being] acts of language that not only describe worlds but also circumscribe the stories we tell about them and what and how we see in them" (1691). Indisputably, the Great War contributes to constructing the time of modernism, describing and circumscribing the stories we tell about modernism, what modernism is about, and how we read modernist literature.

<h3>WOOLF AND MEMORIALIZATION</h3>

In the 1920s, Woolf indirectly contributed to what Valentine Cunningham calls the "war book boom" (44). To look at Woolf's novels of the 1920s is to see the inescapable influence of war on young men, women on the home front, concepts of nation, and the nature of narrative itself. Although *Mrs. Dalloway*'s (1925) Septimus Smith gives the legacy of the war not only a face but also a voice, both *Jacob's Room* and *To the Lighthouse* explore the Great War obliquely through the politics of memorialization. I briefly touch upon these two novels, emphasizing a familiar context within which I would like to include Christopher Isherwood and *The Memorial*.

Many scholars have read *To the Lighthouse* as Woolf's memorial to her mother, Julia Stephen. "[Y]ou have given a portrait of mother which is more like her to me than anything I could ever have conceived of as possible," writes Vanessa Bell after reading the novel (*L3* 572). Woolf responds, "I'm in a terrible state of pleasure that you should think Mrs. Ramsay so like mother" (*L3* 383). Such comments have fostered a reading of the novel as an elegy: personally, an elegy to Julia Stephen, to a family torn apart by death, and to a childhood irrevocably marked by loss. Placing Woolf's personal grief within a larger historical and national context, the novel also elegizes an imperfect yet cherished era, the necessary but still disruptive alterations in the gender roles that shaped and reflected Victoria's reign (which, Woolf argues, continued until 1914), and the millions who died in the Great War.

However, like architects of Great War monuments attempting to memorialize absence and mitigate the anger that attends it—so many fallen soldiers and so few bodies—Woolf struggled to memorialize a woman she barely knew and an era by which she felt confined and from which she was happy to escape. Allyson Booth's attention to space, physical and narrative, connects Woolf's memorial impulse in *To the Lighthouse* with the nation's struggle to memorialize the millions lost on foreign fields during the Great War. According to Booth, *To the Lighthouse* is a modernist example expressing "civilians' relation to the war in terms of architecture or [that] actually situate the home-front experience of war at a specific architectural site" (43), in Woolf's case a family home. In the "Time Passes" section of the novel, the war is "textually bracketed, numerically limited, and architecturally contained," narrated from "inside an empty house" (3): "the buildings of modernism may delineate spaces within which one is forced to confront both war's casualties and one's distance from those casualties…even when war itself seems peripheral to modernist content" (4). As nature threatens to overtake the Ramsey's summer home, war and death interrupt. But their interruption is not as overwhelming as the nature that is beginning to run wild through the hallmarks of civilization: looking glasses, teacups, clothes, books. War and death are contained and bracketed, made accessible while simultaneously recognized as distant and absent.

The tension between presence and absence, proximity and distance, marks Woolf's most evocative experiments in memorialization and, according to Robert Reginio, sets Woolf's work apart from the architectural monuments being erected across the nation that sought to embody memorial impulses in the face of mass absence and a war geographically and, increasingly, temporally distant. Reginio argues that national war memorials like the Cenotaph "implied a return to the unity the nation once represented" while Woolf's narrative experiments in memorialization sought to expose and critique national unity as a mythology deliberately constructed (89). Following Reginio, I propose that like the Cenotaph, an empty tomb, *Jacob's Room* foregrounds absence thematically and structurally; however, while absence is entombed within the structure of the Cenotaph—absence made present—absence is put into relief in Woolf's novel. In other words, whereas the Cenotaph materializes and maintains absence through physical architecture buttressed by national rhetoric and ritual, *Jacob's Room* explores, in Reginio's words, "how the absence is created, constructed, and maintained"; in "leav[ing] her novel decentered," explains Reginio, Woolf erects a counter-monument "to create a memorial embodying failure, indeterminacy, and forgetting" (90). Like Jacob's empty shoes at the end of the novel, I suggest that Woolf's novel emphasizes the inadequacy of memorial efforts attempting to give shape and form to absence that, like the character Jacob, is ever-present but elusive, shaping us as readers (of the novel) and national subjects (postwar), rather than us shaping it (vis-à-vis memorials).

CHRISTOPHER ISHERWOOD AND MEMORIAL INHERITANCE

It seems appropriate that the Woolfs should publish *The Memorial* in 1932 because, as I will argue, it shares with *Jacob's Room* and *To the Lighthouse* a critique of national memorialization through the use of absence and distance. Generational differences aside, Woolf and Isherwood are sympathetic in their critical examination of memorialization, offering a discourse of affiliation that reveals the role the Great War plays in connecting, not separating, younger and older novelists struggling to come to terms with loss, personal and national, in the interwar period: an ostensibly peaceful period saturated with military memorials.

In *The Memorial*, Mrs. Lily Vernon, the doll-like war widow, reluctantly realizes that "[h]istory meant different things to different people" (61) while her stammering, student-at-Cambridge son, Eric, reads to her from his history books. Although it is not the history Lily recognizes, antiquarian societies and monarchical family trees, "Lily took a great pleasure in hearing Eric read…for it was all History" (61).

This rather mundane domestic scene in a novel subtitled "Portrait of a Family" captures the essence of Isherwood's examination of national and familial memorialization.

Ensemble and episodic, *The Memorial*, like Woolf's two novels, examines the war death of Richard Vernon obliquely and associatively as the novel focuses on the lives of his widow, son, sister, and friend in the wake of his death. Richard is approached only through characters' memories as they reflect back upon the years before the war from the vantage points of 1928, 1920, 1925, and 1929 (in that order). The absence of Richard—highlighted through the dedication of the town's war memorial in the 1920 section—shifts the focus from the war's casualties to the war's survivors, both familial non-combatants and fellow friends-in-arms. In this manner, Isherwood's twofold critique emerges: Isherwood, like Woolf, seeks to reveal the inadequacy of national memorialization in the wake of the Great War; Isherwood, like Woolf in "The Leaning Tower," explores the nuances of postwar generational politics that are often over-simplified and exploited in service of national and literary discourses.

The father and son dynamics provide a productive entry point into the generational focus of the novel. Eric, Richard's son, is away at public school when his father is declared "killed in action": "This was his first year as a public school boy, and the telegram, with Mother's letter following it, had seemed merely to add to the darkest tinge to an already melancholy life of war rations, fagging, loneliness, discomfort, strangeness" (96). Eric's mourning evolves in tandem with his adjustment to public school. By the time he returns to the Vernon estate for winter break, Eric has come to terms with his father's death, a man turned memory, "remote and sad" (97). However, upon his return, Eric is shocked and rebuffed by the memorial atmosphere and by his mother, Lily, still deep in the throes of grief; his home had become a living memorial to his parents' marriage and his father's life, both ended prematurely by war. Guilt overcomes Eric and, torn between his duty towards Lily and his frustration at her emotional paralysis, he begins grieving his living mother more than his dead father.

In the 1920 section of the novel, when Eric and Lily escort the senior Mr. Vernon to the dedication of the war memorial, the inadequacy of national memorialization is put into relief as all the members of the Vernon family respond differently. (Only Lily actualizes the national memorial rhetoric and, as such, quickly becomes an unsympathetic character.) Old Mr. Vernon speaks incoherently after a stroke and, despite his healthy appearance, is suspected of being oblivious to the ceremony and its significance. Mary Scriven, Richard's estranged sister, reflects upon the way time heals social wounds: having eloped with her husband Desmond before the war, a single mother by the time the war ended, Mary would have never imagined she'd be welcome again in her home village, let alone that she would have become so socially and culturally indispensable. Eric, worked up to distraction worrying about his mother, discovers unexpected excitement in the new knowledge announced by the Bishop presiding over the ceremony: that a young boy had lied about his age in order to fight—and be killed—in the war. Over the course of the novel, readers learn that Eric regrets having not followed in the boy's footsteps; if he had, he would have been a hero instead of an awkward, fatherless, young man crippled by guilt that he doesn't share his mother's endless suffering. Consequently, when the Bishop asks the village crowd "What did the war mean to you?", each Vernon has a different answer and only Lily's resembles the nationally endorsed response (70). "History meant different things to different people" reverberates.

The memorial fails to bring the Vernon family together in their loss and instead highlights the way in which nationally endorsed modes of memorialization are inadequate, exacerbating familial fissures across generational and gendered vectors. The character Edward Blake, Richard's best friend who has survived the war, represents a familiar male type in the postwar world and functions as a bridge connecting the Lost Generation and the Younger Generation, represented by Eric and his cousin, Mary's son Maurice. Edward Blake, a closeted homosexual who never bent under the force of authority, survived adolescence because of his friendship with Richard, a friendship that continued through adulthood and the war. With Richard's marriage to Lily and then his death in the war, Edward slowly devolves, swinging from adventurous highs to drunken lows culminating in a botched suicide attempt in Berlin at the ten-year anniversary of the war's end. Edward's extreme lifestyle, however, is but an amplified version of his Younger Generation counterparts, Eric and Maurice. Eric, stuttering, bespectacled, awkward, is nothing like his father and thus spends the first two decades of his life trying to make him proud. Well-known as a rising intellectual star at Cambridge, Eric imagines his life as a respected don but, after the General Strike, unable to negotiate his academic work with his emerging moral and political commitment, abruptly leaves academia and the confines of this imagined duty to his father in order to advocate for the poor. Maurice, at the opposite end of the spectrum, is eventually forced down from Cambridge because of fun-loving, debt-accruing antics. Unlike his cousin Eric, Maurice is attracted to the charms of the eccentric and haunting Edward Blake and, the narrative insinuates, risks crossing over to the "disrespectable" side of homosociality in order to save himself from debt.

Isherwood's triangulation of Eric, the dead soldier's son, Maurice, the charming but wayward son of the Vernon fallen daughter, and Edward Blake, the "lucky" soldier who returned from the Front irrevocably damaged, bracket the actual war as the parentheses in Woolf's "Time Passes" section do. In the space created around these men, Richard exists in absence, connecting and simultaneously driving a wedge among them. Richard comes to represent the war itself: mourned and cursed, distant and inaccessible. As with Richard's name carved into the stone memorial at the center of town, it is the stone around the letters that give the letters their meaning: Richard and, by extension, the war, mean everything and nothing to the surviving soldier and the Younger Generation featured in the novel; Richard and the war derive their meaning from the fabric of friends and family that surround their absence. And it is their stories, Isherwood implies, that constitute the truest although most complex memorial. This is best illustrated in the novel's final scene wherein Edward tries to explain to his young German lover, Franz, that the scar at his hairline is from his failed suicide attempt not combat on the Western Front. Disbelieving, Franz reflects: "'that War…it ought to never have happened'" (189). Those words could never be spoken at the village dedication of the war memorial despite the fact that they expressed the only sentiment shared by all the novel's characters.

THE YOUNGER GENERATION WRITERS AND THE WAR NOT FOUGHT

Woolf's 1940 essay, "The Leaning Tower," offers a context for understanding Woolf in conjunction with the Younger Generation of writers, like Isherwood. In it, Woolf investigates the work of the Younger Generation of leaning tower authors whose autobiographically-inflected fiction betrays not only their egotism, self-consciousness, and entitlement but also their rightful position as inheritors—and by extension executors—in the family of English authorship (a point often overlooked in the shorthand summaries of the essay). Also, Woolf's essay is a literary call to arms, challenging writers and readers to bridge the gulf between the dying world and the world yet to be born by claiming literature as common ground where we should "trespass freely [...] and find our own way for ourselves" (154).

Overshadowed by her inspiring conclusion, Woolf's generational analysis reveals the prominent position of the Great War in her historical thought even as the next war loomed heavily on her intellectual and psychological horizon. Here Woolf examines the state of writing produced by the Younger Generation, identifying not only their self-consciousness but also their *historical consciousness*. For Woolf, it is the Great War that *connects* the Younger Generation of writers with the older generation of writers. In assuming their place in the inherited ivory towers of education, class, and privilege (from which they refuse to descend), the Younger Generation of writers inherits the world the older generation had created, including the Great War and its consequences, and, because their angle of vision has changed (the once-steady towers now lean), they have realized that the tower upon which they sit was built upon injustice and tyranny. Through this difficult realization, the Younger Generation writer has mustered up the courage to "tell the truth, the unpleasant truth about himself" (149).

Conscious of their class, gender, and educational privilege, the members of the Younger Generation—too young to fight in the Great War, shaped and scarred by it nonetheless—were also conscious of themselves as exceptions. They emerged into adulthood confronting the historical fact that they, unlike their fathers and older brothers, would not be sent off to the Front, would not fight in the war that to them was *not* First but *only* Great. Isherwood articulates it best in *Lions and Shadows* (1938) when he proposes that men of his generation are "obsessed by a complex of terrors and longings connected with the idea of 'War'" (75–6). War was the test of "your courage, of your maturity, of your sexual prowess" and, Isherwood confesses, "I longed to be subjected to this test... [although] I also dreaded failure" (76).

The void left by war-dead fathers and older brothers was often filled by a larger-than-life hero mythology, leaving male adolescents not only fatherless and brotherless but also burdened by national expectations both inflated and artificial. In this manner, absent fathers and elder brothers were a familial corollary to national heroes. But truth-telling veterans-turned-authors revealed that "the hero became the victim and the victim the hero" (Eksteins 146): disillusioned veteran-authors (Siegfried Sassoon, Wilfred Owen, and Robert Graves) exposed the futility of war, the tragedy of the trenches, and the impossibility of heroism. Thus, for the Younger Generation, the military masculinities reinforced by patriotic national rhetoric through the erection of national memorials—and inescapable thanks to veterans-authors—were both reminders of personal loss and outdated models for their development as contributors to, and citizens of, Britain after the Great War. Consequently, the Younger Generation could not help but conceive of themselves within and against a paradigm dominated by military heroes. Great War heroism became the test that, without a war of their own to fight, the Younger Generation would never pass.

For the Younger Generation, it is not only fathers and older brothers that are absent as they enter adulthood; war is also absent and ironically mourned by young men burdened by national expectations that, with no war to fight, they will never meet. They, like Woolf, find national memorial efforts inadequate and even insulting. Similar to Woolf in *To the Lighthouse* and *Jacob's Room*, they seek to make visible and to honor absence by attending to the impact of war in their present reality rather than constructing mythologies of presence and proximity oriented towards the ideals and values of a prewar past. In this manner, we can perceive how the Great War creates lines of affiliation between writers traditionally characterized as antagonistic, extending our understanding of modernism to truly include all those impacted by war, even those too young to fight.

Works Cited

Bluemel, Kristin. *Intermodernism: Literary Culture in Mid-Twentieth-Century Britain*. Edinburgh: Edinburgh UP, 2009.
Booth, Allyson. *Postcards from the Trenches: Negotiating the Space between Modernism and the First World War*. Oxford: Oxford UP, 1996.
Cole, Sarah. *At the Violet Hour: Modernism and Violence in England and Ireland*. Oxford: Oxford UP, 2012.
Cunningham, Valentine. *British Writers of the Thirties*. Oxford: Oxford UP, 1988.
Deer, Patrick. *Culture in Camouflage: War, Empire, and Modern British Literature*. Oxford: Oxford UP, 2009.
Eksteins, Modris. *Rites of Spring: the Great War and the Birth of the Modern Age*. New York: First Mariner Books, 2000.
Esty, Jed. *A Shrinking Island: Modernism and National Culture in England*. Princeton, NJ: Princeton UP, 2003.
Fussell, Paul. *The Great War and Modern Memory*. Oxford: Oxford UP, 1975.
Isherwood, Christopher. *Lions and Shadows*. New York: New Directions, 1947.
——. *The Memorial*. London: Hogarth, 1932.
Reginio, Robert. "Virginia Woolf and the Technologies of Exploration: *Jacob's Room* as Counter-Monument." Ed. Helen Southworth and Elisa Kay Sparks. *Woolf and the Art of Exploration*. Clemson, SC: Clemson U Digital P, 2006.
Schroeder, Steven. "Mother of All Battles." *PMLA*. 124.5 (2009): 1690–1703.
Sherry, Vincent. *The Great War and the Language of Modernism*. Oxford: Oxford UP, 2004.
Tate, Trudi. *Modernism, History and the First War World*. Manchester, UK: Manchester UP, 1998.
Tylee, Claire. *The Great War and Women's Consciousness: Images of Militarism and Womanhood in Women's Writings, 1914–64*. Iowa City: U of Iowa P, 1990.
Winter, Jay. *Sites of Memory, Sites of Mourning: The Great War in European Cultural History*. Cambridge: Cambridge UP, 1998.
Woolf, Virginia. *Jacob's Room*. 1922. New York: Harcourt, 1923.
——. "The Leaning Tower." 1940. *The Moment and Other Essays*. New York: Harcourt Brace Jovanovich, 1948.
——. *The Letters of Virginia Woolf*. Vol. 3: 1923–1928. Ed. Nigel Nicolson and Joanne Trautmann. New York: Harcourt Brace Jovanovich, 1977.
——. *To the Lighthouse*. 1927. New York: Harcourt, Inc., 1927.

Taking Up Her Pen for World Peace:
Virginia Woolf, Feminist Pacifist. Or Not?

by Paula Maggio

Words. Virginia Woolf used them. And she described them. She called them wild. She called them free. She spoke of them as irresponsible but sensitive, democratic but un-teachable, self-conscious but unwilling to be confined. Words, she said in her 1937 BBC radio broadcast, are changeable.[1] They take on one meaning, then another. They convey truths that are many-sided. They mean one thing to you, another thing to me. Words, she knew, have power. They have the power to express our thoughts and our emotions and the power to provide meaning that transcends generations. Words also have the power to liberate our thinking from the routine and from the stale—whether we are writing of the world at home or the world abroad.

In this paper, I will discuss two words that have been applied to Woolf, two words used to stamp her with an indelible label. These two words are used to deny her charmingly contradictory nature and to disallow her the changeability she grants to words themselves. The first word is feminist. The second word is pacifist. Like others before me, I will make the case that Woolf was both. Like others before me, I will also make the case that Woolf rejected both. Woolf, like words, was unwilling to be confined to one meaning. Woolf, like words, was changeable. Woolf, like words, can't be caught and sorted into a certain kind of order.

To make the case for Woolf as feminist and pacifist, as well as her refusal to label herself as either, I will provide a brief overview of her work as it relates to her feminist war resistance at home and abroad. I will then look at specific diary entries and letters dating from 1916 through 1938 in which Woolf refers to her own feminism and pacifism. I will also review passages in *A Room of One's Own* (1929) and *Three Guineas* (1938) that mention those concepts in general terms. In conclusion, I will discuss her 1940 essay, "Thoughts on Peace in an Air Raid," which I argue she wrote from a feminist pacifist perspective that persisted throughout her life, despite her changeability.

It is well documented that Woolf's feminist war resistance found expression in both her fiction and her non-fiction. Shaped by her childhood experiences, such as the sudden aversion to violence she felt during a squabble with her brother Thoby ("A Sketch of the Past" 71), and reinforced by her wartime experiences as an adult during the Great War, Woolf's pacifist attitude informed the aesthetic of her post-war fiction. As Karen Levenback, Jane Marcus, and Mark Hussey[2] have so aptly argued, Woolf's experiences of war—and the vision those experiences brought her—provided her with the material for an artistic and feminist argument against war and its underlying patriarchal structure. In novels such as *Mrs. Dalloway* (1925), *To the Lighthouse* (1927), and *The Years* (1937), Woolf argues against the hierarchies and inequities of patriarchal culture and connects them to the origins and culture of war.

But Woolf herself did not consistently identify as either a feminist or a pacifist. Like the words she used and loved, she was changeable. The word "feminist," for example, shows up infrequently in her private and public writing, but it does appear just often enough to indicate her complicated and changeable attitudes about identifying as one. And when the word does show up in her diaries and letters, it always appears in connection with politics and war, paralleling the way feminism and anti-militarism are linked throughout the history of the women's peace movement.[3] In a January 23, 1916 letter to lifelong friend and fellow feminist and pacifist Margaret Llewelyn Davies, Woolf notes her growing feminism in response to the Great War and its coverage in the popular press: "I become steadily more feminist, owing to the Times, which I read at breakfast and wonder how this preposterous masculine fiction [the war] keeps going a day longer—without some vigorous young woman pulling us together and marching through it" (*L2* 76). Reading about the war in the newspaper strengthens Woolf's feminism and inflames her anger about the connection between patriarchy and war. In her passion, she imagines young women uniting the female sex in a march right onto the battlefield, as if that battlefield, that "preposterous masculine fiction," doesn't actually exist as a separate reality. And indeed it does not, for Woolf has already seen the line between battlefront and home front dissolve. She has heard the sounds of war from across the English Channel and overhead at Asham. She has seen the war come home in the form of damaged soldiers on the streets and in the homes of London.

Once World War I is over, though, Woolf abandons her private identification with feminism, believing herself to have moved on in her thinking. In her October 17, 1924 diary entry, she considers making a feminist response to a political brouhaha covered in the popular press. But this time she speaks of her own feminism in the past tense. She notes, "If I were still a feminist, I should make capital out of the wrangle" (*D2* 318). With this remark, she recognizes the power feminism can lend to a political stance. But she sees herself as having progressed much further than that. Quoting Katherine Mansfield, she describes herself as "a ship far out at sea" (318), a ship that she believes has travelled some distance beyond feminist ideologies—so that she now has a wider view.

Five years later, in October 1929, we know that Woolf has not abandoned her feminism, although she is still conflicted about being publicly identified as a feminist. In the same month that she publishes her openly feminist polemic, *A Room of One's Own* (1929), she clearly expresses the conflict she feels about being identified as a feminist. While her text bravely makes a long public argument about the inequities between the sexes—and makes it with what she describes as "ardour and conviction"—she is privately insecure about how the book will be received if she is identified as an advocate for womankind. She frets that her friends will respond with only evasion and jocularity. She worries that the book has a "shrill feminine tone." She is concerned she "shall be attacked [by critics] for a feminist" (*D3* 262). If she is subject to such attacks, though, she has a self-protective strategy steeped in stereotypically feminine behavior at the ready. She will simply dismiss the book as "a trifle" (262). By minimizing the import of her own work, she can also minimize the criticism it receives because of its feminist philosophy.

Interestingly enough, Woolf tells just such a story, which she calls a "psychological puzzle," within the text of *Room*. She describes the irate reaction of a male acquaintance when he reads Rebecca West's characterization of men as snobs. The man, dubbed Mr. Z and described as the "most humane, most modest of men," brands West an "arrant feminist" because of her criticism of his sex. Woolf feigns surprise, arguing that the characterization is "possibly true if uncomplimentary" and that Mr. Z is suffering from wounded vanity because West has infringed on "his power to believe in himself." According to

Woolf, West has wounded him by refusing to serve as a looking glass that reflects "the figure of man at twice its natural size" (35). Instead, West, the "arrant feminist," has dared to tell the truth. Woolf, too, dares to tell the truth—about men, about patriarchy, about war—but she is not comfortable with being labeled a feminist.

Woolf's reluctance to be branded as a feminist even while she is writing a feminist tome shows up again in 1932 as she is working on *Three Guineas*. In a diary entry dated February 16, she speculates about a title for a book that she is "quivering & itching to write." What should she call it, she wonders? She suggests a title, "Men are like that." But she immediately scraps that idea as "too patently feminist" (*D4* 77). For Woolf, it is one thing to write a thoughtful book that has well-documented support for its feminist views but another thing entirely to advertise that feminism on its cover. Within *Three Guineas* itself, Woolf uses the word "feminist" only three times, all within two pages. And in that passage she makes the point that "feminist" is "a dead word, a corrupt word" (101) that is obsolete now that men and women are working together for the rights of all (102). Yet her claims are made with tongue in cheek. For in the next breath, Woolf admits that though women have entered the professions, the monster of the patriarchal state is still operating at home and abroad. And men and women working side by side must fight its tyranny (103).

We know that Woolf disliked appearing didactic in her writing, and that is one reason why she is reluctant to allow her work to be easily categorized as feminist. But there may be two additional reasons for her reluctance. First, because of her own perfectionism as a writer and her insecurities about how that writing would be received, she wants her audience, whether friends or critics, to accept her work. Knowing both groups well, she is aware that overt feminism was not likely to go down easily. So while Woolf understands that the personal is political—that tyranny in the patriarchal home breeds tyranny abroad—she is unable to stand up to the tyranny of disapproval from her friends and critics. Second, perhaps she did not want to use her intellectual energy and its power to fight every feminist battle that came her way. In a letter to pioneering suffragette and composer Ethel Smyth dated April 15, 1931, Woolf mentions listening to "two love lorn young men" who "caterwaul—with an egotism that, if I were a feminist, would throw great light on the history of the sexes—such complete self absorption: such entire belief that a woman has nothing to do but listen" (*L4* 312). Woolf looks at the situation through a feminist lens but at the same time she denies being a feminist. For her, the proper response would necessitate a good deal of intellectual work—writing an entirely new history of the sexes, no less. And she does not seem willing to take on the project.

We find somewhat similar contradictions regarding Woolf's identification as a pacifist, contradictions that can be partially explained by her inclination to tailor her message to her audience. In a May 18, 1931 letter to Smyth, who had spent time in Holloway Prison in 1912 as a result of her militant suffragette activities, Woolf admits to being a pacifist. She then qualifies her statement. "Of course, and of course, I'm not such a pacifist as to deny that practical evils must be put to the sword: I admit fighting to the death for votes, wages, peace, and so on" (*L4* 333). Woolf identifies as a pacifist, but only up to a point. When the cause is right—and when she is writing to someone who has endured prison to help the cause of women's suffrage—she claims she, too, will abandon a pacifist stance and take up the sword.

Critics disagree regarding the lifespan of Woolf's pacifism. In "A Writing Couple: Shared Ideology in Virginia Woolf's *Three Guineas* and Leonard Woolf's *Quack, Quack!*,"

Patricia Laurence maintains that Woolf renounced her pacifism in 1935 after she and Leonard drove through Germany (128). During their trip, the Woolfs were troubled by swastikas, anti-Semitic banners, a ten-minute delay at customs, and crowds lining the street to salute a Nazi official. In her diary, Woolf complains of hers and Leonard's "obsequiousness gradually turning to anger. Nerves rather frayed. A sense of stupid mass feeling masked by good temper" (D4 311). Laurence writes that after this experience, Woolf was unable to continue as both anti-fascist and anti-war (128). Phyllis Lassner disagrees. In *British Women Writers of World War II: Battlegrounds of Their Own*, she lists Woolf among the women writers who became lifelong pacifists as a result of WWI, viewing the horrors of the second war as a continuation of the first (12).

Woolf's personal writing contains evidence to back up Lassner's view, with which I concur. In a diary entry of March 13, 1936, Woolf ascribes Aldous Huxley's refusal to sign a manifesto[4] to his pacifism, and she does not equivocate about her own. "He's a pacifist. So am I," she affirms just one week after German troops marched unopposed into the Rhineland (D5 17). Here we see Woolf sticking to her pacifist stance despite Germany's militancy. She was not alone. By the mid-1930s and continuing until just before its entry into the war, Britain boasted the greatest mass pacifist movement in its history, according to Richard A. Rempel in "The Dilemmas of British Pacifists During World War II" (D1 214). Although Woolf expresses her disapproval of what she calls "idiotic letter signing and vocal pacifism" in a July 4, 1938 letter to Davies, she remains an articulate advocate for peace (L6 250). In the letter written soon after *Three Guineas* was published, Woolf admits that she wrote her pacifist polemic because she could not stay silent when there was "an obvious horror in our midst." She explains that the tyranny of Hitlerism abroad "finally made my blood boil into the usual ink-spray" (250). She adds that in *Three Guineas* she quoted—perhaps verbosely—from "such a mass of material" to attract the attention of a mass audience she described as common, reluctant and "easily bored" (251). She notes that she found it necessary to "slip quotations down people's throats" in jelly—"too much jelly"—in order to make her feminist anti-war argument palatable to the masses (251).

Just before Britain declares war against Germany in 1939, the peace movement falls apart. In little more than a year, membership in the Peace Pledge Union, Britain's secular pacifist group, plummets to its lowest level. But Woolf's feminism and pacifism endure. Perhaps they endure because she recognized Britain's shared responsibility for the war. Perhaps they endure because she admitted that her country shared tyrannical characteristics with Germany. Rempel explains that a number of individuals remained pacifists throughout the war and he argues that some did so because they clearly recognized Britain's role in World War II as well as its own tyrannical practices (D1 215). Whatever Woolf's reasons, her feminism and pacifism permeate her final essay on WWII.

"Thoughts on Peace in an Air Raid," written in August of 1940 for an American audience, casts a spell of peace. Using the conceit that she is writing her essay while German fighters zoom above her Sussex home in the dark of night, Woolf describes the experience of thinking about peace while living in the midst of war and she structures her tale within a feminist framework. She imagines the young airmen, both English and German, fighting each other overhead, piloting winged hornets that "may at any moment sting you to death" (243). She wonders how women, without political power and without military weapons, are expected to fight for England's freedom. They must, she says, fight with their minds, even if their thoughts are limited to the private realm, even if their thoughts are limited to the tea-table, even if their thoughts must come up against the loud and furious "spate of words from the loudspeakers and the politicians" (244). Woolf argues that both men and women are victims of war, prisoners of "a subconscious Hitlerism in the hearts of men," the "desire for aggression; the desire to dominate and enslave" (245). In Woolf's eyes, war does not recognize gender. Everyone, man and woman, soldier and civilian, is its victim.

As a feminist peacemaker and a writer, in "Thoughts on Peace in an Air Raid," Woolf recognizes the power of words to liberate men and women of all nations from fear and hate. She recognizes their power to free us from the desire to dominate others. Having written *A Room of One's Own* and *Three Guineas* from a feminist pacifist perspective, she knows what it is like to fight the tyranny of patriarchy and militarism with her mind. She now recommends that tactic for the world at large. We must think against the current, she advises. We must think peace into existence. If we don't, she writes, "we [...] will lie in the same darkness and hear the same death rattle overhead" (243). If we don't, we will no longer be able to think. If we don't, we will be without words. If we don't, we will fail to create. And in Woolf's view, that is darkness indeed.

Notes

1.   "Craftsmanship" was part of a series titled "Words Fail Me." The text was published as an essay in *The Death of the Moth and Other Essays* (1942).
2.   See Levenback 83–113; Marcus 271–74; and Hussey 2–3.
3.   For an in-depth discussion of the women's peace movement and its feminist connections, see Liddington, *The Long Road to Greenham*.
4.   While Leonard Woolf supported the League of Nations' collective security system, Huxley became a sponsor of the Peace Pledge Union. When Italy invaded Abyssinia, sanctions were imposed. Huxley considered them a maneuver that would push Italians into rallying around Mussolini and make the establishment of peace more difficult.

Works Cited

Hussey, Mark, ed. *Virginia Woolf and War: Fiction, Reality, and Myth*. Syracuse, New York: Syracuse UP, 1991. Print.

Lassner, Phyllis. *British Women Writers of World War II: Battlegrounds of Their Own*. London: Macmillan, 1997.

Laurence, Patricia. "A Writing Couple: Shared Ideology in Virginia Woolf's *Three Guineas* and Leonard Woolf's *Quack, Quack!*" *Women in the Milieu of Leonard and Virginia Woolf: Peace, Politics, and Education*. Ed. Wayne K. Chapman and Janet M. Manson. New York: Pace UP, 1998. 125–43.

Levenback, Karen. L. *Virginia Woolf and the Great War*. Syracuse, New York: Syracuse UP, 1999.

Liddington, Jill. *The Long Road to Greenham: Feminism and Anti-Militarism in Britain Since 1820*. London: Virago, 1989.

Marcus, Jane. "'No more horses': Virginia Woolf on Art and Propaganda." *Women's Studies* 4.2/3 (1977): 265–89.

Rempel, Richard A. "The Dilemmas of British Pacifists During World War II." *The Journal of Modern History* 50.4 (1978): D1 213–D1 229.

Woolf, Virginia. *A Room of One's Own*. 1929. New York: Harcourt, 1981.

——. "A Sketch of the Past." *Moments of Being: A Collection of Autobiographical Writing*. Ed. Jeanne Schulkind. New York: Harcourt, 1985.

——. "Craftsmanship." Words Fail Me. British Broadcasting Corporation. London, 29 Apr. 1937. Radio.

——. *The Diary of Virginia Woolf*. Ed. Anne Olivier Bell. 5 vols. San Diego: Harcourt, 1978–84. *Major Authors on CD-Rom: Virginia Woolf*. CD-ROM.

——. *The Letters of Virginia Woolf*. Eds. Nigel Nicolson and Joanne Trautmann. 6 vols. New York: Harcourt, 1975–80. *Major Authors on CD-Rom: Virginia Woolf*. CD-ROM.

——. *Mrs. Dalloway*. 1925. New York: Harcourt, 1981.

——. "Thoughts on Peace in an Air Raid." 1940. *Death of the Moth and Other Essays.* New York: Harcourt Brace, 1942. *Major Authors on CD-Rom: Virginia Woolf.* 243–48. CD-ROM.

——. *Three Guineas.* 1938. New York: Harcourt, 1966.

——. *To the Lighthouse.* 1927. New York: Harcourt, 1955.

——. *The Years.* 1937. New York: Harcourt, 1965.

THE SEX WAR AND THE GREAT WAR:
WOOLF'S LATE VICTORIAN INHERITANCE IN *THREE GUINEAS*

by Christine Haskill

L ong neglected by critics, Virginia Woolf's indebtedness to the Victorians has come to the attention of recent scholars. Even so, their work tends to focus on her relation to mid-Victorianism. This paper interrogates how Woolf's construction of feminist pacifism in *Three Guineas* (1938) resonates with late Victorian literary feminism. Specifically, I examine the narrator's internal debate within *Three Guineas* over whether to reform or burn down the women's college. This dialogue reflects a division among New Woman writers between the reforming vision of Olive Schreiner and the radical tactics of George Egerton. Schreiner and Egerton represent an important tension in feminism between equality and agency and this tension operates as a dialogue in the narrator's pursuit of expanding women's options in the public sphere and resisting war in the private sphere. Woolf's debate with late Victorian feminists informs her critique of modern war as an outsider. When she contextualizes the tyranny of war alongside the tyranny of the separate spheres, the Great War and the sex war of the late nineteenth century become inextricable in *Three Guineas*.

Many scholars have considered Woolf's use of the past, the way she "thinks back through her mothers" as she contends in *A Room of One's Own* (1929, 97), but her relation to the Victorians is often seen as oppositional, in part because Woolf herself emphasized these breaks. More recently, critics have analyzed this rich literary and cultural relationship between Woolf and the Victorian past. As Gillian Beer writes, "The Victorians are not simply represented...in her novels...the Victorians are also *in* Virginia Woolf. They are internalized, inseparable, as well as held at arm's length" (93). I agree with Jessica R. Feldman, who writes that "when modernist writers insist upon radical discontinuity, we should not take them at their word....What is dismissed is also summoned" (454). Seeing the affinities rather than the radical ruptures between New Woman writers and Woolf locates a different kind of Victorian inheritance present in her work. Such an undertaking emphasizes finding resonating ideas, echoes, and imagery, or as Feldman contends, interpreting "patterns" that "link to other patterns" (456). In order to trace a Victorian inheritance, my focus has been less on locating biographical connections than on examining, in Feldman's language, these "works of art as webs of relations" (453) which share common themes and political ideas.

Woolf returns to the Victorians and the separate spheres ideology in *Three Guineas* to argue against war as a feminist pacifist. Responding to the question—how can women prevent war?—Woolf turns to women's status in society, their access to education, and the professions which will enable them to exert influence over wars. But at a deeper level, her answer to the question of how to prevent war lays bare the violence embedded in both the private and public spheres and she advances pacifism by returning to Victorian feminism and reworking women's identities as outsiders. I argue this reflects, in part, the writing and thinking of New Woman writers such as Egerton and Schreiner. While Woolf often contrasted herself to the Victorians, her thinking reflects a consistent return to them in an effort to excavate the legacies of the patriarchal house as well as its connection to the violence of war. While carrying forward Schreiner's call for equality, Woolf remains skeptical of institutional reform and locates feminist resistance within private sphere reconfigurations, a position which I argue is more reflective of Egerton.

By returning to the Victorian ideology of the separate spheres as a way to advocate pacifism in *Three Guineas*, Woolf traces a genealogical link between the tyrannies of gender and the tyrannies of war. In arguing for the advancement of the daughters of educated men, she explains they are the "weakest of all the classes in the state" and they "have no weapon with which to enforce [their] will" (16). While it might seem curious to utilize the language of weaponry within a pacifist argument, such language was a common feature of New Woman writing and the suffrage movement. The supposed "sex war" was a cultural response to the Woman Question and the emergence of New Woman writers and feminists in the nineteenth and early twentieth centuries. New Woman feminists challenged the complementarity of the separate spheres in order to argue that, rather than leading to harmony, separate spheres created antagonism. Consequently, they argued that changing women's social and political status would result in a peace between the sexes. As historian Susan Kingsley Kent explains, "The feminist movement, and more singularly the suffrage campaign, aimed to supply women with the weapons necessary to repulse male attacks and to establish a condition of 'sex peace'" (164). The conditions for "sex peace" included access to education, the professions, legal protections, sexual equality, and the vote as central issues; these are causes that New Woman writer Schreiner also advocated in *Woman and Labour* and in her fiction.

For Egerton, the sex war is fought primarily within the sexual economy and marriage. In "Virgin Soil," the protagonist Flo insists that her mother did not furnish the sexual knowledge she needed for marriage and motherhood, leaving her defenseless: "You gave me not one weapon in my hand to defend myself against the possible attacks of man at his worst. You sent me out to fight the biggest battle of a woman's life…with a white gauze… of maiden purity as a shield" (132). In other words, the separate spheres ideology constructs marriage within a sexual economy that creates a sex war. The language of weaponry, antagonism, and battle reflects a broader cultural conversation about gender, the separate spheres, and the sex war of the late Victorians. Woolf continues this language by utilizing the imagery of the sex war in her discussion of pacifism.

In the first section of *Three Guineas*, Woolf argues that the daughters of educated men require entrance to university education in order to prevent war. This point echoes traditional feminist calls for equality through access to institutions. But Woolf becomes skeptical that admission to the universities will necessarily lead to war-prevention because education teaches students the value of "force and possessiveness" and, she asks, "are not force and possessiveness very closely connected with war?" (38). This line of questioning leads to an internal dialogue within *Three Guineas* about the terms for asserting and accepting women's equality in the public sphere. If equality grants access to institutions, this access, she argues, does not necessarily prevent war, as the institutions themselves are implicated in the dominant values that justify war. Responding to a women's college secretary also seeking funds and support, Woolf asks: "If I send [the guinea], what shall I ask them to do with it? Shall I ask them to rebuild the college on the old lines? Or shall I ask them to rebuild it, but differently? Or shall I ask them to buy rags and petrol and Bryant

& May's matches and burn the college to the ground?" (42). In other words, should the college continue the dominant traditions, reform them with new values, or simply be declared irredeemable and subsequently destroyed?

On the surface, this internal dialogue looks like a reflexive discussion between Woolf and the secretary, but I would argue that at a deeper level these three options reflect a recurring debate within feminism over methods of engagement. To rebuild the college on the "old lines" represents an equality based on patriarchal culture; to rebuild it differently represents reform; and to destroy it represents a radical rejection of the institution as inherently corrupt. These methods reflect a divide between Schreiner and Egerton's political strategies, and these strategies are not limited to Schreiner and Egerton; they represent broader divisions in feminist thinking as well.

In *Woman and Labour* (1911), Schreiner argues that women's equality in education, work, and government is essential to war prevention; women must extend their influence into the public sphere, working from within to challenge the institutions that lead to war. Asserting that "there is no closed door we do not intend to force open" (59), Schreiner emphasizes finding work based on suitability rather than sex, and this argument is further reflected in her New Woman heroine Lyndall's lament over gender roles and her utopian vision of a sex peace when "love is no more bought or sold"; "when each woman's life is filled with earnest, independent labour, then love will come to her" (*The Story of an African Farm* 161–62). This visionary imagery of sex harmony through equality is further reflected in Schreiner's maternal pacifist arguments, in which she contends that women's roles as mothers furnish a special insight into the system of war. Schreiner argues that women must "enter in the domain of war and… labor there till in the course of generations [they] have extinguished it" (*Woman and Labour* 63). Her call to end war is a reforming vision; women's participation in the public sphere will end war when their voices are heard and their maternal knowledge is made visible. Schreiner's thinking represents a tension between gaining access to masculine institutions and reforming those institutions from within. She reflects the first two options in Woolf's questions about access and reform—to inherit on the old lines or rebuild differently.

Figure 1: "Women of Britain Say 'Go!'," 1914 poster, The British Library.

Egerton, by contrast, remains skeptical of institutional reform, arguing instead for an oppositional stance to patriarchal institutions and a different kind of liberation based on redefining women's identities and constructing a home that remains separate from the corruption of patriarchal culture. She maps the sex war onto the individual—the battle over gender is within identity—and she rejects the patriarchal association of women with altruistic domesticity. Unlike Schreiner, Egerton distances herself from the formal interests of the women's movement, stating: "I am not greatly concerned in the social, so-called educational, or political advancement of women. They are exotics—what interests me is her development from within out as a female" (qtd. in "Women in the Queen's Reign" 216). This emphasis on self-development and wholeness is reflected in her popular short story collections *Keynotes* (1893) and *Discords* (1895). In her stories, she dismantles the separate spheres divide by showing how the public discourses on morality and sexuality corrupt the private sphere and she reinforces an oppositional stance to the public sphere of patriarchal discourse by creating outcast or outsider characters who embrace their outcast status as a site of liberation. Rather than emphasize women's self-sacrifice as the Angel in the House, Egerton advocates a coming to self and utilizes the language of moral integrity through her characters. As the fallen woman in "A Psychological Moment at Three Periods" asserts, "No power on earth, no social law, written or unwritten, is strong enough to make me tread a path on which I do not willingly set my own foot" (92). This cultivation of moral integrity is often set within reconfigured domestic spaces, as in "The Regeneration of Two," in which the protagonist Fruen transforms from a decadent widow to a fiery New Woman who turns her large empty house into a home for social outcasts (151). Egerton evinces a radical suspicion of patriarchal institutions and often rejects masculine culture in favor of separate women's communities, reworking the domestic space as a site of feminine self-development rather than feminine self-sacrifice. This radical suspicion and rejection of patriarchal institutions is reflective of Woolf's option of rejecting the college and burning it to the ground.

Woolf's line of questioning in *Three Guineas* is a consideration of inheritance: what are the legacies of patriarchy within the education system and how might women enter that system while still pursuing both equality and peace? This is an attempt to define feminism on pacifist terms—access is not enough to intervene in war—and she favors rebuilding the college differently. She recognizes, however, that fundamentally changing the directives of the education system will be impractical and thus she considers burning it to the ground, drawing on generational imagery as the daughters and mothers rejoice in the "blaze" of the fire (45). If an institution cannot be rebuilt on new lines and must continue perpetuating the ideals of war, then Woolf advocates for its radical destruction. Her options reflect a fundamental tension within feminist thinking—does social reform come from the individual or the institution? This tension is reflected in the different perspectives of Schreiner and Egerton.

Ultimately, Woolf concedes that neither feminist strategy is practical. In order to achieve equality, the daughters must have access to education; "they must follow the old road to the old end" (46). Woolf feels compelled to commit her first guinea, even on the troubled terms of the college, because it signifies the possibility of opening the professions to women, creating an alternative to the singular confines of the private house (49). She reveals the limitations of social reform because, within masculine-dominated institutions, the most practical course is simply to inherit the old system on the old lines. This inheritance may eventually lead to equality that can prevent war but it is troubled by its connection to the systems of war.

Rather than reform dominant ideals as Schreiner does, Woolf locates resistance in reconfiguring experiences of exclusion and oppression in her construction of an outsiders' society, a move that she shares with Egerton. Woolf's argument that women must have equality in education and the professions in order to prevent war is set alongside her assertion that inequality has provided an outsider's advantage. This argument might appear contradictory because she seems to argue that equality is both desirable and undesirable. Here Woolf reflects a broader tension within feminism between public reform and private liberty. When she makes the case that women must enter the professions but must do so differently than men, she brings both Schreiner and Egerton together. Now "the daughters of uneducated women" do not burn down the house but rather dwell in a new house and sing: "We have done with war! We have done with tyranny!" as the mothers "laugh from their graves" (100). Defiance against the tyranny of the separate spheres is envisioned through the construction of a new house in which mothers and daughters dwell; Woolf reconfigures women's association with the home as a way of engaging the public sphere on feminist pacifist terms.

Rejecting public values leads Woolf to analyze the tyrannies of the private sphere and she contextualizes war and pacifism within a longer trajectory of the Victorian separate spheres, mapping her discussion of war onto both the private sphere and the individual. In her analysis of Victorian fathers, Woolf contends that in order for daughters to resist patriarchal control—as she highlights in her example of Sophia Jex-Blake—they will need to resist their class and their sex because "when the lady was killed the woman still remained" (159). The separate spheres ideology relies upon making women *the Sex*, as Woolf explains: "It was the woman, the human being whose sex made it her sacred duty to sacrifice herself to the father" (159). In this passage, Woolf strikes at the root of the separate spheres: the daughter's identity as a "woman" is defined by the patriarchal value of feminine self-sacrifice.

It might seem contradictory to argue for "killing the woman" and establishing the society of outsiders on the basis of sexual difference, but this can be clarified by examining Egerton's distinction between an artificial patriarchal construction of "woman" and an authentic female-defined identity. In "The Regeneration of Two," Fruen declares that women are "always battling with some bottom layer of real womanhood that [they] may not reveal," as they wrestle with "the outside husk of [their] artificial selves" (148). This distinction between authentic and artificial womanhood is reflected in Woolf's argument both for and against the category "woman," as she argues for killing the "woman" but also locating a more authentic womanhood beneath the trappings of patriarchy.

Echoing utopian visions described by New Woman writers, Woolf constructs a sex peace by asserting that the causes of feminism and pacifism are the same. In order to describe these goals, Woolf returns to the Victorians: "What were they working for in the nineteenth century—those queer dead women in their poke bonnets and shawls? The very same cause for which we are working now" (*TG* 121). Woolf is shifting the terms away from the sex war to focus on a common enemy of both men and women—tyranny: "Thus we are merely carrying on the same fight that our mothers and grandmothers fought" (121). Beneath the imagery of the sex war lies a deeper, more fundamental conflict between freedom and the tyranny of the dictator who is "interfering now with your liberty; he is dictating how you shall live; he is making distinctions not merely between the sexes, but between the races" (122). In order to challenge the tyranny of the separate spheres, she synthesizes the public equality of Schreiner with the woman-defined identities of Egerton, arguing that gaining access to education and the professions will help establish "that weapon of independent opinion which is still their most powerful weapon. […] a mind of their own and a will of their own" (71). It is not simply that the dictator determines women's equality under the law but that they are not granted the individual freedom and will to determine their own lives and identities. Woolf asserts that the sex war is an "embryo" of the tyranny that exists on an international scale (65). While she advances a feminism reflective of both Schreiner and Egerton, her emphasis on identity, self-development, and radical destruction of patriarchal constructions echoes Egerton more clearly.

Much of the propaganda and rhetoric of World War I draws on and reinforces the separate spheres division between a feminine private sphere and a masculine public sphere, between the women and children of the home front and the chivalric men of the battlefield, as we see in the famous poster "Women of Britain say 'GO!'" (See Fig. 1). Although the realities of war disrupted the separate spheres, the ideology—the cultural gender narrative—remained pervasive and, while legal and institutional barriers to women's participation in the public sphere started to crumble after the war, a significant gender backlash ensued, reinstating the separate spheres, as Kent discusses in *Sex and Suffrage* and *Making Peace*. Woolf intervenes in this gender backlash by connecting the tyrannies of the Victorian patriarchal house to the violence of the Great War in order to challenge the emerging threat of Fascism and a second world war. Postwar society is reinvesting in the separate spheres at the same time that Woolf is being asked how women can prevent war. By returning to the Victorian separate spheres in order to understand the legacies of war, Woolf challenges the separate spheres as a site of war and reconfigures Victorian feminism as a basis for pacifism. The New Woman writer's critiques of the separate spheres offered her a discourse from which to develop her own analyses. Furthermore, her writing not only attempted to intervene in a cultural discourse of war but also in the early discourse of feminism. Woolf contends that in order for feminism to continue its goals of equality and freedom, feminism should be pacifist. While the narratives of WWI and modernism traditionally reflect a break from the Victorians, Woolf interrogates the legacies of feminism and war by reaching back to her Victorian foremothers. Part of this legacy can be traced back to two New Woman interventions in the separate spheres debates—the sex war of the fin de siècle—represented by Schreiner and Egerton.

Works Cited

Beer, Gillian. "The Victorians in Virginia Woolf: 1832–1941." *Virginia Woolf: The Common Ground.* Ann Arbor: U of Michigan P, 1996. 92–111.

Egerton, George. *Keynotes* and *Discords.* Ed. Sally Ledger. Birmingham, UK: U of Birmingham P, 2003.

——. "A Psychological Moment at Three Periods." Ledger. 67–94.

——. "The Regeneration of Two." Ledger. 135–69.

——. "Virgin Soil." Ledger. 127–34.

Feldman, Jessica R. "Modernism's Victorian Bric-a-Brac." *Modernism/Modernity* 8.3(2001): 453–70. *Project Muse.* Web. 24 Mar. 2014.

Kent, Susan Kingsley. *Making Peace: The Reconstruction of Gender in Interwar Britain.* Princeton, NJ: Princeton UP, 1993.

——. *Sex and Suffrage in Britain, 1860–1914.* Princeton, NJ: Princeton UP, 1987.

Schreiner, Olive. *The Story of an African Farm.* Oxford: Oxford UP, 2008.

——. *Woman and Labour.* New York: Dover, 1998.

"Women in the Queen's Reign." *The Ludgate* 4 (Jun 1897): 213–17. *British Periodicals.* Web. 7 Aug. 2013.

Woolf, Virginia. *A Room of One's Own.* 1929. San Diego: Harcourt Brace Jovanovich, 1957.

——. *Three Guineas.* 1938. Annot. and intro. Jane Marcus. Orlando, FL: Harcourt, 2006.

Sky Haunting: The British Motor-Car Industry and the World Wars[1]

by Ann Martin

Virginia and Leonard Woolf bought their first automobile in the summer of 1927. It was a used Singer, and while Woolf expressed her enthusiasm for motoring in letter after letter, the car itself was not always reliable. "My God, how you would have laughed yesterday!" she wrote to Vita Sackville-West on August 3: "Off for our first drive in the Singer: the bloody thing wouldn't start. The accelerator died like a duck—starter jammed. All the village came to watch—Leonard almost sobbed with rage. At last we had to bicycle in and fetch a man from Lewes. He said it was the magnetos—would you have known that? Should we have known? Another attempt today, we are bitter and sullen and determined. We think of nothing else. Leonard will shoot himself if it dont start again" (*L*3 407). Though the motor-car in *Mrs. Dalloway* (1925) has been pulled off to the side of Bond Street with a punctured tire, the Singer's starter mechanism places Woolf in a similarly stalled position; and while she exaggerates her frustration to typically comical ends, the violence of the tone and imagery connects the breakdown to its equally disruptive twin: the accident.

The Woolfs had a few of those too, though of a minor sort. Leonard backed their Singer into gate posts, hedges, and—after a visit to Charleston—their own garage: "we knocked a bit off the car getting it into the shed" (*L*3 405). Woolf describes her own driving practice to Janet Case as "wobbling round and round Windmill Hill, every day, trying to avoid dogs and children" (*L*3 403) and notes in a letter to Ethel Sands that she has "driven from the Embankment to the Marble Arch and only knocked one boy very gently off his bicycle" (*L*3 400). Though she states to Sands that she "would rather have a gift for motoring than anything," it did not seem forthcoming, at least according to that year's Charleston Bulletin:

> The less said about July the better.
> Mrs. Bell drove from Hyde Pk-Corner to Marble Arch.
> Mr. Woolf drove from Marble Arch to Hyde Park Corner.
> Mrs. Woolf knocked a boy of [sic] his bicycle.
> Mrs. Bell killed a cat.
> The less said the better. (Woolf and Bell 113)

More disturbing, of course, were the serious motor accidents she encountered: Angelica's in 1924, which Woolf comes to see—with relief—as "only a joke this time"(*D*2 299), and a fraught experience the year following:

> London […] is shot with the accident I saw this morning & a woman crying Oh oh oh faintly, pinned against the railings with a motor car on top of her. All day I have heard that voice. I did not go to her help; but then every baker & flower seller did that. A great sense of the brutality & wildness of the world remains with me—there was this woman in brown walking along the pavement—suddenly a red film car turns a somersault, lands on top of her, & one hears this oh, oh, oh. (*D*3 6)

The impact of the machine retains a violent potency beyond the moment; and while it does not diminish the pleasure Woolf obviously took in motoring, the car's disruptive potential casts a shadow over its place in Woolf's writing.

It is not just the accident or the breakdown that links the car to violence, however; it is also the commodity's imbrication in systems of capitalism and imperialism, which relates directly to the historical role of motor-car manufacturers in wartime industries, including the production of aircraft. In imagery from *Mrs. Dalloway*, the car is often contiguous with war: the punctured tire on Bond Street is heard as a "violent explosion" and compared to a "pistol shot" (*MD* 14), and Septimus finds "himself unable to pass" (15), rooted to the pavement as the present becomes the past in a revisitation of trauma. More subtly, in a scene before Peter Walsh reflects upon the boys in uniform returning from the Cenotaph, he sees himself in the window of an automobile manufacturer. These moments in which war and the motor-car are linked, and linked to loss, may allow us to consider another association: that of the automobile with the skywriting airplane, which haunts this London as an unresolved signifier of war regardless of memorials to a distanced past or celebrations of post-war progress.

Madelyn Detloff has argued that, in her responses to acts of remembrance and commemoration, Woolf "critique[s] the logic of substitution" that informs compensatory gestures: "When loss is figured metaphorically, the particularity of the reference is lost, becoming something else—insight, the consolation of philosophy, the occasion for building character, the impetus for a beautiful elegy—anything but loss *as* loss" (24). Detloff suggests that Woolf attends to these elisions in part through an "associative use of metonym to figure the 'negative space' of absence precipitated by loss" (23). Applying such concepts to *Mrs. Dalloway*, the boys' compensatory performance of military patriotism in having taken the commemorative wreath to the "empty tomb" is recognized by Peter Walsh (*MD* 56); but consolation is resisted through his historicizing gaze, as he sees, for example, that the "weedy" cadets do "not look robust" (55). His awareness and judgment of their lack appear to be informed and necessitated by Walsh's unsettling exchange with Clarissa Dalloway. Before following the boys, and failing to keep up, he has confronted his own image: "And there he was, this fortunate man, himself, reflected in the plate-glass window of a motor-car manufacturer in Victoria Street" (53). As Makiko Minow-Pinkney has pointed out (161), Peter uses the reflection to assure himself of his unity and coherence as a subject and uses the automobiles to enact a compensatory narrative of masculinity: "Clarissa had grown hard, he thought; and a trifle sentimental in the bargain, he suspected, looking at the great motor-cars capable of doing—how many miles on how many gallons? For he had a turn for mechanics; had invented a plough in his district, had ordered wheel-barrows from England, but the coolies wouldn't use them, all of which Clarissa knew nothing whatever about" (*MD* 53). His defensive narration of mechanical know-how seems to enable Peter to parget over a sense of personal and public failure: powerful car as pen-knife.

The car-manufacturer, like the Cenotaph, would seem to be a realistic detail: a company known as Swallow was located in Westminster on Victoria Street until it folded around 1922 (Baldwin 185). But Swallow did not make large automobiles. Indeed, the vehicle they displayed at the 1921 White City Motor Show was a four-cylinder two-seater. Peter's reference to "great cars" may thus be read as a literary device associating the automobiles behind the plate glass with the chauffeur-driven motor-car that arrives at Buckingham

Palace and the "low, powerful, grey" automobile owned by Sir William Bradshaw (*MD* 103). These are the vehicles that Minow-Pinkney identifies as "luxury [objects] associated with royalty, the upper classes, and Empire" as well as with "the patriarchal power game and establishment ideology" (161). Peter's mind is following a symbolic route, then, where motor-cars are metonymic of Whitehall, Britishness, and capitalist production. And yet these references to male privilege and imperialism are again complicated in Peter's thoughts by their association with lack and loss: the pathos of "poor Gordon" and other Great Soldiers (*MD* 56), the "'coolies'" resistance to colonial power, Clarissa's ignorance of his "turn for mechanics," and—most suggestive of all—the implicit place of motor-car manufacturers in the production of wartime arms and aircraft.

In the associative slide between cars and airplanes in *Mrs. Dalloway*, as in *Between the Acts*, war's bases in political and economic systems are anything *but* absented. It is the particularity of Woolf's cultural references that is striking here; or more specifically, the historical particularity of the link between peacetime automotive manufacturing and wartime airplane manufacturing: the bridge between World War I and World War II military technology that was supported by the civilian consumption of motor-cars in the interwar period. A connection between British automotive companies' design and production of motor-cars, and their design and production of engines and guns used in fighter planes and bombers, may not be deliberate on Woolf's part. Nevertheless, the realities of industrial practices in Coventry and Birmingham, and their particular connections to British military production, suggest another dimension of Woolf's references to motor-cars that may recontextualize the significance of airplanes in her work too. In this approach, the interwar commodity of the luxury marque is located in a nexus of historical relations that refuses an elision of wartime violence and loss.

Distinctions have been made between the place of cars and the place of planes in Woolf's writing. Where airplanes are often read as suggesting the interpretative possibilities that individuals can and must realize, automobiles seem to reinforce social divides. Michele Pridmore-Brown argues, for example, that the airplanes interrupting the Reverend's speech in *Between the Acts* (1941) prompt the need for active, critical listening in the face of war (419)—a necessary form of agency that is less evident in the pageant-goers' dispersal to their expensive cars, as noted by a departing member of the audience: "I shouldn't have expected either so many Hispano-Suizas…That's a Rolls…That's a Bentley…" (*BTA* 180–81). The plane in *Mrs. Dalloway*, and its wind-blown skywriting, would thus seem to stand in contrast to the hierarchies signalled by the prestigious cars on Bond Street and at Bradshaw's establishment. In *Mrs. Dalloway*, writes Christina Britzolakis, "[c]ar and aeroplane are both emblems of technological modernity, yet opposed to each other as symbolic forms of imagined community," for the plane "distracts" the crowd from the motor-car's "aura of state power" and "momentarily unites them in a collective effort to decipher its message" (133). And however much that activity places the citizens as consumers (134), the plane and its skywriting—"egalitarian and open to all" as Andrew Thacker puts it (165)—suggest for Michael North "the ineluctable subjectivity and idiosyncrasy of the individual" (83). Thus "the aeroplane figures as the free spirit of the modern age returning the eye to the purity of a sky which has 'escaped registration'" (Beer 276).

There is, however, an historical, material reality to the skywriting plane that complicates these readings. Thus, when Gillian Beer asserts that "[t]he aeroplane in *Mrs. Dalloway* is no war-machine. Its frivolity is part of postwar relief. It poignantly does *not* threaten those below it. It is a light aircraft, perhaps a Moth" (276), she is not entirely correct. As she notes, the de Havilland Moth first flew in 1925, but in late February, too late for *Mrs. Dalloway*. Instead, and as suggested by Elaine Showalter, Woolf's inspiration was likely the skywriting plane that first appeared above Epsom Downs at the 1922 Derby on May 31 (xxiv). A Special Correspondent for the *Times* provided an account of the event. While the initial mood he describes is reminiscent of the impulses Beer and others associate with the plane—"Homely, free-and-easy, and democratic is Derby Day"—by one o'clock, the audience's attitude has changed: "We have all got tired of watching that aeroplane write in a smoke-trail on the sky the title of a popular newspaper" ("The Derby" 17). And "that aeroplane" was indeed a war machine: the Royal Aircraft Factory S.E.5a designed for battle and deployed in WWI.

The S.E.5a was a highly maneuverable combat plane, praised by pilots as "an excellent fighting aircraft" given its "speed in a dive and its stability as a gun platform" (Campbell 115). It was outfitted with a Lewis gun on an "overwing mounting" and a Vickers gun on the fuselage ("Royal"). A relatively inexpensive fighter, costing £837 to manufacture (Everett 125), it was also fast, powered by a 200hp engine. That inline engine, constructed initially to produce 150hp, had been designed by the Spanish-Swiss car company, Hispano-Suiza—one of the luxury marques remarked upon in *Between the Acts*. The Hispano engine was further developed by Wolseley, however, a car company owned by the armaments and aviation manufacturer Vickers Limited, which had a plant at Brooklands beside the famed race track. Under license, Wolseley developed the Viper V8 based upon Hispano's design, and by June 1917, this more reliable engine was powering the Royal Aircraft Factory S.E.5a.

Following the war, thirty-three surplus S.E.5as were purchased by Major John Clive or "Jack" Savage, formerly of the Royal Naval Air Service. He adapted them for skywriting, and the plane became known as the Savage-Wolseley S.E.5a. Having served from 1914–1918 in a branch of the Navy that merged with the Royal Flying Air Corps to become the Royal Air Force, Savage had noted that the Hispano-based, Wolseley Viper V8 engine possessed long exhaust tubes that produced smoke when oil dripped upon them. He extended those pipes and used the mounting area of the Vickers gun for the canister of smoke-producing oil ("Major Savage's"). He patented this technology and in a successful business venture travelled to the U.S., India, Australia, and throughout Europe with his fleet. He seems to have donated the last of his planes to the Science Museum of London in June 1939—an example is currently located at the Shuttleworth Collection—and moved on to develop searchlight technology, which culminated in his collaboration on the Leigh light, used in the detection of U-boats in WWII ("Death" 350).

Savage's work in WWII connects back to a *Times* feature from August 18, 1922, which discussed the implications of skywriting for its London readership. That story, "Sky Writing by Aircraft," was subtitled "Wide Scope in War and Peace," and it addressed the wartime potential and value of the Savage Wolseley S.E.5a as a supplement to military communications systems. "Like the royal car," John Young notes in his reading of the piece, "Woolf's skywriting plane functions in public discourse as a reminder of Britain's military and technological might" (99). The same may be true of the Hispano-Suiza and the British marques, Rolls Royce and Bentley, that are parked in *Between the Acts*. Rolls Royce is connected consistently with class privilege in Woolf's work, but the armoured cars it built for the British Army in WWI—associated most famously, perhaps, with T.

E. Lawrence—spoke also to the company's long-term involvement in military industry, including the production of the Merlin engine for the Spitfire and the Lancaster at Crewe, following Rolls Royce's acquisition of Bentley in 1931. Closer to home, Virginia Woolf's third car, a 1933 Lanchester, was built by the marque's parent firm BSA, the Birmingham Small Arms Company Limited. In WWI, they had manufactured the Lewis guns mounted on S.E.5as. By WWII, BSA owned the only rifle factory in Britain, producing Browning .303 machine guns at the initial rate of 600 per week for the Air Ministry ("Birmingham"). In this historical relationship between automotive marques and aircraft manufacturing, civilian uses of technology are linked to its wartime application, development, and production, just as peacetime machines are linked to wartime loss—of pilots and civilians and those making arms. When BSA's Small Heath factory was bombed by the Luftwaffe in November 1940, fifty-three workers were killed ("Birmingham"). In September of that year, a bombing run on the Vickers factory at Brooklands resulted in the deaths of eighty-three workers and injuries to over 400 more (Catford).

Woolf depicts such violence from the skies in "Thoughts on Peace in an Air Raid," but she suggests the overlapping contexts that link military and civilian uses of technology in an earlier essay, "Flying Over London," written in the winter of 1928, just months before she and Leonard bought their second Singer. At a moment when she is still preoccupied with motor-cars, she is transported by "Flight-Lieutenant Hopgood" into a transcendent experience: "Wraiths (our aspirations and imaginations) have their home here; and in spite of our vertebrae, ribs, and entrails, we are also vapour and air, and shall be united" (187). Time and space shift and combine from the vantage point of the plane, as the individual parts of London are joined and juxtaposed through the Zeiss glasses. But she also sees a traffic jam of "eleven or twelve Rolls Royces in a row with city magnates waiting furious" (191). Their privileged progress has been disrupted by the frustrating complications of civilian technology, which are mirrored in the glitch that besets Hopgood's Gypsy Moth. "As a matter of fact," Woolf writes in conclusion, "the flight had not begun; for when Flight-Lieutenant Hopgood stooped and made the engine roar, he had found a defect of some sort in the machine, and raising his head, he had said very sheepishly, ''Fraid it's no go to-day'" (192).

While Erica Delsandro has noted that in "Thoughts of Peace," as in this imagined flight over London, "Woolf positions herself in the role of the airman" (120), I suggest that Woolf is already there, has already *been* there: she has written this deflatingly "comic" ending before (Deer 92) in depicting the faulty magneto of the Singer. She has herself experienced the frustrating breakdown of machines that would bring power of movement to those privileged enough to own or command them; but machines haunted also by disruption and violence, random and deliberate, civilian and military, in peacetime or war. It is not surprising that Flight-Lieutenant Hopgood is twice characterized as Charon: as well as breakdowns and accidents, this imagined flight connects to the RAF training that will take place in Tiger Moths beginning in the early 1930s, and his plane prefigures the military aircraft that will interrupt the Reverend Streatfield's speech as well as the Woolfs' lives at Monk's House. German bombing runs over Rodmell and Lewes will bring back memories of air raids on London from the Fall of 1917 (Levenback 123) and bring about the destruction of Tavistock Square in the Fall of 1940 (Lee 742–43)—not by Mercedes-powered Gotha bombers, this time, but rather by Junkers 88s and by Dorniers and Heinkels, their engines designed and built in Germany by Daimler-Benz and BMW.

Note

1. My thanks to Gill Lowe and Maggie Humm for their invaluable contributions to my research, and to Rob Leigh for sharing his photographs of the Shuttleworth Collection. This essay is for W. Norton Martin and F. R. McColl.

Works Cited

Baldwin, Nick. *A-Z of Cars of the 1920s*. Bideford, Devon: Bay View Books, 1994.

Beer, Gillian. "The island and the aeroplane: the case of Virginia Woolf." *Nation and Narration*. Ed. Homi K. Bhabha. London: Routledge, 1990. 265–90.

"Birmingham Small Arms Company Limited." *Wikipedia*. 29 May 2014. Web. 16 June 2014.

Britzolakis, Christina. "'The Strange High Singing of Some Aeroplane Overhead': War, Utopia and the Everyday in Virginia Woolf's Fiction." *Utopian Spaces of Modernism: British Literature and Culture, 1885–1945*. Ed. Rosalyn Gregory and Benjamin Kohlmann. New York: Palgrave Macmillan, 2012. 121–40.

Campbell, Christopher. *Aces and Aircraft of World War I*. Toronto: Methuen, 1981.

Catford, Nick. "Brooklands—Vickers-Armstrong air raid shelter." *Subterranea Britannica*. 4 January 2011. Web. 16 June 2014.

"Death of Jack Savage." *Flight*. 27 Sept. 1945. 350.

Deer, Patrick. *Culture in Camouflage: War, Empire, and Modern British Literature*. Oxford: Oxford UP, 2009.

Delsandro, Erica. "Flights of Imagination: Aerial Views, Narrative Perspectives, and Global Perceptions." *Virginia Woolf: Art, Education, and Internationalism. Selected Papers from the Seventeenth Annual Conference on Virginia Woolf*. Ed. Diana Royer and Madelyn Detloff. Clemson, SC: Clemson U Digital P, 2008. 117–24.

"The Derby: Great Day on the Downs." *The Times*. London. 1 June 1922. 17.

Detloff, Madelyn. *The Persistence of Modernism: Loss and Mourning in the Twentieth Century*. Cambridge: Cambridge UP, 2009.

Everett, Susanne. *World War I: An Illustrated History*. Greenwich, CT: Bison, 1980.

Lee, Hermione. *Virginia Woolf*. London: Vintage, 1996, 1997.

Levenback, Karen. *Virginia Woolf and the Great War*. Syracuse, New York: Syracuse UP, 1999.

"Major Savage's Sky-Writing Aeroplane." *The Scarf and Goggles Social Club: Land, Sea and Air in the Age of Adventure*. 22 Mar. 2013. Web. 24 January 2014.

Minow-Pinkney, Makiko. "Virginia Woolf and the Age of Motor Cars." *Virginia Woolf in the Age of Mechanical Reproduction*. Ed. Pamela L. Caughie. New York: Garland, 2000. 159–82.

North, Michael. *Reading 1922: A Return to the Scene of the Modern*. Oxford: Oxford UP, 1999.

Pridmore-Brown, Michele. "1939–40: Of Virginia Woolf, Gramophones, and Fascism." *PMLA* 113.3 (1998): 408–21.

"Royal Aircraft Factory S.E.5.a." *Palmflying.com*. 6 May 2014. Web. 2 June 2014.

Showalter, Elaine. Introduction. *Mrs. Dalloway*. Ed. Stella McNichol. London: Penguin, 2000.

"Sky Writing by Aircraft. Wide Scope in War and Peace." *The Times* (London). 18 August 1922. 5.

Thacker, Andrew. *Moving Through Modernity: Space and Geography in Modernism*. 2003. Manchester, UK: Manchester UP, 2009.

Woolf, Virginia. *Between the Acts*. 1941. Ed. Frank Kermode. Oxford: Oxford UP, 2000.

——. *The Diary of Virginia Woolf*. Ed. Anne Olivier Bell. 5 vols. London: Hogarth, 1978–1984.

——. "Flying Over London." *The Captain's Death Bed and Other Essays*. London: Hogarth, 1950. 186–92.

——. *The Letters of Virginia Woolf*. Vol. 3. Ed. Nigel Nicolson and Joanne Trautmann. London: Hogarth, 1977.

——. *Mrs. Dalloway*. 1925. Ed. Stella McNichol. Annot. and intro. Elaine Showalter. London: Penguin, 2000.

——. "Thoughts on Peace in an Air Raid." 1940. *The Crowded Dance of Modern Life*. Ed. Rachel Bowlby. London: Penguin, 1993. 168–72.

—— and Quentin Bell. *The Charleston Bulletin Supplements*. Ed. Claudia Olk. London: British Library, 2013.

Young, John. "Woolf's *Mrs. Dalloway*." *Explicator* 58.2 (2000): 99–101.

THE 1914 "EXPURGATED CHUNK":
THE GREAT WAR IN AND OUT OF *THE YEARS*

by Eleanor McNees

Correctly identified by Karen Levenback as set in 1914 instead of 1917, the first of two "expurgated chunks" from *The Years* originally served to bridge the prewar 1914 section, ending with Kitty Lasswade's arrival at her home in the north of England, and the 1917 section of the novel beginning with Eleanor Pargiter's exit from the omnibus into the wartime blackout of a winter's night in Westminster. Set in the late afternoon and evening of September 1914 (in the first holograph version October), this section, omitted late in the galley proof stage in 1936, provides an unusually vivid range of responses to the war from diverse class perspectives. It illustrates what Mark Hussey has called the "polyphony of private and public voices" that one detects in Woolf's late fiction and nonfiction (12). It also provides a signal instance of what John Whittier-Ferguson terms Woolf's "inventively exhausted prose" in her late writings of the1930s (231) as the characters try to find words to articulate their responses to the first phase of the war. In what follows, I read the omitted 1914 section both in its more expansive holograph form and in the considerably amended galley proof stage as Woolf's attempt to give, like both war memoirist D. Bridgeman Metchim and historian R.H. Gretton, a lived, authentic experience of the war outside of both newspapers and trenches.

Beginning with "A View From the Street," as Woolf titled her 1919 review of Metchim's book on the war, the expurgated section follows the pensioned Pargiter servant Crosby as she marshals her landlady's children across a Richmond street into Kew Gardens. The section affords an unusual glimpse into Woolf's original method of delineating a range of civilian responses to the early stages of the war. Moreover, the holograph version reveals a deeper engagement with the disparate civilian views and offers a far more astute commentary on how representatives of lower, middle, and upper-middle classes responded to one of the early disasters of the war—the sinking of three British cruisers in the North Sea on September 23, 1914—than do the galley proofs. The newspaper headline, "Three British Cruisers Sunk," serves as the truncated narrative thread that allows for Crosby; Bert Parker, a "traveller in men's underwear"; Ray Sargent, an accountant; and Miriam Parrish, a friend of Eleanor Pargiter, all to reveal their class-inflected responses to the early stage of the war. By the galley proof stage, Ray Sargent has become an anonymous man irritated by the "garbage in the newspapers," his considerable commentary on the war and its causes deleted. Likewise, much of Eleanor's self-interrogation about her inability to prevent the war has also disappeared. Together Ray Sargent and Eleanor Pargiter in their separate internal monologues perseverate on the role of educated men and uneducated women as complicit in instigating war (a theme Woolf will extend into the holograph section of 1917 during the air raid discussion in Maggie's cellar). Their thoughts contribute to the central but ultimately ineffectual debate of the expurgated section, Sargent's exasperated repetition of "What for?" balanced against Eleanor's guilt at not somehow acting to stop a dead acquaintance from going to war.

Woolf employs her familiar trope of public transport in the 1914 section to assemble civilian attitudes toward the war—indifference, anger, patriotism, guilt. The section quickly leaves Crosby and the children at Kew and follows the salesman Bert Parker as he boards a train to central London. It closes twenty-three pages later with Eleanor Pargiter in her flat off the Bayswater Road prompted to search the casualty lists after she reads the headline "Three British Cruisers Sunk." Eleanor recognizes the name of an acquaintance in the casualty lists and conjures up a vivid picture of the dead sailor buoyed up by the waves, a recurring image that will need to be excised from the Present Day section of the holograph with the deletion of this 1914 section.

The movement of the 1914 chunk from Crosby's obliviousness to the war to Eleanor's sense of guilt and impotence at being unable to prevent Captain Rankin's death would have prepared the reader for the more intimate and extended war scene in Maggie's Westminster home during an air raid in 1917. More importantly, taken together with the brief 1918 section on Armistice Day, November 11, 1918, and narrated from Crosby's point of view, the expurgated chunk would have bracketed the war years within the consciousness of the old Pargiter servant walking in Richmond in 1914 and 1918, and thus would have explicitly countered the "official" public versions in the "Northcliffe papers" Woolf criticizes in a diary entry toward the end of the war (*D1* 200). As she notes in her review of Metchim's *Our Own History of the War: From a South London View,* "[n]o one who has taken stock of his own impressions since 4 August 1914, can possibly believe that history as it is written closely resembles history as it is lived" (*E3* 3). As Karen Levenback has suggested, Woolf follows Metchim's technique of presenting war as lived within the civilian consciousness (120). Woolf eschews any attempt, as she writes to Stephen Spender shortly after the publication of the novel, to "bring in the Front [...] partly because fighting isnt within my experience, as a woman" (*L6* 122). In 1917, however, she had reviewed a war memoir by Evelyn Spearing, Newnham tutor turned V.A.D. and sent to the Belgian front. In that review, Woolf quotes the first part of Spearing's statement: "'I have had horrors enough to last me my whole life, but still I don't think I would have missed it if I had been given my choice'" (*E2* 113). Woolf omits, however, Spearing's actual participation in those horrors and her sense of communion with the soldiers that Woolf's characters in the 1914 section are denied. Spearing confesses, "It is something to feel that one has shared in any way in what the men have had to bear....There is a curious community of suffering in which one is glad to have been allowed to take one's part" (S 59). This community of suffering is present only in a subdued and remote way throughout both deleted and extant war sections from 1914 to the nearly omitted 1918 section.

The late omission of the 1914 chunk shifts the focus of the published novel away from the centrality of war and its impact on those civilians beyond the Pargiter family. It also diminishes Eleanor Pargiter's role as a key recorder of nuanced impressions of wartime London and prevents readers from hearing what Grace Radin calls "reverberations" or what Anna Snaith terms a "haunted text" where "[b]eneath the most fleeting of references lie layers of contextual meaning" (Snaith lxiii). Building on Radin's textual excavations in the early 1980s, recent critics have addressed Woolf's techniques of embedding her late cultural criticism in her deletions from the published text, but neither Alice Wood's genetic approach to the novel with its attention to the composition process nor Elizabeth Evans's discussion of the late insertions of the preludes as providing an authoritarian perspective at odds with the deletion of Woolf's social criticism, mine the holograph notebooks for specific textual evidence. Only Snaith's exhaustive investigation tackles Woolf's pattern of submerging the major historical moments in fleeting individual observations to drive home the material conditions of wartime London (lxxxix). Similarly, the severe shortening of the published 1917 wartime section from the earliest holograph version serves, like a third expurgated section, to abort the links between education and war at the heart of the 1914 holograph. The truncation of the 1917 section from the original holograph version erases the civilian views of the two male outsiders and "foreigners," Renny, a Frenchman, and Nicholas, a Pole, who polarize the debate about education and women's suffrage.

Two days after the war began, Virginia and Leonard Woolf were vacationing in Northumberland. Woolf writes to Katherine Cox on August 12 of their proximity to the North Sea where they might be "in the midst of it" should a naval battle occur (*L2* 51). This could account for the prominence of the *Times* headline a little over a month later in the omitted 1914 section about the sinking of the three British cruisers as well as for the ending of the published prewar 1914 section in the north on Kitty Lasswade's husband's estate. In addition, both Metchim and Gretton note the sinking of the British cruisers in September 1914 as a significant turning point in civilian attitudes toward the war. The entire expurgated chunk is characterized by a tone of despondency that pervades each character's consciousness as each reacts in turn to the naval disaster.

In the omitted 1914 section of the holograph, Crosby is the first of the characters to read the headline "Three British Cruisers Sunk" on newspaper placards on Richmond High Street. Both the headline and Crosby's response, "Tut tut tut," are omitted in the galley proof stage. Omitted too in the galley stage is a comment by a man sitting on the park bench by Crosby to another woman, "There's nothing more about it," and the woman's response, "Just sunk." The prominence of the newspaper headline and the lack of information available to the public echoes throughout the section, another instance of the reverberations that Radin argues structure the entire novel.

As Crosby watches Bert Parker walk toward the station, the point of view shifts to his consciousness. In both holograph and galley proofs, Parker finds the train crowded with young soldiers joking and laughing, but in the holograph we hear that "[h]e had a good mind to join up himself," thinking their job preferable to his own as he jots down earnings in his notebook. Once the soldiers exit at Hammersmith, the remaining passengers turn again to their newspapers, collectively reading the same headline, "Three British Cruisers Sunk," and searching for further information. Again the newspaper serves as the connective tissue allowing an old lady (later we learn it's Eleanor's friend Miriam Parrish) to ask to borrow another passenger's paper. His silent response in the holograph, "What for?" derives from his fury and frustration at the war and is triggered once again by the headline in the holograph but not in the galley proof. In the holograph, Ray Sargent, unnamed and considerably reduced in the galley proofs, assumes the role of the angry, educated upper-middle-class commentator on the folly of the war. Too old himself to join up, he vindictively looks across at the salesman Bert Parker and conjures up an image of a dead sailor that will resurface in Eleanor's vivid picture of the dead Captain Rankin towards the end of the section: "They'll get you one of these fine days.... You'll be floating in the North sea one of these days—What for? What for? What for? He had said the same thing many thousand times since the 4th of August." We learn that Sargent has worked as an accountant at the

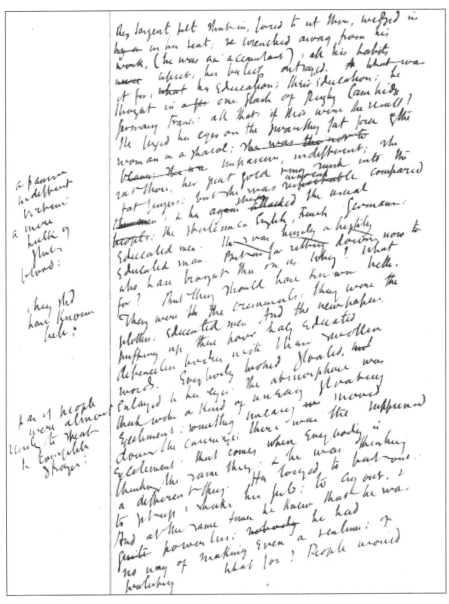

Figure 1: Notebook 5:52, Berg Collection, New York Public Library, reproduced by permission of The Society of Authors as the Literary Representative of the Estate of Virginia Woolf

Education Office, a position that presumably triggers his diatribe about the uselessness of a Rugby and Cambridge education in preventing war: "What was it for: his education; their education; he thought in one flash of Rugby Cambridge, Germany France: all that: if this were the result?" For Sargent sitting amidst "impassive" and silent passengers evidently less educated than he is, the culprits are the "educated men" like himself and the newspapers:

They were the criminals; they were the plotters: educated men. And the newspapers, puffing up the poor half educated defenceless bodies with their swollen words. Everybody looked bloated, enlarged in his eyes. The atmosphere was thick with a kind of uneasy gloating excitement; something uneasy moved down the carriage; there was the suppressed excitement that comes when everybody is thinking the same thing; & he was thinking a different thing. He longed to [burst] out, to perhaps shake his fist; to cry out, & at the same time he knew that he was powerless; he had no way of making even a sentence...What for? People would roll over the words...(Notebook 5:52)

Woolf may have culled Sargent's response to his fellow passengers from her diary entry toward the end of the war in which she criticizes the class leveling the war has generated: "Perhaps the horrible sense of community which the war produces, as if we all sat in a third class railway carriage together, draws one's attention to the animal human being more closely" (*D1* 153). Unable to remain on the train any longer, Sargent exits at Knightsbridge before his stop. This passage is significantly shortened in the galley proofs where "[e]verybody seemed...to have fed on the garbage in the newspapers; and to be passively chewing the cud" (Radin transcription, "The Years" 182). The original holograph passage echoes Woolf's comment about Metchim's point of view in her review of his book: the civilian south London view is that of the "anonymous monster the Man in the Street. He is not an individual himself, nor is the anonymous 'you' who merges into the gentleman in South London an individual; both together compose a vast, featureless, almost shapeless jelly of human stuff taking the reflection of the things that individuals do, and occasionally wobbling this way or that as some instinct of hate, revenge, or admiration bubbles up beneath it" (*E3* 3). The train journey that indiscriminately jostles Bert Parker, Ray Sargent, and Miriam Parrish together combines in its portrayal of these characters these same instincts. The journey allows Woolf a brief chance to draw faces from a crowd, to "catch the general readers attention" as she indicates in her letter to Spender (*L6* 123). Their dispersal one by one at the various stations en route to central London is highlighted by Miriam Parrish's disappointment at exiting the train onto the Leicester Square platform and feeling that briefly they had "all belonged to one family, were moving on, united, to one high goal victory" (Notebook 5:57). In her diary for November 11, 1918 and for the following day, Woolf remarks on the way the war had brought people, especially civilians, together. She speculates about how that togetherness will disappear now that the war has ceased: "We are once more a nation of individuals" (*D1* 217).

The end of the 1914 holograph focuses on Eleanor Pargiter as she travels home towards Bayswater from the theatre. Throughout this and subsequent sections, Eleanor will voice a central theme of the novel in her frustrated attempts to understand and identify with others. As she overhears a remark about Britain's commitment to France, she realizes guiltily that she had forgotten about the war during the play: "One was not allowed to forget about the war for long, she thought rather bitterly. She had been to the play; for the past hour she had been absorbed; wondering how it would end...She had forgotten the war completely. Now here it was again...She had an uneasy feeling of guilt. It was childish to become so absorbed in a mere story; in something that was only made up, inside a warm well lit theatre. When she ought to be thinking—what?" (Notebook 5:58).

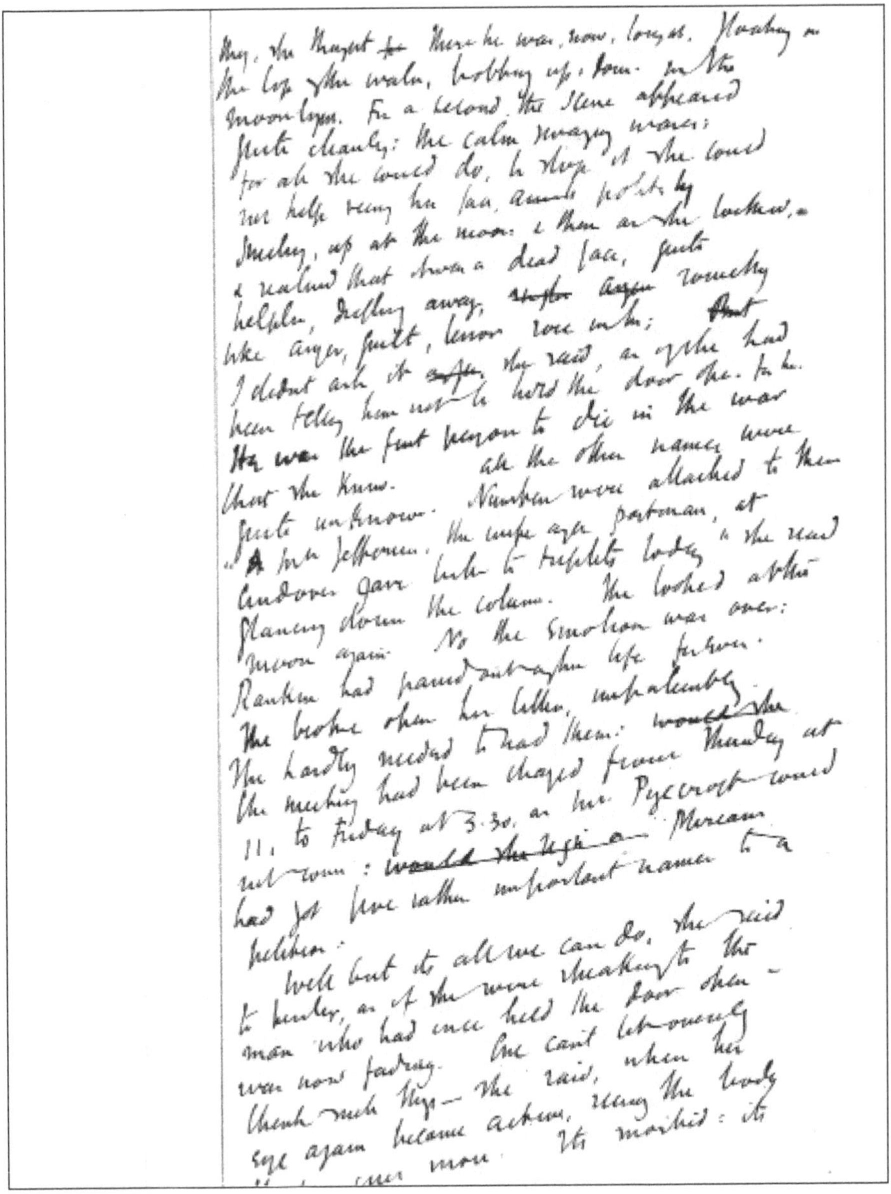

Figure 2: Notebook 5:65, Berg Collection, New York Public Library, reproduced by permission of The Society of Authors as the Literary Representative of the Estate of Virginia Woolf

She castigates herself for having "no strong convictions" and therefore being unable to prevent the war. Reviewing her upbringing, she regrets not having read the newspapers or followed "the course of politics" or formed a society or "headed a procession and gone to Whitehall, and said, if you don't stop what you're doing," but she concludes that these are "ridiculous" thoughts since she still couldn't have influenced the course of events. Ultimately, she faults her lack of education, an omission she will remark to Renny and Nicholas in the holograph version of the 1917 air raid scene.

Once on the omnibus, Eleanor continues to speculate on the war but, unlike Ray Sargent, she does not blame the politicians. The former leaders, Gladstone and Parnell, who she thinks might have "done something," have been replaced by a government of shopkeepers, "business men; lots of typewriters and departments. [...] These men toil away; we never listen to what they say. Who could read their speeches!" (Notebook 5:60). Her thoughts revert to the people on the bus as she wearily concludes that none of them could have done anything to prevent war: "Look at us—little, ordinary, commonplace" (Notebook 5:61). Like Sargent on the train, she gets off before her stop, but unlike Sargent who wants to cry out in protest, Eleanor tries to quell her sense of inadequacy and responsibility. Woolf symbolically offers Sargent, the educated civilian man, along with Eleanor, the uneducated civilian woman, as gendered responses to the commencement of war.

Eleanor's most personal connection to the actual fighting is triggered by the same newspaper headline others had perused on the train. Browsing the casualty lists, she recognizes a name, L.R. Rankin, among the officers drowned in the North Sea battle. With a jolt, she recalls meeting him at a dinner party at her brother Morris's house before the war: "Pale, pink colored, with a nice smile; very clever with his hands. He had shown them different ways of tying knots. [...] Well, he was dead. She remembered how he had held the door open for her as she went in" (Notebook 5:64). In an involuntary effort to reify his death, she suddenly becomes an eye witness and abandons her civilian detachment:

Floating on the top of the water, bobbing up and down in the moonlight. For a second the scene appeared quite clearly: the calm swaying water; for all she could do, to stop it she could not help seeing his face politely smiling, up at the moon and then as she looked, and realized that it was a dead face, quite helpless, drifting away, something like anger, guilt, terror rose in her; I didn't ask it she said, as if she had been telling him not to hold the door open for her. He was the first person to die in the war that she knew. (Notebook 5:65)

The image of the dead captain floating on the waves becomes for Eleanor a synecdoche for the faceless men who die in the war.

Apart from the late insertion of the opening preludes, the short published 1918 section that closes the sections on war differs only in small details from the holograph. The published version dramatizes Crosby's thoughts more explicitly as she vents her irritation with having to clean a Belgian tenant's bath—"Dirty Brute"—she mumbles several times. In both versions, Crosby (hobbling out to do her shopping), a housepainter, and a woman carrying a loaf of bread—all ordinary civilians—hear sirens followed by an explosion (guns *booming* in the holograph). In the holograph, Crosby hears the woman tell the housepainter that the war is over; in the final version, she hears this news later when she enters a shop. The holograph is explicit: "The guns were announcing armistice had been signed. That was the meaning of the booming guns and the wailing sirens" (Notebook 5:145). Woolf drew heavily on her single-paragraph diary entry for November 11, 1918 for the 1918 section of the novel. She recounts the sirens hooting, the guns going off, the rooks wheeling. She is one of the civilians looking out the window at a housepainter and at an old man carrying a loaf of bread. That she chose to render the section through Crosby's consciousness intensifies the sense of anticlimax and indifference from the civilian point of view. Old and insecure about her ability to pay rent on a diminishing pension, Crosby can focus only on her own dilemma and on the loss of respect and politeness within and between classes the war has seemingly encouraged. Grounding the first and last civilian responses to the war within Crosby's consciousness would have reinforced Woolf's intention *literally* to present the war from the street—from Metchim's south London view. Without the expurgated 1914 section, we are left with the much-revised 1917 section that omits the other servant's (a nurse to Maggie's two children) perspective as she presumably huddles in the upstairs kitchen with the children. Instead the raid scene depicts an array of mostly detached philosophical positions as the bombs draw closer and then recede.

Throughout the expurgated 1914 chunk of *The Years* as well as in the 1918 section, Woolf tried to render the physical reality of the Great War through repetitive textual, visual, and auditory images as those images viscerally impacted a variety of civilians from a range of classes. Perhaps most of all, the omission of the 1914 section diminishes this visceral voice from the street, railway carriage, or omnibus and narrows the focus to the early working title of the novel, "The Pargiters."

Works Cited

Evans, Elizabeth F. "Air War, Propaganda, and Woolf's Anti-Tyranny Aesthetic." *Modern Fiction Studies* 59.1 (2013): 53–82.

Gretton, R.H. *A Modern History of the English People 1880–1922.* London: Martin Secker, 1929.

Hussey, Mark. Introduction. *Virginia Woolf and War: Fiction, Reality, and Myth.* Ed. Mark Hussey. Syracuse, NY: Syracuse UP, 1991.

Levenback, Karen. "Virginia Woolf's 'War in the Village' and 'The War from the Street': An Illusion of Immunity." Hussey 40–57.

——. *Virginia Woolf and the Great War.* Syracuse, NY: Syracuse UP, 1999.

Metchim, D. Bridgman. *Our Own History of the War from a South London View.* London: Arthur H. Stockwell, 1918.

Radin, Grace. *Virginia Woolf's The Years: The Evolution of a Novel.* Knoxville, TN: U of Tennessee P, 1981.

Snaith, Anna. Introduction. *The Years.* By Virginia Woolf. Ed. Anna Snaith. Cambridge: Cambridge UP, 2012. xxxix–xcix.

Spearing, E.M. *From Cambridge to Camiers Under the Red Cross.* Cambridge: W. Heffer & Sons, 1917.

Whittier-Ferguson, John. "Repetition, Remembering, Repetition: Virginia Woolf's Late Fiction and the Return of War." *Modern Fiction Studies* 57.2 (2011): 230–53.

Wood, Alice. *Virginia Woolf's Late Cultural Criticism: The Genesis of 'The Years,' 'Three Guineas' and 'Between the Acts.'* London: Bloomsbury Academic, 2013.

Woolf, Virginia. "A Cambridge V.A.D." 1917. *The Essays of Virginia Woolf.* Vol. 2. Ed. Andrew McNeillie. San Diego: Harcourt, Brace, Jovanovich, 1987. 112–14.

——. *The Diary of Virginia Woolf.* Ed. Anne Olivier Bell. 5 vols. New York: Harcourt Brace Jovanovich, 1977–1984.

——. *The Letters of Virginia Woolf.* Ed. Nigel Nicolson and Joanne Trautmann. 6 vols. New York: Harcourt Brace Jovanovich, 1975–1980.

——. *The Pargiters.* 1932–1934. Notebook 5. MS Berg 42.

——. "The War from the Street." 1919. *The Essays of Virginia Woolf.* Vol. 3. Ed. Andrew McNeillie. San Diego: Harcourt, Brace, Jovanovich, 1988. 3–4.

——. *The Years.* 1937. Annot. and intro. Eleanor McNees. Orlando, FL: Harcourt, 2008.

"BEAUTY, SIMPLICITY AND PEACE":
FAITHFUL PACIFISM, ACTIVIST WRITING, AND *THE YEARS*

by Charles Andrews

In the constellation of values central to Virginia Woolf's ethical belief, pacifism remains one of the most controversial. Though it is fairly easy to celebrate her uncompromising opposition to the First World War or her youthful dabbling in political performance art during the Dreadnought Hoax or to sympathize with her devastation at losing her nephew Julian in the Spanish Civil War, these highlights of her pacifist stance can be overshadowed by her persistent pacifism at the end of her life.[1]

Critical biographers have often portrayed these years as ones of tragic failure. Herbert Marder describes Woolf's perspective in 1940 as such: "if hearty patriotism was suspect, pacifism no longer served her either, and she had nothing to put in its place" (296). Even more pithily, Alex Zwerdling entitled the penultimate chapter of *Virginia Woolf and the Real World* "Pacifism Without Hope." There is all too often an uneasiness with Woolf's later pacifism which emerges in descriptions like Zwerdling's: "To [Woolf], nonviolence was an article of faith rather than a discretionary tactic—the closest thing to a religion her secular skepticism permitted" (274). For Zwerdling, it seems, the only way to explain Woolf's lack of realism, her clinging to a belief in spite of evidence, is to regard her pacifist convictions as religious.

It was not uncommon among Woolf's contemporaries to follow this line of thought and regard pacifism as essentially religious—either as a faith in its own right or as a political value that fundamentally arises from religion. One of the largest peace organizations of the 1930s was the Peace Pledge Union, a secular group founded by the charismatic Anglican Canon Dick Sheppard, whose personal religious beliefs motivated his peace activism even as he attempted to preserve his organization's secularity.[2] Sheppard's Christian pacifist views were espoused by other PPU members, like Max Plowman who even offered a thoroughgoing defense of pacifist convictions as a religion in his book *The Faith Called Pacifism* (1936).[3]

But these religiously inclined peace activists adopt a position markedly different from Woolf's own. Woolf's refusal to join established peace organizations as well as her resistance to literature as propaganda perpetuate her role as an Outsider, not only from the patriarchal establishment she criticized in *Three Guineas* (1938) but also from institutionalized political activities whose positions she in many respects affirmed.

Critics like Zwerdling who see Woolf's pacifism as religious might be critiqued for working with a crude definition of "religion" which means something like "belief in spite of facts." I will not be engaging here with the ways religious faith is construed but I find the notion of "pacifism as religion" for Woolf suggestive beyond Zwerdling's superficial meaning. Not only is Woolf's pacifism a deeply-held conviction that remained intact even when its supposed "effectiveness" had been debunked, her pacifism was religious in the sense of praxis. This belief was not held in some merely propositional form or solely as a matter of affect; rather, pacifism animates much of Woolf's intellectual and creative labors of the 1930s. This praxical dimension of Woolf's pacifist thought takes shape in several forms—the public lecturing and polemical writing she did on peace despite her reluctance to formally join any particular organization; the ways she (along with Leonard) created a network of artists, intellectuals, and activists who regularly engaged with political concerns; and, most intriguingly, her fiction writing which sought high artistic quality along with anti-war contentions.

Her desire for politically engaged literature that would sacrifice neither politics nor artistry appears to be Woolf's biggest intellectual challenge during the 1930s. While tangling with revisions to *The Years* in 1935, she expressed in her diary disdain for Aldous Huxley's preachy fiction: "A very difficult problem; this transition business. And the burden of something that I wont call propaganda. I have a horror of the Aldous novel: that must be avoided" (*D4* 281). Selecting Huxley as her literary *bête noire* is particularly intriguing given their friendship, shared commitment to pacifism, and Huxley's own struggles at the time to write his modernist, pacifist novel *Eyeless in Gaza* (1936) with its complex experimental form and explicit political agenda.

Several of Woolf's 1920s novels exhibit her capacity for rich literary fiction that conveys a strong sense of anti-war feeling without becoming agitprop. Jacob Flanders's boyhood with a cow's skull on the beach and later his empty shoes in an empty room, or Septimus Warren Smith's damaged psyche and ultimate suicide, or Andrew Ramsey's death in brackets all manage to be complex, symbolic, and aesthetically full, avoiding the "incomplete" quality Woolf criticized in novels by Edwardian realists while still leaving no doubt that war is evil and should be eliminated.[4] These twenties works memorialize dead young men whose absence matters as much as their presence and Woolf calls attention to the infusion of the past into the present. Turning to *The Years* (1937) offers a contrasting mode where the growing threat of war and concern for a new and better world emphasizes what Tamar Katz has described as the novel's "future" obsession (3). *The Years* has often been seen as less introspective than Woolf's earlier works and her own ambivalence about the published novel has shaped some of its reception. Woolf's contemporary, the novelist, essayist, and PPU activist Storm Jameson sounded an early yet persistent critique of *The Years*, writing in 1937 that the novel is notable for its "sense of deadness, of falsity" which Jameson ultimately found indicative of their emotionally impoverished world (282).

What is at one level a criticism of the novel in fact becomes one of its greatest attributes: its quietly ambiguous yet explicitly political nature. Many scholars have poured over the long period of writing and revision which took Woolf's proposed "Novel-Essay" *The Pargiters* to its much less explicitly political final published form, as well as the kinship between *The Years* and its didactic sibling *Three Guineas*. My attention here is not to the writing process but rather to the ways that *The Years* is still "activist writing" and retains a political form even without overt, feminist-pacifist didacticism.

Referring to a novel as "activist writing" can sometimes sound like unfavorable criticism, the literary critical equivalent of being "funny-looking but having a good personality." And certainly, the 1930s produced a good deal of well-intentioned pacifist writing of this type. But I would argue that, without lapsing into mere propaganda, *The Years* can be read as literary activism. Nancy Knowles has provided the most useful framework for examining what she calls Woolf's "narrative pacifism," a theoretical model that helps to explain how literary form is crucial to pacifist writing. All too often when the resources of peace studies are brought into conversation with literary studies, the emphasis is on content alone. This critical sifting through literature for scenes of hideous war violence or trauma can mean that works which avoid explicitly violent scenes or overt discussion of war seem not to fit.[5] Likewise, the sheerly propagandistic literary works often fail on aesthetic terms because their content and message obliterate the ambiguity and complexity that we tend to value in high-quality fiction. Borrowing from Knowles here, there are several elements that comprise Woolf's narrative pacifism, including: 1) a focus on structural inequality in the foreground; 2) juxtaposition of this inequality with war in the background; and, 3) an unconventional narrative structure that requires readers to assemble fragments (242).

Knowles's test case from Woolf's fiction is *Between the Acts* (1941), a novel that readily displays these components. For my purposes, *The Years* is even more telling since it less obviously projects its pacifist values.

Additionally, we might supplement Knowles' theory with Judith Butler's analysis of the "frames of war," that is, the conditions under which societies agree that killing is acceptable when it is recognized as warfare rather than murder. Butler observes that "the frame initiates (as part of weaponry) or finishes off (as part of reporting) a whole set of murderous deeds…its success depends upon a successful conscription of the public" (xiii-xiv). Butler's call to action implores us: "Our responsibility to resist war depends in part on how well we resist that daily effort at conscription" (xiv). Anti-war literature thus might be seen as an intercession into that frame, a way of interrupting the frame's persuasive hold on the public narrative of war and a means for recasting that narrative in terms less favorable to war's success.

Few novels undertake this effort at intervention in "the frame" with the sophistication and the subtlety of *The Years*. Woolf's critique of what Butler calls "the conditions of [war's] possibility and probability" is quite subtle and for that reason has sometimes drawn unfavorable criticism (ix). However, it is the subtlety in her narrative—her ultimate decision to excise anything overtly didactic—which gives the novel its rhetorical power and makes it truly oppositional rather than merely reactionary.

In the "1917" episode, notable for Woolf's depiction of the air raid, a discussion among Sara, Maggie, Renny, and Eleanor reveals the powerful way the frame of war conscripts these otherwise peace-minded non-combatants. As with much of the novel, the primary narrative business attends to the mundane, in this case the plates from Maggie and Eleanor's "drawing-room at home," plates which Renny snidely observes are broken at the rate of one a week (269). Maggie blankly responds: "They'll last the war" (269). Renny's face changes, assuming a "curious mask-like expression" that Eleanor attributes to an underlying French patriotism. Regarding herself, Eleanor feels "a little light-headed" and "blurred" from wine-drinking which seems to her like "light after the dark; talk after silence" (269). This mixture of emotion and observation culminates in a free indirect moment with Eleanor supposing that it was "the war, perhaps, removing barriers" (269). This removal of barriers, flush of wine and patriotism, and time passing marked by broken dishware are all signals of war's frame. Each moment in their lives, no matter how mundane and seemingly removed from the center of power and from the diplomatic hierarchies that generate war, each of these minute changes in affect and apparently trivial action takes some of its shape from the context of war. Through Renny's gibe about the plates, his insinuation that women in the household cannot be trusted to manage responsibly even the small domestic duties entrusted to them, Woolf renders a scene with patriarchal inequality in the foreground that is heightened by the background of war.

All of these characters are effectively conscripted by the War, even in their opposition to it. Sara is the most overtly pacifist character here, ridiculing North's exuberant militarism by calling him a lieutenant in the "Royal Regiment of Rat-catchers or something" (270). Though Sara expresses views we might readily associate with Woolf's own—particularly her longstanding mockery of military pomp—Woolf resists propaganda by lacing Sara's character with bitterness and militancy that undermine the virtuousness of her position. Sara describes her last encounter with North, sitting in what she calls his "mud-coloured uniform, with his switch between his legs, and his ears sticking out on either side of his pink, foolish face"—a description that fails to contain her rage at his attitude and appearance (270). Most infuriating seems to be his impassiveness as he simply repeats to her "Good, Good" while manipulating his switch, a lame yet still irksome reminder of his phallic power sustained by militarism. But rather than finding a thoroughly pacifist response to North, Sara indulges in militancy herself and displays her own grasping at phallic power. She drowns out North's murmuring by taking up a "poker and tongs [...] and play[ing] 'God save the King'" (270). While relating this anecdote to Eleanor and the others, she repeats her performance with silverware, holding "her knife and fork as if they were weapons" (270). In Sara's militant pacifism, even her anti-war protests grow violent and link her with the militant suffragette Rose whom we later learn has patriotically joined the war effort.

In this scene, Sara is not merely hindered or oppressed by patriarchal social structures, she reproduces them, displaying an inability to imagine some moral alternative. The problem with Sara's behavior is not that her rhetoric is forceful or associated with violence. After all, Woolf herself can be found using similarly violent metaphors on behalf of peace, as in her often-quoted diary entry about *Three Guineas* where she notes that she has "collected enough powder to blow up St Pauls" (*D4* 77) or her entry from May 1940: "This idea struck me: the army is the body: I am the brain. Thinking is my fighting" (*D5* 285). Rather, the problem with Sara's position is its failure to be more than reactionary; hers is a politics based in response to the thing she despises and she conducts her opposition by using the enemy's very terms. Though her language could be seen as a form of reclaiming or as a mode of using the enemy's tools against himself, Woolf's broader agenda in *The Years* shows that violence cannot successfully bring about an end to violence and what is needed must be a far more revolutionary change in the social structures that make war inevitable.

Woolf suggests the failure of a "war for peace" by puncturing the emotional uplift experienced by the characters once the raid ceases. When the raid is over, no one can remember what they were talking about before it started and its interruption—like the devastating interruption of the Great War itself—forever separates them from their prior train of thought. The broken form of the scene enacts the content of Woolf's critique. Sara proposes a toast to the New World and they all momentarily join in exhilarated optimism at the thought of the post-war world to come. But in the distance, they hear the guns still firing and "a sound like the breaking of waves on a shore far away" (277). Not only are they reminded that the end of war has not yet begun, a more sinister element resurfaces in Renny's angry effort at reassurance when he kicks a wooden box and "savagely" says: "They're only killing other people" (277). As with his previous eruption of patriotic sentiment, his appearance changes and we are told that "the mask had come down over his face" (277). Not simply a shift in facial expression, the "mask" signifies a hardened submission to violent impulses and callous self-preservation—precisely the attitudes that allow otherwise good people to affirm a war conducted for their benefit. The emotional uplift felt during the cessation of active violence is thus undercut by a reminder that peace is not the same thing as the absence of immediate warfare. So long as Renny and others like him perpetually sink into violence, and thoughtful yet ambivalent people like Eleanor are conscripted by the frame, and politically active people like Sara resort to militancy, then the socially-structured preconditions of war remain intact.

Those violent social structures are subtly yet powerfully attacked in the novel's elliptical, allusive form with its fragmentary assemblage of voices that require active readership. The final "Present Day" chapter set in the early 1930s exhibits most clearly Woolf's choral mode, bringing together many of the characters, voices, themes, and incidents into a collage that demands readerly synthesis.[6] Sara and North discuss their last meeting, years before in 1917, and engage in a process of reconciliation while eating a wretched meal whose centerpiece is a deeply symbolic joint of lamb, a "rather stringy disagreeable object which was still bleeding into the well" on "[t]he willow-pattern plate" now "daubed with gory streaks" (304). This religiously evocative, sacrificial feast suggests Sara and North's earlier disagreement about military killing and the blood between them, yet it is through this meal that they come to terms with each other and restore something of their former friendship. In numerous examples like this throughout the "Present Day" chapter, Woolf returns to sites of conflict, presents the ineffaceable stain of bloodshed, war, and violence, and still manages a glimmer of hope for "another world, a new world"—the mantra of her characters during the lull in the air raid and in the aftermath of the novel's final party (401).

This last party does not eliminate conflict or neutralize the structural violence inherent in a society barreling toward another war but Woolf infuses the final scene with some of her most Romantic optimism. The revelers at Delia's party emerge into the strange light of dawn to realize that tubes and omnibuses have stopped running and the usually belligerent Rose invites them to walk home together: "Walking won't do us any harm," she says (411). In the open air, the concluding single-sentence paragraph offers a last look at the seasonal weather which marked the passage of time throughout the novel: "The sun had risen, and the sky above the houses wore an air of extraordinary beauty, simplicity and peace" (412). This calm ending may seem insufficiently ironic and skeptical, a Romantic excess in a work so thoroughly shot through with cynicism about the progress of time and the violence of "civilization." Yet I would suggest that this last paragraph is not a solution to the problems posed by the rest of the narrative but instead functions like the last heard voice in a choral work—meaningful as the concluding tone but not wholly dismissive of the range of voices preceding it. Instead, the active reader must work to make connections and assemble fragments and hold together disparate voices in opposition to the ideologies of patriarchy and militarism. The novel thus becomes an artistic testament against bloodshed, challenging the frame of war through Woolf's narrative pacifism.

Notes

1. Space limitations prevent an engagement with the argument that *Between the Acts* signals Woolf's abandonment of absolute pacifism. See MacKay 27–32.
2. In a PPU pamphlet which presents a transcript of an interview with Sheppard and Aldous Huxley, Sheppard responds to the question "On what principles is the Movement based?" by saying "Speaking for myself, I believe this issue is a spiritual one. I am a pacifist because I am a Christian, and I think that a large number of our members have fundamentally the same convictions as myself. At the same time, we welcome every sincere pacifist, whatever his views. There is no kind of religious test. Personally, I repeat, I profoundly believe that the Movement has got to be founded on a spiritual basis" (4).
3. Plowman's ideas are echoed in other books by PPU charter members, such as John Middleton Murry's essay collection *The Pledge of Peace* (1938) and Canon Charles E. Raven's *War and the Christian* (1938). The later peace movement historian Martin Ceadel followed this formulation in the subtitle of his first book—*Pacifism in Britain, 1914–1945: The Defining of a Faith* (1980).
4. In her famous "Character in Fiction" (1924), Woolf criticized novels whose completion could only be achieved by a reader compelled "to do something—to join a society, or, more desperately, to write a cheque" (*E3* 427).
5. Sarah Cole has argued that "in the canonical literature of the First World War, the disenchanting of violence becomes in many ways the primary work of the writer," creating a tendency among poets like Siegfried Sassoon to depict bodily horror as the main mode of their anti-war protest (63). Knowles's narrative pacifism uncovers additional methods whereby writers resist war.
6. Woolf used this musical metaphor for the ending of *The Years* in her diary: "I want a Chorus. a general statement. a song for 4 voices" (*D4* 236).

Works Cited

Butler, Judith. *Frames of War: When is Life Grievable?* London: Verso, 2009.

Ceadel, Martin. *Pacifism in Britain 1914–1945: The Defining of a Faith.* Oxford: Oxford UP, 1980.

Cole, Sarah. *At the Violet Hour: Modernism and Violence in England and Ireland.* Oxford: Oxford UP, 2012.

Jameson, Storm. *Civil Journey.* London: Cassell, 1939.

Katz, Tamar. "Pausing, Waiting, Repeating: Urban Temporality in *Mrs. Dalloway* and *The Years.*" *Woolf and the City: Selected Papers from the Nineteenth Annual Conference on Virginia Woolf.* Ed. Elizabeth F. Evans and Sarah E. Cornish. Clemson, SC: Clemson U Digital P, 2010. 2–16.

Knowles, Nancy. "Active Pacifism in a World at War: The Legacy of Virginia Woolf's Pacifist Theory on Narrative Structure." *The Theme of Peace and War in Virginia Woolf's War Writings: Essays on Her Political Philosophy.* Ed. Jane M. Wood. Lewiston, NY: Edwin Mellen, 2010. 237–260.

MacKay, Marina. *Modernism and World War II.* Cambridge: Cambridge UP, 2007.

Marder, Herbert. *The Measure of Life: Virginia Woolf's Last Years.* Ithaca: Cornell UP, 2000.

Murry, John Middleton. *The Pledge of Peace.* London: Herbert Joseph, 1938.

Plowman, Max. *The Faith Called Pacifism.* London: J. M. Dent and Sons, 1936.

Raven, Charles E. *War and the Christian.* London: SCM Press, 1938.

Sheppard, Dick and Aldous Huxley. "100,000 Say No! Aldous Huxley and 'Dick' Sheppard Talk about Pacifism." London: Athenaeum, 1936.

Woolf, Virginia. *The Diary of Virginia Woolf.* Ed. Anne Olivier Bell. 5 vols. San Diego: Harvest/Harcourt, 1977–1984.

——. *The Essays of Virginia Woolf.* Vol. 3. Ed. Andrew McNeillie. San Diego: Harcourt Brace Jovanovich, 1988.

——. *The Years.* 1937. Annot. and intro. Eleanor McNees. Orlando, FL: Harvest/Harcourt, 2008.

Zwerdling, Alex. *Virginia Woolf and the Real World.* Berkeley and Los Angeles: U of California P, 1986.

Virginia Woolf, Katharine Burdekin, and Britain's Cosmopolitan Musical Culture

by David Deutsch

Important recent work has demonstrated how Virginia Woolf found in music and sound a fascinating means to engage the political violence and nationalism that preoccupied Europe during the 1930s. Michele Pridmore-Brown, for instance, has proposed that in *Between the Acts* (begun in 1938, published posthumously in 1941) Woolf depicts how music can serve as a violently "controlling" force symbolic of "fascism's emphasis on acoustic communion," while "noise" or "static" can lead to the disruption of coercive musical meanings (411–12). Emma Sutton has suggested that in *Between the Acts* and elsewhere Woolf used "musical allusions [to] critique the nationalism character- istic of much contemporary British music and discourses about music" (122). While not discounting these persuasive claims, I want to argue that Woolf likewise drew on popular British discourses that promoted the peaceful connotations of classical music and that she even anticipated the British public's widespread reassertions of these peaceful connota- tions during World War II.

I want to emphasize, in other words, how Woolf's depictions of music promoted and even predicted the continuation of what I will call Britain's popular musical cos- mopolitanism, a widely acknowledged, shared European heritage developed specifically and uniquely in Britain through the music of Bach, Beethoven, Handel, Mozart, and even Wagner. Consequently, my analysis draws on Melba Cuddy-Keane's suggestion that in Woolf's work an "*objet sonore*" can provide a "bridge between the individual and the world" and can convey "a wholeness, a comprehensiveness, that embraces the communal life of the universe" (90). The "*objet sonore*" on which I wish to focus is classical mu- sic with a German provenance, which with its "comprehensiveness" actually reinforces conceptions of a "communal" European culture. A significant portion of Britain's early twentieth-century public was intensely invested in classical music, much of it associated with Germany.[1] Individual amateurs listened to and performed Bach, Beethoven, and Handel; Sir Henry Wood offered weekly "Wagner Night[s]" at the Queen's Hall; and the BBC dispersed a plethora of nominally German compositions from 1922 onward, interweaving German music into British everyday life.[2] This was part of the democratiz- ing force of radio technology, which, as Pamela Caughie has noted, from its inception fostered an "emerging mass culture" the "aesthetic implications" of which Woolf consis- tently, if cautiously, engaged (333). Indeed, when Woolf recreated a similar interweaving in her fiction, she did not just reflect the world around her. She projected public hopes that European musical traditions could represent long-lasting, international humanistic sympathies despite fascist atrocities in the years leading up to and during WWII.

I will investigate this claim for Woolf's popular musical cosmopolitanism from two new angles, one literary, political, and contemporary to Woolf and one more broadly cultural and historical. First, I wish to place Woolf in dialogue with Katharine Burdekin in order to argue that both novelists similarly used German classical music to imagine the rejuvenation and the peaceful reunification of Europe in the context of Hitler's remilitarization of Germany and the destruction of WWII. Woolf in *Between the Acts* and Burdekin in *Swastika Night* (1937) both intimate that classical music can promote international socio-cultural sympathies, although not political ones, amidst international strife. Subsequently, I will use letters written to the BBC's *Radio Times* to argue that Woolf's and Burdekin's prediction that music by German composers could provide a common means to advance the comforting idea, if not the political fact, of a united Europe proved remarkably accurate during WWII in Britain.

꩜

Initially, Woolf envisioned the potential for music as a healing cosmopolitan force in her post-World War I "String Quartet" (1921). A concert attendee announces that "Regent Street is up, and the Treaty signed," evoking England's commercial revitalization and a move towards stabilizing European politics after the Treaty of Versailles (132). "Still," someone insists, "the war made a break" and people are "seeking something" (132, 133). These people seek to heal Europe's still broken culture. A "Mozart" string quartet, Woolf proposes, can help with these reconciliations (133). At Woolf's concert, Mozart's German music recalls "the waters of the Rhone," a French and Swiss river, in a British room, inspiring "sorrow" and "joy" to grow "inextricably commingled" (133, 134). This cosmopolitan musical mingling promises that Europe's culture will heal as joy returns to temper an enduring pain.

Woolf insightfully rejects a naïve optimism but draws on Neo-Platonism to portray music as offering a balanced opposition to excessively nationalist ideologies. Warning that "the worst of music" is the "silly dreams" it inspires, she cautiously imagines a Mozart quartet conjuring a Platonically idealized city, a musical reimagining of Plato's Republic (134). This immaterial city consists of "neither stone nor marble," but "hangs enduring;" remaining free from political divisions, it has no "flag," is "auspicious to none," yet is "resplendent" and "severe" (135). Resplendently undamaged by war, Woolf's musical city symbolizes a severely neutral meeting ground. This musical city cannot stop war, and therefore offers no false joy, but it can counteract excessive nationalism by representing an indestructible international community.

During the lead up to and the commencement of WWII, Woolf intensified her interest in the unifying force of music even in the midst of international violence. In *Between the Acts*, her pageant audience decides that "[m]usic makes us see the hidden, join the broken" (120). Highlighting the cosmopolitanism of this "join[ing]," this miscellaneous audience listens together to music that might be by "Bach, Handel, Beethoven, Mozart" or be "merely a traditional tune" such as "Home Sweet Home" or "Rule Britannia," the latter of which Beethoven, Handel, and Wagner each borrowed to weave into their own music (188).[3] The "hidden" subtleties of these diverse musical influences "join" into a recognizably cosmopolitan musicality. This music, then, makes the "distracted united," uniting audience members from a range of social circumstances and, more symbolically, nations distracted from their common humanity and shared interests. It conjures "warriors straining asunder" getting "recalled from the edge of appalling crevasses; they crashed; solved; united" (189). This cadenced ending symbolizes both a musical resolution, in the "unit[ing]" of a final chord, and an anticipated resolution to the discord of WWII, as Britain and Germany's shared musical culture implies the potential for peace.

In this context, Woolf's use of music resonates remarkably with Burdekin's in the latter's *Swastika Night*. In Burdekin's dystopian, futuristic novel, the Nazis appropriate Germany's musical discipline to mythologize their superiority and to justify their having dominated Europe for some "seven hundred years" (78). Alfred, however, an enslaved British man, begins to challenge the myth of Nazi superiority by drawing on his own fondness for music. Warming to Alfred's musical interests, Friedrich von Hess, a high-ranking Nazi official, confesses that Germans can no longer compose good music due to the social limitations of Nazism. "No one" in Germany, von Hess admits, "has written anything for hundreds of years, except the most flagrant hash-ups and plagiarisms" (120). Contemporary Germans have "technical skill," but under the Nazis' rigid authoritarianism and extreme nationalism German creativity has become "stagnant" (121). Contemporary performances, moreover, falter due to the Nazis' ban on foreign instruments, such as Christian whistles. Most "Germans despise the Christians," whom they consider international outcasts, and so refuse to use Christian instruments (195). Yet, the "bird-music" from Wagner's *Siegfried*, von Hess insists, "should always be played on Christian whistles" because it does "not *fit* with the more sophisticated instruments" produced by the Nazis (145). Von Hess asserts the cosmopolitanism of *Siegfried* by arguing that even Germans cannot perform it properly without the international outcasts' whistles. To over-exaggerate a Wagnerian German nationalism, as the actual Nazis did, debilitates Wagner's music. Through von Hess, then, Burdekin argues that the cosmopolitan elements of Wagner's music contest Nazi claims to Germany's pre-Nazi art and the alleged benefits of oppressive, anti-cosmopolitan Nazi regulations.

Music, accordingly, provides a catalyst for defying Nazism. Nazi laws forbid trading with Christians but, when von Hess orders his servants to collect Christian whistles for him, they "forgive" him this infraction because of his rank and because they are "musical men themselves" (145). This appreciation for good music inspires an anti-xenophobic exchange, which challenges the mythology of Nazi superiority and, consequently, other aspects of the Nazis' seeming omnipotence. Alfred had believed that "some, both individuals and races, have special *abilities*. The Germans have musical ability, for instance. And martial ability" (106). If the Nazi Germans' musicality can weaken, Alfred realizes, their militarism may weaken, too. Correspondingly, if the Christians have untapped musical abilities, they may have new ways of combating the Nazis. Alfred, then, inspired by von Hess's confessions, encourages the conquered British to cooperate with the Christians to overthrow the Nazi tyranny and Burdekin implies that their shared efforts will eventually defeat Nazism. Burdekin anticipates, therefore, not just another European war, but its conclusion, which is advanced, in part, by a longstanding musical cosmopolitanism.

Alfred considers that Bach, in particular, could provide a peaceful humanist rallying point for ending war by representing a non-violent universal culture. Burdekin's Nazis claim Bach as their compatriot but Alfred believes him to be "great in a way no man of action was great…a kind of peak civilisation in general," as much British as German (99). Bach affirms Alfred's belief that a "rebellion" against the Nazis can come but that it "must be spiritual, out of the soul. The same place where Bach got his music from" (100). Alfred increasingly rejects the Nazis, who betray Bach's cosmopolitanism, as he seeks to establish a pacifist, spiritual Europe opposed to violence and terror. Burdekin thereby joins Woolf to advance the hope that a shared European musical culture, even one stemming from Germany, might unite various nationalities into a harmonious, although not homogenous, community. A common musical culture, these authors suggest, will not end war but it can remind us how Europe benefits from peaceful international exchanges.

❧

Burdekin's *Swastika Night* was published in 1937 and Woolf had nearly finished *Between the Acts* in 1941, but their anticipation of the British public's continued engagement with German classical music throughout WWII proved to be a veritable foreshadowing of actual events. Significant sections of the British public did, in fact, continue to manifest widespread admiration for classical composers associated with Germany and, simultaneously, with a broader European culture. They found in this musical cosmopolitanism some reprieve, however inadequate, from Nazi threats to Britain during and after the Blitz, as well as some reminder of non-violent European sympathies. Letters written from 1940 to 1945 to the BBC's *Radio Times* provide a unique insight into how the British public found a familiar peaceful comfort in wartime broadcasts of German music.

It is difficult to assess the precise popularity of the BBC's classical programming during these years, much less the representativeness of these letters, but both indicate that classical music did appeal to much of the British public. Asa Briggs notes that from 1939 to 1945 there were anywhere from 8,577,354 to 9,940,210 radio licenses in Britain and he puts contemporary sales of the *Radio Times* at anywhere from 2,282,422 to 4,058,650 (Briggs Appendix B). Not everyone, naturally, was focusing on classical composers, but, as Briggs argues, "'serious music' gained a wider and more knowledgeable audience during the course of the war" (526). This last claim is bolstered not only by the BBC's own achievements but also by the diverse successes of Myra Hess's National Gallery concert series (1939–1946) and the continued popularity of Sir Henry Wood's Promenade concerts (founded in 1895), not to mention provincial concert series and the wartime efforts of the Council for the Encouragement of Music and the Arts (CEMA), among other groups promoting music.

These letters, then, through the briefly public words of generally private individuals, give an important indication of how elements of British society turned to classical music to find comfort during the war. Notably, these individuals define this music in calming, spiritual, and international terms that recall the musical themes of Woolf and Burdekin. In 1940, for instance, M. F. Woollard wrote to express appreciation for a broadcast of Schumann's piano concerto. Woollard reported that amidst the "wailing" of air raid warnings "the remembrance of its calm beauty was a distinct comfort" (*Radio Times* 12 July 1940: 9). Soon after, Kathleen Hassard praised a broadcast of "Beethoven's Appassionata Sonata," as Beethoven's sonatas offer intimations of a "permanence" that would "live on after the dangerous toys of mankind have done their worst" (*Radio Times* 16 Aug. 1940: 8). At the present time, Joan Booth wrote, "many people want and need the healing power found in the music of such old masters as Handel" and "Haydn" (*Radio Times* 14 June 1940: 9). In 1941, during the Blitz, Hedley Matthews wrote to praise a performance of Handel's *Messiah* and noted how "soothing" and yet "thrilling" it was to hear "something both sane and human in these mad days (and nights) of bombs and guns" (*Radio Times* 3 Jan. 1941: 8). British listeners also enjoyed music by Finnish, French, Polish, and Russian composers, yet it was German music that most consistently symbolized a shared, peaceful international spirit. Most directly, German music broadcast into people's homes could counter the discordant noises of war. More symbolically, hearing familiar and even occasionally more modern German composers recalled a calm, healing, international humanism that would survive despite the violence of war.

The above letters were likely from civilians, yet service members of a variety of ranks and classes also wrote to the *Radio Times* in support of broadcasting music by German composers. In 1940, for instance, Lt. Rice, M. E. C., R. E., B. E. F., wrote to ask the BBC to give troops "*one* decent concert a week—composers like Beethoven, Brahms, Mozart." Noting the "rather trying and 'nervy' life" of being in the Armed Forces, even when not in imminent danger, Rice reported that "to a large number of people a concert would give real mental—almost spiritual—relaxation" (*Radio Times* 29 Mar. 1940: 9). As might be expected, not everyone considered classical music, German or otherwise, to offer a desirable spirituality or cultural sustenance. Complaining of Proms broadcasts, G. W. W., Petty Officer, H. M. Ships, argued that "the Services need entertainment....Forcing things that they don't want on men is *not* democracy" (*Radio Times* 1 Aug. 1941: 8). V. N., a sailor writing from Portsmouth, nonetheless challenged this politically inflected claim. He questioned whether G. W. W. contemplated "the tolerance of the, admitted, minority on the Lower Deck," whose requests for "'once a month' opera, and 'once a year' Proms" were "crushed" by majority tastes (*Radio Times* 22 Aug. 1941: 8). J. A. F., a coder, sparked a similar exchange by arguing that "[e]minent music critics of the lower deck must have jive, jazz, and boogie-woogie....Bach, Beethoven, Mozart...must on no account be listened to" (*Radio Times* 9 Feb. 1945: 4). "Lofty" Dell, Petty Officer, Royal Navy, however, retorted that he had "spent well over ten years on the lower deck" and that he "learned to love the music of Tchaikovsky, Handel, Mozart, Gounod, etc.,...through the eminent music critics of the lower deck" (*Radio Times* 16 Mar. 1945: 4). Despite being a self-confessed minority, there were a substantial number of service members, including those of the "Lower Deck," men who were generally not of the relatively educated and affluent officer class, who wished to hear classical music, including music by German composers.

Occasionally, the BBC even presented Wagner's music, so often associated with German nationalism, as part of a liberal international culture. The *Radio Times*, for instance, remarked of an upcoming broadcast of Wagner's "Rule Britannia Overture" (perhaps akin to the tune played by Miss La Trobe) that Wagner had used the tune "as a symbol of liberty battling against tyranny," which was "a slap for the Nazis who claim Wagner as a prophet of their ideology!" (*Radio Times* 26 Mar. 1943: 3). Here the BBC agreed with Woolf, Burdekin, and Philip Bailey, an enthusiastic listener who had suggested that Wagner's music, too, was part of "an international language" and was valuable to "people of all nations" (*Radio Times* 16 Feb. 1940: 9). The BBC, then, facilitated a widespread public embrace of German music as a comforting, culturally unifying tradition that countered Nazism and xenophobia. In this endeavor, the BBC found support in a significant, if incalculable, proportion of its listeners.

❧

Throughout the first half of the twentieth century, British authors and audiences frequently enjoyed German classical music, often through public institutions such as Promenade concerts and BBC broadcasts. Early in the century, this effective integration of German music into British culture occasionally troubled even those who admired it. E. M. Forster in *Howards End* (1910) and G. B. Shaw in *The Music Cure* (1914), for instance, anxiously use sophisticated German music, musicians, and audience members as allegories for German expertise dominating British amateurism. More intensely, E. F. Benson in *Mike* (1916) and H. H. Munro in *When William Came* (1913) depict the attractions of this German musicality subverting British patriotism and confidence and thereby facilitating German influence over British hearts and minds. For these authors, music provides an ostensibly non-threatening means to question whether Britain was prepared to compete with Germany's expertise or efficiency in other intellectual, technical, and psychological arenas, all of which converged, horrifically, in modern war.

Britain, of course, outlasted Germany in WWI, passing what Harold Perkin has called the "supreme test of national efficiency" (186). Moreover, despite the relatively limited, yet unfortunately virulent, musical nationalism rightfully noted by Pridmore-Brown and Sutton, a musical cosmopolitanism inclusive of German composers returned to Britain with renewed vigor after 1918 and thrived right up to and throughout WWII.[4] Paul Kennedy has observed that such "shared cultural traditions" had "little or no weight in the changing relationship" between Britain and Germany in the years leading up to 1914 (386). This seems all too true for political relationships in advance of and during both world wars. Yet, German music undoubtedly remained an influential cultural trope. Both Woolf and Burdekin indicate how, while German music inevitably symbolized foreign influence in Britain, it also came to symbolize an aesthetic heritage shared between these nations and with Europe itself, which benefits from peaceful international associations. These novelists, then, evidence and promote the importance of Bach, Beethoven, Mozart, and even Wagner for imagining a liberal humanist harmony that could temper and resist, if not overcome, divisive nationalisms. Notably, they present this as a public rather than a private or factional sentiment and anticipated that it would last despite war. Individual letters written to the BBC prove them to have been right. As such, Burdekin and Woolf were joined by many all but anonymous individuals in reinforcing and advancing music as a means not to prevent war—this is beyond the power of music—but to soften violent nationalisms and to imagine a sympathetic cosmopolitan peace and post-war reconciliations.

Notes

1. From the late-nineteenth century onwards in Britain, the concept of "German" music was broadly conceived to include the efforts of Austrian composers; see, *Grove's* reference in 1880 to Mozart's interest in "the advancement of German art" (Grove 519).

2. For music in British homes and the BBC, see Rose (197, 204, *et passim*); for Wood and Wagner, see Cox (32).

3. For Beethoven, Handel, and Wagner's use of "Rule Britannia," see Richards (99).

4. For German music and musicians during the First World War, see Hynes and Foreman.

Works Cited

Briggs, Asa. *The History of Broadcasting in the United Kingdom: The War of Words*. Oxford: Oxford UP, 1995.

Burdekin, Katharine. *Swastika Night*. London: Lawrence and Wishart, 1985.

Caughie, Pamela L. "Virginia Woolf: Radio, Gramophone, Broadcasting." *Edinburgh Companion to Virginia Woolf and the Arts*. Ed. Maggie Humm. Edinburgh: Edinburgh UP, 2010. 332–347.

Cox, David. *The Henry Wood Proms*. London: British Broadcasting Corporation, 1980.

Cuddy-Keane, Melba. "Virginia Woolf, Sound Technologies, and the New Aurality." *Virginia Woolf in the Age of Mechanical Reproduction*. Ed. Pamela L. Caughie. New York: Garland, 2000. 69–96.

Foreman, Lewis. "The Winnowing-Fan: British Music in Wartime." *Oh, My Horses! Elgar and the Great War*. Ed. Lewis Foreman. Rickmansworth: Elgar Editions, 2001. 89–131.

Grove, George, ed. *Grove's Dictionary of Music and Musicians*. Vol. 2. London: MacMillan, 1880.

Hynes, Samuel Lynn. *A War Imagined: The First World War and English Culture*. New York: Atheneum, 1991.

Kennedy, Paul. *The Rise of the Anglo-German Antagonism, 1860–1914*. Boston: Allen and Unwin, 1980.

Perkin, Harold. *The Rise of Professional Society: England Since 1880*. London: Routledge, 1989.

Pridmore-Brown, Michele. "1939–40: Of Virginia Woolf, Gramophones, and Fascism." *PMLA* 113.3 (1998): 408–421.

Radio Times. British Broadcasting Corporation. 1940–45.

Richards, Jeffrey. *Imperialism and Music: Britain 1876–1953*. Manchester, UK: Manchester UP, 2001.

Rose, Jonathan. *The Intellectual Life of the British Working Classes*. New Haven: Yale UP, 2001.

Sutton, Emma. *Virginia Woolf and Classical Music: Politics, Aesthetics, Form*. Edinburgh: Edinburgh UP, 2013.

Woolf, Virginia. *Between the Acts*. 1941. New York: Harcourt, 1969.

——. "String Quartet." 1921. *Complete Shorter Fiction of Virginia Woolf*. Ed. Susan Dick. London: Hogarth, 1985. 132–35.

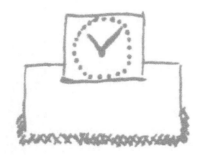

DEATH IN THE AIR: VIRGINIA WOOLF AND SYLVIA TOWNSEND WARNER IN WORLD WAR II

by Maud Ellmann

This evening I shall hear the news on the wireless.
This man, that man—
A thatcher in Essex may be, a downland shepherd—
Dead at that stroke,
Escaped to a civil death from the impending

Death in the air.

—Sylvia Townsend Warner

In a diary entry of April 3, 1941, Sylvia Townsend Warner notes: "A very noisy evening. We have lost Benghazi to the German advance. Today the news that Virginia Woolf, missing since Friday [March 28], is now presumed drowned in the Sussex Ouse. I was thinking of her while I weeded, and suddenly received a powerful impression that the reason of her going was the leader in the Times about a fortnight ago, called Disappearance of The Highbrow, and a flood of filthy letters that followed it" (Warner, *Diaries* 110). These poignant reflections provide a preview of the themes I examine in this essay. The first of these themes is war and how it reverberates in Woolf's and Warner's fiction. In the case of Woolf, I focus on *The Years* (1937), which was completed during the Spanish Civil War; in the case of Warner, I conclude with her short stories about wartime Britain, most of which were originally published in *The New Yorker*.

The second theme is news and how it travels across the airwaves. War and news occupy the same airspace; note that Warner's phrase "a very noisy evening" could refer either to the nightly din of aerial bombardment or to the wireless broadcasts reporting the German advance on Benghazi. A further source of noise is propaganda, epitomized by the *Times* leader that Warner suspects of having driven Woolf to suicide. This leader, entitled "Eclipse of the Highbrow," which was published in *The Times* on March 25, 1941, proclaimed that the conditions of this war "can hardly give rise to arts unintelligible outside a Bloomsbury drawing-room, and completely at variance with those stoic virtues which the whole nation is now called upon to practice" (5). This rhetoric exemplifies "the endless snubbing and nagging of war" that irritates the heroine of Patrick Hamilton's wartime novel *The Slaves of Solitude* (1947); the "gauntlet of No's and Don'ts thumped down on her from every side" (100–01).

Although it is unlikely that this stupid *Times* editorial was responsible for Woolf's suicide, its contempt for Bloomsbury reveals the obstacles to literary innovation during World War II in Britain. The official culture of wartime, with its insistence on "stoic virtues," drove experimental writers to assume what Patrick Deer has recently described as "camouflage." In many cases, writers resorted to traditional literary forms to mask their resistance to the noise of propaganda. Sylvia Townsend Warner, among others, reworks the conventions of realism, pastoral, and lyric to challenge the ideology of war, with its insistence on "patriotic Englishness, fortified masculinity, and compliant femininity…a disciplined

Home Front and loyal Empire at war" (Deer 5). Woolf, meanwhile, attacks this ideology head-on in *Three Guineas* (1938), but challenges it more obliquely in *The Years* by jettisoning the conventions of the novel, notably those of hero, courtship, climax, and resolution.

Woolf's reputation has soared in recent decades, thanks largely to feminist criticism, and her canonical status has now become impregnable. Warner's works, by contrast, have languished in critical neglect. For this reason my essay begins with a brief sketch of Warner's career, highlighting some of her affinities to Woolf. The following section examines how Woolf's *The Years* responds to the "dead bodies and ruined houses" of war (to quote the shellshocked refrain of *Three Guineas*) by disrupting the protocols of historical narrative (165, 180, 198). One such disruption consists of the preludes to each section inserted in the late stages of the novel's agonizing composition.[1] These preludes take an aerial perspective on the movements of the weather and the traffic in the streets. The narrator, transported "somewhere among the clouds above," looks down on London from the same position as the bomber, suggesting an uneasy complicity between these viewpoints (Yeats 184).[2]

Figure 1: RAF Gloster Gladiators, 1930s.

My essay considers what these prefaces reveal about war and air: "that thin, fluid, diaphanous, compressible and dilatable Body, in which we breathe, and wherein we move, which envelops the Earth on all sides," in the words of Robert Boyle (the seventeenth-century author of the infamous air pump experiments in which so many hapless sparrows suffocated) (qtd. in Lewis, *Air's* 46).[3] In World War II, this invisible "Body" becomes the site of global warfare, where weather, weaponry, and wireless communication compete for the same airspace. In this age of "atmoterrorism," to borrow Peter Sloterdijk's coinage, war consists of battles in the air and for the air, in which the very medium we breathe becomes the instrument of our destruction. "We must remind ourselves that there is such a thing as atmosphere," Woolf advises the common reader (*On Being Ill* 26). My essay examines how Woolf and Warner remind us of the atmosphere of war—an atmosphere in which the thunder and lightning of the bombing raids can scarcely be distinguished from the weather.

※

Sylvia Townsend Warner was born in 1893 at Harrow-on-the-Hill in the outskirts of London, home to Harrow, the famous public school in which her father was a much-loved history master. Like Woolf, Warner received little formal education but learned a lot more from her father's library than she would have imbibed in the traditional classroom. Her schooling was cut short in kindergarten due to her mimicry of the teachers, which irritated them so much that her parents withdrew her after a single term. The only word of praise in her report card was that "Sylvia always sings in tune" (Harman 8). This compliment was prescient: Warner was to become an accomplished composer and musicologist, and was planning to study with Schoenberg in Vienna before the outbreak of the First World War scuppered this ambition (Harman 26).

As self-taught "daughters of educated men," Woolf and Warner were not unusual among the middle-class women writers of their generation, few of whom attended university.[4] Outsiders in education, Woolf and Warner were also outsiders in love. Both formed erotic attachments to women at a time when such passions were taboo. Woolf's love affair with Vita Sackville-West inspired her fantasy novel *Orlando* (1928), while Warner's union with the poet Valentine Ackland contributed to some of her finest writing, including the 1936 novel *Summer Will Show*, a lesbian romance set during the French Revolution. As writers, both Woolf and Warner were tireless experimenters, unwilling to settle in a single fictional mode. It has been remarked that each of Warner's seven novels could have been written by a different person (Simon). Similarly, each of Woolf's novels strives to overturn the fictional conventions of the last. As Elizabeth Bowen writes in a moving tribute to Woolf: "she recognised her own virtue—the untouched ice, the savage intractability of the spirit that must experiment....Never once did she do the same thing over again" (*Mulberry* 179).

On March 26, 1926 the newly established American Book of the Month Club chose Warner's novel *Lolly Willowes* as its inaugural selection. In this novel, middle-aged Lolly Willowes flees her brother's home in London, where she has languished in the role of serviceable maiden aunt, to set herself up as a witch in the Dorset village of Great Mop. Lolly's plea for a "life of one's own, not an existence doled out to you by others" anticipates Woolf's title *A Room of One's Own*, published two years later (*Lolly* 239). The popular success of *Lolly Willowes* provided the occasion for the Warner's only meeting with Virginia Woolf at a luncheon party organized by *Vogue*. When Woolf asked how Warner came to know so much about witches, the younger author replied, "Because I am one" (Harman 66).

Warner lived through two World Wars, whereas Woolf committed suicide before the end of World War II, but war reverberates through both their works. Warner's first published article recounted her experience as a shell-machinist in a munitions factory in 1916, where the regular workers, "bone-weary, working long hours of necessity, living in the vitiated air of the shop, where the noise eats them like a secret poison," referred to well-heeled female volunteers like Warner as "Miaows" (Harman 30–2). Although grateful for this first-hand experience of factory-work, Warner later regretted having been a scab. In 1935, she followed her partner Valentine Ackland in joining the Communist Party of Great Britain, and the couple travelled twice to Spain to aid the republican cause.

In contrast to Woolf, who responded to the Spanish Civil War with the anti-war polemic of *Three Guineas*, Warner wholeheartedly supported the armed struggle against fascism. Indeed she never formally left the CPGB; instead she went so far as to lament the death of "Uncle Joe" [Stalin] in 1953, and dismissed as capitalist propaganda the mounting evidence of Stalinist atrocities. If her politics ossified in later life, however, her fiction remains too "sly," her irony too slippery for absolutism.[5] Despite recent attempts to recast her as a lesbian crusader, Warner's work evades the stranglehold of identity-politics. As Jane Garrity has shrewdly observed, "Warner resists collusion with existing models of 'deviant' sexuality and elects, instead, to employ an individualized discourse of inversion that relies on elements of fantasy, evasion, dissimulation, and displacement" (142).

Elizabeth Bowen, who wrote the history of her Anglo-Irish family during the London Blitz, later remembered that "the past mattered more than ever" in "the savage and austere light of a burning world" (*Bowen's Court* 464). Like Bowen, Woolf and Warner responded to the burning world by turning to the past in their historical novels in the 1930s. Warner's *Summer Will Show*, set in 1848, was followed by *After the Death of Don Juan* (1938), described by the author as "a parable…or an allegory…of the political chemistry of the Spanish War, with the Don Juan—more of Molière than of Mozart—developing as the Fascist of the piece" (Warner, *Letters* 51n1). In 1931, Woolf started collecting material for the novel-essay that ultimately morphed into *Three Guineas* and *The Years*, which the author regarded as "one book" even after their division (*D5* 148). Single or double, both books were completed during the Spanish Civil War, in which Woolf's nephew Julian Bell was killed in 1937.

❧

Turning now to *The Years*, the title of this novel is misleading, given that the narrative actually consists of a handful of days plucked out of the decades between 1880 and the early 1930s. "The Hours," which was the provisional title of *Mrs. Dalloway*, would be closer to the mark (Briggs 143–44).[6] It is well-known that Woolf was impressed by Turgenev's selectiveness in the use of detail, "the long process of elimination" that "clears the truth of the inessential" (*CE1* 248; *D4* 172). In *The Years*, Woolf emulates this technique to somewhat baffling effect. Things and actions stand out for their inconsequence: instead of gesturing to hidden depths, their superficiality marks the loss or repression of meaning. Like cinders, or "obscure remainders from a silent conflagration," these traces signify the absence of the whole from which they have been torn (Millot 208).

On January 20, 1931, Woolf noted in her Diary: "I have this moment, while having my bath, conceived an entire new book—a sequel to a Room of Ones Own—about the sexual life of women: to be called Professions for Women perhaps—Lord how exciting!" (*D4* 6). Even at this early Eureka moment in the composition of *The Years*, there is a striking discrepancy between the prim and proper title "Professions for Women" and the book's projected subject-matter, as if a process of self-censorship had already been set in motion.[7] Wary of writing what she called an "Aldous" [Huxley] novel (*D4* 281), Woolf pruned *The Years* of anything that could be taken for grandstanding, drastically curtailing the provenance of the narrative voice. "I'm afraid of the didactic," she noted in her diary in January 1933 (*D4* 145). Yet by suppressing what she criticized as the "loud speaker strain" in 1930s writing, Woolf also ended up suppressing the sexual life of women ("Leaning Tower" 272).

The opening sections of *The Years* create the expectation of a Victorian family chronicle, complete with straying patriarch and dying matriarch. But instead of a continuous history, the novel offers a series of vignettes, most of which are too banal to qualify as epiphanies or moments of being. Each of these vignettes provides a glimpse of the Pargiters and their acquaintances as they grow older, poorer, fatter, but no wiser. In the Proustian conclusion of the novel, entitled "The Present Day," the surviving Pargiters reassemble for a party. But time is not regained in this reunion; there is no artist, as there is in Proust, to make sense of these thwarted and inconsequential lives. Although Sara (or Elvira in earlier drafts) was originally cast as the writer in the family, this would-be novelist degenerates into a scatterbrained, eccentric drunk, notorious for a visceral outburst of anti-Semitism (*TY* 322–24). The novel therefore resists what Leo Bersani has described as the "culture of redemption," probably because the language of redemption has been co-opted by the war machine.

Hermione Lee describes *The Years* as a "crippled" novel, and there's some justice to this verdict (677). In a diary entry of November 3, 1936, Woolf herself likened the much-cut manuscript to a dead cat (D5 23).[8] It is as if she had responded to the "dead bodies and ruined houses" of the Spanish war by blasting her own narrative to smithereens. Much as the Victorian family breaks apart, its childless daughters scattered among London bedsits, so the novel's episodes float free of past and future, obliging the reader to interpolate the missing years. This fragmented structure also bears the scars of Woolf's research, the newspaper articles that she cut and pasted into a scrapbook.[9] These clippings, which amount to a dossier against patriarchy and its endemic war-mongering, provide the background for the pacifist polemic of *Three Guineas*. Woolf describes the daily paper in *Three Guineas* as "history in the raw" (159), and she preserves this rawness in *The Years* by presenting history as a series of disconnected days, in which the characters, trapped in the present, are deprived of either foresight or hindsight.

This disintegration corroborates Barry McCrea's argument that the novel as a genre is bound up with the fate of the bourgeois family. McCrea points out that the typical ending of the *English* fairy-tale, "they lived happily ever after," is usually rendered in *French* as "ils eurent beaucoup d'enfants" (133–35). They had lots of children: the sense of an ending therefore depends on the perpetuation of the family. In *The Years*, by contrast, daughters remain spinsters, with exceptions such as Delia, whose adolescent crush on Charles Stuart Parnell lures her into marriage to a disappointing Anglo-Irishman.[10] The other central female characters, as David Trotter has pointed out, end up not in families but in "a network of single women of different generations connected primarily by the telephone." In contrast to the 1880s, when the Pargiters had orbited around the mother's deathbed where her children were conceived and born, the 1930s see the orphaned siblings scattered into mobile privacies, the mother's gravitational pull having been supplanted by the matrix of telephony (Trotter 79–83). In a similar way, the isolated moments that form the novel's episodes hover in the void, marooned in time.

In this sense they resemble the "one-day" world of the newspaper, which "obliterate[s] the day before," as Woolf observes in *Between the Acts* (146).[11] The daily paper also forecloses the day to come. Hegel famously remarked that the newspaper serves as a substitute for morning prayers (Anderson 35). But the diurnal distribution of the newspaper, governed by the natural rhythms of sunrise and sunset, belongs to a different tempo from the news itself. As the term implies, the news has to be new, unprecedented, unrepeatable. Yet the interruptions it records are cushioned by the daily resurrection and obsolescence of the medium, a rhythm that testifies to continuity and cyclicality, as opposed to the brusque irruption of the "new."

For this reason the news would seem to be diametrically opposed to the everyday. But it makes more sense to view the everyday as a defence-formation, constructed in response to the newspaper's daily diet of violence, in which the traumatic events of war, rape, torture, revolution, and murder, along with natural catastrophes like earthquakes and tsunamis, feature side-by-side with ads and gossip columns. Thus the newspaper ensures that the character of the everyday is both "repetitive and veiled by obsession and fear," in Lefebvre's formulation ("Everyday" 10). In the newspaper, as on the radio and the TV, war is brought into the home but also distanced as a spectator sport. This means that war is "not very near. Even when it is here," as Gertrude Stein observes (*Wars* 9). Yet war is also never very far away, even when it takes place on a distant continent, because it is instantly transmitted through the media.

In a media-saturated world, the traumatic infiltrates the everyday, suggesting an affinity between these seeming opposites. What they have in common, Mary Favret has proposed, is that neither trauma nor the everyday can ever "know or tell itself" ("Everyday" 618).[12] Freud conceives of trauma as a shock that the ego can't absorb, Lacan as a fragment of the real that cannot be incorporated into the symbolic order. This troubling fragment, which can neither be remembered nor forgotten, induces the syndrome of compulsive repetition. In this sense trauma bears a structural resemblance to the everyday, which is characterised by routine, habitual practices, repeated unconsciously or semi-consciously, which cannot account for their own origins. The everyday, it has been argued, is "practically untellable" because it "eludes the grip of forms" (Lefebvre, *Everyday* 182; qtd. in Favret, *War* 160).

The most conspicuous instance of trauma in *The Years* is the scene where Rose is accosted by a flasher during her secret flight to Lamley's toyshop. Although there is no sequential link between Rose's trauma and the theme of war, they are connected by recurrent images of scars. In the section headed 1908, we discover that Rose bears a white scar on her wrist as a result of a self-inflicted injury: "I dashed into the bathroom and cut this gash," she belatedly explains (*TY* 116). Rose's scarred wrist recalls the manual injuries suffered by her father, who lost two fingers in the British suppression of the Sepoy Rebellion of 1857, as well as her brother Morris, who cut his hand bathing—a bathetic version of his father's wound (*TY* 80). In fact *The Years* contains a remarkable 322 references to hands, twice the number to be found in Woolf's other novels.[13] In *The Years*, some hands are scarred and mutilated, while others are presented as repellent: Gibbs's "great red paw" looks like "a piece of raw meat," and North is "disgusted" by Milly's "fat little hand," its diamond rings engulfed in flab (*TY* 38, 273). Associated with these hands are references to claws and gloves, such as the disturbing image of Sara peeling a banana: "the banana-skin was like the finger of a glove that had been ripped open" (*TY* 236).

Paradoxically, this obsession with hands coincides with a virtual embargo on touching in *The Years*. When hands reach out to other people in *The Years*, their attentions are usually unwelcome, like the flasher's hand that grabs at Rose, or the "heavy hand" deposited on Kitty's knee by the lecherous historian "Old Chuffy" (*TY* 48). In the early scene where Colonel Pargiter visits his mistress, "the hand that had lost two fingers began to fumble rather lower down where the neck joins the shoulders" (*TY* 7). This hand, grammatically dismembered from the Colonel's body, functions as an independent agent, at once priapic and castrated, fumbling at anonymous body-parts: "where the neck joins the shoulders." Apart from a few handshakes and the odd peck on the cheek, Woolf's characters rarely touch each other; their customary mode of salutation is a distant wave. This distance reflects the narrator's perspective on her characters, which grows increasingly external as the narrative proceeds: "there's a good deal of gold," Woolf notes, "in externality" (*D4* 133).[14] The consequence of intimacy, by contrast, is defilement: *The Years* teems with images of dirt, stains, and smudges, such as the infamous "line of grease" that Sara expects the Jew to deposit on the boarding-house bathtub (*TY* 249).[15] In this novel to touch is to smear, to stain the surfaces of walls, bathtubs, and paper with greasy traces of embodiment.

Hands also write: "Eleanor was sitting at her writing-table with her pen in her hand" (*TY* 66). The marks her pen deposits on the paper correspond to the marks the Jew deposits on the bath, insofar as both are means of blackening white surfaces. Specifically Eleanor is drawing "on her blotting paper; a dot with strokes raying out round it"—the same spiderish blobs that Woolf doodled on her manuscripts.[16] Despite her resemblance to the author in this scene, however, Eleanor is not a writer but a drudge who, far from writing a novel, is totting up her father's accounts. Like Sara, Eleanor never blossoms as a writer, despite the frequent hints about the sisters' literary promise. This elimination of the figure of the writer from the text probably reflects Woolf's sense of incapacity as she agonized over the revision-process. Meanwhile the recurrent images of injured hands reflect the lacerations that Woolf inflicted on her manuscripts or "handicraft"; Rose's cut wrist, for example, marks a cut scene from the draft novel-essay that was later published as *The Pargiters*.[17]

These images of wounded hands are also implicated in the theme of war, a connection clinched by Colonel Pargiter's dismembered fingers. Suggestive of impotence, these missing fingers also foreshadow the dismemberment of empire. Furthermore, they mark the obsolescence of manual warfare, which has now been superseded by aerial bombardment, in the same way that handwriting has been overtaken by communication through the airwaves, or physical intimacy by telephony. Heidegger argues that the hand is in danger from the typewriter, which threatens to uncouple thinking from writing (80–1, 85–6). In Woolf, however, the hand is in danger from the air, the new domain of both the media and the military. Writing has migrated from the page into the atmosphere, a transition signaled by the famous scene of skywriting in *Mrs. Dalloway*.

Instead of dropping bombs, this airplane is advertising toffee. Its threat of violence, however, is not entirely dispelled; such displays contributed to the glamorization of air power in the aftermath of World War I. The German Zeppelin raids on London, which Woolf portrays in the 1917 section of *The Years*, sparked an arms race in which the British high command struggled to catch up with German advances in air power. In the interwar years, the colonies provided the RAF with a convenient testing ground for this proliferating arsenal. As Paul Saint-Amour has shown, Churchill as secretary of state, together with his chief of air staff Hugh Trenchard, began to step up RAF operations in the colonies after the Great War, "hoping to demonstrate that air power could efficiently and affordably contribute to 'imperial defense'" ("Partiality" 438).

In the 1930s, when Woolf was struggling with the composition of *The Years*, war was both "in the air" and "on the air." In the air, in the sense that there was "wind" of its imminence in Britain; on the air, in the sense that war was constantly bruited over the airwaves. Furthermore, war in the air had already begun in Spain, as in the colonies, although RAF attacks on civilians were rarely reported *on* the air. Even so, destruction and the communication of destruction occupied the same medium in this period. Hence Sylvia Townsend Warner, in a diary entry of June 14, 1940, reflects that "the giving of news by wireless, which is *non*-geographical, has tended to give the war-news something of the quality of news of a pestilence. It has made it, in a fashion, an atmospheric rather than a territorial phenomenon" (*Diaries* 104). Wireless communication means that war is not just reported

Figure 2: POLICEMAN ON BICYCLE, LONDON 1917.

but actually conducted on the air, through the medial dissemination of news and propaganda.

With the exception of the atmospheric preludes in *The Years*, Woolf and Warner tend to portray the experience of air war from the ground, resisting the panning shots of total war by zooming in to close-ups of the home front. Many writers of the 1930s, dazzled by the rise of air power, had idealized the airman and his God's-eye view. The view from the ground, by contrast, is necessarily partial and occluded. From this position, the ear rather than the eye bears witness to the battle in the sky. "A long-drawn hollow sound wailed out," Woolf writes in *The Years* (210), referring to the air raid siren that compels the household to retreat into the "crypt-like" cellar (211). In fact, Woolf remarked that her strongest memory of World War I was darkness, due to the long hours she was forced to spend in cellars (Lee 346).

The psychoanalyst Edward Glover, in a study of war neurosis published in 1942, notes that civilians suffered from a pathological inability to "interpret sounds in the night." Their "obsessive concern with the interpretation of sound," Glover contends, arose from the confusion of real violence with the threat of violence transmitted over the airwaves (19).[18] Such threats, as Paul Saint-Amour has shown, induce a kind of "pre-traumatic stress syndrome" in their auditors, in which anticipation becomes "a new medium for delivering injury" ("Traumatic" 7–8). Contrary to the Freudian model that attributes psychic trauma to the failure to anticipate shock, the forewarnings of bombardment, particularly sirens, terrorized civilians as much as the "avalanches of noise" that proceeded from the bombs themselves (Hanley 86).[19]

Figure 3: NEAR TOWER BRIDGE, LONDON, JUNE 11, 1914, REPRODUCED BY PERMISSION OF LONDON METROPOLITAN ARCHIVES

During the air raid in *The Years*, the huddled company is forced to guess at the significance of sounds that penetrate their cellar, the ominous crescendo of the guns that culminates in "a violent crack of sound, like the split of lightning in the sky" (*TY* 212). If the guns are "like" a lightning-bolt, a thunderstorm is also "like" aerial bombardment; in these similes, the tenor is hard to distinguish from the vehicle, since war and weather are easily mistaken for each other. Warner records a similar confusion in her diary of December 10th, 1940: "A long distant growl. An explosion? Not until the third of these did we realize it was only a thunderstorm. One of the advantages of a thunderstorm is that one feels no need to locate it. I don't know why not being allowed to know where *noises off* take place should irk one so. If a bomb falls, a bomb has fallen, and that should suffice a contented mind. But it doesn't" (*Diaries* 107). Thus war in the air is experienced as "*noises off*," as sounds disconnected from their source, those unsettling sounds that film theorist Michel Chion describes as "acousmatic" (32–3 and passim).

Warner's confusion of the sounds of war with those of weather contradicts the usual assumption that war, as a man-made upheaval of the natural order, represents the very opposite of weather. War tends to be regarded as an irreversible catastrophe, weather as an everlasting contest of the elements; war therefore belongs to the linear time of Western historiography, weather to the cyclical time of nature. At the cultural level, weather is a byword for banality, associated with small-talk and what Woolf calls the "cotton wool of daily life" ("Sketch" 72). "[W]hen two Englishmen meet," Samuel Johnson famously observed, "their first talk is of the weather; they are in haste to tell each other, what each must already know" (qtd. in Favret, *War* 126). War, on the contrary, implies the destruction of the everyday and its phatic commonplaces.

On inspection, however, this apparent opposition between war and weather falls apart. This is because weather is more catastrophic and war more everyday than common wisdom acknowledges. The current climatological crisis shows that weather, as a natural phenomenon, can no longer be uncoupled from the human, "artificial" world of culture. As Sloterdijk remarks, "what human beings meet in the weather are the expectorations... of their own industrial-chemotechnical, militaristic, locomotive, and tourist activities" (Sloterdijk 89). Today weather *is* war, insofar as it has been coopted by the military-industrial complex; likewise, war *is* weather. In the near future, the US military plans to consolidate its control of the ionosphere, weaponizing the weather so that blizzards, whirlwinds, thunderstorms, and droughts can be unleashed on refractory populations (Sloterdijk 64–5). Thus Warner's confusion between thunderstorms and bombs foretells the shape of things to come, a future in which human war converges with the weather.

Figure 4: UP HOUSEWIVES AND AT 'EM, 1940.

The everyday, on the other hand, could be seen as the by-product of modern war, its unspectacular counterpart. In modern war, which has come to enlist every aspect of life, including the very air we breathe, it no longer makes sense to conceive of the everyday as an insulated zone of peace, or of war as a bounded event that can be declared and entered. Now that war has taken to the air, it is no longer a crisis but a presence: "there is always war," as Gertrude Stein declares (Stein 7). Today's battle-cries about the "war on terror," the "war on drugs," and recently the crazy "war on fat," are symptomatic of the ubiquity of militarism in contemporary life.

In *The Years*, the notion of war as climax is replaced by war as climate. Plot gives way to "friction," to borrow Clausewitz's term for the humdrum complications—including the weather—that thwart the plots of military strategists (von Clausewitz 119–21). One of Woolf's most conspicuous revisions to the novel was to preface the sections with lyrical descriptions of the atmosphere, thereby evoking the weather forecasts that had become a daily feature of BBC radio since March 26, 1923. Woolf's set-pieces on the weather were interpolated in the proofs during the last two months of 1936, thereby coinciding with the bombing of Madrid.

Elizabeth Evans, in a discerning study of *The Years*, proposes that Woolf's prefaces, by exposing the limitations of the God's-eye view, ironize their own totalitarian ambitions. Without disputing this argument, I also want to make the case that the airminded language of the prefaces should be read as symptomatic rather than totalitarian. Having forbidden herself to proselytize, Woolf seems to have displaced her anxiety about the war on to the weather. Take the section headed "1914," which is set on a "brilliant spring" day shortly before the June 28th assassination of the Archduke Franz Ferdinand of Austria (*TY* 164). No such world-historical event, however, is recorded in this episode; instead Martin runs into Sara, treats her to a tipsy lunch, and accompanies her to the Round Pond in Kensington Gardens, where they meet up with their cousin Maggie and her baby. While this terrestrial activity is thoroughly inconsequential, the sky is full of omens of destruction. "Even the air seemed to have a burr in it as it touched the tree tops; it vibrated, it rippled"—with intimations of aerial bombardment. The leaves, moreover, are described as "sharp," the fields as "red with clover," foreshadowing the bloodbath and the poppyfields of World War I (*TY* 164). H.G. Wells, in his 1921 preface to his prophetic 1908 novel *War in the Air*, claims that the notion of military "fronts" (first used in print in 1375) has now been outdated by air war (7). But this military term had already migrated into meteorology (first usage 1921). Given that London's climate is affected by weather-fronts across the globe, Woolf's bulletins indicate that England's "daily island life" is constantly besieged by global airflows—both climatic and informational.[20] "Dispersed are we," the gramophone sings in *Between the Acts* (95–103, 196–98): in the preludes to *The Years*, things and persons are dispersed into currents of affect, creating something like the "weather-maps of public feeling in a crisis" envisaged by the founders of Mass Observation (Harrisson et al. 155).

While reporting on the fluctuations of the weather, Woolf also charts the movements of the streets, and it is worth noting that updates on traffic, along with those on weather, are longstanding daily features of the radio. In *The Years*, the movements of traffic evoke the advance of armies, thwarted by the gridlock of competing forces that mirror the diurnal skirmish of the clouds. Woolf also stresses the cacophony of traffic—blasting horns, booming motors, screeching brakes—which resembles the soundscape of war, with its shrieking sirens, zooming planes, and roaring bombs. When the church clocks strike, the word "strike" bristles with military innuendoes. These clocks, moreover, are irregular, "as if the saints themselves were divided" (*TY* 164). This failure of synchrony seems to confirm Karl Popper's view that clocks are clouds, as opposed to the deterministic view that clouds are clocks. In *The Years*, the mistimed striking of the clocks suggests that time is out of joint in London 1914, and that the nation, like the saints, is divided from within, as well as threatened with division from without.

ﾞ✿

To conclude, I turn briefly to Warner's wartime fiction, first to her short story "English Climate." This title seems to endorse Woolf's view that "we must remember there is such a thing as atmosphere" (*On Being Ill* 26). In Warner's story, this atmosphere is governed by the English climate, which produces incessant rain, as well as by the mental climate of the war, which produces incessant admonitions. Gunner Brock, having been granted a short leave from his regiment, travels nineteen hours to his family home in Dunbridge, where "a regular downpour" threatens to inundate the village's proud "Book Mile," the "dingy caterpillar" of "disgraced books" donated for National Salvage Week (63, 69). Just as the rain soaks the island in the democracy of damp, uniting all regions in soggy equivalence, so books are reduced to a democracy of paper, their contents and provenance obliterated.

To his horror, Brock discovers his own books among the salvage. His mother, energized with a new sense of her own importance—like the many bustling matrons who form a comic chorus in the fiction of this period—has nobly sacrificed her son's possessions to the war effort. This donation indicates that the "war-climate," as Bowen calls it, has effected a transvaluation of values (Preface vii).[21] Books are no longer prized for the thoughts that they purvey, nor even for their marks of ownership, "the unmistakable warmed look of a well-read copy" (63–4), but merely for the reuse-value of their board and paper.

"What a clearance!" (63) a housewife cheers, gazing in triumph at the sodden Book Mile. The term "clearance" recalls the German "*Säuberung*" or purge, which was the term used for the Nazi book-burning of 1933. To Gunner Brock's mind, however, even an *auto-da-fé* would restore some dignity to these dishonored, soggy cast-offs; besides, he sneers, the villagers might "get some fun" out of the bonfire (68). Mrs Brock is horrified by this suggestion. "*Burn a book?*" she exclaims. "Why, for months

Figure 5: PUTTING THE LID ON HITLER, 1940.

now we've been lighting the fires with gorse and shavings. There's no paper burned in this house, I can tell you. Every scrap of it goes into salvage. Burn a book? Why, your father's even given up his shaving calendar!" (68).

This funny story first appeared on May 1, 1943 in *The New Yorker*, which Warner described as her "gentleman friend" because it provided her with a reliable income by publishing over a hundred of her short stories (Harman 145). The title "English Climate" indicates that the story is addressed to American curiosity about the everyday life of the Home Front. Its concern with books and their misfortunes resembles Warner's other wartime stories, which often focus on the fate of objects as a sign of the times. The most ambitious of these stories is "The Museum of Cheats," which traces the fortunes of an eighteenth-century skeptic's collection of religious and superstitious objects, ranging from reliquaries and indulgences to witch-knots and toad-skins. These objects alter with the centuries, their physical decay accompanied by their semantic transformation. Uprooted from their origins in magic and religion, and vilified as flimflam by their own collector, these "cheats" owe their longevity, as well as their semantic mutability, to their enshrinement in the museum. Here they are reinterpreted by each succeeding generation as relics of folk culture, vendible commodities, sacrosanct antiques, and finally as noxious junk, after spending World War II in a flooded cellar.

The fate of this collection suggests that all objects are cheats insofar as they promise to be solid—an illusion shattered by aerial bombardment. "All my life I have said, 'Whatever happens there will always be tables and chairs'—and what a mistake," Bowen wrote to Virginia when the Woolfs' home in Tavistock Square was destroyed by a bomb (*Mulberry* 216–17).[22] In their wartime writings, Woolf and Warner portray objects as remains or debris, much as *The Years* portrays history as the fragments of an irrecoverable narrative. In these works, the damage inflicted on bodies and buildings by war and weather indicates that things are no longer to be understood as monadic entities in which subjective sovereignty has been rehoused, but "disgraced" and disgraceful refuse, "swollen and blained, like the dead," as Warner describes the cheats after their ordeal in the cellar (126–27).

These remains could be compared to Bataille's notion of the "*informe*" or the formless, defined as that which "has no rights in any sense and gets itself squashed everywhere, like a spider or an earthworm," yet is dressed up by philosophy in the "frock coat" of form (31). Air war demystifies form by reducing objects to clouds and crowds of atoms; in effect to a disturbance of the weather. It is not just the weather in the streets, however, but the atmospherics of the text that partake of this disintegration. By reducing realism to shrapnel, to the fallout after an explosion, Woolf exposes the everyday in all its unredeemed and uninflected bathos, deprived of the frock-coat of narrative continuity. In this way *The Years* partakes of

Figure 6: Dresden, 1945. (Credit: SLUB Dresden/ Deutsche Fotothek, Walter Hahn)

the air war that it represents, pre-empting the shattering effects of bombing. "*Consider the gun-slayers, bomb droppers here and there. They do openly what we do slyly,*" booms the megaphone in *Between the Acts* (187). In *The Years,* Woolf does slyly what bomb droppers do openly by disclosing the *informe,* the unformed that lurks within the formed, the ruins of ontology without a frock-coat. Perhaps this is what she meant by asserting that *The Years* was a deliberate failure (*D5* 65).

Notes

1. For the composition history, see Radin and Snaith. A succinct account of the novel's composition may be found in Jeri Johnson's learned and insightful introduction to her edition of *The Years,* cited throughout.
2. Gillian Beer remarks of the first prelude: "Something odd and uneasy occurs in this writing with its mixture of Dickensian super-eye and the autocracy of the air, gazing *de haut en bas.* The aerial view affords a dangerous narrative position" (151). See also Evans 53–4.
3. See also Shapin and Schaffer.
4. The phrase "daughters of educated men" resounds bitterly through Woolf's *Three Guineas,* e.g. pp. 155, 163, etc. For a useful summary of the education received by middle-class women writers of the 1930s, see Montefiore 23–4.
5. Warner writes, "Women as writers are obstinate and sly" ("Women as Writers" 380). I discuss this essay at greater length in "The Art of Bi-Location: Sylvia Townsend Warner."
6. The holograph draft of "The Hours" is housed in the British Library: Add. MS 51045, f.136.
7. As Christine Froula has pointed out, no sooner had Woolf announced her subject "than repression intervened…as if in an involuntary hystericization of her text" (214).
8. In *The Pargiters,* Elvira is a hunchback and, as Julia Briggs points out, her "status as a physical cripple (and a wise fool) indirectly exposes other characters as emotionally or psychically damaged" (284). In *The Years,* I argue, the image of the injured hand performs a similar function to Elvira's deformity, but also marks the damage inflicted by the author on the novel, and vice versa. See also Froula 244.
9. See the Monks House Papers in Silver.
10. Woolf was reading R. Barry O'Brien's *The Life of Charles Stewart Parnell* (1898) in January 1933 (*D4* 143) while writing *The Pargiters.*
11. In "The Revolutionary Simpleton," Wyndham Lewis attributes the "one-day" world of modernist novels like *Ulysses* to the ubiquity of advertising: "The world in which Advertisement dwells is a one-day world" (23). Much the same charge could be laid against the newspaper.
12. See also Favret's *War at a Distance* 160.
13. Emily Dalgarno, who has also drawn attention to Woolf's frequent references to hands, argues that "in nearly all of the more than one thousand appearances of *hand* in [Woolf's] novels it is used to hold objects, grasp another hand, beat time, wave, etc." (172). In *The Years,* however, hands tend to fumble, fidget, shake, and suffer laceration, thereby thwarted in the purposeful actions listed by Dalgarno. As Steven Connor has pointed out, "the knitting and grasping and clasping and fidgeting and fumbling…that occupy so much attention in *The Years* are ghostings of the hand that is writing them." Furthermore, these restless hands could be seen as ghostings of the sexual material occluded or repressed in the final version of the text.
14. *The Years* could be seen as Woolf's voyage out, as opposed to her previous novel, *The Waves,* which represents her voyage in, her ultimate attempt to plumb the inner life. By contrast, the narrator of *The Years* bears more resemblance to Katherine Hilbery in *Night and Day,* with her love of mathematics and distaste for literary sentiment, as if Woolf were giving voice to her own opposite.
15. See Connor.
16. Reinforcing this resemblance to the author, Eleanor's pose harks back to the scene at Elvedon in *The Waves,* where a mysterious lady sits writing at a table. In a later passage in *The Years* (109), Eleanor seems to be assembling a scrapbook, as Woolf did in preparation for her critique of the patriarchal war-machine in *Three Guineas* and *The Years.*
17. See *The Pargiters* 54–6, where Rose, after her encounter with the flasher, locks herself in the bathroom and holds a "Grand Council of War" against her brother Bobby and his sex. By cutting this scene and substituting Rose's cut, Woolf implies that the little girl has reversed her declaration of war against herself.
18. Thanks to Matthew Boulette for drawing my attention to this reference.

19. The phrase "avalanches of noise" is James Hanley's in his Blitz novel *No Directions* (86).
20. The phrase "daily island life" comes from Gertrude Stein's lecture "What is English Literature" (33 and passim).
21. See Fleming on the word "Klime" and the interconnections between social and meteorological climate (7). See also Boia 18–19.
22. Bowen's letter to Virginia Woolf is dated January 5, 1941.

Works Cited

Anderson, Benedict. *Imagined Communities*. Rev. ed. London: Verso, 2006.

Bataille, Georges. "Formless." *Visions of Excess: Selected Writings, 1927–1939*. Ed. and trans. Allan Stoekl. Manchester, UK: Manchester UP, 1985.

Beer, Gillian. "The Island and the Aeroplane: The Case of Virginia Woolf." *Virginia Woolf*. Ed. Rachel Bowlby. London: Longman, 1992. 132–61.

Bersani, Leo. *The Culture of Redemption*. Cambridge: Harvard UP, 1990.

Boia, Lucian. *The Weather in the Imagination*. London: Reaktion, 2005.

Bowen, Elizabeth. *Bowen's Court*. 1942. *Bowen's Court and Seven Winters*. Ed. Hermione Lee. London: Virago, 1984.

———. *The Mulberry Tree: Writings of Elizabeth Bowen*. Ed. Hermione Lee. London: Virago, 1986.

———. Preface. *Ivy Gripped the Steps*. By Bowen. New York: Knopf, 1946.

Briggs, Julia. *Virginia Woolf: An Inner Life*. New York: Harcourt, 2005.

Chion, Michel. *Audio-Vision: Sound on Screen*. Trans. Claudia Gorbman. New York: Columbia UP, 1994.

Connor, Steven. "Virginia Woolf, the Baby and the Bathwater." Introduction. *The Years*. By Virginia Woolf. New York: Vintage Classics, 1992. Web.

Cuomo, Chris J. "War is Not Just an Event: Reflections on the Significance of Everyday Violence." *Hypatia* 11.4 (1996): 30–45.

Dalgarno, Emily. *Virginia Woolf and the Migrations of Language*. Cambridge: Cambridge UP, 2012.

Deer, Patrick. *Culture in Camouflage: War, Empire, and Modern British Literature*. New York: Oxford UP, 2009.

"Eclipse of the Highbrow." *The Times*. London. March 25, 1941: 5.

Ellmann, Maud. "The Art of Bi-Location: Sylvia Townsend Warner." *The Palgrave History of British Women's Writing*. Ed. Mary Joannou. Vol. 8: 1920–1945. London: Palgrave, 2012. 78–93.

Evans, Elizabeth F. "Air War, Propaganda, and Woolf's Anti-Tyranny Aesthetics." *Modern Fiction Studies* 59.1 (2013): 52–82.

Favret, Mary A. "Everyday War." *ELH* 72.3 (2005): 605–33.

———. *War at a Distance: Romanticism and the Making of Modern Wartime*. Princeton, NJ: Princeton UP, 2010.

Fleming, James Rodger. *Fixing the Sky: The Checkered History of Weather and Climate Control*. New York: Columbia UP, 2010.

Froula, Christine. *Virginia Woolf and the Bloomsbury Avant-Garde: War, Civilization, Modernity*. New York: Columbia UP, 2005.

Garrity, Jane. *Step-Daughters of England: British Women Modernists and the National Imaginary*. Manchester, UK: Manchester UP, 2003.

Glover, Edward. "Notes on the Psychological Effects of War Conditions on the Civilian Population." *The International Journal of Psychoanalysis* 23 (1942): 17–37.

Hamilton, Patrick. *The Slaves of Solitude*. New York: New York Review of Books, 2007.

Hanley, James. *No Directions*. London: Faber and Faber, 1943.

Harman, Claire. *Sylvia Townsend Warner: A Biography*. London: Minerva, 1991.

Harrisson, Tom, Humphrey Jennings, and Charles Madge. "Anthropology at Home." *The New Statesman and Nation*. January 30, 1937: 155.

Heidegger, Martin. *Parmenides*. 1942–43. Trans. Andre Schuwer and Richard Rojcewicz. Bloomington: Indiana UP, 1992.

Lee, Hermione. *Virginia Woolf*. London: Vintage, 1997.

Lefebvre, Henri. "The Everyday and Everydayness." Trans. Christine Levich. *Yale French Studies* 73 (1987): 7–11.

———. *Everyday Life in the Modern World*. Trans. Sacha Rabinovitch. Piscataway, NJ: Transaction, 1984.

Lewis, Jayne Elizabeth. *Air's Appearance: Literary Atmosphere in British Fiction, 1660–1794*. Chicago: U of Chicago P, 2012.

Lewis, Wyndham. "The Principle of Advertisement and its Relation to Romance." *Time and Western Man. Book I: The Revolutionary Simpleton.* London: Chatto and Windus, 1927. 23–5. Web.

McCrea, Barr. *In the Company of Strangers: Family and Narrative in Dickens, Conan Doyle, Joyce, and Proust.* New York: Columbia UP, 2011.

Millot, Catherine. "On Epiphanies." *James Joyce: The Augmented Ninth.* Ed. Bernard Benstock. Syracuse, NY: Syracuse UP, 1988. 207–209.

Montefiore, Jan. *Men and Women Writers of the 1930s: The Dangerous Flood of History.* London: Routledge, 1996.

Popper, Karl. "Of Clouds and Clocks: An Approach to the Problem of Rationality and the Freedom of Man." *Objective Knowledge: An Evolutionary Approach.* Oxford: Oxford UP, 1979. 206–55.

Radin, Grace. *Virginia Woolf's "The Years": The Evolution of a Novel.* Knoxville: U of Tennessee P, 1981.

Saint-Amour, Paul. "On the Partiality of Total War." *Critical Inquiry* 40.2 (2014): 420–49.

———. "Traumatic Earliness." Introduction. *Tense Future: Modernism, Total War, Encyclopedic Form.* New York: Oxford UP, 2015. 1–46.

Shapin, Steven and Simon Schaffer. *Leviathan and the Air-Pump: Hobbes, Boyle, and the Experimental Life.* Princeton, NJ: Princeton UP, 1985.

Silver, Brenda R., ed. *Virginia Woolf's Reading Notebooks.* Princeton, NJ: Princeton UP, 1983.

Simon, David Carroll. "History Unforeseen: On Sylvia Townsend Warner." *The Nation.* January 25, 2010. Web.

Snaith, Anna, ed. *The Years.* By Virginia Woolf. Cambridge: Cambridge UP, 2012.

Sloterdijk, Peter. *Terror from the Air.* Trans. Amy Patton and Steve Corcoran. Los Angeles: Semiotexte, 2009.

Stein, Gertrude. *Wars I Have Seen.* 1945. London: Brilliance Books, 1984.

———. "What is English Literature." *Look At Me Now and Here I Am: Selected Works, 1911–1945.* Ed. Patricia Meyerowitz. London: Peter Owen, 2004. 31–57.

Trotter, David. *Literature in the First Media Age.* Cambridge, MA: Harvard UP, 2013.

Von Clausewitz, Carl. *On War.* Ed. Michael Howard and Peter Paret. Book 1. Princeton, NJ: Princeton UP, 1984.

Warner, Sylvia Townsend. *The Diaries of Sylvia Townsend Warner.* Ed. Claire Harmon. London: Virago, 1995.

———. *Letters.* Ed. William Maxwell. London: Chatto and Windus, 1982.

———. *Lolly Willowes.* 1926. London: Virago, 2012.

———. "English Climate." *The Museum of Cheats.* New York: Viking, 1947. 59–69.

———. *The Mulberry Tree: Writings of Elizabeth Bowen.* Ed. Hermione Lee. London: Virago, 1986.

———. *New Collected Poems.* Ed. Claire Harman. Manchester, UK: Fyfield Books, 2008.

———. "Women as Writers." *Royal Society of Arts Journal* 107.5034 (1959): 379–86.

Wells, H. G. *The War in the Air.* Harmondsworth: Penguin, 1973.

Woolf, Virginia. *Between the Acts.* 1941. New York: Harcourt, Brace, Jovanovich, 1970.

———. *Collected Essays.* 4 vols. New York: Harcourt, Brace, and World, 1967.

———. *The Diary of Virginia Woolf.* Ed. Anne Olivier Bell. 5 vols. London: Penguin, 1983.

———. "The Leaning Tower." 1940. *The Essays of Virginia Woolf.* Vol. 6: 1933–1941. Ed. Stuart N. Clarke. London: Hogarth Press, 2011.

———. *On Being Ill.* 1926. Ashfield, MA: Paris Press, 2006.

———. *The Pargiters: The Novel-Essay Portion of "The Years."* Ed. Mitchell A. Leaska. New York: Harcourt Brace Jovanovich, 1977.

———. *A Sketch of the Past. Moments of Being.* Ed. Jeanne Schulkind. New York: Harcourt Brace, 1985.

———. *Three Guineas.* 1938. Ed. Morag Shiach. Oxford: Oxford World's Classics, 2008.

———. *The Years.* 1937. Ed. Jeri Johnson. London: Penguin Books, 2002.

Yeats, W. B. "An Irish Airman Foresees his Death." 1919. *The Poems.* Ed. Daniel Albright. London: Everyman's Library, 1992.

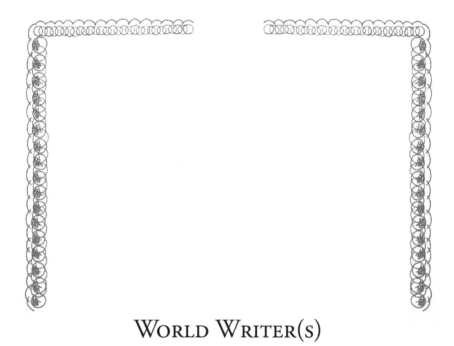

WORLD WRITER(S)

TEACHING PRIVILEGES:
THREE GUINEAS AND THE COST OF GLOBAL CITIZENSHIP

by David J. Fine

Virginia Woolf's *Three Guineas* (1938) teaches its readers to hold fashion in suspicion. Scanning men's clothing in the 1930s, Woolf's speaker notices that "every button, rosette and stripe seems to have some symbolical meaning" (24). This dress "not only covers nakedness, gratifies vanity, and creates pleasure for the eye," she maintains, "but it serves to advertise the social, professional, or intellectual standing of the wearer" (26). There is indeed a thread, fine though it may be, tying the "sartorial splendors of the educated man" (26) to the peacocky labels of his fashion, to the "emotions which, as we need scarcely to draw on biography to prove, nor ask psychology to show, have their share in encouraging a disposition toward war" (27). These seemingly innocuous bonnets, buttons, and badges draw lines, demarcate notoriety, and incite envy. War has its material base. Thus, *Three Guineas* takes care to demonstrate that "both sexes have a very marked though dissimilar love of dress": a difference arising from sex that shrouds commonality through the "hypnotic power of dominance" (177). I will return to this power later, but now I shift registers slightly. For this paper will not assess the fashion of educated men: that battle is, I fear, quite lost. It will dilate, rather, on what is fashionable *in* the academy: not on what intellectuals wear as much as on the threads that, at whatever historical moment, weave together their cogitations. Style has its place there, too, and it is hardly an innocuous one. Woolf's analysis, in this mode, not only underscores the need to think critically about global injustices but also problematizes the privileges of higher education itself.

In this essay, I focus on the academic fad closest to my heart—that nebulous neologism, "global citizenship"—and reflect on my experience teaching *Three Guineas* to two cohorts of (largely privileged) seniors in Lehigh University's Global Citizenship Program. My argument first examines the various academic discussions concerning global citizenship education before turning to an analysis of how *Three Guineas* productively complicates students' engagement with communities both local and global. I then assess sympathetic attachment and the political benefits of such good feeling. In the end, my paper shifts, with Woolf's aid, from a cosmopolitan framework rooted in moral sensibility to a decisively political one, asking urgent questions of higher education and its implication in systemic injustice.

Lehigh University's certificate program in Global Citizenship, the oldest of its kind in the United States, draws students from three undergraduate colleges—arts and sciences, engineering and applied sciences, business and economics—and presents them with opportunities for interdisciplinary, experiential learning. The mission statement, written in the wake of September 11, 2001, reads as follows: "The Global Citizenship Program prepares students for engaged living in a culturally diverse and rapidly changing world. Emphasizing critical analysis and value reflection, the program structures educational experiences through which students learn to negotiate international boundaries and develop their own sense of personal, social, and corporate responsibility to the global community" (*Global Citizenship*). Courses in globalization, literature, urbanism, and political theory complement community engagement and foreign travel. Each year, Global Citizenship takes a cohort of sophomores abroad, with recent trips to India, Malaysia, China, Costa Rica, and Ghana. A university-sponsored scholarship covers most of the travel costs for admitted students. Upon return, participants reflect on the intersession trip by reading literature and writing analytical essays. In the third year, students turn decidedly toward the local community of Bethlehem, Pennsylvania. A course on cities and citizenship prepares them for their senior capstone projects, through which they attempt to put their understanding of global citizenship into practice. After four years, seniors graduate not with a discipline-specific knowledge but rather with a set of diverse experiences from which they can draw as they make informed decisions about their lives as political animals.

As an instructor and an administrator, I have worked with the Global Citizenship Program for over four years. I have created syllabi, written articles, and organized intersession trips, but I would never attempt to define the term that overarches my profession. This reticence exists, in part, because I am neither sure global citizenship means anything clearly nor convinced that it should. On a recent visit to Lehigh, Gayatri Spivak rightly groaned about "meaningless terms like global citizenship," and let us admit, in the privacy this society affords us, that postmodern humanists often find themselves engaging with fashionable though meaningless terms. Surely the greenest of novices can think of a few: sustainability, animal studies, digital humanities, object-oriented ontology, etc. Sometimes these trendy terms pay the bills, as in my case, where my company credit card brews coffee after coffee automatically; sometimes these fads do not pay the rent but merely point in new directions for thinking or demand, in their emptiness, to be thought about more carefully. As you will have rightly guessed, there are many scholars thinking about global citizenship, and their scholarship threatens the term with definition. But I will hold out with Spivak: global citizenship means nothing clearly, and that is the beginning rather than the end of its pedagogical promise.

While there is no critical consensus on what the term "global citizenship" might mean, all appear to agree that, as one trio of educated men—Michael Peters, Harry Blee, and Alan Britton—has suggested, "[t]he underlying political concepts of the notions of citizenship struck during the Enlightenment are in disarray as though they have melted under the constant sun of the combined and sometimes contradictory processes of globalisation, localisation and regionalisation" (1). Notions of citizenship grounded in the nation-state have worn thin and prove, practically speaking, grossly inadequate. If this trio of educated men is correct that the sun never sets on the "contradictory processes of globalisation, localisation, and regionalisation," then it makes sense that university administrators increasingly intuit global citizenship's relevance. Students must think and experience citizenship anew. Global citizenship provides administrators with a conceptual goal toward which they might move their institutions. As such, they insist higher education must address the radical particularity of both international and local communities. This push toward global citizenship maintains, in this sense, the threefold, seemingly impossible demand for vigilant global awareness, increased democratic participation, and responsible community engagement.

The problem with global citizenship, though, is that the adjective, *global*, eclipses the noun, *citizenship*, by its sheer scope and voguish appeal. Egoistic creatures with very busy world-saving schedules, human beings will warmly welcome the weak-willed global as a substitute for citizenship's implied imperative. *Global* suggests the complimentary cosmopolitan; in a word, it captures the tepid liberal predilection: nothing threatening to the market, of course, and in fact, as an adjective, quite re-marketable. And so, in *global*, the worm again lays the eggs of her imperial ambitions, and dictators breed from the best intentions. Labels deceive, and, correctly Woolf adds, "in our age of innumerable labels, of multicoloured labels, we have become suspicious of labels; they kill and constrict" (163). "The Arts of Maintaining Imperial Dominance," while a fine and accurate categorization of the corporatization of higher education, lacks the selling power of the sleek and thereby attractive "Global Citizenship." So the phrase that means nothing sticks, because it fills classrooms and brews coffee, however fairly.

Addressing this tension, Brazilian educator Vanessa Andreotti distinguishes between what she calls "soft" and "critical" global citizenship, arguing in favor of the latter. Soft global citizenship approaches poverty, for instance, "as a lack of resources, services and markets, and of education" (45). Without capitalist development, the poor cannot participate in the global market; hence they drag behind. The structures, institutions, and individuals that act as a barrier to economic growth must go, and the West can make that change happen. This mode of education for global citizenship is soft to the extent that it refuses the hard questions of justice. It centers instead on moral obligations to help those less fortunate. Through a backdoor, it reifies Western industrialism and its colonial legacy as the global universal. Indeed, this developmental approach, as Andreotti notes, "may end up promoting a new 'civilising mission' as the slogan for a generation who take up the 'burden' of saving/educating/civilising the world" (41). Andreotti argues, in response, for a critical approach to cosmopolitanism. This method "is not about 'unveiling' the 'truth' for the learners, but about providing the space for them to reflect on their context and their own and others' epistemological and ontological assumptions: how we came to think/be/feel/act the way we do and the implications of our systems of belief in local/ global terms in relation to power, social relationships and the distribution of labour and resources" (49). From this angle, Global Citizenship's purpose is not to build a bridge in China, however necessary, but to articulate the specific cultural values and epistemological biases that make bridge-building in China appear the natural solution to poverty. In class, students practice articulating the assumptions shaping their answers and animating their approaches. This classroom foregrounds listening and conversation, for which Anthony Appiah has argued passionately, and helps diverse citizens "get used to one another" (85). It facilitates cognizance of the knowledge Global Citizenship students lack.

With so much of my students' energy invested in soft global citizenship—this brand, after all, makes students *feel* good because there *is* a solution and they *are doing* something—it takes inhuman, if not inhumane, effort to create the space for critical distance. Therefore, I open the Global Citizenship Capstone course with *Three Guineas*, because this text unsettles the educative ground on which these seniors stand. It is an attempt to move students from three years of watered-down Martha Nussbaum to a more rigorous interrogation of their privileges. The decision echoes Andreotti's call to develop a critical global citizenship based on "the strategic assumption that all knowledge is partial and incomplete, constructed in our contexts, cultures and experiences. Therefore, we *lack* the knowledge constructed in other contexts, cultures and experiences" (49, emphasis added). Poverty, from this angle, is a function of inequality and injustice, resulting from complex structures, systems, assumptions, and power relations that create, maintain, and obscure exploitation. Inequity here results not from inadequate moral feeling but from ordinary political structures and decisions. My choice to teach Woolf echoes, too, the aforementioned trio of educated men and accepts their invitation to investigate, in global citizenship education, "the following assertions: that war and globalisation go hand in hand; that contemporary globalisation *is* a form of war (and war may be a form of globalisation); that militarisation and war are integral parts of the neo-liberal agenda; and that there are inextricable links between the US military-industrial complex, the free market, and world order" (Peters *et al.* 10). All in a day's work, and, if thinking is our fighting, then this class is war.

Of course, my Global Citizenship students despise *Three Guineas*, simply hate it. They find its "rambling" confusing. They criticize Woolf for failing to posit *a* solution. They find her "novel" a period piece, something no longer necessary in the generation of independent women like Beyoncé. The frustrated emotion it engenders seems to mark, however, the extent of its unsettling. So what exactly does *Three Guineas* accomplish in the global citizenship classroom? As many will recall, Martha Nussbaum has been a major advocate for cosmopolitan education. In their first semester at Lehigh, Global Citizenship students study Nussbaum's essays on cosmopolitanism and then her *Poetic Justice* in the second-semester Global Literature course. Significantly, Nussbaum links not only the humanities but literature in particular to the promotion of world citizenship (302). Literature allows students to exercise their "ability to think what it might be like to be in the shoes of a person different from oneself, to be an intelligent reader of that person's story, and to understand the emotions and wishes and desires that someone so placed might have" (299). Readers envision what it would be like to live in other places, in different unfortunate circumstances, and "[e]nlisting students' sympathy for distant lives is thus a way of training, so to speak, the muscles of the imagination" (300). The narrative imagination stirs compassion and sympathy for the other; this feeling will, ideally, lead global citizens to act in more informed ways. Nussbaum promises that this witness is not "uncritical" (299), but, while Nussbaum's argument in favor of world citizenship is laudable, it reduces cosmopolitanism, especially in the hands of Instagram-ready young adults, to feeling with, feeling for those the world has chosen to ignore. This good feeling proves selfie-centric, if not politically moot. As Andrew Dobson has helpfully illustrated, the intellectual recognition of common humanity and the feelings it proffers fail to lead to political action (182). These suffering strangers remain too far away, too disconnected to make a living demand on one's conscience.

Lauren Berlant's "*subject of feeling*" underscores the political stakes of sympathetic identification (145). "Compassionate liberalism is," as Berlant insists, "a kind of sandpaper on the surface of the racist monument whose structural and economic solidity endures" (6). The sympathetic subject fabricates justice through the substitution of moral feeling for democratic praxis. She feels better about her part in systemic injustice, because she emotes rightly. Correct feeling thus becomes the mark of good politics, but it merely scratches the surface and leaves the base intact. "Salt tears have gone bowling down his cheeks," as Muriel Spark describes, but then—and here is the catch—he returns to the business of ordinary living, "refreshed, more determined than ever to be the overdog" (35). Is this desire to remain the overdog not at the heart of global citizenship education? We must answer, to a large extent, yes. The goal of my interaction with *Three Guineas* is, however, to disrupt students' sympathy and to reorient their vision toward their implication in political systems that systematically and historically privilege certain groups of insiders.

I assign *Three Guineas* precisely because it does not show the photographs of dead bodies and ruined houses. The multilayered, tortuous text frustrates one's desire for sympathetic attachment to the victim and, instead, reorients the subject of true feeling toward ridiculous pictures of the victors. These photographs of English professional men alert readers, as Jane Marcus and many others have noted, to the origins of the war impulse and its contemporary manifestations. Importantly, Woolf not only shares these pictures but she also mocks them, showing the deep blindness buffering the bourgeoisie and their privileges. She asks, in a footnote on "the clothes worn by the educated man" (23), "what degree of social prestige causes blindness to the remarkable nature of one's own clothes? Singularity of dress," she insists, "when not associated with office, seldom escapes ridicule" (177). In this footnote, a judge "wearing a scarlet robe" and "vast wig of artificial curls" sentences a woman to "prudence and proportion" in her fashion (177). The judge's clothes go unremarked, un-ridiculed, because, Woolf suspects, the "hypnotic power of dominance" mystifies.

But, if Spark is correct that "ridicule is the only honorable weapon we have left," then mock we must. Art must be, again in Spark's terms, desegregated and our minds liberated "from the comfortable cells of lofty sentiment in which they are confined and never really satisfied" (36). Like Woolf, Spark writes with direct reference to fascism and argues against cultured sentimentality. *Three Guineas* accomplishes Spark's goal—"to see less emotion and more intelligence in these efforts" (35)—as it pushes frustrated, fourth-year students to see themselves in the ridiculous procession of men. They will, soon, enter it. The clock ticks. Therefore, "we have to ask ourselves, here and now, do we wish to join that procession, or don't we? On what terms shall we join the procession? Above all," Woolf wonders, "where is it leading us, the procession of educated men?" (76) I have students keep a scrapbook in which they collect current events to remind themselves of the outside world. I ask them, in their final paper, to reallocate the per-person expenses of the intersession trip in order to promote global citizenship today. I invite them to see themselves, most importantly, in the procession of educated men and to consider whether and on what terms they will join it. After all, it is not terribly difficult to find a picture from Lehigh's graduation ceremony that mirrors, almost exactly, Woolf's picture of the academic procession. This harsh juxtaposition of images encourages students to see themselves as implicated in war and its injustices and to hazard renewed questions of gendered equity.

These processes of implication are crucial, Andrew Dobson argues, in the cultivation of a thick cosmopolitanism in learners. Global citizenship conceptually fails, he claims, because appeals to common humanity and sympathy mystify, through tears, political accountability. Modern globalization brings with it, however, the opportunity to underscore "casual responsibility," which clarifies for students both the role they play in systemic injustice and "takes us more obviously out of the territory of beneficence and into the realm of justice" (172). In a globalized capitalist economy, it is easier to show how Western actions affect distant neighbors. Justice grounded in a materialist analysis of power relations makes a stronger claim on citizens' action than regarding the suffering of distant others, because it embroils them in the injustice. Neither feeling for others nor engaging in short-term charitable projects is enough if one sees clearly justice's demand. *Three Guineas* forces American students in a global citizenship curriculum to view themselves as heirs of the educated men. The missing pictures of dead bodies withhold the moment for emotional catharsis. The text pushes all of its readers, myself included, to look directly at social injustice and to begin the process of tallying debt and of planning for reparation.

Academic fashions lead scholars to try on this idea, then another, as if they were changing hats, adjusting their belts. We dress up vintage readings of *Orlando* with a fashionable term here and a materialist approach there. Teaching *Three Guineas* to a group of largely privileged undergraduates at a wealthy private university has taught me, however, to look more closely at how I am dressing myself up: for my students, for the university, for the market. To what extent does dominance's hypnotic power keep me from seeing the fashions with which I cloak my teaching privileges? I will admit I enjoy feeling like an outsider, but, as long as my plastic breeds coffee, however fairly, I must wonder if my "attempt to influence the youth against war through the education they receive at the universities" (*TG* 38) amounts to much. Remember: one "must earn enough to be independent of another human being and to buy that modicum of health, leisure, knowledge and so on that is needed for the full development of body and mind. But no more. Not a penny more" (*TG* 97). In addition, do not Woolf's facts from history and biography "prove that education, the finest education in the world, does not teach people to hate force, but to use it? Do they not prove that education, far from teaching the educated generosity and magnanimity, makes them on the contrary so anxious to keep their possessions, [that 'tenure track' of which the ancients speak], in their own hands, that they will use not force but much subtler methods than force when they are asked to share them? And are not force and possessiveness very closely connected with war?" (38). Isn't it all too much?

Woolf's outsider confesses that, "as a woman, I have no country. As a woman I want no country. As a woman my country is the whole world" (129). She remains true to the four teachers of the daughters of educated men, embracing poverty, chastity, derision, and freedom from unreal loyalties. *Three Guineas* maintains that cosmopolitanism's very possibility rests on the lessons of these teachers. In this sense, global citizenship is far from sympathetic but bespeaks instead "other and more complex emotions. It suggests that we cannot dissociate ourselves from that figure but are ourselves that figure" (168). That figure is the dictator and not the victim. In a rapidly changing profession, scholars and teachers of Woolf must take justice's materiality seriously. We must remember poverty, chastity, derision, and freedom from unreal loyalties. We must, most importantly, reflect critically on our work, before it goes out of fashion.

Works Cited

Andreotti, Vanessa. "Soft Versus Critical Global Citizenship Education." *Policy & Practice: A Development Education Review* 3 (Autumn 2006): 40–51.

Appiah, Kwame Anthony. *Cosmopolitanism: Ethics in a World of Strangers.* New York: Norton, 2007.

Berlant, Lauren. *The Female Complaint: The Unfinished Business of Sentimentality in American Culture*. Durham, NC: Duke UP, 2008.

Dobson, Andrew. "Thick Cosmopolitanism." *Political Studies* 54.1 (2006): 165–184.

Global Citizenship. Lehigh University, n.d. Web. 3 June 2014.

Nussbaum, Martha. "Education for Citizenship in an Era of Global Connection." *Studies in Philosophy and Education* 21.4–5 (2002): 289–303.

Peters, Michael A. *et al*. "Introduction." *Global Citizenship Education: Philosophy, Theory and Pedagogy*. Ed. Michael A. Peters, *et al*. Rotterdam: Sense Publishers, 2008. 1–13.

Spark, Muriel. "The Desegregation of Art." *Critical Essays on Muriel Spark*. Ed. Joseph Hynes. New York: G.K. Hall & Co., 1992. 35–6.

Woolf, Virginia. *Three Guineas*. 1938. Annot. and intro. Jane Marcus. Orlando, FL: Harcourt, 2006.

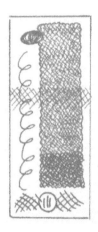

FROM GUINEAS TO RIYALS: TEACHING WOOLF IN THE MIDDLE EAST

by Erin Amann Holliday-Karre

I entitle this essay "Teaching Woolf in the Middle East" not because I see Qatar as representative of all of the Middle East but because of the fact that, due to the large importation of expatriate labor, Qatar brings people from all over the Middle East and indeed the world. While Qataris make up only 10% of the overall population, about 40% of my female students are Qatari. The rest hail from Jordan, Syria, Lebanon, Bahrain, the United Arab Emirates, Saudi Arabia, Egypt, Tunisia, Sudan, and Libya. We also have young women from South Asian countries like Pakistan, Bangladesh, and India. Except in rare circumstances, Qatar does not allow foreigners to become citizens; therefore, while many students claim allegiance to different nationalities, most of them were born in Qatar and many of their parents were born there as well.

Despite the title of this paper, I do not wish to generalize about the experience of all Middle Eastern women. While I believe that my background as the great granddaughter of Lebanese immigrants creates a cultural bond between me and my students, I am fully aware of my status as a Western white female and the ethical challenges of teaching Western literature and feminism to young (mostly) Arab women. The purpose of this paper is to explore the limits of Western feminist ideology in the Middle East through Virginia Woolf's *Three Guineas* (1938). Because Woolf refuses to champion the ideology of liberal humanist thought, my students are introduced to the kind of argumentation that allows them to challenge an all-too-common tenet of liberal humanist feminism that insists upon the oppression of women in the Middle East.[1]

I define liberal humanist feminism by the ideology of the International Women's Alliance (IWA) which, during the time that Virginia Woolf was writing *Three Guineas*, embarked on a world tour in an effort to recruit and mobilize women internationally around the common goals of suffrage and social equality. The IWA recorded their experiences with non-Western women in a journal entitled *Jus Suffraggii* or *The Right to Vote* and worked under the assumption that all women shared the common experience of patriarchal oppression. In the reports gathered between the years of 1911–1950, the IWA expressed many concerns over the status of women in the Middle East and detailed many customs which they saw as impeding Arab women's social and political emancipation. Among the issues raised by the IWA are: a need for education among Arab women, the relegation of women to the domestic sphere, the veil (a catchall word used to describe the Abaya, hijab, shayla, niqab, burqa, and the chaodor—items of clothing distinct in appearance as well as cultural and religious meaning), and the strong sense of nationalism that they perceived in women from Egypt, Palestine, Lebanon, Syria, and Jordan.

In "Unveiling Scheherazade: Feminist Orientalism in the International Alliance of Women," Charlotte Webber argues that, while the belief in the shared experience of all women allowed the IWA, in some cases, to transcend the orientalist distinction between East and West, the organization still worked under the premise that Western women were advantaged: "Western feminists rarely considered themselves to be equally oppressed"

(150). I start with the history of the IWA not only to situate Woolf's writing within the context of Western feminist thought in the early twentieth century but also because the view of Middle Eastern women has not much changed. Despite Nawar Al-Hassan Golley's argument that the Arab world is socially structured around the family and cannot be easily separated into the division between public and private and her contention that the dictates of women's dress in the Arab world are ideologically parallel to the "capitalist" forces that pressure women to be sexual and seductive, general consensus among Western feminists is that Western women are far more liberated than our Middle Eastern counterparts. While alternative narratives have been proposed among non-Western feminists, such as Lama Abu Odeh's claim that the veil has an empowering effect on women, or Leila Ahmed's claim that contrary to the belief that Arab men segregated women, "it was women who were doing the forbidding, excluding men from their society" (521), these arguments remain marginalized in favor of the master narrative that insists upon women's oppression in Middle Eastern society.

It is within the context of Western feminist belief about the oppressed status of women in the Middle East that I introduce students to Woolf's *Three Guineas*. Over a period of two weeks, the students read small sections of *Three Guineas* and each day I ask them to respond in writing for ten minutes. The responses vary widely and include: the role of women in religion, the difficulty of imagining a life without war, censorship in Qatar, and the issue of women driving in Saudi Arabia. Many students, after reading Woolf's section on the role of women in the religious profession, go to great lengths to write about the ways in which Islam gave women access to education, a role in society, and protected them from a life of servitude and slavery. In this paper, however, I want to focus on student responses to the issues addressed by both Woolf and the IWA, responses that deal with women's nationalism, the veil (or, in Woolf's case, clothing and gender), and the question of women's education.

Of course, *Three Guineas* is ideologically opposed to *Jus Suffraggii* on the question of education. In a 1929 piece on women in Syria and Palestine, the writers at *Jus Suffraggii* urged Western teachers to find work in the Middle East on the premise that "ignorance and the stifling influence of long tradition can only be overcome by training and example" (Webber, 140). The suggestion in this piece that Western tradition and education are *not* based on ignorance and stifling influence is a belief that is challenged by Virginia Woolf in her assertion: "[Education] is good for some people and for some purposes. It is good if it produces a belief in the Church of England; bad if it produces a belief in the Church of Rome; it is good for one sex and for some professions, but bad for another sex and other professions" (26). The women of the IWA suggest that a Western education is a neutral education whereas Woolf shows the ways in which British education is designed to exclude, promote discrimination, and establish hierarchies. Woolf goes on to argue that education is responsible for British obsession with property and the desire to go to war. One can only assume, based on Woolf's careful critique of Western education, an institution that goes unquestioned by the writers at *Jus Suffraggii*, that educating women in Syria and Palestine would only perpetuate a new and different kind of "stifling influence."

Many students remark that Woolf was "ahead of her time" or that "what she says is still relevant today." No doubt this is due to the similarities they see between their own lives and those of the "daughters of educated men" that Woolf describes in *Three Guineas*. While the majority of students in my classroom claim that women are not inferior to men, they still do not see education as the means to equality.[2] Education is generally viewed in one of three ways: education is a status symbol that allows women to become more attractive on the "marriage market;" education is what allows women "to be better mothers and to raise healthy children;" or education is a kind of insurance in the case of divorce or death of one's father. One student writes, "I consider my education as a shield as I do not trust men. If I ended up married without an education and then at some point I got divorced, I would not be able to take care of my children and would end up back in my parents' house." The concern over divorce amongst students is high, largely due to recent studies about the growing divorce rate in Qatar. Conservative analysts often cite women's education as responsible for the high divorce rate—independently thinking women lead to unhappy homes.[3] Even so, few students assert that that education allows women to have independence or employment. Of the students who argue, with Woolf, that education is "among the greatest of all human values" (24), many go on to acknowledge the fact that education does not change the social status of women. A student writes, "We are left as the educated daughters in society and not as a valuable asset in society. Education has not enlightened life for us." Contrary to the belief of the IWA that education leads to equality for women, students are more likely to agree with Woolf that education is largely designed to strengthen dominant social structures.

Where *Three Guineas* differs from *Jus Suffragii* in terms of education, both texts hold a similar view regarding the question of nationalism. Members of the IWA who visited Palestine negatively recall the "excessive nationalism" of Palestinian women, while Woolf warns the women of Britain against asserting any sort of national pride: "The educated man's sister—what does patriotism mean to her? Has she the same reasons for being proud of England, for loving England, for defending England? Has she been greatly blessed by England?" (9). Woolf's questions to the educated man's sister lead us to the conclusion that England has not offered her the same advantages that it has offered to men and therefore women have fewer reasons for nationalistic pride. In response to Woolf's writing on nationalism, students are quick to point out that, just like women during Woolf's lifetime, a woman in the Gulf and the Levantine cannot give her nationality to her children. In class, students almost never use direct quotations from the text, but on this day I got an uncommon number of responses that included the words, "as a woman I have no country" (109). And yet, historically, women's movements in the Middle East are tied to nationalistic causes.[4] The most prolific feminist scholarship in the Middle East is undeniably from Egypt, where the fight for the rights of women ran parallel to the call to Arab nationalism (a point that is underscored by my Egyptian and non-Egyptian students alike). While we do discuss the pitfalls of nationalism in class, I am aware that nationalism is easy to decry when your country has a strong national identity. But for those countries in the Middle East who are ravaged by civil war and struggling to form their identity, nationalism allows women a forum in which to participate in public discourse. And in Qatar, where expatriates are denied the right to citizenship, many students hold tightly to their national identity as a way to assert their difference, prove their modernity, or to establish a sense of belonging—even if they've never been to the country whose name appears on the cover of their passport.

But what nearly all of my students have in common, regardless of their nationality, is the fact that roughly 85% of them wear the Abaya,[5] (about 6% wear the niqab, which covers the entire face leaving room only for the eyes, another 6% wear only the hijab, an elastic headband and scarf that completely covers the neck and head, with otherwise Western clothing, and 3% do not cover their head at all). While none of my students would claim that the Abaya is linked to oppression, the writers of *Jus Suffragii* were insistent upon the fact that discarding the veil was the only means to Middle Eastern women's liberation. Charlotte Webber sees this political move as responsible for the failed relationship between IWA and Middle Eastern women: "By establishing its abolition as an essential condition for women's emancipation, they may unwittingly have stifled the growth of feminism within Muslim societies" (144). Western feminists have to get over this hurdle before we can establish a feminist dialogue between the West and the Middle East. I suggest that one of the ways to achieve this goal is to remember to critique our own societies even as we look outwards to critique the dress of others. In reading Woolf, students are introduced to a powerful example of one such critique.

In her section on men and public dress, Woolf writes, "Not only are whole bodies of men dressed alike summer or winter [...] but every button, rosette, and stripe seems to have some symbolic meaning" (19). Like my students, professional men wore one form of dress out of doors and another inside. They wore clothing that made them all look alike and yet no one ever suggested that their gowns, wigs, and robes, which they wore in both summer and winter, symbolized their oppression. Woolf also provides students with the forum to speak critically about women's dress in the West when she writes, "Besides the prime function of covering the body, it has two other offices—that it creates beauty to the eye, and that it attracts the admiration of your sex" (20). Where Western women tend to see ourselves as liberated by our Western dress, Woolf asserts that our dress is not liberating at all; it has "offices," which can be defined as either workplaces or responsibilities, and under both definitions "offices" demand allegiance, conformity, and hard work. In responding to this quotation, a student writes, "I love how she writes about how England is supposed to be about freedom and liberty and then goes on to write about the different purposes of clothing for men and women." Many of my students argue that Western dress for women is tied to the approval of men, forcing women to appear sexually attractive at all times; thus, women in the West are not more liberated than Middle Eastern women. Western women dress in order to be sexually pleasing or, as one student puts it, "guys hunt for women who are half naked." Being familiar with Western stereotypes about Middle Eastern women, students took this opportunity to address the fact that not all Middle Eastern women are required to wear the veil; "[They say that] men are free and the woman have to wear the Abaya and hijab. We're not under pressure or anything of that sort that Westerners believe." Unlike the laws in Saudi Arabia that prohibit women from uncovering their head, women in Qatar are not so legally bound. In the course of three years, I have seen students both shed and adopt the Abaya. *Legally*, there is no pressure. But the social pressure to conform, for Muslim women, does exist.

In teaching feminism in the Middle East, I have been challenged to think about the ways in which feminism, historically, has perpetuated Western male values from Mary Wollstonecraft's argument for women's education, to Charlotte Perkins Gilman's belief that women should find employment outside the home, to Simone de Beauvoir's assertion that women's equality is dependent upon recognizing that she too possesses sexuality. While these early feminists were instrumental in building the argument against a biological definition of gender, rarely did they critique the values of the social institutions that were excluding women. Because of this, it is easy for many of my students to define Western feminism as irrelevant to the Middle East (or as the perpetuation of Western male ideology). And while I recognize that students must be challenged to think in ways that are often directly opposed to their cultural and religious beliefs, it is also necessary to provide students with the tools to analyze and contest Western feminist ideology— particularly when that ideology disempowers them. What students learn from Woolf is that feminism is not just about the values that we uphold but also a method of scholarly inquiry and social critique. I believe that Woolf's writing models the kind of practice that not only allows initially hesitant students to identify as feminist but also teaches them how to respond to a liberal humanist discourse that insists upon their "oppression."

Notes

1. I do not mean to suggest here that women's oppression does not exist in the Middle East. Indeed, women's oppression exists globally. But, following the work of Chandra Talpade Mohanty and Gayatri Chakravorty Spivak, we must certainly now recognize that essentializing about the lives of all Middle Eastern women not only serves to underscore the superiority of Western social values but also alienates Middle Eastern feminists who fight oppression across diverse cultural, political, and class contexts.

2. In Qatar, there are two major institutions of higher education: the country's only national university where I teach, and the American and European universities that have satellite campuses at the Qatar Foundation in Education City. Qatar University enrolls the majority of students in Qatar. The student body is 70% female and 30% male. This gender disparity is explained by the fact that most male nationals go overseas to acquire an education. Realizing this inequality, and in an effort to allow women access to the same education as men, Her Royal Highness Shaykha Mozah bint Nasser Al Thani established the Qatar Foundation to allow women whose parents would not allow them to leave the country the same access to Western education as men. Qatari citizens, however, being largely conservative, still prefer the gender-segregated classrooms at Qatar University to the coeducational classrooms at Qatar Foundation and thus Qatar University enrolls the majority of female Qataris.

3. The leading English speaking newspaper, *The Peninsula Qatar*, has fixated on Qatari divorce rates for the past four years. In 2010 they cite "intellectual incompatibility" as a primary factor in the rising divorce rate, stating "After they are legally married (but still courting), her academic achievement threatens him, while his lax opinion of formal education may be unappealing to her" (Jassim Al-Nasr). Two years later, in 2012, still citing "intellectual incompatibility" as a primary cause of divorce, *The Peninsula Qatar* goes on to report that "36 percent of early divorce cases take place due to wives disobeying their husbands."

4. In "Is Feminism Relevant to Arab Women," Nawar Al-Hassan Golly asserts, "In the Arab world, feminist consciousness has developed hand in hand with national consciousness since the early 19th century" (521).

5. Al-Hassan Golley asks Western feminists to be mindful of the fact that "the Abaya, a full length cloak, and the matching head cover, worn by women in Gulf countries…is traditional dress for women in the Gulf in the same way the sari is the traditional outfit for Indian women" ("Is Feminism Relevant" 522).

Works Cited

Ahmed, Leila. "Western Ethnocentrism and Perceptions of the Harem." *Feminist Studies* 8.3 (1982): 521–534.

"Experts Blame Host of Factors for Rising Divorce in Qatar." *The Peninsula Qatar*. N.p., 23 Feb. 2012. Web.

Golley, Nawar Al-Hassan. "Is Feminism Relevant to Arab Women?" *Third World Quarterly* 25.3 (2004): 521–536.

———. *Reading Arab Women's Autobiographies: Shahrazad Tells Her Story*. Austin: U of Texas P, 2003.

Jassim Al-Nasr, Tofol. "Qatar's Divorce Rate Is among the World's Highest. But Is It Divorce?" *The Peninsula Qatar*. N.p., 10 May 2010. Web.

Odeh, Lama Abu. "Post-Colonial Feminism and the Veil: Thinking the Difference." *Feminist Review* 43 (1993): 26–37.

Webber, Charlotte. "Unveiling Scheherazade: Feminist Orientalism in the International Alliance of Women, 1911–1950." *Feminist Studies* 27 (2001): 125–157.

Woolf, Virginia. *Three Guineas*. 1938. New York: Harcourt, Brace, 1966.

FASHIONABLE MISCONCEPTIONS:
THE CREATION OF THE EAST IN VIRGINIA WOOLF'S *ORLANDO*

by Matthew Beeber

In Virginia Woolf's *Orlando* (1928), Constantinople plays the role of an androgynous, Othered space. The relation between fashion and gender—a relationship particularly strong in England—breaks down in the East, allowing Orlando to wear non-gendered clothing and to act in ways which transgress typical gender roles. The use of Constantinople as an Orientalized, sexualized, and yet un-gendered space in the novel has been well noted by critics. What has not been explored is that Woolf's portrayal of Constantinople and of the East is a *mis*representation; there is no evidence to suggest that the fashion or culture of Turkey or the Ottoman Empire was ever more androgynous than that of England. This paper explores Woolf's purposefully inaccurate portrayal of Turkish fashion in *Orlando* and argues that such misrepresentation serves as a critique of a Victorian literary tradition which portrayed the colonized East as feminized, androgynous, and Sapphic. In making such an argument, I first discuss the role of satire in *Orlando* and the novel's position in relation to the English literary tradition as seen in the dedicatory preface. I then examine the depiction of Eastern fashion in the Constantinople scenes of *Orlando*, suggesting that the ironic portrayal of the East as androgynous and feminized can be read as an engagement with a specific element of the Victorian literary tradition: the eroticization and over-sexualization of the East and the xenological discourse which dominated Victorian perceptions of the Other. I track such discourse beginning with the letters of Lady Mary Wortley Montagu, one of the first Western women to write from and about Constantinople and with whose work Woolf was familiar. Montagu's *Turkish Embassy Letters* can provide insight into the Victorian misconceptions against which Woolf levies a critique through her satirical portrayal of Turkish fashion in *Orlando*.

Turkey, the setting for Orlando's sex change, plays the role of Woolf's androgynous ideal. While still in his official capacity as an ambassador to the British Empire, Orlando wakes every morning and "wrap[s] himself in a long Turkish cloak" (*O* 88); following the rebellious uprising and his sex change, she "dresse[s] herself in those Turkish coats and trousers which," the narrator tells us, "can be worn indifferently by either sex" (103). When she wakes as a woman, Orlando wears clothes no different from when she was a man; the supposed sartorial androgyny of the East has allowed him the freedom to switch from one gender to another. On her return to England, Orlando, according to the narrator, thinks for the first time about her gender. He suggests that "[p]erhaps the Turkish trousers, which she had hitherto worn had done something to distract her thoughts" (113). Because Turkish clothing is androgynous, the Turkish people become androgynous; the narrator writes that "the gipsy women, except in one or two important particulars, differ very little from the gipsy men" (113). Woolf, in the voice of the biographer, has created an androgynous space through the description of sartorial fashion. The biographer's Constantinople, his exotic East, is a place where robes and trousers are worn "indifferently by either sex," where androgynous fashion, in contrast to the strictly gendered fashions of the British Empire, allows for a less gendered society.

Yet fashion in Constantinople was not (and is not) any more androgynous than the fashions of England. Woolf writes in her diary in 1906, when she was twenty-four, of a trip to Greece and Turkey with Vanessa and Violet Dickinson.[1] Fewer pages are dedicated to fashion than one might expect; and her observations focus on the differences between men's and women's fashion—men wear turbans or fezzes—rather than any similarity. She calls "the national dress—a fez & a frock coat [...] disappointing," and later qualifies that it is only the men, with "an occasional nose like a scimitar," who wear these "red caps" (*PA* 349, 352). These observations are important because they further discredit the representation of Constantinople found in *Orlando*. Not only does Turkish society differ from its androgynous representations in the novel but it was well known that gender distinctions were in fact stricter and had greater implications than in England. Thus, there is a disconnect between Woolf's androgynous portrayal of Turkish fashion and the actual fashions of the Ottoman Empire. We can begin to address this disconnect by examining Woolf's use of satire and the way that she positions *Orlando* in (or against) a Victorian literary tradition.

Orlando begins with a preface which is instrumental in defining its genre as a satire. "Many friends have helped me in writing this book," it begins, followed by a list which includes persons both real and imaginary, from literary figures to members of Vita Sackville-West's extended family, to friends and acquaintances (*O* 5). The list begins with members of the British literary tradition such as "Defoe, Sir Thomas Browne, Sterne, Sir Walter Scott, Lord Macaulay, Emily Brontë, De Quincey, and Walter Pater"; includes Bloomsbury affiliates such as Roger Fry, Ottoline Morrell, and Duncan Grant as well as family members such as Vanessa and Quentin Bell; and ends with a sarcastic thanks to "a gentleman in America, who has generously and gratuitously corrected the punctuation, the botany, the entomology, the geography, and the chronology of previous works of mine and will, I hope, not spare his services on the present occasion" (5–6). This list has been given significant scholarly attention, with critics suggesting a range of interpretations from sincere to satirical. Critics such as David Daiches take the preface seriously, suggesting that it is an earnest acknowledgment of debt to the British literary canon. J.J. Wilson ridicules this interpretation, asserting instead that the preface leaves no doubt that the text is to be read satirically. It is in *Orlando*'s preface, she writes, that "the mask drops, the hoax is obvious," and that "the arbitrariness and acerbity of sentiment and tone are unmistakable" (176). More recent critics have noted the profound ambivalence of the preface. Helen Southworth claims that the preface is "multi-functional: Woolf acknowledges family ties with Quentin and old friendship with Cecil and Sanger; she recognizes real intellectual and professional debts with Sanger and Quentin and, at the same time, pokes fun at the literary establishment" (78). Jane de Gay shows that *Orlando* is a critique of Leslie Stephen's methods—especially his gender biases—as a Victorian literary biographer while at the same time suggesting that there is an element of earnest acknowledgement of certain individuals mentioned in the preface (65).

I analyze the preface here for two reasons: first, I would like to point out simply that the literary tradition and the British canon in particular were subjects of intense fascination for Woolf and that *Orlando* displays Woolf's complicated position both in, and at times against, this tradition. Second, like Wilson, I want to assert that to whatever degree the preface is in earnest, we must acknowledge the presence of satire. I suggest that the satire of the literary tradition in the preface can function as a signpost, alerting us to the presence of similar satire in the main text and helping to inform our reading of Woolf's treatment of fashion in the East. The ironic treatment in the preface of the mainly patriarchal literary tradition problematizes the possibility of an earnest reading throughout and it is through this same lens of irony that we must view Woolf's depictions of Constantinople.

Many critics have addressed Woolf's depictions of androgyny in the East without, however, recognizing that such descriptions depart from the reality of Turkish fashions. David Roessel, in particular, has exhaustively catalogued Woolf's references to that city throughout her fiction, as well as her biographical connections, such as the death of her brother, Thoby, whose typhoid was contracted there, as well as her sister Vanessa's miscarriage there in 1911. Roessel cites Woolf's description of Turkish fashion as being androgynous without exploring the inherent misrepresentation in such a description. He instead treats as fact the notion that one "could more easily disguise one's sex" in the Ottoman Empire than in England, or at least that Woolf believed this to be true (404). As a root cause of this perception, Roessel cites the essay "Lady Hester Stanhope" (1910), in which Woolf summarizes the life of that lady, a wealthy and eccentric Englishwoman who lived the second half of her life as a kind of lord in the Ottoman Empire. In the essay, Woolf claims that Stanhope adopted the wearing of "the trousers of a Turkish gentleman" (*E1* 327). Although it is true that traditional Ottoman dress included baggy trousers for both men and women, these trousers were not identical; in addition, the wearer's sex would have been clearly demarcated by other elements of the costume. Woolf's brief mention of only Stanhope's trousers is thus somewhat misleading in its suggestion that Ottoman costume was perhaps androgynous. She is using Stanhope's trousers as a trope, a symbol of androgyny and sexual freedom in the East, a symbol especially powerful in the imaginations of Victorian women for whom the trousers might appear mannish in comparison to burdensome crinolines. Indeed, Roessel goes on to write that "[i]t makes sense, then, for the sexual transformation [in *Orlando*] to take place in an area where the gap between the two sexes is not perceived to be wide" (404). Yet, the very premise of this statement must be questioned. We know that the gap between the sexes was in fact wide, and, from Woolf's account of Constantinople in her diaries, we know too that she was aware of this fact. Thus, the incorrect portrayal of Turkish fashion in *Orlando*, as in her earlier essays, must be seen, I argue, as the leveling of a critique of a Victorian literary tradition which portrayed the East as androgynous, feminized and Sapphic.

As Roessel, Alison Winch, and others have suggested, Woolf was aware of an Orientalist tradition of associating the East, and Constantinople specifically, with Sapphism. In an oft-quoted diary entry describing the inchoate "Jessamy Brides," a project which preceded and eventually became part of *Orlando*, Woolf writes that "Sapphism is to be suggested. Satire is to be the main note. [...] The Ladies are to have Constantinople in view" (*D3* 131). Although the "Jessamy Brides" never came into being, both its satire and its theme of Sapphic love in connection with the East have carried over to *Orlando*. Irving Schick, in *The Erotic Margin,* discusses the long history of the West's sexualizing of the East, claiming the "practice of gendering and sexualizing geography" to be ancient (108). He writes that "Western attitudes towards Turkey, and Islam generally, have, for several centuries, been shaped by...the trope of 'oriental sexuality'" (1). In making this point,

Schick employs the concept of xenotopia, which casts foreign places as feminine, linked with virginity, and ready to be conquered. Woolf, it seems, advances a kind of xenotopia in her portrayal of Constantinople; it is portrayed as not only inferior to the British and available for conquest, but also feminized, androgynous, and Sapphic. Schick claims that "this image of the 'Other' as omnisexual, prone to engage in sexual relations with anyone or anything, animate or inanimate, is common in xenological discourse" (119). It is this xenological discourse which Woolf is recognizing and satirizing in her deliberate and ironic misrepresentation of Turkish fashion.

As post-colonial studies has shown us, one element of Orientalism is the practice of displacing anxiety-inducing elements of a society (such as female sexuality) onto the colonized Other. The East thereby becomes a blank space, able to be filled in the colonizer's mind with what is paradoxically both threatening and erotic. One of many places to begin tracing this Orientalist narrative is in women's travel writing in the 18th century. Lady Mary Wortley Montagu arrived in Constantinople in 1718, the same year as the first round of "reforms" to Westernize the Ottoman Empire, on a journey which "constitutes the beginning of women's secular travel accounts about the Orient" (Konuk 393). Montagu has been written about frequently and some critics, such as Winch, consider her work to be the direct inspiration for the Constantinople episode of *Orlando*. As I have noted, Woolf was familiar with Montagu's work; in 1908, two years after her first trip to Constantinople and almost twenty before she writes *Orlando*, Woolf writes in a letter to her sister, "I'm probably going to write about Ly. May [*sic*] Montagu" (*L*1 *337*). Montagu was the wife of the British ambassador to the Ottoman Empire and her letters written during the year she spent in Constantinople with him served as the inspiration for *The Turkish Embassy Letters*. The work itself is the site of some controversy, as scholars have debated to what degree the letters have been fictionalized over the course of their long and successful publication in the 18th and 19th centuries. The letters contain descriptions of both the fashions and customs of Ottoman women and many accounts of Montagu disguising herself as an Oriental woman. Montagu's letters from Constantinople were written in roughly the same time period in which Orlando visits that city in the novel.[2] My purposes for reading Montagu's letters are twofold. First, they further indicate the actual disparity between the genders and their fashions in Constantinople, not only in Woolf's time but also in the early 1700s, the supposed timeframe of Orlando's ambassadorship there. Second, they provide insight into the origins of the inaccurate Victorian beliefs about Eastern cultures and offer a seminal example of the Orientalizing literary tradition which Woolf satirizes in *Orlando*. This may seem paradoxical but, as I will show, Montagu's description of the strictly divided Ottoman society contains the seed of an Orientalist argument for the supposed sexual promiscuity of the East.

Montagu's letters provide no indication of androgyny in the fashions or culture of eighteenth-century Constantinople. In a 1718 letter to her younger sister, Lady Montagu gives a detailed description of the typical dress of women. "[N]o woman," she writes, is ever "permitted to go in the streets without two muslins, one that covers her face all but her eyes and another that hides the whole dress of her head" (71). She adds that "their shapes are also wholly concealed by a thing they call a *ferace* which no woman of any sort appears without" (71). Such description confirms that a strict dress code was enforced within Ottoman society, a dress code which differed markedly between sexes. Like Woolf,

Montagu devotes little space in her diary to the description of male fashion, except to comment on the wearing of turbans.[3] The distinction between male and female headdress is noted again in Montagu's description of burial yards: "[t]hey set up a pillar with a carved turban on the top of it to the memory of a man" whereas "[t]he ladies have a simple pillar without other ornament" (99–100). Billie Melman, in *Women's Orient*, aptly notes that Montagu "emphasises not the similarities, but the differences between Ottoman men and women" and that "women [in Ottoman society] are constantly characterised as *mothers*" (95). All of this is to confirm what we already suspected, that Turkish fashion was not androgynous in the eighteenth century any more than in the twentieth. The cultural and sartorial divide between men and women was wide in Ottoman society.

Yet despite the clarity with which she describes the contrast between sexes, Montagu's letters are in part responsible for the misconceptions Victorians harbored about the East. In the letter to her sister quoted above, directly preceding the description of women's veils and robes, Montagu writes that "'[t]is very easy to see they have more liberty than we have" (71), meaning that Muslim women, required by custom to cover their faces and disguise the shapes of their bodies, are thus afforded more liberty than enjoyed by Western women. As both Robert Halsband and Melman have noted, "the paradox of liberty in bondage is driven *ad-captandum*" (Melman 86). That is, Montagu's argument is somewhat specious, glossing over the inequities of Ottoman society and focusing on a single advantageous byproduct of women's oppression. More so, "liberty," in Montagu's usage, "spelt out *sexual freedom*. And it meant one's ability to follow one's 'inclination' and 'indulge' oneself (Montagu's words) in that inclination, regardless of one's sex" (Melman 86). The trope of a greater sexual freedom in the Orient is taken up by Lady Elisabeth Craven, another eighteenth-century Englishwoman and travel writer, who describes the custom of women leaving a pair of slippers outside their door to signify the need for privacy. Victorian readers of Montagu and Craven (of which there were many) gravitated towards such implications of women's privacy and ability to disguise themselves, however misguided those descriptions may have been, and worked them into a larger narrative of the East as promiscuous and over-sexualized.

As Woolf was a reader of Montagu, she must certainly have been aware of Montagu's misguided argument regarding women's "liberty" within the deeply patriarchal Ottoman society. Winch reads *Orlando* as being deeply influenced by Montagu's work. She writes that it is "an elucidation, a re-enactment, [and] an imitation, using Montagu's texts as sources or prototypes" (53). Yet, missing from this characterization is the fact that *Orlando* is a satire. With its obvious misrepresentation of Turkish fashion, its casting of Ottoman society as androgynous, and its simplification of foreign custom (in the East they all just wear robes), *Orlando* can be read as a *response* to Montagu, a critique of the imperial and Orientalist narratives which stemmed from her work and which informed the patriarchal literary traditions of the Victorians.

Notes

1.   Thoby and Adrian were also travelling in Greece and Turkey at this time and the two parties converged at various points. Hermione Lee explains the relative scarcity of diary entries describing Constantinople, claiming that "[t]here was no literary entry-point for her to Muslim culture" (225).

2.   The timeline of *Orlando* is of course inconsistent and fantastical and it is therefore difficult to assign specific years to Orlando's ambassadorship, yet when he returns to England he becomes acquainted with Alexander Pope who is one of the recipients of Montagu's letters in the year 1718. Other details may place Orlando's time in Constantinople slightly earlier than Montagu's, such as his acquaintance with Dryden upon his return to England; Dryden died in 1700.

3.   Montagu comments on turbans whereas Woolf mentions fezzes—one of the many changes in national dress enacted as a part of the 1839 fashion edict, an effort of continued westernization.

Works Cited

De Gay, Jane. "Virginia Woolf's Feminist Historiography in *Orlando*." *Critical Survey* 19.1 (2007): 62–72.

Konuk, Kader. "Ethnomasquerade in Ottoman-European Encounters: Reenacting Lady Mary Wortley Montagu." *Criticism* 46.3 (2004): 393–414.

Lee, Hermione. *Virginia Woolf.* New York: Vintage, 1999.

Melman, Billie. *Women's Orients, English Women and the Middle East, 1718–1918: Sexuality, Religion, and Work.* Ann Arbor: University of Michigan, 1992.

Montagu, Mary Wortley, Lady. *Turkish Embassy Letters.* Intro. Anita Desai. Ed. Malcolm Jack. New York: Little, Brown, 1994.

Roessel, David. "The Significance of Constantinople in *Orlando*." *Papers on Language and Literature* 28.4 (1992): 398–416.

Schick, Irvin C. *The Erotic Margin: Sexuality and Spatiality in Alteritist Discourse.* New York: Verso, 1999.

Southworth, Helen. "Virginia Woolf's *Orlando* Preface, the Modernist Writer, and Networks of Cultural, Financial and Social Capital." *Woolf Studies Annual* 18 (2012): 75–107.

Wilson, J.J. "Why Is *Orlando* Difficult?" *New Feminist Essays on Virginia Woolf.* Ed. Jane Marcus. Lincoln: U of Nebraska P, 1981. 170–84.

Winch, Alison. "'in plain English, stark naked': *Orlando*, Lady Mary Wortley Montagu and Reclaiming Sapphic Connections." *Critical Survey* 19.1 (2007): 51–61.

Woolf, Virginia. *A Passionate Apprentice: The Early Journals, 1897–1909.* Ed. Mitchell A. Leaska. San Diego: Harcourt, 1990.

——. *The Diary of Virginia Woolf.* Vol. 3. Ed. Anne Olivier Bell. New York: Harcourt Brace Jovanovich, 1980.

——. *The Essays of Virginia Woolf.* Vol. 1. Ed. Andrew McNeillie. San Diego: Harcourt Brace Jovanovich, 1986.

——. *The Letters of Virginia Woolf.* Vol. 1. Ed. Nigel Nicolson and Joanne Trautmann. New York: Harcourt Brace Jovanovich, 1975.

——. *Orlando: A Biography.* Annot. and intro. Maria DiBattista. Orlando, FL: Harcourt, 2006.

From London to Taipei: Writing the Past in "Wandering in the Garden, Waking from a Dream" and *Mrs. Dalloway*

by Shao-Hua Wang

Hsien-yung Pai's "Wandering in the Garden, Waking from a Dream" (1968) is one of the most famous short stories in post-1949 Taiwanese literature.[1] "Wandering" delineates a banquet among a group of "exiled" Mainland Chinese, many of whom are former female recitalists of K'un-ch'ü and whose social and economic status ascends through marriage. The work is famous for its stream-of-consciousness technique and its collage of references to traditional Chinese literature, as well as its representation of the very refined art of K'un-ch'ü opera, "an exclusive art for aristocratic connoisseurs" ("Wandering" 382).[2] It is not surprising that Pai's writing is influenced by Western modernisms; after all, he graduated from the Department of Foreign Languages and Literatures at National Taiwan University before pursuing further studies in the United States. However, in a response to Sher-shiueh Li's question after a talk in 2003, Pai himself asserted Woolf's partial influence on his "Wandering." Li then published "Towards a Poetics of Parentheses," which compares *Mrs. Dalloway* (1925) with "Wandering." Li argues that the usage of parentheses by both authors reveals a deeper reality in characters' minds (167–68).

Indeed, there are many similarities between *Mrs. Dalloway* and "Wandering." Both stories focus on one main female character and her past love. The contrast between Bourton and London resembles that between China and Taipei; in both cases, memories of the past saturate the present-day settings. The opera lyrics she sings reflect Madame Ch'ien's own desire, evoking memories of her pre-war extra-marital love affair in China. However, there appears to be a more profound link between the two works. Woolf's influence on Pai lies not merely in the parallel construction of the plots. Even stating that Pai's narrative technique is similar to that of Woolf seems to reduce the depth of the connection between the two works. Pai's "psychological realism" can be understood in phenomenological terms since it is a realism that aims to stay true not to the external reality but to the inner self. On the surface, such a realism seems to be achieved through symbols, internal monologues, and other literary techniques. More importantly, however, I propose to draw upon Maurice Merleau-Ponty's phenomenological understanding of language in order to argue that both Pai's and Woolf's writings allow an openness toward the external world and ultimately their works emphasize a lived life. Such an emphasis is best demonstrated in their fundamental similarity in evoking the past and in describing the unsayable truth of life.

Merleau-Ponty's phenomenology builds on Husserl's thought, rejecting the traditional Cartesian dualism of mind and body. Existence, in Merleau-Ponty's terms, is neither purely transcendental nor purely physical; instead, it features an intermediating "being-in-the-world" (82). Consciousness, as he further argues, "is being toward-the-thing through the intermediary of the body" (138–39). As consciousness is always conscious *of* something, Merleau-Ponty views it as the power to give a form to experiences while it features "a network of intentions" (121). In Merleau-Ponty's own words, to perceive things is to "live them" as the subject must open up and reach out toward the external others (325–26). Hence, one's existence relies on external others. Such an existence or a being-in-the-world unfolds in time: the body creates time (239–40). Indeed, the living present opens up a lived past and a not-yet future (433). Merleau-Ponty further postulates that being co-exists with "all the other landscapes which stretch out beyond [one's surrounding], and all these perspectives together form a single temporal wave, one of the world's instants" (331).

Such a temporal take renders the comparison between the work of Woolf and that of Pai more fruitful. After all, phenomenology stresses not merely the here and now but also their relationships with an elsewhere in the past or in the future. In *Mrs. Dalloway*, it is this openness to the external world that enables Clarissa to plunge into Bourton in the past: "What a lark! What a plunge! For so it had always seemed to her, when, with a little squeak of the hinges, which she could hear now, she had burst open the French windows and plunged at Bourton into the open air" (*MD* 3). The present moment is a threshold to Clarissa's past, through the French window's "little squeak of the hinges" (3).[3]

The same openness is at work when she recalls her love for Sally; she stresses "the moment" repeatedly: "[o]nly for a moment; but it was enough" (*MD* 27). To plunge into the very heart of the moment, as Clarissa asserts, is to transfix it and to see herself: "Clarissa (crossing to the dressing-table) plunged into the very heart of the moment, transfixed it, there—the moment of this June morning on which was the pressure of all the other mornings, seeing the glass, the dressing-table, and all the bottles afresh, collecting the whole of her at one point (as she looked into the glass), seeing the delicate pink face of the woman who was that very night to give a party; of Clarissa Dalloway; of herself" (31). The openness toward the outside world and toward the mirror allows her to see her own existence.[4] The verb "plunge" in the two passages points to a profundity that is not limited to the present moment, for each present is teeming with the past.

In "Wandering," the protagonist Madame Ch'ien also plunges into her "moment." It is very difficult to summarize "Wandering" due to its collage of past and present events. Post-1949 Taipei in the short story is constructed upon a past in China when Madame Ch'ien was an excellent K'un-ch'ü recitalist in the group "the Terrace of the Captured Moon." Along with other female recitalists, Madame Ch'ien performed in Nanking and attracted numerous admirers. However, the recitalist's social status was low and her "sisters" in the group tended to marry military officers as concubines. In contrast, Madame Ch'ien's singing skills had won her the heart of the widower His Excellency General Ch'ien. General Ch'ien is quite senior to Madame Ch'ien; as Madame Ch'ien's sister, nicknamed "Red-red Rose," sarcastically puts it, the General "might as well be her granddaddy" ("Wandering" 352). Despite their difference in age, however, General Ch'ien wanted to have Madame Ch'ien, then nicknamed "Bluefield Jade," sing to amuse him so that he would "be content for remaining years of his life" (342). As a result, Madame Ch'ien married General Ch'ien as his proper wife. She married for wealth and status rather than for love and desire; she worked hard to fulfil the role of a proper general's lady. Nevertheless, after her marriage, she fell in love with her husband's *aide-de-camp*, Yen-ching Tseng. This extramarital love was short-lived as it was soon revealed at a banquet that Tseng had a love affair with Madame Ch'ien's own sister "Red-red Rose," also a recitalist. We know of these past stories only indirectly through Madame Ch'ien's memories during a banquet held in post-1949

Taipei by "Fragrant Cassia," now Madame Tou, a former recitalist and concubine. The whole K'un-ch'ü group has retreated from Mainland China to Taiwan. Now that the General is dead, Madame Ch'ien has lost her glory. Many of her other sister-recitalists, however, have gained a higher social status thanks to their husbands. In the banquet in Taipei, they perform K'un-ch'ü and talk about the good old days in China. During this banquet, Madame Ch'ien recalls her love affair with Tseng, her dead husband, love, desire, betrayal, and death, all through K'un-ch'ü singing and imagery retrieved from memories.

One particular passage best demonstrates how Pai uses colors and the art of singing to symbolize the desire at work. The passage starts with Madame Ch'ien's K'un-ch'ü singing in the past. The lyrics reveal a girl's desire: "Spring fever/ that did me by stealth surprise/ I cannot send away/ Unspoken discontent/ too suddenly/ wells all within my heart" ("Wandering" 370). The very K'un-ch'ü piece that Madame Ch'ien was singing is eponymous to Pai's short story. It is clear that the lyrics speak of Madame's Ch'ien's own desire and discontent. Then comes a plunge into another past, an erotic moment with Tseng, and these two moments in the past intertwine:

Fiercely the ball of red flame shot up again, burned till those loftily-raised eyebrows glistened dark green with sweat. The two wine-red faces were once more closing in on each other, showing their white teeth, smiling....*(Master Wu, a bit lower please, I've drunk too much tonight). And yet he has to come over with a winecup in his hands, saluting: Madame. His riding boots, raven-glossy, water-smooth, click together, the white copper spurs sting your eyes. His eyelids peach pink with wine, still he salutes: Madame. Allow me to help you mount, Madame, he said; in his tight-fitting breeches his long slender legs looked muscular, trim, like a pair of fire-tongs clasping the horse. His horse was white, the road was white, the tree trunks were white, and his white horse shone in the blazing sun.... They say that all along the wayside the road is full of white birch trees. The sun, I cried, the sun has pierced my eyes. And then he whispered in a gentle voice: Madame. General Ch'ien's lady. General Ch'ien's aide-de-camp. General Ch'ien's—Fifth, Ch'ien P'eng-chih called, his voice choked. Fifth, my dear, he called, his voice dying, you'll have to take care yourself.... Worldly glory, wealth, position—but I only lived once, Understand? Sis, listen to me, Sis. But Red-red Rose comes over with that cup of wine in her hands and says, Sister won't do me the honor, her liquid eyes flashing. (Master Wu, I've drunk too much* hua-tiao)—
Languishing
where may I tell
my unquiet heart
Seething
how shall I redress this life
so ill-fulfilled
except I sue to Heaven—
Right at the moment, this life so ill-fulfilled
—she sits down beside him tight at that moment, all red and gold, at that moment, the two wine-red faces slowly closing in on each other, right at that moment, I see

their eyes: her eyes, his eyes. It's over, I know, right at that moment....It's over, my throat, feel my throat, is it quivering? (371–74, translator's emphasis)

The banquet scene features the colors red and white, which indicate Madame Ch'ien's sister "Red-red Rose" and Tseng respectively; the "wine-red faces" and white teeth subtly reveal their relationship. Then the scene shifts to Madame Ch'ien and Tseng's affair. The whole erotic scene is dominated by Tseng's representative color white—the horse, the road, and the tree trunk; the piercing sun is loaded with sexual implication. Tseng's gentle whisper "Madame" forms a stark contrast with General Ch'ien's dying and choked voice. Through both the visual and auditory senses, Pai skillfully unravels Madame Ch'ien's past. Life and desire confront death and wealth. Madame Ch'ien finally realizes that she had "only lived once," as her own sister, Red-red Rose, intervenes. As the singing continues, Madame Ch'ien is actually acting out the lyrics, her "ill-fulfilled life." The moment when she discovers that Tseng is in love with her sister, when all is turned *"red and gold,"* she finds herself losing her voice and her life.

Such a plunge into Nanking in the past results in a deep understanding of life that *Mrs. Dalloway* shares with "Wandering." Clarissa and Sally's kiss, that one precious moment, was interrupted by Peter's asking "[s]tar-gazing?" (*MD* 30). In this horrible moment of interruption, Sally was "mauled," life is torn apart (31). In this way, Clarissa's life seems to be as "ill-fulfilled" as that of Madame Ch'ien.

Above all, however, it is the voiceless elements in the two works that deserve more attention. They are particularly important in "Wandering" on two levels. First, K'unch'ü is a very refined art form that requires skills and virtuosity. However, there is no voice without a real life. As Laurent Jenny argues, art and life are not opposed to each other; instead, aesthetic apprehension requires a real usage of art in life—*"l'art dans la vie"* (13–15). Secondly, the passage from "Wandering" is in itself a "performance" of literary skills. Words here demonstrate the protagonist's openness to the past and create a lament and voicelessness. It is in the silence that the regret is most resounding. This voicelessness is also very evident in *Mrs. Dalloway*. In fact, the voicelessness and the unsayable are to be found in the beggar woman's failed attempt to articulate:

> ee um fah um so
> foo swee too eem oo (*MD* 69)

The woman's undistinguishable sound is repeated; it interrupts Peter Walsh's thoughts of Clarissa, whom he thought of as "cold as an icicle" (68). In fact, David Bradshaw has noted that "Woolf's London is a city that embraces the marginalized and accommodates the voiceless and yet everywhere confronts them with a built environment" (232). Indeed, near Regent's Park Tube station, among "middle-class people" vanishing like leaves to be trodden under, a beggar woman cries out the unrecognizable sound (*MD* 61). It is "a frail quivering sound, a voice bubbling up without direction, vigour, beginning or end, running weakly and shrilly and with an absence of all human meaning" (68). The beggar woman's voice is comparable to Madame Ch'ien's quivering throat, both have lost their essence—the former points to civilization's inability to understand this love "which has lasted a million years" (*MD* 69) whereas the latter is a life that had only lived once. In both cases, however, existence is demonstrated through the characters' physical bodies—singing seems to reveal one's profundity, which is not limited to the here and now. In "Wandering," singing is the trigger to the past; Pai uses K'un-ch'ü to present art's embodiment of life and Madame Ch'ien's failure to live and love. In *Mrs. Dalloway*, it reveals an alienated society in which the possibility of communication is put into question. In a phenomenological reading, voices represent the body's extending movement toward the outside, an outside of the here and now. However, instead of an all-inclusive understanding of the external, the body also suggests partial perception and fragmentary memories. In the light of Merleau-Ponty, Elizabeth Grosz develops the body's existence in time and space; she argues that external space can only be understood "through certain relations we have to our body or corporeal schema" (90). Limited as this bodily perspective may seem to be, it nonetheless reflects the fragmentary nature of existence; after all, Grosz points out that "[the body's] modes of access to objects are always partial or fragmentary, interacting with objects but never grasping or possessing them in their independent and complete materiality" (90–91). Both voices and voicelessness offer the reader a glimpse of the characters' existences. Singing is a particular physical action. The words sung imply a specific profundity of existence; as a result, singing surpasses the circumscription of the physical body. Through sounds, the past is revisited and what could not be sung is revealed.

Woolf seems to be interested in sounds in her depiction of the age in "Characters in Fiction": "[t]hus it is that we hear all round us, in poems and novels and biographies, even in newspaper articles and essays, the sound of breaking and falling, crashing and destruction. It is the prevailing sound of the Georgian age—rather a melancholy one if you think what melodious days there have been in the past" (*E3* 433–34). The "prevailing sound of the Georgian age" features cacophony. What is more important, however, is how Woolf portrays an unrecognizable sound in *Mrs. Dalloway*; it may not be as audible as "the sound of breaking and falling" found in "poems and novels and biographies"; what makes Woolf's novel aligned with and yet distinct from them, is the beggar woman's cry in the busy London streets. The sound points not to the audible but to a silence that characterizes a profundity.

Indeed, silence is the unwritten side of modern life rooted in Woolf's work. I argue that it is this concern with the unnamable that inspires Pai's short story. Madame Ch'ien embodies art, life, desire, and death. Her virtuosity in K'un-ch'ü makes her an artist; nonetheless, she had lived only once. She is not a real artist and she ultimately lost her voice. Madame Ch'ien cannot articulate her real desire and her true love. In a similar way, the beggar woman's song is "an ancient spring" and "love which has lasted a million years"; however, it could not be understood. Michel Collot comments on this kind of poetic silence, which he links to the blank space on the page, a blank that speaks more than words could speak (99).

As my brief comparison attempts to make clear, Woolf's modernist agenda is present in Pai's work. After all, as Jean Guiguet puts it, Woolf transposes into writing what modernity dramatizes:

> It does away with time and space and makes possible the telescoping of past and present, of the here and the elsewhere, the self and the non-self; it disintegrates objects and personalities and replaces them by that universal participation which

Virginia Woolf's vision so disturbingly reveals. And this disintegrated world harbours and gives rise to anguish. Here the scattered personality, in search of self, experiences nothingness. But, as against this ultimate liability, we must count as an asset the quest itself; along the path that leads to the abyss, it oscillates between despair and joy, between solitude and communion; although it ends in doubt, yet the trail is blazed with certainties. (461–62)

It is a similar trail that Pai has traversed. It is a similar self that the two authors search for. It is a lived life that they pursue. A phenomenological approach reveals that Woolf's influence on Pai lies beyond literary techniques, as Pai also pursues the being-in-the-world that Woolf is passionate for.

Notes

1. In 1949, a group of Chinese retreated to Taiwan with the government after the civil war against the Communist Party. The year 1949 marks the political separation of Taiwan and China, followed by political and economic turmoil.
2. K'un-ch'ü (昆曲) K'un-ch'ü is a traditional Chinese fine art entailing music, dance, and poetry, demanding "high standards of its singers" ("Wandering" 382).
3. It is worth noting that the motif of the window is complicated and does not always suggest a positive way out in the city. For instance, Septimus, who is another Clarissa in many respects, finds the window open up to his suicide: "[t]here remained only the window, […] the tiresome, the troublesome, and rather melodramatic business of opening the window and throwing himself out" (*MD* 111).
4. For an analysis of Clarissa and herself in the mirror, see Mickalites.

Works Cited

Bradshaw, David. "Woolf"s London, London's Woolf." *Virginia Woolf in Context*. Ed. Bryony Randall and Jane Goldman. Cambridge: Cambridge UP, 2012. 229–42.

Collot, Michel. *La poésie modern et la structure d'horizon*. Paris: Presses Universitaire de France, 1989.

Grosz, Elizabeth. *Volatile Bodies: Toward a Corporeal Feminism*. Bloomington: Indiana UP, 1994.

Guiguet, Jean. *Virginia Woolf and Her Works*. Trans. Jean Stewart. London: Hogarth, 1965.

Jenny, Laurent. *La Vie Esthétique: Stases et Flux*. Lagrasse: Éditions Verdier, 2013.

Li, Sher-Shiueh. "Towards a Poetics of Parentheses: A Reading of Pai Hsien-yung's 'Youyuan jingmeng' in Light of Virginia Woolf's *Mrs. Dalloway*." *Bulletin of the Institute of Chinese Literature and Philosophy*. 28 (2006): 149–170. Web. 15 March 2014. <http://www.litphil.sinica.edu.tw/home/publish/PDF/Bulletin/28/28-149-170.pdf>.

Merleau-Ponty, Maurice. *Phenomenology of Perception*. Trans. Colin Smith. London: Routledge, 1989.

Mickalites, Carey James. "Alienated Vision and the Will to Intimacy, or Virginia Woolf and 'the Human Spectacle'." *Modernism and Market Fantasy: British Fictions of Capital, 1910–1939*. New York: Palgrave Macmillan, 2012. 133–69.

Pai, Hsien-yung. "Wandering in the Garden, Waking from a Dream." *The Taipei People*. Trans. Hsien-yung Pai and Patia Yasin. Ed. George Kao. Hong Kong: Chinese UP, 2000. 328–384.

Woolf, Virginia. *The Essays of Virginia Woolf*. Vol. 3. Ed. Andrew McNeillie. London: Hogarth, 1988.

———. *Mrs. Dalloway*. 1925. Ed. David Bradshaw. Oxford: Oxford UP, 2000.

AN ESTRANGED INTIMACY WITH THE WORLD:
THE POSTCOLONIAL WOOLF'S PLANETARY LOVE IN *THE VOYAGE OUT*

by Alan Chih-chien Hsieh

What does Virginia Woolf, a canonical English modernist writer, have to do with the postcolonial? Doesn't the juxtaposition of Woolf and the postcolonial sound out of place? Is it appropriate to make up such an awkward phrase as the "postcolonial Woolf"? While general readers of Virginia Woolf might feel confused about the combination of Woolf and the postcolonial, many thematics in postcolonial studies—nation, imperialism, race, etc.—have been frequently discussed in Woolf studies, often along with a feminist or poststructuralist reading. Indeed, as evidenced by an increasing body of Woolf scholarship on the relationship between Woolf and British cultural imperialism, motivated by the emblematic debate between Jane Marcus and Patrick McGee, it is fair to say that (post/anti)coloniality is actually essential to the cultural politics of Woolf criticism. Despite the intimacy between Woolf and the postcolonial, however, when we leave out the conjunction to create the term "postcolonial Woolf," this awkward phrase at once elicits not only an estrangement or an intimacy but an "estranged intimacy" that foregrounds a tension in this unusual combination. Building upon this disciplinary "estranged intimacy" evoked by the term "postcolonial Woolf," in what follows I focus on Woolf's first novel *The Voyage Out* (1915). I argue that the protagonist Rachel's reading and exploration of life embody an "estranged intimacy with the world" that informs an ethical imagination of our being-in-the-world and an ethical reading of others that can be set against a narrative of triumphalism in this explicitly "colonial" novel. In so doing, I hope to open up new possibilities of reading Woolf through a postcolonial lens in response to the recent call for an ethical (re)turn in postcolonial studies.

As a *Bildungsroman*, Woolf's first novel describes Rachel's journey to South America and her parallel rite of passage in which her quest for knowledge and her desire to "see life" are accompanied not only by people she encounters but also by the books suggested by these "mentors." Full of intertextual references and book titles, the novel foregrounds reading as a trope for Rachel's initiation into the social order and her cultivation of normative values. Rachel's "voyage in" the world of books and her reaction to those mentors become the crucial elements if we intend to tease out the significance of Rachel's reading. As Susan Stanford Friedman has pointed out, reading as a trope in the novel is gendered and represents two different cultural initiations—women excel in reading the book of life while men hold sway over the printed word. But for Friedman what distinguishes Rachel from others is that she challenges these gendered distinctions in her intense intertextual reading of both books and life. However, despite noticing the potential of Rachel as a privileged reader in the novel, Friedman still interprets Rachel's abortive *Bildung* literally as a warning and claims that her death indicates not only the oppression of patriarchy but her complete identification with what she reads and her ignorant acceptance of male authority. Turning to the ideal model of readers that Woolf articulates in her later essays, Friedman suggests that Rachel is a predecessor to this more judicious common reader and interprets Woolf's killing Rachel off as a defiant act against the literary taste dominated by male critics.

Building upon Friedman's reading of Rachel as a privileged reader in the novel, I would like to qualify her literal interpretation of Rachel's abortive *Bildung*. I suggest that if we see Rachel not merely as an intertextual reader in an entirely textualized world but rather as a singular being truly living at every moment of this living-world, we can note that Rachel's exploration of life brings out an alternative relationship with the world, what I call an "estranged intimacy" with the world. By estranged intimacy, I mean a close relationship with the world, a togetherness, that is at the same time estranged because this being-in-the-world, emerging from encounters with others, is never an enclosed space but an open whole. Rachel's estranged intimacy with the world thus anticipates the unexpected possibilities of life, arising from our being-in-the-world, our situatedness within the living-world, our embodied experiencing of the world. In this respect, my conception of Woolf's estranged intimacy with the world corresponds to David Herman's project of "re-minding modernism" and his emphasis on the enactive aspect of cognition. According to Herman, our understanding of the world does not follow a Cartesian model of one-directional cognition with a perceiving subject and the perceived reality. Rather, it is a dynamic interplay between agent and environment. Cognition is profoundly entangled with the contexts of actions and interactions with surrounding environments. It is a moment-by-moment process of experiencing the world. We are always in a process of both affecting and being affected by others, completely open to any contingent encounters.

This new focus on the inseparable relationship between the interior reality and the exterior environment brings us to an oft-noticed characteristic of Woolf's writing—her interest in the common mind. As Michael Whitworth puts it, in the contemporary intellectual atmosphere dominated by Nietzschean individualism, Woolf's interest in sympathy, communal living, and common consciousness distinguishes her from other modernist writers.[1] But I would like to emphasize at the same time that Woolf's representation of common consciousness is never an enclosed entity insulated from the world outside. It is always an intimacy, a coming-together, and at the same time an estrangement, an openness, that keeps the singularity of each being and retains the contingency of every new encounter. In her novels, Woolf is always in search of an interpersonal (or even transcendental) connection that does not curb the singularity of each being, a connection that I term an estranged intimacy with the world. I suggest that if we focus less on how Rachel fails to engage critically with the world of books and more on her irreducible experience of life and on her search for interpersonal connections, we can discover that the novel itself registers a planetary love that entails an ethical reading of alterity.

Rachel's estranged intimacy with the world is vividly embodied first through a comparison with a traditional heterosexual romantic love envisioned by Terence. This comparison is instigated, at least in part, by the gaze of the colonial "other" in the scene in the village along the river. In fact, Rachel's relationship with the native women, established by the sight of the native women with their daunting gaze, not only brings to Rachel and Terence the immediate feelings of coldness and melancholy but profoundly influences Rachel's reflection on her engagement with Terence. Their confrontation with the native village as an absolutely alienating world that cannot be contained by the gaze of the Westerners makes Rachel question traditional marriage with its fixed gender roles. Uncertain about their engagement and marriage, after their return from the native village, Rachel and Terence discuss different natures of man and woman, discovering that there is an insurmountable gulf between them. Disturbed by the prescribed process of engagement and marriage, Rachel emphatically denies falling in love with Terence and disputes the common definition of love: "I never fell in love, if falling in love is what people say it is, and it's the world that tells the lies and I tell the truth. Oh, what lies—what lies!" Appalled by the thought that "any one of these people had ever felt what she felt, or could ever feel it, or had even the right to pretend for a single second that they were capable of feeling it" (*VO* 342), Rachel wonders "[w]ould there ever be a time when the world was one and indivisible?" (345). "Why don't people write about the things they do feel?" (346).

Rachel Bowlby has succinctly pointed out that being "in love" in Woolf's writing, particularly in *The Voyage Out*, is starkly portrayed as elusive and inadequate because of the gap between the bodily passion of love and social conventions of marriage.[2] Indeed, as Julia Kuehn's reading of the native village scene suggests, Rachel's encounter with the natives collapses the self-other binary and makes her realize that she will be the same as the native women with the same entrenched patriarchal oppression and gender inequality, once she steps into the marriage with Terence. For Kuehn, the cause of the fever that kills Rachel lies in the "impossibility of ever being happy in such a 'strange' union" (143). Thus, instead of a traditional romantic love, what Rachel truly desires, I argue, is a different kind of love that goes far beyond the restraint of "the love of one human being" (*VO* 352). Rachel is in search of a kind of love that is derived from an "estranged intimacy" with the world, an interconnected yet indeterminate relationship with the world. She wants "[t]o be flung into the sea, to be washed hither and thither, and driven about the roots of the world—the idea was incoherently delightful" (*VO* 347). Invoking the imagery of voyaging, the narrator tells us that Rachel "seemed to be able to cut herself adrift from [Terence], and to pass away to unknown places where she had no need of him." Dissatisfied with the limiting circuit of romantic love, "[Rachel] wanted many more things than the love of one human being—the sea, the sky" (352). With all these suspicions of their marriage, Rachel abruptly bursts out and decides to break off with Terence. Although the narrator comments that Rachel's remarks unite them even more than ever, we can tell that this intimacy is never as satisfactory as it may seem and that the world can never be "one and indivisible." As the silence that creeps into the conversation between Rachel and Terrence connotes, the native women's "motionless inexpressive" gaze reminds Rachel of the existence of an absolute alterity, hinting at the insignificance of their tour of the native village, the uncertainty of the future, and the indescribable pain of being in love. Although Rachel and Terence now stand together in front of a looking-glass, the narrator reveals that "it chilled them to see themselves in the glass, for instead of being vast and indivisible they were really very small and separate, the size of the glass leaving a large space for the reflection of other things" (353).

Unsatisfied with the love of one human being and the suffocating heterosexual marriage, Rachel searches for a "planetary love" that surpasses the limits of traditional love. Here I draw from the notion of "planetarity" proposed by Gayatri Spivak in *Death of a Discipline*. Insisting on an ethical exigency of comparison and translation, Spivak urges us to imagine ourselves as planetary creatures rather than global entities. As she remarks, "[t]he globe is on our computers. No one lives there. It allows us to think that we can aim to control it. The planet is in the species of alterity, belonging to another system; and yet we inhabit it, on loan" (72). Spivak's statement seems paradoxical; if the planet is in the species of alterity and belongs to another system, how can we still inhabit it, on loan? For Spivak, however, this is not a contradiction in that "[t]o be human is to be intended toward the other" (73). In this respect, a "planetary love" cannot be confused with the traditional romantic love in which two lovers are locked within an enclosed space. Rather, as "estranged intimacy with the world" suggests, it is a love of the world as an open whole, a love that is embodied in our indeterminate relationship with others, a love that anticipates the unexpected possibilities of life emerging from our moment-by-moment encounters with other singular beings.

Before Rachel falls ill, she comes to a realization about the nature of her love for Terence. Closely observing Terence's face and remembering her differences from Terence and all the possible quarrels in the future, Rachel asserts her individuality, independence, and the singularity of life even though she is going to be with Terence from now on: "But all this was superficial, and had nothing to do with the life that went on beneath the eyes and the mouth and the chin, for that life was independent of her, and independent of everything else. So too, although she was going to marry him and to live with him for thirty, or forty, or fifty years, and to quarrel, and to be so close to him, she was independent of him; she was independent of everything else" (*VO* 367–68). But her independence of Terence does not mean that her love with Terence is absolutely a burden to her life. Rather, it is her love of Terence that makes her realize what the love that she is always searching for is like: "Nevertheless, as St. John said, it was love that made her understand this, for she had never felt this independence, this calm, and this certainty until she fell in love with him, and perhaps this *too* was love. She wanted nothing else" (368, emphasis added). Here two difference conceptions of love can be recognized. One is the romantic love that cannot satisfy Rachel's desire to "see life." The other is the planetary love that entails an estranged intimacy with the world. But in this revelatory moment of love, it is her love of Terence that makes her discover the planetary love that she is always searching for. Why is that? Isn't the romantic love contrary to the planetary love? Perhaps the problem lies in our definition of love. I suggest that we can look at Woolf's excitement and expectation brought about by her love and marriage with Leonard described in a letter to him: "We both of us want a marriage that is a tremendous living thing, always alive, always hot, not dead and easy in parts as most marriages are. We ask a great deal of life, don't we? Perhaps we shall get it; then, how splendid!" (*L1* 497). While both Rachel and Woolf reject traditional love with its established rules and gender roles, what they suggest is that the love between man and woman, the love between human beings, should be conceived as part of the planetary love that invites us to maintain an estranged intimacy with the people we love, with the world that surrounds us, with the planet we inhabit.

So does my discussion of Rachel's estranged intimacy with the world and the ethical refrain of planetary love have anything to do with the "postcolonial Woolf" I mentioned in the beginning? Through my alternative postcolonial reading of *The Voyage Out*, I aim to respond to the ethical turn/return proposed by the postcolonial scholar Simon Gikandi. In an interview entitled "Postcolonialism's Ethical (Re)Turn," Gikandi observes the impact of the emergence of global literary studies on postcolonial studies. For Gikandi, globalization is a double-edged sword in that while it leads to a global cultural phenomenon and opens up possibilities, at the same time it causes problems of homogenization in the process of uneven cultural exchange. In thinking about the notion of global identities in postcolonial studies, therefore, Gikandi asks us always to keep in mind this gap between the ideal of cultural infusion and concrete material experiences of globalization. In terms of global literary studies, he urgently reminds us of the "vanishing of the Third World" in the global scene of literary production due to the predominance of legitimizing institutions in the West and "the collapse of the cultural infrastructure" in the Third World. As Gikandi prudently indicates, however, the core of the entire issue perhaps does not lie in the way the postcolonial paradigm has been appropriated by the hegemony of institutions. Rather, it is possible that these problems are inherent in postcolonial studies itself: how can the project of postcolonial studies that tends to distance itself from historicism, nationalism, and humanism not be at odds with the ethical project of decolonization? At the end of the interview, touching upon the recent proposals by scholars such as Paul Gilroy and Gayatri Spivak and conceiving them together as a call for a return to the ethical project, Gikandi suggests that an ethical (re)turn might be a new point of departure for us to reconsider the project of postcolonial studies.

So is it possible for us to reconsider the postcolonial scholarship on Woolf? Can we propose another reading of Woolf than a critique of cultural politics in Woolf's work? To what extent can Woolf's liberal thinking correspond to this call for an ethical (re)turn in postcolonial studies?

In response to Lytton Strachey's comments on *The Voyage Out*, Woolf writes: "What I wanted to do was to give the feeling of a vast tumult of life, as various and disorderly as possible, which should be cut short for a moment by the death, and go on again—and the whole was to have a sort of pattern, and be somehow controlled" (*L2* 82). Woolf's thinking on her own work recalls the final scene of the night of storm when all the people in the hotel return to bed after expressing their concerns about the death of Rachel. At this final moment, the focus of the narrative is on St John Hirst: "All these voices sounded gratefully in St. John's ears as he lay half-asleep, and yet vividly conscious of everything around him. Across his eyes passed a procession of objects, black and indistinct, the figures of people picking up their books, their cards, their balls of wool, their work-baskets, and passing him one after another on their way to bed" (*VO* 437). How should we interpret this bewildering ending? Should we condemn the hotel guests' indifference and cold-bloodedness merely because they need to go back to their path of life? If we can remember Woolf's and Rachel's belief in maintaining an estranged intimacy with the world, along with the planetary love that it embodies, perhaps Rachel's abortive *Bildung* can be taken metaphorically as an exigency of planetary love in our ethical reading of alterity across the world.

Notes

1.　According to Michael Whitworth, Woolf's interest in sympathy, communal living, and common consciousness is often interpreted as the influence of *Unanimisme*, a literary movement in France founded by Jules Romains. See Norrish, McLaurin, and the entry "Common Mind, Group Thinking" in Cuddy-Keane *et al.*, *Modernism: Keywords*.

2.　In "Virginia Woolf's 'in Love'," Rachel Bowlby suggests that what distinguishes Woolf's writing of love from others is that Woolf's figuration of love is less concerned with "what" happens in narrative than "how" it is articulated. Being in love as a smooth narrative thus appears in Woolf's work as being "in love" with the quotation marks to foreground the problem of language. Bowlby argues that it is in her first novel *The Voyage Out* more than any other text that being "in love" is starkly portrayed as an ineffably distressing state that requires words to express but will necessarily fail. For Bowlby, then, the language of love in this novel serves as a bridge that attempts to connect two radically distinctive states: the physical attraction of love and the social world of engagement and marriage. The predicament of the novel for its author and characters thus lies in a contradiction: while it is acknowledged that a marriage should involve sexual attraction, at the same time sex and marriage are said to belong in different categories. Building upon Bowlby's cogent reading, I argue that the Woolf's figuration of love not only registers the anxiety and distress resulted from the division between the private and the public, but also gestures towards a planetary love that embodies the ethos of an estranged intimacy with the world.

Works Cited

Bowlby, Rachel. "Virginia Woolf's 'In Love.'" *Feminist Destinations and Further Essays on Virginia Woolf.* Edinburgh: Edinburgh UP, 1997. 173–90.

Cuddy-Keane, Melba, Adam Hammond, and Alexandra Peat, eds. *Modernism: Keywords.* Malden, MA: Wiley-Blackwell, 2014.

Friedman, Susan Stanford. "Virginia Woolf's Pedagogical Scenes of Reading: *The Voyage Out, The Common Reader,* and Her 'Common Readers.'" *Modern Fiction Studies* 38.1 (1992): 101–25.

Gikandi, Simon. Interview by David Jefferess. "Postcolonialism's Ethical (Re)Turn: An Interview with Simon Gikandi." *Postcolonial Text* 2.1 (2006): n. pag. Web. 13 Dec. 2013.

Herman, David. "1880–1945: Re-minding Modernism." *The Emergence of Mind: Representations of Consciousness in Narrative Discourse in English.* Ed. David Herman. Lincoln: U of Nebraska P, 2011. 243–72.

Kuehn, Julia. "*The Voyage Out* as Voyage In: Exotic Realism, Romance and Modernism." *Woolf Studies Annual* 17 (2011): 126–50.

McLaurin, Allen. "Virginia Woolf and Unanimism." *Journal of Modern Literature* 9.1 (1981–82): 115–22.

Norrish, P. J. "Romains and L'Abbaye." *Modern Language Review* 52 (1957): 518–25.

Spivak, Gayatri Chakravorty. *Death of a Discipline.* New York: Columbia UP, 2003.

Whitworth, Michael. "Virginia Woolf and Modernism." *The Cambridge Companion to Virginia Woolf.* Ed. Sue Roe and Susan Sellers. New York: Cambridge UP, 2000. 146–63.

Woolf, Virginia. *The Voyage Out.* 1915. New York: Oxford UP, 1992.

——. *The Letters of Virginia Woolf.* Ed. Nigel Nicolson and Joanne Trautmann. 6 vols. New York: Harcourt, Brace Jovanovich, 1975–80.

"Shakespeare's Sister":
Woolf in the World before *A Room of One's Own*

by Susan Stanford Friedman

Virginia Woolf tells us in *A Room of One's Own* (1929) "a woman writing thinks back through her mothers" (97), an observation that took on allegorical weight in generations of feminist criticism establishing what Elaine Showalter famously called *A Literature of Their Own*, shifting the pronoun slightly to emphasize the need to construct a literary history of women's writing as a distinctive tradition. And yet, when we turn once again to *A Room of One's Own*, we must be struck by how entirely English Woolf's lineage of women writers is in this particular polemical essay. George Sand does make a momentary appearance, alongside Currer Bell and George Eliot, notable for their use of ambiguous or male pseudonyms. But her snapshots of women writing—from Lady Winchelsea and Margaret Cavendish to Austen, the Brontës, and the fictionalized Mary Carmichael—are resolutely English. And by "English," I mean an ethnic and national designation, not only a linguistic one. How does this Englishness shape the reflections Woolf makes about women's writing more generally in *A Room of One's Own*? For a writer so deeply associated with a gender-based cosmopolitanism in *Three Guineas* (1938)—"as a woman I have no country. As a woman I want no country" (129)—Woolf's lineage of writing "mothers" in *A Room of One's Own* seems parochial, especially in the context of the 2014 Virginia Woolf Conference theme, Writing the World. *A Room* does *not* look back through literary mothers of the world beyond England, nor does it even consider the kinds of issues the resonant phrase "writing the world" suggests.

I propose, however, a different framework for rethinking *A Room of One's Own* as a text that is both in the world and writes the world: namely Woolf's astounding ability to create iconic figures and tropes that travel to and incorporate the world. Woolf was a gifted phrase-maker, a crystallizer of concepts that she embodied in condense, resonant, unforgettable, image-based, metonymic or metaphoric terms: Shakespeare's sister; a room of one's own; 500 pounds a year; killing the angel in the house; Chloe liked Olivia...; she broke the sentence, she broke the sequence; the daughters of educated men; dead bodies and ruined houses; round and round the mulberry tree; as a woman I have no country—and many more such iconic figures or phrases from *A Room of One's Own*, "Professions for Women," and *Three Guineas* in particular. Woolf's most potent theory typically takes figural, metonymic, or metaphorical form, all of which invite translation and the multiple meanings that translation entails.[1]

An image becomes an icon only when it travels: when it moves from place to place in the world, taking on new meanings from its new contexts, like a motif. The travels of an icon also move high and low, into the mainstream, into a broad-scale public imaginary, and across national borders, as Brenda Silver has shown in *Virginia Woolf Icon*. The advent of 21st-century social media and the daily use of icons on our desktops and smart phones have exponentially intensified this kind of globalizing iconic process. So disseminated, an icon does not have to be deeply or accurately understood for it to have its impact, or for it to be translated into different contexts, adapted, indigenized, vernacularized, even transformed. Rereading *A Room of One's Own* within these contemporary frameworks of circulation can track the travels of her iconic tropes to determine the nature of their vibrant afterlife around the world, with writers, artists, activists, and entrepreneurs transforming her image-phrases into everything from new revolutionary poetics to fetish commodities.

Tracking how writers *after* Virginia Woolf interact with and transform her iconic tropes is one very valuable way of reading Woolf "in the world." But I would like to suggest yet another way, one that sees their iconic nature and functioning not as a point of origin but rather as part of a wider, even potentially world-wide discourse for which she remains central, but only as part of the story. For thinking about feminism in general, I have used the metaphor of mushrooms springing up after the rain, here and there, connected through invisible networks underground. I use it to critique the center-periphery or diffusionist models of power relations in the world, the very model that ends up making so-called Western feminism the dominant originator of discourse that must be set aside, challenged, attacked, and so forth to be relevant to the rest of the world. I suggest that we read *A Room of One's Own* in the context of texts in the world that came *before* Woolf created those iconic phrases, texts that play with closely related issues and even images. In short, I propose a way of reading Woolf in the world before Woolf was in the world.

My case in point focuses on the pre-existence of Shakespeare's sister in India *before* Woolf created her in *A Room of One's Own*. First, to re-look at that icon, Shakespeare's sister, from a new angle (46–51). At the heart of Woolf's iconic fiction about Judith Shakespeare is a sibling story about the differential treatment of and conditions for gifted brothers and sisters in the same family. Patriarchy, of course, provides the overarching context, the gender system which favors men and destines women to confinement in a life defined through sexuality and procreation. But the focus on Woolf's narrativization of patriarchy is the brother-sister relationship: both William and Judith are born with the same inner genius, she imagines. What happens to the brother with the gift? Shakespeare: arguably the greatest writer in the English language. What could happen to the sister with the same gift? Sexual exploitation, unwanted pregnancy, gift thwarted, madness, suicide. Woolf carefully contextualizes her Judith Shakespeare in the material and ideological conditions of sixteenth-century England and bookends her literary lineage of literary mothers with another fictionalized, "modern" writer, Mary Carmichael, thus implying that conditions have changed so that an innovative 20th-century woman writer can flourish.

Underneath this familiar historicized argument about change is Woolf's sense of an ongoing and still contemporary rivalry between talented brothers and sisters. In her own family, the tension of "Shakespeare's sister" is re-enacted in Virginia's competitive relationship with her gifted brother Thoby, sent off to school with the family's scant funds, while she herself was educated haphazardly, if at all, at home. This foundational brother-sister rivalry permeates *Three Guineas* tropically and reappears strikingly in "A Sketch of the Past," where Woolf recounts an early childhood scene of bitterly fighting with Thoby, then letting him beat her up, and finally using the kind of shock effect the beating produced as the basis of her drive to create (71–72).

What has led me to see the significance of the brother-sister rivalry in Woolf's trope of Shakespeare's sister has been rereading *A Room of One's Own* in relationship to the early prose of Rabindranath Tagore and then finding out to my great surprise that he had a supremely talented older sister, the best-known of the fourteen Tagore children after Rabindranath himself. Swarnakumari Devi (1855/6–1932) was Bengal's first substantial woman writer, publishing thirteen novels, two collections of short stories, two volumes of poetry, four plays, an opera, several farces, literature for children, travelogues, memoirs, and essays on scientific and reform issues. She also composed music and songs and edited the literary journal *Bharati* for decades with her daughters, a journal that "shaped the literary and cultural tastes of a generation," according to Rajul Sogani and Indira Gupta. A number of her aesthetic innovations—e.g., the first short stories and the first opera in Bengal—were later credited to Rabindranath, erasing her influence.[2]

Even in the reform-minded Tagore family, the boys and girls lived very different lives. The brothers were sent off to school while the sisters were educated at home, married off as children, and confined to the inner quarters of the house, the zenana. Swarnakumari did all her writing in seclusion, while her talented brother Rabindranath went out to administer the vast family estates in Bengal, where for ten years he wandered among the people, gathering much of the material and oral patterns of narrative that inform his prose of the 1890s and early twentieth- century. Nonetheless, Swarnakumari was an active feminist and reformer, an advocate for girl's and women's education (her daughters went to college), an opponent of child brides and mistreatment of widows, a member along with the whole Tagore family of the reformist Bramho sect of Hinduism, and an anti-colonial nationalist who served as a voting delegate at the Indian National Congress.

Before Woolf created the trope of Shakespeare's sister, Tagore and Swarnakumari played out its subterranean sibling rivalry in their lives and work. Swarnakumari, for example, dedicated her first volume of poems in 1880 to Tagore with playful lines that hint at the competition between them.

> To my younger brother.
> Let me present these poems: carefully
>   gleaned and strung
> To the most deserving person.
> But you are so playful. I hope you will not
> Snap and scatter these flowers for fun. (Tharu and Lalita 237)

Tagore's unsuccessful efforts to prevent the publication of Swarnukari's translation of her 1898 novel *Kahake* (1898) as *An Unfinished Song* in England (1913) suggests that he too felt the competition. Ostensibly wanting to spare her the criticism of English reviewers, he writes to William Rothenstein in 1914: "She is one of those unfortunate beings who has more ambition than ability. But just enough talent to keep her alive for a short period. Her weakness has been taken advantage of by some unscrupulous literary agents in London and she has had stories translated and published. I have given her no encouragement but have not been successful in making her see things in the proper light" (qtd. in Tharu and Lalita 238). In fact, *An Unfinished Song* was positively reviewed in London and went into a second edition in 1914, belying his need to keep her novel in the "seclusion" of Bengali. An ongoing, subterranean competition between older sister and younger brother anticipates and re-enacts the trope-to-be of Shakespeare's sister.

As a nationalist, feminist reformer, and advocate of Bengali literature and culture, Swarnakumari Devi also read extensively in English literature, as did her brother Rabindranath. For both, the Victorian novel, with its capacity to probe the subtleties of family and communal life, must have seemed ideally adaptable for representing the hybrid lives of the Bengal elite as they sought a prose form rooted in the life and language of Bengal. George Eliot was among Swarnakumari Devi's favorite writers. And George Eliot appears in contestation with Shakespeare, gratuitously, unnecessarily, in a full chapter of *An Unfinished Song*. The novel is a scandalous first-person novel about Moni, a woman who narrates the interiority of her dreams and passions. Moni backs out of a public engagement she had made herself, refuses a marriage her father arranges, and insists on a love marriage of her own choice. As a striking confirmation of Moni's choice, Swarnakumari Devi devotes a whole chapter to a passionate debate about whether George Eliot's genius equals that of Shakespeare, with the pro-Eliot side argued by the man Moni loves and the anti-Eliot side argued by her brother-in-law.

Did Woolf know this novel? Possibly. It was published in English in two different translations, the second in England in Swarnakumari Devi's own translation in 1913. But there is no evidence that Woolf had even heard of Tagore's sister or even that she had ever read Tagore. Their significance for Woolf lies not in the circulation of their texts to Woolf's library, but rather in the circulations between brother and sister as an instance of the sibling rivalry that Woolf herself would later recreate in iconic form in *A Room of One's Own* with world-wide and still growing circulation *after* 1929.

The contemporary brother/sister rivalry embedded in Woolf's trope of Shakespeare's sister permeates Tagore's early short stories and novellas written from the 1890s through the early twentieth century. Tagore does not invoke Shakespeare or pose the debate about women writers the way Swarnakumari Devi and Woolf do. Rather, the trope appears within the broader context of narratives about girls and women who resist but are often destroyed by the demands of the joint family structure, about the practice of child brides, and about the vulnerable position of child widows and widows in general. Many of Tagore's female characters crave to learn, love to read, and sometimes find a way to write, often secretly and, for elite women, within the confines of the zenana. Tagore spun story after story out of the feminist issues his sister raised in her own fiction, the multidimensional reform for which his family stood, and the lives he learned about in East Bengal. Often, the agonistic plots revolve around a contest of wills between a girl or woman and her age peers in the family—a brother, a husband, in-laws of both sexes.

At times, Tagore uses these sibling contestations to work through questions of aesthetics, particularly the contrast between the "modern" aesthetics he himself promotes and what he regarded as the highly elaborate artifice of Bengali Renaissance writing. With an interesting twist on what Woolf would later formulate in *A Room of One's Own*, Tagore's stories about male writers almost invariably mock the men, ironizing their literary and intellectual pretensions, making fun of their style and their egos. In short stories like "Kata" (1891)/ "The Notebook" (1991) or novellas like *Nashtanir* (1901)/ *The Broken Nest* (1971), Tagore activates the brother-sister rivalry, but creates the girl as invariably bolder, truer, and *more* gifted than the man. These sisters in Tagore's tales become a persona for himself as the modern writer who, in the 1890s, began to seek a literary language fed by, though not limited to, the oral traditions of the rural poor, especially of women.[3]

In conclusion, I'd like to return to the question with which I opened: how can we approach reading *A Room of One's Own* "in the world" and as a text that "writes the world"? How in particular can we construct a lineage of writers for Woolf that sets aside the limited genealogy of English literary mothers that she proposes in *A Room of One's Own* and that also acknowledges her particular gift to create unforgettable, condensed figures and phrases that achieve iconic status and travel the world *after* she creates them, tropes like "Shakespeare's sister"? I have suggested that one way to achieve this is a different form of literary genealogy, one that is transnational, one that is not dependent on arguments of influence, one that unpacks the issues embedded in her condensed trope, and one that identifies these issues at work in lives and literatures *before* Woolf. Ultimately, I am also interested in using this approach to global works written *after* Woolf's tropes begin to circulate globally. To approach the *pre-* and *afterlife* of Woolfian tropes on a global stage, I believe we need to move well beyond Woolf's once influential request that we "read back" through our literary mothers. Reading Woolf "in the world" and "writing the world" might well construct global lineages that include male as well as female writers: the literary fathers, brothers, and sons as well as the literary mothers, sisters, and daughters. In short, I propose a way of reading Woolf in the world *before* Woolf was in the world. Then, perhaps, we can read Woolf in the world *after* she was in the world in a different way, one that doesn't perpetuate the notion of that feminism was invented in the West and spread to the Rest, one that emerges out of a different framework for reading world literatures in circulation across space and time.

Notes

1. For discussion of the trope of "as a woman I have no country" in *Three Guineas*, see Friedman, "Wartime Cosmopolitanism;" for the tropes of "a room of one's own" and "the angel in the house," see Friedman, "Migration."
2. Swarnakumari Devi's publications also appear under the names Swarnakumari Debi, and Swarnakumari Debi Ghosal. "Devi" and "Debi" were largely honorifics for women in Bengal not known by a family name in the late 19th century.
3. For extended discussion of Tagore's stories, see Friedman, "Towards a Transnational Turn."

Works Cited

Ghosul, Swarakumari Debi. *Khahake.* 1898. *An Unfinished Song.* Ed. C. Vijayasree. New Delhi: Oxford UP, 2008.

Friedman, Susan Stanford. "Migration, Encounter, and Indigenisation: New Ways of Thinking about Intertextuality in Women's Writing." *European Women's Writing in English in a European Context.* Vol. 13. Ed. Patsy Stoneman, Vita Fortunati, and Eleanora Federici. Germany: Peter Lang, 2005.

——. "Towards a Transnational Turn in Narrative Theory: Literary Narratives, Traveling Tropes, and the Case of Virginia Woolf and the Tagores." *Narrative* 19.1 (2011): 1–32.

——. "Wartime Cosmopolitanism: Cosmofeminism in Virginia Woolf's *Three Guineas* and Marjane Satrapi's *Persepolis.*" *Tulsa Studies in Women's Literature.* 32.1 (2013): 23–52.

Showalter, Elaine. *A Literature of Their Own.* Princeton: Princeton UP, 1977.

Silver, Brenda. *Virginia Woolf Icon.* Chicago: U of Chicago P, 1999.

Sogani, Rajul and Indira Gupta. Introduction. *The Uprooted Vine.* By Swarnakumari Debi. Trans. Rajul Sogani and Indira Gupta. New Delhi: Oxford UP, 2004.

Tagore, Rabindranath. "Khata." 1891. "The Notebook." *Selected Short Stories of Rabindranath Tagore.* Trans. Krishna Dutta and Mary Lago. London: Macmillan, 1991. 43–50.

——. *Nashtanir.* 1901. *The Broken Nest.* Trans. Mary M. Lago and Supriya Sen. Columbia: U of Missouri P, 1971.

Tharu, Susie and K. Lalita. "Swarnakumari Devi." *Women Writing in India: 600 B.C. to the Present.* Vol. 1, *600 B.C. to the Early Twentieth Century.* Ed. Susan Tharu and K. Lalita. New York: Feminist Press, 1991. 235–38.

Woolf, Virginia. "Professions for Women." *The Death of the Moth and Other Essays.* New York: Harcourt Brace Jovanovich, 1942. 235–42.

——. *A Room of One's Own.* 1929. San Diego: Harcourt Brace Jovanovich, 1957.

——. "A Sketch of the Past." *Moments of Being: A Collection of Autobiographical Writing.* Ed. Jeanne Schulkind. 2nd ed. San Diego: Harcourt, 1985. 61–159.

——. *Three Guineas.* 1938. Annot. and intro. Jane Marcus. Orlando, FL: Harcourt, 2006.

LEONARD WOOLF: WRITING THE WORLD OF PALESTINE, ZIONISM, AND THE STATE OF ISRAEL

by Steven Putzel

There is no record of Virginia Woolf's attitude toward Leonard's interaction with British Zionists and Assimilationists and the question of Palestine, though her disparaging remarks about the Woolf family's Jewishness and her purported anti-Semitism continue to spark debate. Yet she responded enthusiastically to Leonard's plan to write a book on the Wandering Jew (*D2* 111); she wrote a heart-rending diary account of a starving young Jewish girl (*D5* 19); and she railed against the plight of English and European Jews in *Three Guineas*: "[t]he whole iniquity of dictatorship, whether in Oxford or Cambridge, in Whitehall or Downing Street, against Jews or against women, in England, or in Germany, in Italy or in Spain" (*TG* 103). She may have come to understand and sympathize with the plight of European Jews, but it was Leonard who immersed himself in the immensely complex politics of "the Jewish question."

Leonard Woolf's long life and life-long involvement with international politics, law, and economics created a body of work that serves as a lens through which we can better see and understand virtually every major historical event and movement of the twentieth century. In fact, his willingness to take on controversial issues, to build policy arguments and express unequivocal convictions, and then to revisit and reassess these arguments and convictions as times and circumstances change, can still help us comprehend current events and controversies.

From his skepticism over the Balfour Declaration of 1917 and the British Mandate for Palestine that lasted until 1948, to the many articles concerning Palestine published in *Political Quarterly* and *The New Statesman* throughout the forties, to his visit to Israel in 1957, and finally to his letters written to Lord Fisher (former Archbishop of Canterbury) in defense of Israeli military strikes in 1968, Woolf demonstrated a complex and constantly evolving attitude toward Israel and Arab-Jewish relations. In 2013, the American Studies Association and many academic organizations around the world moved to boycott Israeli universities over Israel's Palestinian policies, the Presbyterian and Methodist churches divested themselves of their Israeli investments, and the MLA resolved to "criticize" Israel for denying scholars access to Palestinian universities (though the vote to endorse the resolution was not adopted because only 6% of the membership voted). Accusations of anti-Semitism are rampant. Anti-boycott legislation is pending in New York, Maryland, Illinois, Pennsylvania, Florida, and in the U.S. House of Representatives (McMurtrie). Though it serves little point to ask how Leonard Woolf would respond to these boycotts, sanctions, and the anti-boycott movements, the evolution of Woolf's thoughts on Palestine, Zionism, and the State of Israel can help us navigate this international, national, and educational controversy in a broader historical context, and can increase our appreciation for the ways Woolf's essays, letters, Labour Party white papers, and his autobiography helped to "write the world." I have selected three vantage points from which to examine Woolf's evolving views: 1922, 1949, and 1968.

1922: IMPLEMENTATION OF THE BRITISH MANDATE FOR PALESTINE

For Woolf, the debate over the fate of Palestine began in the early years of World War I with Jewish intellectuals and political activists split into two main groups, Assimilationists and Zionists. The Ottoman Empire, which belatedly joined the Axis Powers, controlled the Middle East. Consequently, the British government viewed both Arab groups and International Jewish groups as essential allies against Turkey. We all know the story of T. E. Lawrence and the importance of the Arab campaign against the Ottomans to the Allied war effort. In his work for the Labour Party, however, Woolf was directly involved with the Zionist/Assimilationist debate, which culminated in Zionist diplomatic victory with the 1917 Balfour Declaration: "[h]is Majesty's Government view with favour the establishment in Palestine of a national home for the Jewish people, and will use their best endeavours to facilitate the achievement of this object, it being clearly understood that nothing shall be done which may prejudice the civil and religious rights of existing non-Jewish communities in Palestine, or the rights and political status enjoyed by Jews in any other country" (Schneer 341). As the debate between Zionists and Assimilationists raged, Woolf wrote "Three Jews" (1917). Although Leena Schröder places "Three Jews" in the context of anti-Semitism in Britain during WWI (314), what may be more directly significant to our understanding of this short story is Woolf's involvement with Labour Party politics, the wartime coalition government's flirtation with both Jewish Assimilationists and Zionists, and the resulting 1917 Balfour Declaration. In Leonard's story, the second Jew, who, like the first Jew, is a religious skeptic, agrees with the first that the beautiful English day in Kew Gardens "doesn't belong to us" and adds "we belong to Palestine still, but I'm not sure that it doesn't belong to us for all that" (5). This leads him to tell a story about a third Jew that delineates this cultural belonging, but also illustrates a dangerous miscegenation and obsession with wealth that the second Jew rejects.

Throughout the 1920s, Woolf remained adamantly anti-Zionist. Looking back in *The Journey Not the Arrival Matters*, Woolf recalls a two-hour meeting in 1921 with the influential and persuasive Chaim Weizmann, President of the World Zionist Organization. As head of the British Admiralty laboratories during WWI, Weizmann had developed the process of industrial fermentation to cheaply produce large quantities of acetone, a key ingredient in the cordite used in munitions (Rose 152–53). This work helped Weizmann gain access to David Lloyd George, Prime Minister of the Wartime Coalition Government. Woolf explains that even Weizmann could not "convert" him: "I think that the whole of history shows that the savage xenophobia of human beings is so great that the introduction into any populated country of a large racial, economic, religious, or cultured minority always leads to hatred, violence, and political and social disaster.... That is why I thought originally that the Balfour Declaration and the introduction of a Jewish minority and a Jewish state in a country inhabited by a large Arab population was politically dangerous" (*Journey* 185–86).

We get a clearer understanding of Woolf's view of Palestine and its people—both Arab and Jew—with his description in *Beginning Again* of the Russian translator and Ukrainian Jew, S. S. Koteliansky (Kot), whom he met at the 1917 Labour Party Conference. When Leonard and Virginia invited Kot to Asheham, the topic of discussion was "Jews, Judaism, the relation of Jews to other people, their differences, their faults, and virtues" (Glendinning 198). Some of this talk finds its way into the autobiography. For example: "[t]here are some Jews who, though their ancestors have lived for centuries in

European ghettoes, are born with certain characteristics which the sun and sand of the desert beat into the bodies and minds of Semites." Woolf adds, "I have felt the same qualities of steely, repressed, purged passion burnt into a Semite by sun and sand, in an ordinary Arab pearl diver from the Persian Gulf." Woolf listened as this man eulogized a dead comrade, noting, "It was in Arabic and I did not understand a word, and yet I understood every word. It was Isaiah and Jeremiah and Job—and Kot" (*Beginning* 249–50). In other words, Arabs and Jews are Semitic cousins.

At the end of the war, the British military occupied the former Ottoman-controlled Palestine, until The Council of the League of Nations officially created The British Mandatory of Palestine in July 1922, which was to set up limited self-governance and implement the terms of the Balfour Declaration. Woolf's May 1, 1920 commentary on Article XXII in the *New Statesman* recognizes the "dangerous character of the Middle East problem" and that the UK's violation of at least one of the provisions of the Article already endangered the future of the region. Britain was meant to offer administrative "advice and assistance" to Palestine as an "independent nation," but Palestine was not meant to become "the pawn of the predatory Imperialisms" ("Article XXII" 94). The victorious British and French governments, Woolf tells us, intended to apply the Sykes-Picot agreement of 1916 that would give Britain access to and control over the oil in the region—thus rendering Article XXII meaningless. This, Woolf says, is "the first great test of the reality of the League of Nations" (established 1919). He warns that if the British do not abide by the League's Mandatory system, there will be "perpetual trouble, ending possibly or probably in a blaze, which it will tax all our military resources to extinguish" (95). Prophetic words.

1948–49: ESTABLISHMENT OF ISRAEL AND THE PARTITION OF PALESTINE

In the first British census of Palestine (1922), the population of Palestine was 757,182 with 11% of the population Jewish; in 1930, it was 1,035,154 with 17% Jewish. The estimated population in 1948 was nearly 2,000,000 with 33% Jewish. After the UN sponsored partition granting about 56% of the former Mandatory of Palestine to Israel and 43% to the Arabs (Jerusalem was international), the population of Israel was 873,000, 82% of which was Jewish. Considering these statistics, it is not surprising that the British Mandate spelled trouble from the start. After the 1929 Arab riots, the British government began recommending limitations on Jewish immigration. Woolf makes his views clear in a *Political Quarterly* book review. After praising Norman Bentwich's factual history of the British occupation and the subsequent Mandate, he cites his own views:

> With a little more honesty and firmness of purpose the British politicians and Palestinian administrators might have avoided many of the disastrous and shameful events which have accompanied our administration. I have myself always been very doubtful of the wisdom of the Zionist ideal. The world is already suffering not from too little, but from too much nationalism.... That Palestine should be the territory which had to be converted into the home for this new Jewish nationalism was peculiarly unfortunate, in view of the exacerbated condition of indigenous nationalism everywhere in the Near East after the war. (Rev. of *England and Palestine* 299)

He claims that in the first years of the Mandate "a modus vivendi between the Arabs and Jews might have been secured," if not for Moslem extremists and "the British Government's disingenuous and vacillating attitude after the riots and massacres of 1930" (300).

As a reaction to Arab protests against the Mandatory in the thirties, the Peel Commission of 1937 recommended just what Woolf did not want—the partition of Palestine into Jewish and Arab areas. Arabs rejected this, while the Zionists under Weizmann accepted for purposes of negotiation. In 1939, a British government White Paper rejected partition and proposed creating an independent Palestine to be governed by Palestinian Arabs and Jews in proportion to their numbers in the population in 1939, i.e. 70% Arab to 30% Jewish. It also severely restricted Jewish immigration.

In 1940, musing on the failure of the League of Nations to prevent another world war, Woolf wrote a long article for *Political Quarterly,* "Utopia and Reality," anticipating Foucault on power, force, and violence: "The phenomenon [of Power] is not confined to the relations between states; it can be observed within states in the relation between government and individuals and between individual and individual" (167). He concludes "the attainability of the Zionist policy will depend upon whether Arabs and Jews pursue their separate interests by conflict or whether they pursue their common interests by co-operation" (178).

Woolf had the dubious honor of writing the 1941 Labour Advisory Committee on Imperial Questions Draft Report on Palestine, in which he realized "that it is not possible to reconcile promises made originally to the two communities." But he also recognized that the war had changed the equation. He tells his readers that "[t]he aim should be to establish a regime which will give time and opportunity for healing the breach and composing the difference between the two communities and which, when that has been accomplished, will make it possible for Jews and Arabs to co-operate peacefully in a self-governing Palestine." Crucially, he rejects all proposals to partition Palestine, calling it "a policy of despair and, under existing circumstances, is so desperate as to be almost inevitably disastrous." He was adamant that immigration and land sales must be reasonably restricted to preserve the Arab majority and to "safeguard the Arab cultivator and small owner" (*Letters* 428–30).

Reviewing Richard Grossman's *Palestine Mission* in 1947, just one year before the creation of the State of Israel, Woolf echoes his 1940 views, though the war, Nazi atrocities, and the violent Zionist insurgence against British control of Israel had changed the context. "Both protagonists," he tells his *Political Quarterly* readers, "are right and both wrong, and the blind, unreasoning passions with which they are both afflicted make any reasonable or civilized settlement impossible." His outrage becomes more pointed: "the self-righteous sadism of both sides and of their supporters, masquerading in the hypocritical cloak of misery, patriotism, or impartiality, is revolting" (Rev. of *Palestine Mission* 367).

In 1949, one year after the partition of Palestine, he reviews *Trial and Error: The Autobiography of Chaim Weizmann,* who by that time was the first president of the new State of Israel. What is most fascinating, however, is that Woolf in the same article reviews a new biography of Mahatma Gandhi and Gandhi's own autobiographical account of his early years. Dismissing the obvious dissimilarities between these two nationalists, Woolf sees "a remarkable resemblance in their aims, their methods, and their achievements, and reading their biographies or autobiographies fills me with the same admiration and the same melancholy and despair." Woolf praises both men and characterizes British domination of India and worldwide persecution of Jews as "unmitigated evils." He adds, "[b]ut I cannot accept the implicit assumption of these two great men that freedom and nationalism are intrinsically good and must be pursued irrespective of consequences." He ends his review unequivocally: "I do not believe that the freedom of India or of Israel is going to be of much account so long as people in either country believe that a dead or starving Muslim is of less account than a dead or starving Hindu, or that a dead or starving Arab is of less account than a dead or starving Jew" (Rev. of *Trial and Error* 84–85).

1968: AFTERMATH OF THE ARAB-ISRAELI WAR

In *Downhill all the Way*, ostensibly discussing his journey to Manchester to make a speech in his failed run for Parliament, Woolf goes off on a tangent describing zoos he has visited, including his 1957 visit to the Jerusalem zoo. He compares the ramshackle zoo and its longhaired monkeys to the "ramshackle suburb frequented by those unshaven, long-haired orthodox Jews" whose "self-conscious, self-righteous hair and orthodoxy fill [him] with despair." The monkeys, he says, "gazed at one…with the self-satisfaction of all the orthodox who have learned eternal truth from the primeval monkey, all the scribes and Pharisees who spend their lives making mountains of pernicious stupidity out of molehills of nonsense" (*Downhill* 43). He contrasts the Orthodox in Jerusalem to the energetic, more secular Israeli majority in Tel Aviv, Haifa, and Tiberias. This leads him into a page-long diatribe against what he calls "the horrifying" influence of "Orthodox Judaism" in Israeli politics, reminding him of "how much evil religion has induced human beings to do!" (44).

Woolf's tone and word choice is reminiscent of another wandering Jew, Samuel Jacoby, Woolf's most positive character in his play *The Hotel*. Asked if he believes in God, Jacoby answers, "You can't believe in the old gentleman with the beard…there are so many fools and knaves whom one can see all round one turning the world into hell that there's no point in taking the trouble to invent an invisible super-fool or super-knave in order to put the blame on him" (89). In his autobiography Woolf mocks those who believe in the "old bearded Jehovah sitting up there on Mount Sinai amid the thunder and lightning and once in three thousand years showing his backside to a favoured Moses" (*Downhill* 44). Though this language is disturbing and clearly offensive to many religious Jews, Woolf at the same time recognizes that "the books which we call *Job*, *Ecclesiastes*, and *Micah* had laid the foundations of a civilized morality and a sceptical, rational theism" that would in time become "'the religion of all sensible men'—agnosticism or atheism" (44).

In *Journey, not the Arrival*, Woolf provides a more detailed account of his 1957 visit to Israel, conceding that his early dream of a united Palestine has given way to late 20th century *realpolitik*. "When the Jewish National Home and hundreds of thousands of Jews had been established in Palestine, when Hitler was killing millions of Jews in Europe, when the independent sovereign state of Israel had been created, when the Arabs proclaimed their intention of destroying Israel and the Israelis, Zionism and anti-Zionism had become irrelevant" (186). The kibbutzim impress him, and he sees the Israeli attitude toward Nazareth, which has been called the Arab capital of Israel, as positive and hopeful. Woolf might not be pleased to know that today, old Nazareth, though still predominantly Arab, is now part of Greater Nazareth, ringed by the ever-encroaching Jewish suburban development.

A letter to the editor of *The Times* dated March 25, 1968 and subsequent letters to former Archbishop of Canterbury, Lord Fisher, provide the closest we come to Leonard's last word on Israel and the problem of Palestine. Lord Fisher's wife had written a letter to *The Times* in which she decries an Israeli reprisal against Arab insurgents, likening the Arabs to the French Resistance fighters of World War II. Here is Woolf's letter: "Sir, Lady Fisher of Lambeth says that the Arabs attacking Israelis from Jordan are not terrorists or saboteurs, but heroes and brave men. The act of sabotage for which the Israelis staged the reprisal (which personally I do not defend) was to blow up a bus containing children. I wonder whether the late Archbishop of Canterbury or Jesus Christ would agree with Lady Fisher of Lambeth" (*Letters* 453). In his correspondence with an irate Lord Fisher, Woolf summarizes his view of the Middle East troubles. "From the first moment of the Balfour Declaration I was against Zionism on the ground that to introduce Jews into an Arab occupied territory with the ultimate prospect of establishing an independent Jewish state would lead to racial trouble" (*Letters* 454). In subsequent letters, the eighty-seven-year-old Leonard Woolf demonstrates a keen understanding of the complex and terrible situation between Arabs and Israelis, the new realities wrought by the Holocaust, and the "enormous increase in the Israeli population," adding "there is now an established Israeli state with a large and immensely energetic population." In one of my favorite Leonard Woolf moments, he quotes New Testament scripture to the Archbishop, reminding him of Christ's "uncompromising attitude towards violence and cruelty" (*Letters* 455). Though Woolf was, in the end, a strong defender of Israel, he saw both Arabs and Jews as Semitic protagonists, and he was deeply saddened that a homeland for some descendants of Abraham has meant exile for others. Woolf cuts off the seven-month correspondence with "I think that for anyone anywhere at any time to shoot a policeman in the back or kill a child because he is acting for his own country and homeland when it is under the heel of a conqueror is unjustifiable and morally wrong. The end does not justify the means" (*L* 457–58). As debates over sanctions rage, as rockets rain down on Israeli cities, and as the death toll in Gaza mounts, we realize just how prescient Leonard Woolf had been.

Works Cited

Glendinning, Victoria. *Leonard Woolf: A Biography.* New York: Free Press, 2006.

McMurtrie, Beth. "Controversial MLA Resolution on Israel Fails to Get Enough Votes to Pass." *Chronicle of Higher Education*, June 4, 2014.

Rose, Norman. *Chaim Weizmann: A Biography.* New York: Viking, 1986.

Schneer, Jonathan. *The Balfour Declaration: The Origins of the Arab-Israeli Conflict.* New York: Random House, 2010.

Schröder, Leena Kane. "Tales of Abjection and Miscegenation: Virginia Woolf's and Leonard Woolf's 'Jewish' Stories." *Twentieth Century Literature* 49.3 (2003): 298–327.

Wegener, Susan. "Processing Prejudice: Writing Woolf's Jewish World." 24th Annual International Conference on Virginia Woolf, Chicago, June 7, 2014.

Woolf, Leonard. "Article XXII." *The New Statesman* 1 May 1920. 94–95.

——. *Beginning Again: An Autobiography of the Years 1911–1918.* New York: Harcourt Brace, 1964.

——. "Comments." Editorial. *The New Statesman* 17 Nov. 1917. 145–48.

——. *Downhill All the Way: An Autobiography of the Years 1919 to 1939.* London: Hogarth Press, 1967.

——. Rev. of *England and Palestine*, by Norman Bentwich. *Political Quarterly* 3.2 (April 1932): 298–300.

——. *The Hotel.* 1939. New York: Dial Press, 1963.

——. *The Journey not the Arrival Matters: An Autobiography of the Years 1939 to 1969*. London: Hogarth Press, 1969.

——. *Letters of Leonard Woolf*. Ed. Frederic Spotts. London: Weidenfeld and Nicolson, 1989.

——. Rev. of *Palestine Mission*, by Richard Crossman. *Political Quarterly* 18.4 (Oct. 1947): 367.

——. "Three Jews." 1917. *Virginia Woolf Bulletin* 5 (September 2000). 4–11.

——. Rev. of *Trial and Error: The Autobiography of Chaim Weizmann*, and *Mahatma Gandhi*, by H.S.L. Polak, H.N. Brailsford, and Lord Pethick-Lawrence, and *The Story of My Experiments with Truth*, by M. K. Gandhi. *Political Quarterly* 20.3 (July 1949): 284–85.

——. "Utopia and Reality." *Political Quarterly* 11.2 (April-June 1940): 167–82.

Woolf, Virginia. *The Diary of Virginia Woolf*. Ed. Anne Olivier Bell. 5 vols. San Diego: Harcourt Brace Jovanovich, 1977–84.

——. *Three Guineas*. 1938. San Diego: Harcourt Brace Jovanovich, 1966.

Animal and Natural Worlds

"AND THE DONKEY BRAYS": DONKEYS AT WORK IN VIRGINIA WOOLF

by Elizabeth Hanna Hanson

In summer 2012, when Pamela Caughie and I were proofreading transcriptions of the essays to be included in Woolf Online, I noticed something peculiar. "What is it with Virginia Woolf and donkeys?" I asked. In seemingly every essay we encountered, there was a donkey. And once we started noticing them, they were everywhere. My inbox was soon brimful of emails from Pamela reporting new donkey sightings. Woolf may not have written a novel without one, to say nothing of the hundreds of references scattered throughout her letters, diaries, and essays. The question, once we were confronted with this wealth of examples, became what to do with them. So what is it with Virginia Woolf and donkeys?

In *A Room of One's Own* (1929), Woolf's narrator describes how receiving an income of five hundred pounds a year from her aunt relieved her of the burden of making her "living by cadging odd jobs from newspapers, by reporting a donkey show here or a wedding there" (37). Oddly, Woolf never quite seems to have left the donkey show behind. With the recent emergence of animal studies, scholars have examined her literary treatments of companion species such as dogs and horses, as well as reptiles, amphibians, and insects. No one, however, has yet given sustained attention to donkeys.

Like dogs and horses, donkeys are companion animals but with a different connotation for human observers. We map a certain dignity and grace onto horses, while donkeys serve a traditionally comic function in literature. While the donkey is a figure of toil—particularly for Woolf—it is also a figure of fun. It bears both of these associations vividly in *Between the Acts* (1941), as I will explore in this paper. Like horses, donkeys faced increasing obsolescence as working animals in the modernist period, given the spread of automobiles and other motorized vehicles. Yet it is in their labor that they most often inhabit Woolf's imagination through hundreds of mentions in her writing in all genres. Woolf associates their work with the work of the writer—but generally the less significant, more difficult work, the work less facilitated by ease and inspiration.

Jane Marcus writes in her essay "No More Horses: Virginia Woolf on Art and Propaganda" that Woolf distinguishes between art and propaganda by distinguishing between the "donkey work" of pamphleteers and the "thoroughbred" work of the artist. While Caughie has critiqued Marcus's essay for accepting this distinction as stable and non-contradictory (115–16), Marcus's characterization of Woolf's longstanding distinction between "donkey-work" and "galloping" is useful for clarifying the function of Woolf's donkeys: Marcus regards this distinction as the successor to Woolf's earlier distinction between "'stonebreaking' and 'flying'; writing was to her always divided into two categories, one of hard work and one of speed and release" (154). The opposition between "galloping" and "donkey work" also suggests an opposition between leisure and labor, writing that is pleasurable and writing that is financially necessary for the writer. Although Woolf generally uses "donkey work" as a somewhat dismissive term, I would like to examine "donkey work" of a different kind here—the work that the ubiquitous donkey does in Woolf's writing.

Throughout Woolf's work, donkeys function as figures of humor, ordinariness, or suffering and their often peripheral placement is itself significant. We have no counterpart to *Flush* (1933) in which the donkey's consciousness takes on narrative centrality, but that is precisely the point. The nature of donkey-work, in both of the senses in which I am using it, almost precludes the donkey from being the center of attention. What we have instead is a wealth of passing references. Orlando leaves Constantinople on a donkey and "could not endure to see a donkey beaten or a kitten drowned" (*O* 140, 189). In *The Voyage Out* (1915), a seasick Rachel "had just enough consciousness to suppose herself a donkey on the summit of a moor in a hailstorm, with its coat blown into furrows" (71). Woolf's donkeys are never central; rather, they are pervasively marginal. In the interest of space, I will focus my attention in the remainder of this paper on Woolf's donkeys as they appear in several of her essays and *Between the Acts*.

My initial donkey sightings with Pamela were in the essays Woolf was writing concurrent with the composition of *To the Lighthouse* (1927). Woolf opens the 1926 version of "How Should One Read a Book?" with the observation that many houses contain a space explicitly dedicated to books, then encourages readers to picture themselves in such a space and to envision it as "a sunny room, with windows opening on a garden, so that we can hear the trees rustling, the gardener talking, the donkey braying, the old women gossiping at the pump—and all the ordinary processes of life pursuing the casual irregular way which they have pursued these many hundreds of years. As casually, as persistently, books have been coming together on the shelves" (32). The donkey here is part of "the ordinary processes of life," "casual and irregular," forming part of the background noise to the act of reading. As in Woolf's references to "donkey work," the donkey is distinct, separate, and exterior to literary art but never too remote from it. Indeed, Woolf's analogy draws a parallel between the braying donkey's everyday existence, presumably one of farm labor, and the gradual accumulation of literary tradition. Woolf develops the donkey's role in this tradition in greater detail in *Between the Acts*.

In the introduction to *Victorian Photographs of Famous Men and Fair Women by Julia Margaret Cameron*, Woolf again portrays the donkey's labor as supporting literary endeavors, this time the famous prolixity of the Victorians. Here the donkey is more visible as working than as distracting the reader in the way it does in "How Should One Read a Book?" Both roles are central to the donkey's function, however. Describing Cameron's epistolary excess, Woolf writes, "Volume after volume was despatched through the penny post. She wrote letters till the postman left, and then she began her postscripts. She sent the gardener after the postman, the gardener's boy after the gardener, the donkey galloping all the way to Yarmouth after the gardener's boy" (Introduction). Although donkey work is once again exterior to the creative element of writing, it is essential—humorously so—to the successful transmission of that writing. To be read, Cameron's postscripts must reach the postman, which depends on the speed of the donkey. Reinforcing this association, Julia Margaret Cameron recurs in Woolf's play *Freshwater*, which Woolf described in her diary as "a donkeys work," even going so far as to rent a donkey head to wear when she took her curtain call (*AWD* 229).

Woolf provides the fullest picture of the relationship between the donkey and the literary tradition in *Between the Acts*. The novel features three donkeys, all artificial in some way and all embedded in literary productions. The first is the subject of a fable that Bartholomew recalls and has a typically didactic aspect. The second, comprised of two people in a costume, appears in the pageant. The third is wholly a product of Isa's poetic imagination.

As the characters wait for the pageant to begin and sit wondering about the content of Miss La Trobe's play, Mrs. Swithin remarks that "there's the whole of English literature to choose from." Reflecting on the enormity of this choice, she describes the way she spends rainy days enumerating what she has and hasn't read, with books scattered on the floor around her. Bartholomew then likens her to "the pig in the story; or was it a donkey?" Isa clarifies the comparison: "The donkey who couldn't choose between hay and turnips and so starved" (*BTA* 59). Placed in the context of this comparison, the donkey embodies the anxiety that characterizes the modernist relationship to the enormity of the literary canon. It finds itself paralyzed with indecision when confronted with the task of selection.

Mrs. Swithin's predicament—and the donkey's—bear an uncanny resemblance to the one that Woolf frames at the beginning in "How Should One Read a Book?": "Now, one may well ask oneself…how am I to read these books? What is the right way to set about it? They are so many and so various. My appetite is so fitful and so capricious. What am I to do to get the utmost possible pleasure out of them? And is it pleasure, or profit, or what is it that I should seek?" (32). If we substituted hay and turnips for books, this set of questions might just as well belong to the donkey. Re-imagining reading as eating allows the human reader to enter, in a limited way, into the donkey's world, where the choice of the most desirable kind of food holds more sway than the choice of a mode of reading.

The image of the donkey starving in spite of the abundance around it is not the only image of a donkey in distress that Isa has at her disposal, however. She feels the same sort of historical and literary belatedness as Mrs. Swithin, returning to the same metaphor of excess as she walks alone before the Victorian playlet begins, finally coming to the pear tree in the stable yard, which "was weighted with hard green pears. Fingering one of them she murmured: 'How am I burdened with what they drew from the earth; memories; possessions. This is the burden that the past laid on me, last little donkey in the long cara-vanserai crossing the desert. "Kneel down," said the past. "Fill your pannier from our tree. Rise up, donkey. Go your way till your heels blister and your hoofs crack"'" (*BTA* 155). The donkey that Isa recalled from the story was fatally unable to act when confronted with an excess of food. Here, a similar excess becomes a burden for the donkey. It carries the unripe, inedible fruits of the literary past with no indication that it will have the opportu-nity to enjoy them. In the same way, Isa recites poetry to herself as a sort of solace, but it goes largely unheard, and her loneliness and discontentment remain. Isa's image also calls attention to what Woolf obscures in her myriad references to "donkey work:" the *physical* difficulty, even the acute pain, that the donkey's prescribed work causes it. The implica-tion of donkey work, for the donkey, is suffering. Isa makes us aware of the downside of this labor and of the possibility of failure: there is no end in sight and at some point, the donkey simply may not be able to go on—a possibility that serves as a sobering reminder of the novel's historical moment.

But Isa still sees value in persistence. As the audience returns to their seats on the terrace, "She encourage[s] herself. 'On, little donkey, patiently stumble. Hear not the frantic cries of the leaders who in that they seek to lead desert us. Nor the chatter of china faces glazed and hard. Hear rather the shepherd, coughing by the farmyard wall; the withered tree that sighs when the Rider gallops; the brawl in the barrack room when they stripped her naked; or the cry which in London when I thrust the window open someone cries…'" (*BTA* 156). Isa separates the donkey from the dominant political discourse of the day, directing its attention instead to scenes of everyday reality, as well as this reality's attendant violence. The work of the donkey is the difficult work of engaging with fact.

The donkey's persistence in its task depends on its indifference to the rhetoric of authority, and part of its work in *Between the Acts* consists in subverting that authority. The third donkey in the novel appears in Miss La Trobe's pageant. By its placement there, it participates again in questions of the efficacy and the purpose of literary tradition. The pageant, of course, is acted with the war close at hand—in the newspapers, in the conversations of the audience, and in the twelve airplanes overhead that drown out Mr. Streatfield's attempt to sum up and make sense of the pageant. The pageant donkey, comprised of Albert "the village idiot" and another unnamed actor, suggests how the donkey as a hardworking minor participant in official literary productions can destabilize or disrupt them. Interrupting Mr. Hardcastle's prayer during the Victorian playlet, "the hindquarters of the donkey, represented by Albert the idiot, became active. Intentional was it, or accidental? 'Look at the donkey! Look at the donkey!' A titter drowned Mr. Hardcastle's prayer," and at the end of the scene, "[t]he donkey was captured; hampers were loaded; and forming into a procession, the picnickers began to disappear over the hill" (*BTA* 171). Woolf leaves unresolved the question of whether this moment of levity *is* intentional or accidental, although the necessity of capturing the donkey suggests some improvisation on Albert's part. In what Christopher Ames calls Woolf's "most explicitly carnivalesque novel" (394), we see a mingling of high and low, of serious and comic discourses, and a subversion of authoritative tradition. The donkey's posterior, played by Albert, upstages the scripted reverence for the sacred meant to receive a privileged place in Mr. Hardcastle's prayer.

The other half of the donkey also disorders familiar hierarchies at the end of the play in the midst of a more general jumbling of literary history: "The actors were reluctant to go. They lingered; they mingled. There was Budge the policeman talking to old Queen Bess. And the Age of Reason hobnobbed with the foreparts of the donkey. […] Each still acted the unacted part conferred on them by their clothes. Beauty was on them. Beauty revealed them" (*BTA* 195–196). For Woolf, beauty resides in this scene of carnivalesque instability, and like the idiot—as William Dodge says—the donkey is "in the tradition" (111). Its humble labor and its potential to shock, offend, or disrupt are integral to literature, as Woolf suggests in the revised version of "How Should One Read a Book?" that appears in the *Second Common Reader*. She emphasizes the merits of "rubbish-reading" as well as familiarity with canonical literature, likening this sort of reading to taking a refreshing look out of the library window:

> How stimulating the scene is, in its unconsciousness, its irrelevance, its perpetual movement—the colts galloping round the field, the woman filling her pail at the well, the donkey throwing back his head and emitting his long, acrid moan. The

greater part of any library is nothing but the record of such fleeting moments in the lives of men, women, and donkeys. Every literature, as it grows old, has its rubbish-heap, its record of vanished moments and forgotten lives told in faltering and feeble accents that have perished. But if you give yourself up to the delight of rubbish-reading you will be surprised, indeed you will be overcome, by the relics of human life that have been cast out to moulder. (*CR2* 239)

As Woolf develops this idea, she tellingly discards the "fleeting moments in the lives of donkeys" in favor of "the relics of human life that have been cast out to moulder," as she also shifts from "looking out" to a different kind of reading. Even amidst ephemeral and noncanonical material, the donkey is peripheral. This difference also gives us occasion to remember that the donkey is first and foremost a donkey, not a convenient metaphor.

Jamie Johnson has described how Woolf decenters human subjectivity through the nonhuman animal in *Flush* by drawing attention to the animal perspective in human-animal relationships and to the perspective of the nonhuman animal in itself (34). Is it possible to read Woolf's donkeys against anthropomorphism, or at least as exposing the tendency to anthropomorphism? Doing so is difficult, and I have certainly failed at points in this paper. The donkey, as donkey, has no interest in literature. Its perception of "donkey work" is of the weight of whatever burden is laid upon its back or the speed at which its rider makes it run to catch the gardener's boy. Most of the roles in which Woolf places donkeys, in fact, are those of subservience to human demands, and it is rare for her to bring into focus how the donkey as donkey experiences those roles. Woolf's metaphor of "donkey work" does serve to remind us of writing as working *for* someone or some-thing—whether willingly or grudgingly—persisting in the hard work of writing out of necessity. The donkey has its place *in* the literary tradition, but it can also make us aware of the power relations that have made that tradition possible.

Works Cited

Ames, Christopher. "Carnivalesque Comedy in *Between the Acts*." *Twentieth Century Literature* 44.4 (1998): 394–408. *JSTOR*. Web. 4 June 2014.

Caughie, Pamela L. *Virginia Woolf and Postmodernism: Literature in Quest & Question of Itself*. Urbana: U of Illinois P, 1991.

Johnson, Jamie. "Virginia Woolf's *Flush*: Decentering Human Subjectivity through the Nonhuman Animal Character." *Virginia Woolf Miscellany* 84 (2013): 34–36. Web. 8 May 2014.

Marcus, Jane. "No More Horses: Virginia Woolf on Art and Propaganda." *Critical Essays on Virginia Woolf*. Ed. Morris Beja. Boston: G.K. Hall, 1985. 152–71.

Woolf, Virginia. *Between the Acts*. San Diego: Harcourt Brace Jovanovich, 1941.

——. "How Should One Read a Book?" *The Second Common Reader*. 1932. New York: Harcourt, Brace Jovanovich, 1960. 234–45.

——. "How Should One Read a Book?" 1926. *Yale Review* 16: 32–44. *Woolf Online*. Web. 18 Aug. 2014.

——. Introduction. *Victorian Photographs of Famous Men and Fair Women by Julia Margaret Cameron*. Hogarth, 1926. *Woolf Online*. Web. 15 Aug. 2014.

——. *Orlando: A Biography*. 1928. Orlando, FL: Harcourt, 1956.

——. *A Room of One's Own*. 1929. New York: Harcourt Brace Jovanovich. 1957.

——. *The Voyage Out*. 1915. New York: George H. Doran, 1920.

——. *A Writer's Diary: Being Extracts from the Diary of Virginia Woolf*. Ed. Leonard Woolf. New York: Harcourt, 1954, 1982.

Companion Creatures: "Dogmanity" in *Three Guineas*

by Vicki Tromanhauser

Dogs have played such an integral part in human cultural history that the eighteenth-century novelist Hugh Walpole thought our species might more accurately be dubbed "dogmanity," so inseparable is our evolution from that of canines (qtd. in McHugh 171). As Susan McHugh explains in *Dog*, the *Canis familiaris* is ubiquitous in human communities: dogs' ready availability, remarkable adaptability to extreme conditions, loyalty, and tractability explain their prominence in human households, exploration, and scientific research (171–72). Yet that co-evolutionary story has not been without its tensions. We might remember the turmoil of the Brown Dog Riots in London around that watershed year 1910, when a brown terrier that had been the cruel victim of vivisection in the laboratories of University College gained public sympathy and, temporarily, a memorial statue in Battersea Park (McHugh 138–89; Goldman 60–3). Before its removal, the statue, with a fountain for humans and dogs, attracted a surprising coalition of defenders, including suffragists, organized male workers, and animal welfare advocates, all united in their opposition to the torture of one species for the sake of another's epistemological quest. We might read in the efforts of this impromptu coalition to preserve the short-lived statue early evidence of Woolf's Outsider's Society.

Drawing upon the work of Marshall McLuhan, Tom Tyler argues that "the dog was, originally, a primordial technology that functioned as an extension of human capacities and thereby made possible a whole new way of life" (76). In the laboratory as in the household, humanity has looked to dogs as prostheses, sensory and perceptual technologies through which it might extend its awareness or enlarge its scope of action. In much the same way, *Three Guineas* (1938) shows us how the sisters and daughters of educated men have been cultivated to flourish alongside and to support their male companions. The woman as pet functions as property to shore up the privileged position of a solitary master, a symbolic prosthetic or supplement to the at once masculine and humanistic project of self-definition, esteem, and empowerment.

The nation's somewhat embarrassed reliance on a female labor force during the First World War provoked a misogynistic backlash in the daily papers that Woolf takes pains to document. Applauding women for their "splendid service," without which England might not have proven victorious, one male commentator in the *Daily Telegraph* (January 20, 1936) nevertheless quips that women "were praised and petted out of all proportion to the value of their performances" (qtd. in *TG* 62). The heroic wonder dog in the hour of need becomes no more than a pampered pooch in peacetime.

Yet we need not conceive of such canine technologies solely as a means to augment or enhance human aptitudes and abilities, but instead they can help us to better discern our "default" and "implicitly human mode of apprehension," to perceive our own unnoticed or invisible environments more clearly (Tyler 72). By supplementing feminine perceptual powers with canine aptitudes, Woolf introduces a counterpoint, or even counterenvironment, that works to challenge both masculine and human perceptual norms, what Tyler calls the "unacknowledged perceptual anthroponormativity" that structures our cultural life, our awareness, and our actions (Tyler 72). The particular kind of self-reflection that comes from Woolf's canine perspectivism, her cultural study of dogmanity, might serve as a way of "reminding us that a human point of view is but one immersed, subjective perspective amongst many" (Tyler 77).

Flush (1933), of course, provides Woolf's fullest excursion into a canine world saturated with smells. But five years later *Three Guineas* represents the alterity of female subjective experience for English gentlemen by reproducing a doggy phenomenal world. Women are honorary dogs, domestic animals who must watch the procession of male professionals from the threshold of the private house, or "traps[e] along at the tail end" (*TG* 74), and who have grown tired of, in the words of one 19th-century governess, the "dog trot way of sewing, teaching, writing copies, and washing dishes every day" (*TG* 92). *Three Guineas* generates a virtual experience of the overlapping *Unwelten* (or self-worlds) of the dog and the woman, simulating the shared sensory environments of women and canines. I think here of Jane Goldman's thorough tracking of canine signifiers in Woolf's prequel to *Three Guineas*, *A Room of One's Own* (1929), as a way of "refiguring...central humanist texts" and tropes, and so offering a "(feminist) *enlightening* of the Enlightenment" (Goldman 53).

The growing science of animal cognition has worked to understand dogs' special attunement to humans and their emotions, what cognitive ethologist Alexandra Horowitz describes as dogs' "attention to our attention" (Horowitz 34). It is this mutual interaction and regard that, Jeanne Dubino has shown, characterize coevolutionary stories in Woolf's fiction, the "symbiosis" or "beneficial mutualism" that inheres in the bispecies relationship at its most companionable (Dubino 151–52). I'd like to focus here on the cynomorphic elements of Woolf's critique of English patriarchy, that is, the way in which she endows her narrator with canine aptitudes in order better to navigate the fraught terrain of contemporary social life and sniff out its repressive structures. Derrida has enumerated the ways in which the Western humanistic tradition has conceived of the animal as a *zoon alogon*, a being who cannot properly reason, speak, respond, or return a gaze. Woolf's answers to her various correspondents in *Three Guineas*, in turn, invite a more responsive relationship between men and women, culture and nature, humans and their companion creatures, inspiring a curiosity about what the other animal might experience, imagine, think, or make visible to the English gentleman by returning his gaze. *Three Guineas* provides a dog's-eye view of English culture from below, whether from the bottom ranks of the British civil service or the threshold of the private house.

Woolf's argument addresses our noses as well as our eyes, presenting us with smells that might speak across gender and species borders. The sense of smell has long been connected with animals and sensuality, and through it we apprehend the "trace of our own residual animality" (Lippit 125). Smells are invisible, immersive, and ephemeral, which renders them difficult to represent or translate into language. The fleeting nature of our impressions of smell prevents us from being able to sustain thought about them long enough to record them (Lippit 122–23). We have no semiology of smell, as dogs do through their ability to track a scent. While the human nose contains around six million receptor sites for smell, the canine snout contains two-three hundred million of these receptor sites that then send information to the dog's olfactory cortex, which is forty times larger than ours (Horowitz 71–2; Bradshaw 232). As Vicki Hearne explains, "We don't have a 'sense' of scent" (Hearne 80). In *Dialectic of Enlightenment,* Horkheimer and Adorno maintain that "of all the senses, that of smell…bears clearest witness to the urge to lose oneself in and become the 'other.'…When we see we remain what we are; but when we smell we are taken over by otherness. Hence the sense of smell is considered a disgrace in civilization, the sign of lower social strata, lesser races and base animals" (*Dialectic of Enlightenment,* 184; qtd. in Lippit 123).

In *Civilization and Its Discontents* (1930), Freud turns to that maligned and forsaken sense to uncover the source of its particular "disgrace." Smells recall remote and shameful postures, a time of all fours, filth, and exposed orifices. Displacing humanity's spurned animal instincts onto its doting canine companion, Freud reads in the dog's eyes, or perhaps its snout, the history of "a phase of development that has been surmounted" (Freud 41). Freud was a man devoted to his chows, but the dog's inability to repress its olfactory and sexual instincts explains how the name of man's "most faithful friend in the animal world" has become "a term of abuse" (Freud 42). As he wrote to his colleague, the nasologist Wilhelm Fliess, the transition from dog to human meant the transition from the olfactory to the visual, and a horizontal to a vertical orientation: "upright carriage adopted, nose raised from the ground, at the same time a number of formerly interesting sensations attached to the earth becom[e] repulsive" (qtd. in Stoddart 124). When man "turns up his nose," Freud explains, "he regards himself as something noble" (qtd. in Stoddart 124).

Smells exude "atmosphere"; they pervade spaces despite our best efforts to contain and control them, much like feminine gossip, which "leaks" and spreads through the workplace so perniciously (*TG* 59). Woolf's narrator is not above such nosey methods of gathering information. Seeking what "indirect knowledge" of the professions is available to the disenfranchised female outsider sends her "peeping through doors, taking notes, and asking questions discreetly" (*TG* 61). And this exploratory strategy pitches us downward onto all fours.

By contrast with Freud, Woolf applauds "aroma" for its ability to permeate the artificial partitions of the public space that empower certain classes and species over others, while she celebrates the dog's nose as a subtle social sleuth "hazarding [its] way among imponderables" and detecting even the "most impalpable" of social forces to inhibit women's participation in the public sphere (*TG* 62, 64). Odour, or what Woolf interchangeably calls "atmosphere," "can escape the noses of examiners in examination rooms yet penetrate boards and divisions and affect the senses of those within" (*TG* 64). "Atmosphere plainly is a very mighty power. Atmosphere not only changes the sizes and shapes of things; it affects solid bodies, like salaries, which might have been thought impervious to atmosphere. An epic poem might be written about atmosphere, or a novel in ten or fifteen volumes" (*TG* 64). As a sense that travels across gender or species barriers without need of translation, and penetrates seemingly solid bodies or truths, smell affords a more honest appraisal of the fears and desires that inhibit social mixing and movement. "[B]eing unscientific," as both woman and dog, Woolf's narrator attunes us to the nuances, even poetry, of scent as a way of uncovering what Prof. Grensted calls in psychoanalytic parlance "the infantile fixation" operating at the heart of our social institutions: "We smelt it in the atmosphere; we detected its presence in Whitehall, in the universities, in the Church" (*TG* 151). Woolf associates canine sensibility and the olfactory sense with a kind of disclosure and frank communication that nourishes social life rather than retarding or hindering it (see Weil 94–6).

And as she investigates the employment records of the English Civil Service she comes flush up against "the stench of the unconscious" in all of its fecal and sexual abhorrence (Lippit 127): "there is good reason to think that the word 'Miss,' however delicious its scent in the private house, has a certain odour attached to it in Whitehall which is disagreeable to the noses on the other side of the partition; and [...] it is likely that a name to which 'Miss' is attached will, because of this odour, circle in the lower spheres where the salaries are small rather than mount to the higher spheres where the salaries are substantial" (*TG* 63–4). As Akira Lippit poignantly puts it, "repression stinks" (126). In Woolf's outsider's assessment of English culture, one of the most powerful critical faculties proves to be the olfactory, the sense explicitly shunned by Freud for its connection with animality and female menstruation. In *Civilization and Its Discontents*, Freud maintains that the progress of civilization is doubly impeded by women's inability to sublimate the jealous loves of family life and by humanity's animal origins, which must be assiduously and continually repressed. This work of "organic repression" achieves the tenuous separation of the human from the animal, the process by which man sloughs off the traces of his animality by adopting an upright bipedal posture and thus resists the seductions of the

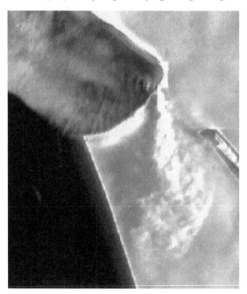

genital and olfactory instincts that continue to govern the world of man's most affectionate beast (Freud 41–2; see Rohman 23–4). The repression of the olfactory coincides with the "taboo on menstruation," so that smell in Freud's anthropological story is connected with animality, sexuality, and sexual difference—the very forces that oppose the interests of civilization (Freud 41). Dogs may not shun their shit, but the "male psyche," he tells us, turns its nose up at women's menstruation, which stinks of "abandoned sexual zones" and the life of the creature tied to its environment (Freud 41; qtd. in Stoddart 124).

And so the "odour thickens" (*TG* 63). If the aroma of "Miss" appears "disagreeable" to the male nostrils in Whitehall, the smell of "Mrs." proves so positively repulsive that not a single married woman appears in its records of

Figure 1: Schlieren image showing the aerodynamics of canine olfaction, reproduced with permission of Springer Publishing

employment (*TG* 64). "As for 'Mrs.,'" Woolf admonishes, "the less said about that word the better. Such is the smell of it, so rank does it stink in the nostrils of Whitehall, that Whitehall excludes it entirely" (*TG* 64).

By training her readers to recognize the interdependency of all life forms that she saw in the politics, economy, and science of her moment, Woolf begins to correct what she found "still so inveterately anthropocentric" in the prevailing cultural ideology (*TG* 172). She cautions readers that "we are sniffing most delicately not facts but savours. And therefore it would be well not to depend on our own private noses" (*TG* 62). Woolf promotes the collective mentality of the pack over the singular perspective of the individual, advancing a cooperative sensibility that characterizes what for Donna Haraway is critical to companionability among species: "we are in a knot of species coshaping one another in layers of reciprocating complexity all the way down. Response and respect are possible only in those knots, with actual animals and people looking back at each other, sticky with all their muddled histories" (42). In fact these knotty and sticky textures shape much of our experience of reading *Three Guineas*: becoming mired in detail, ensnared in extended quotations from Woolf's manifold sources, or entangled in lengthy and digressive footnotes. Such textual knots are partly what has proved so maddening to generations of the text's readers, but are also so crucial to a strategy that promotes inter-species companionability. We cannot trust our own nose, or angle of vision, alone, for "though we look at the same things, we see them differently" (*TG* 7). Appreciating differences of aptitude among species while recognizing interests shared across them is essential to what Haraway calls "companion species" relationships and requires that we learn to live "intersectionally" (Haraway 18).

If it is through sight that "we remain what we are," then smell affords an opportunity to alter our mental and perceptual constitution. Woolf's narrator wagers, "if people are highly successful in their professions, they lose their senses. Sight goes. They have no time to look at pictures. Sound goes. They have no time to listen to music. Speech goes. They have no time for conversation. They lose their sense of proportion—the relation between one thing and another. Humanity goes. [...] What remains of a human being who has lost sight, and sound, and sense of proportion? Only a cripple in a cave" (*TG* 87–88). In one sense, we might read *Three Guineas* as a text that is especially anxious about the difficulty of remaining human in the aggressive climate of late '30s Europe. In a world that bombards us with disturbing images of the human form distorted beyond all recognition—whether in the mutilated bodies of "dead children" in the Spanish Civil War photographs or in the figure of the Führer unnaturally cased in uniform in Woolf's imaginary portrait—Woolf repeatedly asks how we are to "remain civilized human beings" (91). But if we take a different angle, if we look with Woolf's cynomorphic narrator from a different point of view, we might see *Three Guineas* as a text that actively promotes our human disorientation, inviting us to crouch for a moment with the cripple in a cave. This seemingly debilitated creatural posture, this abject state of cultural and ontological privation, is a potentially productive one precisely *because* it demolishes our sense of proportion and undoes our confidence in the right "relation between one thing and another." Woolf's argument thus estranges us from our habitual modes of knowing and presents us with other means by which we might sense the world.

Three Guineas entreats female readers to cast off the chain of submission, to resist "seductions to bribe you into captivity" (97), lest such jingoistic and imperial values as "For God and the Empire" "be written, like the address on a dog-collar, round your neck" (*TG* 85). But it also asks women not to forget their canine training, to celebrate the values that derive from the unpaid-for, informal education women receive to render them fit companions for worldly men: humility, the rejection of egotism and recognition, and a "lack of rights and privileges" (*TG* 94)—in short, an ontology predicated upon privation that, as Derrida argues, has similarly dogged the nonhuman animal in the Western intellectual tradition.

Our excessive reliance upon our visual senses can paralyze, freezing us like a rabbit caught in the glare of a headlamp; it literally captivates us. We have good reason to distrust this vertical orientation and the social hierarchies that accompany it. I'd like to suggest that alongside the text's celebrated photographs, whether featured or described, Woolf attempts to provide us with a kind of smell-ograph—a way of knowing through the nose. Cognitive scientists have recently employed special photographic technology to represent the topography of the dog's olfactory world. Its imaging techniques (see Fig. 1) allow researchers to track "air flow in order to detect when, and how, dogs are sniffing" (Horowitz 69–70).

So in closing, I'd like to invite you to read my favorite photograph in *Three Guineas* (see Fig. 2) as a smell-ograph of sorts and to decipher its rank information. The seasoned sniffer might notice that the heralds' trumpets resemble a proboscis yearning to sniff the horse that wittily turns its rear-end on the elaborate pageantry that celebrates masculine humanist authority. A fuller appreciation of our dogmanity requires us to give more sustained attention to the dog's attention.

Figure 2: HERALDS (*TG* 29).

Works Cited

Bradshaw, John. *In Defence of Dogs: Why Dogs Need Our Understanding*. London: Allen Lane, 2011.

Dubino, Jeanne. "The Bispecies Environment, Coevolution, and *Flush*." *Contradictory Woolf: Selected Papers from the Twenty-first Annual International Conference on Virginia Woolf*. Eds. Derek Ryan and Stella Bolaki. Clemson, SC: Clemson U Digital P, 2012. 150–58.

Freud, Sigmund. 1930. *Civilization and Its Discontents*. Trans. David McLintock. London: Penguin, 2002.

Goldman, Jane. "Who Let the Dogs Out? Samuel Johnson, Thomas Carlyle, Virginia Woolf and the Little Brown Dog." *Virginia Woolf's Bloomsbury, Volume 2: International Influence and Politics*. Ed. Lisa Shahriari and Gina Potts. Basingstoke: Palgrave Macmillan, 2010. 46–65.

Haraway, Donna. *When Species Meet*. Minneapolis: U of Minnesota P, 2008.

Hearne, Vicki. *Adam's Task: Calling Animals by Name*. New York: Knopf, 1986.

Horkheimer, Max, and Theodor W. Adorno. *Dialectic of Enlightenment*. Trans. John Cumming. New York: Continuum, 1972.

Horowitz, Alexandra. *Inside of a Dog: What Dogs See, Smell, and Know*. New York: Scribner, 2009.

Lippit, Akira Mizuta. *Electric Animal: Toward a Rhetoric of Wildlife*. Minneapolis: U of Minnesota P, 2000.

McHugh, Susan. *Dog*. London: Reaktion Books, 2004.

Rohman, Carrie. *Stalking the Subject: Modernism and the Animal*. New York: Columbia UP, 2009.

Stoddart, D. Michael. *The Scented Ape: The Biology and Culture of Human Odour*. Cambridge: Cambridge UP, 1990.

Tyler, Tom. "New Tricks." *Angelaki* 18.1 (2013): 65–82.

Weil, Kari. *Thinking Animals: Why Animal Studies Now?* New York: Columbia UP, 2012.

Woolf, Virginia. *Three Guineas*. 1938. Annot. and intro. Jane Marcus. Orlando, FL: Harcourt, 2006.

Virginia Woolf's Object-Oriented Ecology

by Elsa Högberg

The title of this paper might sound odd, given Virginia Woolf's critique of realism and its privileging of an external object world over the life of the mind. What would the term object-oriented have to do with the writer who claimed that life is "not a series of gig lamps," but "a luminous halo" (*E4* 160)? And how does this relate to ecology? I will begin with Diana Swanson's question in her keynote address during the 2010 conference *Virginia Woolf and the Natural World*: "can Woolf offer insights and approaches useful to us as we grapple with the ecological crisis of the 21st century" (24)?

Swanson, Justyna Kostkowska and Bonnie Kime Scott are among the scholars who have discussed that question, attending to Woolf's work from an ecocritical and eco-feminist perspective. They all highlight her unsettling of binaries such as subject/object, human/non-human, masculine/feminine, and stress the contemporary relevance of her protest against political and financial systems of exploitation, systems that equate women and nature and dominate both. Ecocritical readings also tend to emphasize Woolf's cele-bration of connectivity: the capacity of human subjectivity to enter into close communion with non-human life forms. Thus Louise Westling speaks of our embeddedness in "the flesh of the world," arguing that Woolf's critique of the subject of Western philosophy inspires respect for an "ecosystem in flux" (857). An ecological humanism could be said to unite most ecocritical and ecofeminist readings of Woolf, a stance that foregrounds hu-man responsibility for the natural world.

Responsibility for an Earth community that intertwines human and non-human forms of existence is also central to the object-oriented ontology (hereafter OOO) ad-dressed recently by Graham Harman, Timothy Morton and Mark McGurl, amongst others. However, these thinkers suggest that much ecocriticism "is not thinking coex-istence deeply enough" (Morton, "Here Comes Everything" 165). They speak not of an all-embracing human communion with the non-human world, but of a flat, non-hierar-chical ontology that is also a form of realism. In Morton's words, OOO demonstrates that "real things exist" and that "there are only objects, one of which is ourselves" (165). In this ontology, human subjectivity has object-like qualities and is confronted with an indiffer-ent object world, where objects interact in unforeseeable ways that exceed consciousness. Such a worldview entails a reversal of perspectives: subject-object relations are not just suspended, but superseded by encounters between objects. In *Ecology without Nature*, Morton argues that ecocriticism tends to idealize nature in the same way patriarchy ideal-izes the figure of woman, and that a deep awareness of the current environmental crisis requires an object-oriented worldview (5). Proponents of OOO generally critique "cor-relationism"—the notion that things exist only in relation to human consciousness and language. They see correlationism in the Western philosophical tradition, in postmod-ernism specifically (McGurl, "New Cultural Geology"), and in ecocriticism that values Nature as something at once intelligible and abstract—the environment that surrounds us (Morton, *Ecology* 4–5). In all these ways, OOO is emphatically posthumanist.

What, then, does this ontology have to do with Woolf's work? McGurl suggests that modernism was the first large-scale literary manifestation of "'reflexive modernity,' when the consequences of modernization have become a source of widespread worry." Discussing waste and nuclear waste in particular, McGurl speaks of a "world risk society" where knowledge about the environmental consequences of capitalism is also a fundamental "*nonknowledge*" ("Ordinary Doom" 329). That is to say, the temporality and potentially disastrous consequences of nuclear waste are overwhelmingly real, yet impossible to understand, and processes like global warming and the storage of radioactive materials have uncontrollable and incalculable effects. While Woolf was not concerned with an environmental crisis of today's massive scale, we can detect in her writing a reflexive and arguably ecological thinking about the destructive consequences of modernity that has much in common with OOO. In her recent book, Kostkowska maintains, like Morton, that experimental texts are particularly effective in expressing ecological concerns, even when they do not deal explicitly with nature or the environment.

Following Kostkowska on this point, I propose that Woolf's foregrounding of objects exposes the threat posed by human technology between the World Wars. I suggest that the most unsettling depictions of object encounters appear in her experimental inter-war writing and *Between the Acts* (1941) because the risk of a second devastating war was very much present—real but incalculable—in the years following the Versailles Treaty. Already in 1919, Woolf's friend John Maynard Keynes warned that the peace terms would bring about a "final civil war...which will destroy, whoever is victor, the civilisation and the progress of our generation" (251). This threat grew stronger until she wrote her last novel, and the Woolfs' two London houses were demolished by German bombs while she was composing it. There is an ethical dimension to her object-oriented writing of risk and crisis: McGurl stresses that OOO does not just awaken us to "how doomed we are," but that we can become ethically conscious of our responsibility for the unforeseeable and destructive object interactions we have precipitated ("New Cultural Geology" 388). Such an ethics, I argue, can be traced notably in the "Time Passes" section of *To the Lighthouse* (1927), the interludes of *The Waves* (1931), and in *Between the Acts*.

Central to OOO is the phenomenological notion that all objects have an autonomous existence; they are "closed systems," "irreducible" and "withdrawn" in the sense that they always exceed human access and use (Morton, "Here Comes Everything" 165). Woolf's short story "Solid Objects" (1920) dramatizes precisely this irreducibility. The protagonist John finds a lump of glass that has been shaped by the sea: "it was impossible to say whether it had been a bottle, tumbler or window-pane; it was nothing but glass. [...] [I]t puzzled him" (*CSF* 103). John becomes increasingly obsessed with such objects and is haunted by their inscrutability, as when he spots a beautiful piece of china that he can barely reach with his walking stick: "John was determined to possess it; but the more he pushed, the further it receded. [...] As he seized hold of it he exclaimed in triumph. [...] But how had the piece of china been broken into this remarkable shape?" (104–05). Using them as paper weights does not help; John remains troubled by what he will never know about these objects, and even as he holds them in his hand he does not "possess" them.

Bill Brown offers an insightful reading of "Solid Objects" that addresses the links between capitalism, British wartime economics, and an instrumentalist use of objects that disregards excess. The aestheticized objects in Woolf's story, Brown claims, defy wartime practices such as the collecting of metal and fat for making bombs and explosives (16–21). Seen in contrast to such practices, Woolf's assertion that no object can ever be completely domesticated or instrumentalized takes on political significance, especially if we consider the bomb from an object-oriented viewpoint in the manner of her later text "Thoughts on Peace in an Air Raid." Completed in early September 1940, just before the beginning of the Blitz, the essay opens as follows: "The Germans were over this house last night and the night before that. Here they are again. It is a queer experience, lying in the dark and listening to the zoom of a hornet which may at any moment sting you to death" (*E6* 242). The euphemism of the hornet's sting for a threat not only to "this one body [...] but millions of bodies yet to be born" (242) highlights the incapacity of the mind to conceptualize the disasters that would be caused by exploding bombs in the months, years, and perhaps centuries to come. As Jane Goldman observes, "The deictic marker 'Here' unites reader and writer in the textual locus of a shared vulnerability," forcefully suggesting the incalculable destruction brought about by modern warfare and its mass bombing of civilians, "a new phenomenon in Woolf's era (a commonplace in ours)" (67, 64).

If the expanded temporality of Woolf's essay locates a specific air raid in a longer history of destructive object-relations, her fiction shares with OOO a concern with vast timescapes in which historical time coexists with the prehistoric and primeval. What, for instance, is the temporality of the interludes in *The Waves*, cut off as they are from the anthropocentric perspective in the soliloquies? Do they depict one day, from sunrise to sunset, or a geological time span stretching from the beginning of life on Earth[1] to, say, an imagined future when the sun has set on the British Empire?[2] Perhaps we need to situate any notion of the present in such a "bizarrely humiliating length of geologic time" (McGurl, "New Cultural Geology" 380) as soon as we begin to imagine an object world existing independently of human subjectivity. For McGurl, such efforts to think a "long now" connect literary modernism with what he calls the exomodern, a contemporary tendency in literature, criticism, and theory to depart from the correlationist perspectives of postmodernism in order to interrogate "Western modernity as a disaster" (381; "Ordinary Doom" 337–43).

Gillian Beer in particular has explored the persistence of prehistory and its ominous implications in Woolf's writing (6–28). This persistence is most unsettling in *Between the Acts*: the novel's levelling of the hierarchy distinguishing humans from beasts recalls Freud's works on aggression and war, which Woolf began to read in 1939. Most of the novel was composed in a time of crisis, when a German invasion seemed inevitable and it was generally feared that civilization was coming to an end. As Beer notes about the intrusion of primeval beasts and landscapes into the narrative present: "The *present* is *prehistory*" (18).[3] The novel conveys at once the sense of suspense before an unknown future during a June day in 1939 and the apocalyptic despair of Woolf's diary entry from June 27 the following year: "We pour to the edge of a precipice...& then? I cant conceive that there will be a 27th June 1941" (*D5* 299).

Throughout Woolf's work, the primeval manifests itself in the foregrounding of prehistoric objects such as the beast's skulls in *Jacob's Room* (1922) and *To the Lighthouse*. Theorists of OOO are similarly interested in objects that situate the present in deep time: "the obdurate rock, the dead-cold stone tak[e] center stage as....the physical evidence, in the present, of the time before life on earth, when there existed no entity to which the stone could possibly have been 'given' as an object of consciousness" (McGurl, "New Cultural

Geology" 384). The permanence of the rock, then, highlights the contingent existence of the human species, as does the following passage from *Jacob's Room*: "The rock was one of those tremendously solid brown, or rather black, rocks which emerge from the sand like something primitive. [...] [A] small boy has to stretch his legs far apart, and indeed to feel rather heroic, before he gets to the top" (5). This mode of writing encounters between the human and non-human is quite different from, and arguably less anthropocentric than, the way Woolf ascribes subjectivity to a snail in "Kew Gardens," or (human) feelings to a tree in "The Mark on the Wall" (*CSF* 89).[4] One clear difference relates to affect and mood: her writing of moments where human subjectivity merges ecstatically with non-human forms of life tends to be intensely sensual, immersing the reader in textual pleasure.

But how describe the mood of passages like the one where little Jacob is climbing a rock? It is conveyed, perhaps, in the cry of Jacob's brother Archer, who is looking for him: "The voice had an extraordinary sadness. Pure from all body [...] going out into the world, solitary, unanswered, breaking against rocks—so it sounded" (*JR* 4). The sound of Archer's voice is object-like: disembodied and withdrawn, it does not communicate except as an expression of "extraordinary sadness." This brings to mind John in "Solid Objects," whose initial childlike wonder gives way to his melancholic withdrawal from society and politics; his obsessive pursuit of inscrutable objects makes him abandon his career as a politician and live a life isolated from human contact. According to Morton, melancholia is the dominant affect of OOO, and he defines melancholia as "a mode of intimacy with strange objects that can't be digested by the subject....an object-like coexistence with other objects....The inward, withdrawn, operationally closed mood called melancholy is something we shake off at our peril in these dark ecological times" ("Here Comes Everything" 175–76).[5] If we follow Morton, then, melancholia entails an acute awareness of the reality of objects that is crucial to ecological thinking. Sanja Bahun's recent book *Modernism and Melancholia* is interesting in this respect. Bahun reads modernist aesthetic experiments as strategically melancholic; the aesthetic performance of melancholia, she claims, can be politically as well as ethically effective.[6]

The insights of Morton and Bahun can be applied, I think, to the object-oriented, melancholic mood of "Time Passes" in *To the Lighthouse*. As Ann Banfield observes about the novel's engagement with "[s]ubject and object and the nature of reality" (*TTL* 28), Woolf concurs with Bertrand Russell's epistemology in representing a world that exists independently of human perception. In this sense, "Time Passes" interrogates correlationism in the manner of OOO. Consider the following description of the wind stealing into a bedroom at night: "Here one might say to [...] those fumbling airs that breathe and bend over the bed itself, here you can neither touch nor destroy. Upon which, wearily, ghostlily, as if they had feather-light fingers [...] they would look, once, on the shut eyes and loosely clasping fingers" (*TTL* 138). What emerges here is "an object-like coexistence with other objects," to use Morton's phrase. Woolf's writing in this passage is melancholic in its treatment of human bodies as object-like, in the sense of "objectified"—vulnerable, exposed and passive—while the non-human world is given an uncanny form of being through personification. In this complete reversal of the subject-object hierarchy, the sleepers' "shut eyes" and "clasping fingers" are equated with the objects littering a house abandoned to "the insensibility of nature" (150); their fingers are touched, not touching, and their eyes are seen, not seeing. In this passage, then, the subject is revealed to be what

Morton calls "an (assemblage of) object(s) that can be acted on physically" ("Here Comes Everything" 171). Woolf makes us painfully aware that human bodies are like objects that can indeed be touched and destroyed.

What Woolf terms "the insensibility of nature" is associated with a foreboding sense of disaster. The spring is likened to a virgin, "wide-eyed and watchful and entirely careless of what was done or thought by the beholders" (*TTL* 143). Far from a romantic equation of nature and the figure of woman, Woolf's spring prefigures Prue Ramsay's death, which is reported in square brackets, contained in the text as we tend to think objects can be contained (144). Other objects in "Time Passes," tangible things, are overdetermined in that they signify more than their use value. The sounds of the war reach the empty house "like the measured blows of hammers dulled on felt, which [...] cracked the tea-cups. Now and again some glass tinkled in the cupboard [...] tumblers stood inside a cupboard vibrated too." This passage is followed by the square brackets containing the death of Andrew Ramsay in the war (145). Woolf achieves here something like an ontological equation of objects—the tinkling glasses and the deaths of the Ramsay family members—that foregrounds the catastrophe of war. This makes her writing ecological, if we read it as object-oriented. The feminized and idealized figure of Nature, central to Romantic thought as well as much contemporary ecocriticism, is distorted: "Did Nature supplement what man advanced? [...] With equal complacence she saw his misery, condoned his meanness, and acquiesced in his torture. That dream, of sharing, completing [...] was but a reflection in a mirror" (146). The garden flowers, "beholding nothing, eyeless, and so terrible" (147), are inscrutable, soulless objects that cannot be reduced to anthropocentric fantasies of nature's sympathetic relationship to human subjectivity.

The object-oriented outlook of these passages is melancholic because it dramatizes an impossible mourning of a world that has been lost: it is lost in the moment "I" realize that the world consists of withdrawing and inscrutable objects. As Morton puts it, "We have objects—they have us—under our skin. They are our skin" ("Here Comes Everything" 184). From the perspective of OOO, it is this grating sense of the reality of objects that awakens us to ecocritical awareness and responsibility. This is also an awareness that human acts tend to be object-like: insensitive and destructive, as when the imagery of birds piercing the bodies of worms in the interludes of *The Waves* appears as a metaphor of human violence in the soliloquies. In this sense, Woolf converges with McGurl's notion that an ethical responsibility for the "increasing inextricability of human and natural history" emerges from the insight that "we are the terror…insofar as 'we' are discovered to be 'nonhuman' in precisely the way a stone is—in being careless of the fate of the other" ("New Cultural Geology" 388).

Finally, in Woolf's work, this posthumanist ontology calls for humility and responsibility in a time of crisis; her radical foregrounding of objects exposes the human imprint in those uncontrollable forces of the inter-war years that engendered an apocalyptic sense of the end of civilization. In highlighting the destructive and unforeseeable consequences of modernity, Woolf's object-oriented realism proves relevant for our contemporary, globalized world as a risk society threatened by environmental collapse.

Notes

1. The opening interlude in *The Waves* alludes to Genesis, Ch. 1.
2. See Marcus (155).
3. Beer observes that June 1939 emerges in *Between the Acts* as "the prehistory to a coming war which…may mark the end of this society" (18).
4. Kostkowska (12–28), Scott (154) and Swanson (30–33) cite these stories as examples of Woolf's effort to imagine non-human subjectivity, which they see as central to her ecological thought.
5. Morton cites "Time Passes" in his discussion of melancholy ("Here Comes Everything" 175).
6. Bahun argues that Andrei Bely, Franz Kafka and Woolf made deliberate use of the symptom-concept of melancholia, which is "not simply an escapist frame of mind, but a dual phenomenon with specific resonances and repercussions in the public sphere" (4).

Works Cited

Bahun, Sanja. *Modernism and Melancholia: Writing as Countermourning.* New York: Oxford UP, 2014.

Banfield, Ann. *The Phantom Table: Woolf, Fry, Russell and the Epistemology of Modernism.* Cambridge: Cambridge UP, 2000.

Beer, Gillian. *Virginia Woolf: The Common Ground. Essays by Gillian Beer.* Edinburgh: Edinburgh UP, 1996.

Brown, Bill. "The Secret Life of Things (Virginia Woolf and the Matter of Modernism)." *Modernism/Modernity* 6.2 (1999): 1–28.

Goldman, Jane. "Virginia Woolf and the Aesthetics of Modernism." *The History of British Women's Writing, 1920–1945.* Ed. Maroula Joannou. Basingstoke, UK: Palgrave Macmillan, 2013. 57–77.

Keynes, John Maynard. *The Economic Consequences of the Peace.* 1919. London: Macmillan, 1920.

Kostkowska, Justyna. *Ecocriticism and Women Writers: Environmentalist Poetics of Virginia Woolf, Jeanette Winterson, and Ali Smith.* Basingstoke, UK: Palgrave Macmillan, 2013.

Marcus, Jane. "Britannia Rules *The Waves.*" *Decolonizing Tradition: New Views of Twentieth-Century 'British' Literary Canons.* Ed. Karen R. Lawrence. Urbana: U of Illinois P, 1992. 136–62.

McGurl, Mark. "Ordinary Doom: Literary Studies in the Waste Land of the Present." *New Literary History* 41.2 (2010): 329–49.

———. "The New Cultural Geology." *Twentieth Century Literature* 57.3/4 (2011): 380–90.

Morton, Timothy. *Ecology without Nature: Rethinking Environmental Aesthetics.* Cambridge: Harvard UP, 2007.

———. "Here Comes Everything: The Promise of Object-Oriented Ontology." *Qui Parle: Critical Humanities and Social Sciences* 19.2 (2011): 163–90.

Scott, Bonnie Kime. *In the Hollow of the Wave: Virginia Woolf and Modernist Uses of Nature.* Charlottesville: U of Virginia P, 2012.

Swanson, Diana L. "'The Real World': Virginia Woolf and Ecofeminism." *Virginia Woolf and the Natural World: Selected Papers from the Twentieth Annual International Conference on Virginia Woolf.* Ed. Kristin Czarnecki and Carrie Rohman. Clemson, SC: Clemson U Digital P, 2011. 24–34.

Westling, Louise. "Virginia Woolf and the Flesh of the World." *New Literary History* 30.4 (1999): 855–75.

Woolf, Virginia. *Between the Acts.* 1941. Ed. Frank Kermode. Oxford: Oxford UP, 2008.

———. *The Complete Shorter Fiction of Virginia Woolf.* Ed. Susan Dick. Orlando, FL: Harcourt, 1989.

———. *The Diary of Virginia Woolf.* Vol. 5. Ed. Anne Olivier Bell. New York: Harcourt Brace Jovanovich, 1984.

———. *The Essays of Virginia Woolf.* Ed. Andrew McNeillie and Stuart N. Clarke. 6 vols. London: Hogarth, 1986–2011.

———. *Jacob's Room.* 1922. Ed. and intro. Sue Roe. London: Penguin, 1992.

———. *To the Lighthouse.* 1927. London: Penguin, 1992.

———. *The Waves.* 1931. Ed. and intro. Kate Flint. London: Penguin, 2006.

THE BODIES IN/ARE *THE WAVES*

by Michael Tratner

From around 1860 to 1920, a new concept dominated theories of physiology, a concept curiously similar to the fragmentation of modernist art and literature. Historians of neuroscience describe this as the "era of localization" (Finger 323). Localization is a theory that the human brain does not function as a coherent whole but rather is a collection of separate, localized organs, each of which generates a distinct part of consciousness. What we experience then is not simply a reflection of the world which our intelligence interprets but rather more like a collage painted by multiple painters all working at the same time. The parallel to the fragmented structure of many modernist paintings seems fairly straightforward. And localization provides an intriguing way to understand *The Waves* (1931).

Localization broke down the distinction between mind and body: as scientists demonstrated that physically altering the brain (in accidents or during surgery) altered or even created thoughts, it became commonplace to conclude that consciousness does not derive entirely from a "self" or a "soul" or any other non-physical entity. According to the historian Roger Smith, localization "suggested physical analogues for functions that were previously considered the expression of nonphysical, mental, or vital powers. Localization thus enabled description of living and mental processes as part of the natural world" (17). Localization also extended beyond the brain to suggest that other parts of the body could contribute to consciousness. In 1884, William James defined emotion as "felt awareness of visceral activity," which led to the widespread belief in the early twentieth century that emotions were "inherently bodily, involuntary and irrational" (Dixon, 24, 2). External things then seemed able to directly interact with the "viscera" or with subsections of the brain and produce reactions quite independent of the overall "self." Along with Darwinian conceptions, localization led many writers to see humans as in large part acting as animals, not merely controlling the animal parts of themselves.

In her essay "On Being Ill," Woolf indicates that she saw the power of the body to shape consciousness as undermining what literature had generally presented:

> with a few exceptions [...] literature does its best to maintain that its concern is with the mind; that the body is a sheet of plain glass through which the soul looks straight and clear. [...] On the contrary, the very opposite is true. All day, all night, the body intervenes. [...] The creature within [...] cannot separate off from the body like the sheath of a knife or the pod of a pea for a single instant; it must go through the whole unending procession of changes, heat and cold, comfort and discomfort, hunger and satisfaction, health and illness, until there comes the inevitable catastrophe; the body smashes itself to smithereens. (*Selected Essays* 101)

The Waves, I suggest, is structured to make us feel that unending procession of physical changes. The interludes provide a time sequence that seems utterly natural—the sun rising and setting—and the sections between the interludes mark stages in the lives of characters that have no relation to any plans in the lives of those characters; the only "plot" of these stages seems to be that of moving in accord with the physical flow of time. The interludes gradually come to seem a set of metaphors that define each section of the book as a stage in those six human lives and those stages of the six lives then appear to be waves that flow as a result of natural forces, not human choices or historical events. The novel thus traces the plot which bodies follow on their own, namely, growth, maturation, aging, and approaching death, a sequence as physical and inexorable as sunrise and sunset.

Readers usually see *The Waves* as an ethereal book about consciousness but what I am suggesting aligns with recent developments in Woolf studies, most notably Derek Ryan's essay about the interludes in *The Waves* as presenting a "posthuman" perspective and Craig Gordon's study of the influence of "bioscience" upon Woolf. F. D. McConnell argued in 1968 that the novel was an effort to step outside the human into nonhuman worlds, but I suggest instead that we see it as seeking to find the nonhuman inside each individual. The interludes repeatedly show light passing from natural scenes of animals and plants into human-shaped spaces, into houses, probing, revealing. Like the light in the interludes, the book seeks to illuminate the human world with a non-human light, to imagine peering into human consciousness from a nonhuman perspective. And what is seen is the way that human consciousness emerges from and is shaped by everything material that impinges on it, from inside and from outside. Instead of seeing consciousness as what an individual brings to the world, the book seeks to answer the question Bernard asks: "[H]ow describe the world seen without a self?" (287).

It is not merely the interludes that explore a physical world outside consciousness. Characters comment on the automatic functioning of their bodies. Bernard describes himself at breakfast as having "that feeling of existing in the midst of unconsciousness such as the tree frog must have couched on the right shade of green leaf. [...] Muscles, nerves, intestines, blood-vessels, all that makes the coil and spring of our being, the unconscious hum of the engine, as well as the dart and flicker of the tongue, functioned superbly. [...] [E]ating drinking; sometimes speaking—the whole mechanism seemed to expand, to contract, like the mainspring of a clock" (260–61). Bernard implies that at least sometimes the body simply spits out words and thoughts the way a frog's tongue darts. The streams of words in the novel may then be, as Carrie Rohman puts it, the product of bodies "vibrating" to natural rhythms.

Localization complicates this vision of the natural vibrations of human life by revealing that there are multiple vibrating systems in each individual and each system is in a sense a separate "animal" with its own goals, competing against the other structures that make up the individual. Seeing the book as presenting a localized view of consciousness, the six characters may then be not six separate individuals but six substructures within one body. It is not hard to think of them that way; they do not seem all that separate, their thoughts focusing almost entirely on each other, not on anyone outside the six. We hear briefly about parents, marriages, relationships and children, but without names or defining personalities. Repeatedly the book suggests that the characters are not distinct. Bernard says he cannot tell himself apart from the others, so much so that his "body" registers physical experiences of the others: "Here on my brow is the blow I got when Percival fell. Here on the nape of my neck is the kiss Jinny gave Louis. My eyes fill with Susan's tears" (289). One line in particular hints that all six are parts of one body; at a dinner party, Bernard says, "We saw for a moment laid out among us the body of the complete human being whom we have failed to be" (277).

The failure of the six voices to be one complete human being connects to what I suggest is a second plot of the book, namely the collapse of the centuries-old illusion of centralized control of the body. This illusion is presented as a body, namely Percival, a leader who could unify all the six consciousnesses in the novel. What is striking about Percival is that he emerges when the other characters go to school and he never has a voice of his own; he thus appears as a product of the school system, something everyone learns. If we are conceiving of the book as about substructures of one body which generate various parts of the overall consciousness, Percival is not such a substructure; he isn't a body part, isn't an organ. He is an image, a belief imposed upon the six others.

Now, Percival is an odd vision of that which can control all the parts of the body because we would expect that to be the brain. Percival is not identified with the brain at all. But if we examine what was going on historically as a reaction to the discovery of localization, we can see that Percival actually represents the attempt to restore self-control to the body once the brain is recognized as no longer the center of everything.

To understand what replaced the brain as the way to control the overall body at the end of the 19th century, I want to introduce another technical term from the history of physiology: "inhibition." Roger Smith has written a superb history of the concept, noting that the word had no physiological meaning in English until the 19th century and, when it emerged, it derived from other discourses: "when the word 'inhibition' itself came into common currency, it necessarily had associations with the regulation of the economy and with technology…self-regulating capacities of the governor on the steam engine or the trade cycle" (8). In other words, "inhibition" became applicable to the body via metaphoric parallels between the body and a new kind of machine and a new kind of economic system. The physiological meaning of "inhibition" derived from the rise of industrial capitalism, and indicated at first a quality necessary for that system to work: all must be able to "inhibit" their wild impulses to be good capitalists or workers, good parts of the overall self-regulating machine that is the economy.

"Inhibition" provided a mechanism by which the various localized substructures, the various "organs" within one individual body could direct that body without having the mind be an overall organizing function. Consider this definition from 1883: "By inhibition we mean the arrest of the functions of a structure or organ, by the action upon it of another, while its power to execute those functions is still retained, and can be manifested as soon as the restraining power is removed" (Brunton 419). In other words, inhibition is the power one internal structure has of stopping another internal structure from functioning without demolishing that other structure, just keeping it quiet for a time. This process does not then require the brain to decide which organs can control the body at which time; the organs can control each other or take charge at different moments.

But while scientists were exploring the ways that inhibition allows the various organs to take turns controlling the overall body of an individual, there emerged at the end of the nineteenth century a gradual fear of the power of inhibition. By the end of the nineteenth century, the word almost reversed its meaning. Instead of referring to necessary processes of parts of the body controlling other parts of the body to allow coherent action, it came to be used to describe the body's inability to act, a process more like self-paralysis than self-control. And the culprit blamed for the loss of power was the brain, which started to seem an organ improperly dominating the rest of the body. Thus, what once seemed a coolly self-restrained person began to seem someone too weak to take action. Gail Bederman has traced this shift in her account of concepts of manliness at the end of the 19th century: "During the 1890s, they coined the new epithets 'sissy,' 'pussy-foot,' 'cold feet' and 'stuffed shirt' to denote behavior which had once appeared self-possessed…but which now seemed overcivilized.…The very word 'overcivilized' was coined" (17). Modern civilization seemed to have gone too far; the result predicted by numerous writers was that those who were not so civilized would overthrow civilization. Fear of that result led to theories of how to unleash the primitive body which had been repressed beneath the overcivilized mind. Modernism participated quite enthusiastically in this effort to uncover and unleash the primitive body, as we can see in Picasso's art. In particular, there was a felt need to restore a more aggressive and muscular masculinity. Bederman notes that "in the 1860s the middle class had seen the ideal male body as lean and wiry. By the 1890s, however, an ideal male body required physical bulk and well-defined muscles" (15). The lean and wiry body was the Victorian self-controlled body; the bulky, muscular body of the 1890s resisted inhibition and counterbalanced the brain.

The Waves presents as part of its "plot" the development of the grand masculinity that Bederman traces emerging around the turn of the century. And Percival is that image: a muscular masculine body that is recognized as capable of uniting everyone, replacing the power of the brain. Percival represents what all the other characters cannot be: a complete body. He is particularly valued by the most over-intellectual, over-civilized character, Neville. Neville knows that he will be a great success as a writer "[b]ut I shall never have what I want, for I lack bodily grace and the courage that comes with it. The swiftness of my mind is too strong for my body" (129). Percival is the body which Neville lacks, the body that can be strong enough to equal Neville's mind and so Neville feels a "need […] to offer my being to one god" (52), to Percival.

Percival sets out to establish that this new masculinity can lead the world; he leaves to subdue and organize the "primitive" people Britain has colonized. His death, falling off a horse in India in the precise middle of the life-cycle of the book (when the sun is at its highest), puts his death at "middle age," a life stage when everyone becomes acutely aware that the body is going its own way, losing its strength and overthrowing all efforts to impose a vision of a coherent body upon the fragmented or localized body. Percival's fall represents the inability to do exactly what he was designed to do: control the "animal" body.

The interludes change with Percival's death: before that the scenes are all local scenes of modern houses and gardens. But the interlude that ushers in Percival's death includes a "mosque" and "washerwomen kneeling on hot stones" near "mules" (148–49). The local scenes are for the first time labeled "English fields," making it clear that something other than England is now visibly part of the world of the interludes. Later interludes include views from a location "so distant that no shining roof or glittering window could be any longer seen" (208). What is being revealed in these interludes is the existence of something that is not British, is not upper class, is not male, is not domesticated, is not civilized—and that something is the body. Everybody's body is a physical thing outside civilization.

Woolf essays and novels seek to develop ways of understanding this new vision of the body and in particular to counter the type of masculinity being proposed as the only way to control such a body. Her essays seek to counter political leaders such as Mussolini and Hitler and her novels seek to counter modernists such as Pound who admire such politicians. But what has not been much noted is that Woolf's answer is not an intellectual one but rather another way of giving up control to a localized system of mind and body. In *A Room of One's Own* (1929), Woolf proposes that all minds have both male and female parts and need to have both, but in order to make use of both of these localized portions of the mind, one has to let go of conscious control, to "lie back and let the mind celebrate its nuptials in darkness" and "not look" (108). While this is partly a satiric version of Victorian female sexuality, it is also something else: uniting of male and female parts of the mind while "not looking" is a vision of the mind operating at times quite separate from consciousness, as if male and female parts of the mind were more like bodily organs operating outside consciousness than like mental structures. If we think of the voices in *The Waves* as parts of one mind or one body, then as we read we are passing back and forth across the feminine and the masculine parts. This circulation is, I suggest, Woolf's vision of a way to accept localized biology.

But it is not easy to give up the ancient belief in a unified mind in a controllable body. The chapters immediately after Percival's death suggest a complete break-up of the totality which the six voices make; there are no longer all six voices in a chapter but three in one and four in the next. In these two chapters, the six voices no longer connect all together; the body is not just localized, but broken in half.

However, in the chapter after those two, in which the six gather for a dinner party, there is a renewed effort to bring them all together, to re-organ-ize themselves as a leaderless entity. It is in that chapter that they envision the complete human being they have never been. In that chapter they come close to being what Woolf advocated, an androgynous, gender-balanced entity—a modernist body-in-parts.

But that vision also collapses, as gender becomes unbalanced again with the death of Rhoda. The problem with Rhoda is that she is the opposite of Percival: he is all body; she feels she has no body. She is the most inhibited character, suppressing her impulses, suppressing her body (or the part of the overall body of the six which she represents). Intriguingly, though, she is the one who can see the very essence of the localized body, the modernist body-in-parts, when she says "Percival, by his death, has made me this gift, let me see the thing. There is a square; there is an oblong. The players take the square and place it upon the oblong. [...] The structure is now visible" (163). The structure she sees, of parts that have their own shape and connect together but do not blend into a single whole, is very much the vision of the localized mind and the localized body.

However, Rhoda cannot live out or enact that vision because of her feeling that she has no body, that she herself is just an image like Percival. Her life in images makes her, I suggest, a version of the female poet who, Woolf writes in *A Room of One's Own*, will someday "put on the body which she has so often laid down" (118).

When Rhoda kills herself, the gender balance is once again upset, as it was when everyone accepted the image of Percival. But this time, a male part of the overall body assumes leadership by itself and Bernard becomes the voice of the six. His monologue ends with his imagining becoming Percival and riding against the waves, against the "inevitable catastrophe" of death. His attempt to triumph over the physical flow of nature is the failure of Woolf's dream. Bernard creates unity by resisting the physicality of the human body, by flinging himself against the waves. The novel's separation of the interludes and the monologues is an effort to recognize that the physical flow of the body cannot be easily put together with the mental flow of words, but both are necessary. The book ends with Bernard choosing words and rejecting the multiplicity of the body. For all her own facility with words, Woolf never wanted to make that choice.

Works Cited

Bederman, Gail. *Manliness and Civilization: A Cultural History of Gender and Race in the United States, 1880–1917*. Chicago: U of Chicago P, 1995.

Brunton, T. Lauder. "On the nature of inhibition, and the action of drugs upon it." *Nature* 27 (1883): 419–487.

Dixon, Thomas, *From Passions to Emotions: The Creation of a Secular Psychological Category*. Cambridge: Cambridge UP, 2003.

Finger, Stanley. *Origins of Neuroscience: A History of Explorations into Brain Function*. New York: Oxford UP, 1994.

Gordon, Craig A. *Literary Modernism, Bioscience, and Community in Early 20th Century Britain*. New York: Palgrave Macmillan, 2007.

McConnell, F. D. "'Death Among the Apple Trees': *The Waves* and the World of Things." *Modern Critical Views: Virginia Woolf*. Ed. Harold Bloom. Philadelphia: Chelsea House Publishers, 1986. 53–65.

Rohman, Carrie. "'We Make Life': Vibration, Aesthetics, and the Inhuman in *The Waves*." *Virginia Woolf and the Natural World: Selected Papers from the Twentieth Annual International Conference on Virginia Woolf*. Ed. Kristin Czarnecki and Carrie Rohman. Clemson, SC: Clemson U Digital P, 2011. 12–23.

Ryan, Derek. "Posthumanist Interludes: Ecology and Ethology in *The Waves*." *Virginia Woolf: Twenty-First Century Approaches*. Ed. Jeanne Dubino, Gill Lowe, Vara Neverow, and Kathryn Simpson. Edinburgh: Edinburgh UP, 2014. 148–166.

Woolf, Virginia. *A Room of One's Own*. 1929. New York: Harcourt Brace Jovanovich, 1957.

———. *Selected Essays*. Ed. David Bradshaw. Oxford: Oxford UP, 2008.

———. *The Waves*. 1931. New York: Harcourt Brace, 1959.

Stretching Our "Antennae": Converging Worlds of the Seen and the Unseen in "Kew Gardens"

by Joyce E. Kelley

In "Modern Fiction" (1925), Virginia Woolf famously writes, "Let us not take it for granted that life exists more fully in what is commonly thought big than in what is commonly thought small" (*CE2* 107). She encourages us to look beneath the main "plot" and action of our lives to find the portion which "escapes" (105). In speaking of the "worlds" of Woolf's writing, we must remember that Woolf draws our attention repeatedly to the smaller moments of life, even the smaller beings. In Woolf's fiction, children particularly discover large worlds in minute things; in *To the Lighthouse* (1927), Nancy's imagination changes a tidal pool "into the sea" (75) and in *The Waves* (1931), Bernard, crawling under the canopy, finds the "stalks of flowers are thick as oak trees" (23). Woolf privileges the ability to imagine the world from a perspective unseen by most adults so that objects and ideas previously overlooked become magnified. These passages find a precursor much earlier in "Kew Gardens" (1919) in which Woolf uses an "oval-shaped flower-bed" as a stage and records both the microcosm of action in it and the macrocosm of people passing around it (*AHH* 28). As flowers unfurl, colored lights shift, and a snail crawls, the primary world is established and the people seem mere curious passersby. As Diana L. Swanson has written, the "human world is no longer the center of her writerly universe" (54). By making her focus a sensitive snail, feeling for a path with his retractable horns, who encounters an "angular green insect" with "its antennae trembling" (30), Woolf reveals how much of everyday life we humans miss. The antennae become a symbol of this extrasensory awareness Woolf allows her human characters to achieve in the garden.

The Royal Botanic Gardens at Kew cover 121 hectares and house 30,000 kinds of plants (kew.org). It is then remarkable that Woolf chose for her short story to be confined to such a small space—primarily the world of a snail and what can be perceived from his flower-bed. Woolf also removes the reader from human-influenced narration with a proliferation of insect-related figurative language, suggesting that the narrator, while omniscient and able to shift perspective from ground to sky, might be a butterfly, bird, or dragonfly mentioned elsewhere in the story.[1] Woolf challenges our usual focus by making the snail the single recurring character. The people, oblivious to the snail's existence, are inconsequential to his progress, although he is aware of them as shapes and voices. The snail moves slowly, finding "[b]rown cliffs with deep green lakes" and "blade-like trees that waved from root to tip" (30). As in Bernard's and Nancy's imaginations, minute objects appear large. By the last scene of the flower-bed, the snail is considering crawling over a leaf, testing it with "the tips of his horns" and then deciding to creep beneath it. We see from his perspective as he contemplates "the high brown roof" of the leaf and "the cool brown light" (33). A snail's "horns" are really eye-stalks; an additional metaphor for enriched perception, they allow the snail extrasensory ability to see beyond his body.

Like bees to a flower, four couples move in and out of view during the course of the story.[2] The garden walkers seem carefully selected to show a "cross-section" of people who might appear in the gardens at any moment (Bishop 271). Several critics including Edward L. Bishop and Jeanette McVicker have noted the balance in gender, age, and class, as Woolf shows first a middle-aged married couple, then a "well-to-do" younger and older man (the latter appearing somewhat senile or eccentric) (32), two older women friends "of the lower middle class" (32), and a final young romantic pair.[3] The walkers appear randomly and "straggled" along like "the white and blue butterflies who crossed the turf" (29). The human figures have no more weight in the story than the small creatures, simply representing visitors during a short interval of space and time in Kew Gardens.

While the couples may seem inconsequential, the import of their time spent at Kew is profound. Woolf's story examines why people visit gardens and she is aware that the reasons are complex: not just to experience sights and sounds of nature, but to think and feel, to converse, to clear one's head, to paint, to write, to find creative energy. We can see in Woolf's diary how Kew functioned for her as a meaningful place to walk and be inspired and to share the beauty of nature with friends. When the Woolfs escorted the Minister for Education to the gardens in 1919, Virginia remarked how he took in the beauty of the magnolias "as a man who collects objects for the good of his soul" (*D1* 264). While gardens may function as a respite from the world at any moment, this purpose can be magnified at a time of domestic or national strife. Woolf began "Kew Gardens" in 1917 during the height of the First World War and her diary entries from these years reveal her keen absorption with the garden as a green space where imagination and escape from ordinary concerns are possible.[4] In May 1918, after a visit to Kew with Leonard, Virginia noted, "[t]o the general loveliness & freshness was added a sense of being out when we should have been at home; this always turns things into a kind of spectacle. It seems to be going on without you" (*D1* 148). Woolf captures this feeling in "Kew Gardens"; life and movement are everywhere and we see only snippets of conversations and fragments of characters' relationships and intentions. However, if one can train one's antennae on the scene, there are worlds to witness that one never knew existed. I would like to focus on an organizing principle in "Kew Gardens" that many critics miss: each couple highlights the worlds of the seen and the unseen by tapping into a presence not readily witnessed by normal vision. Standing near the flower-bed, at least one member of each couple has a moment of epiphany realized in the spiritual versus the material world before moving back into his or her usual routine.[5]

The first couple, like the others we will observe, does not come to Kew just to see flowers, but to think. Simon wanders into view, followed by his wife Eleanor, followed by the children; the distance between them allows Simon to delve into memory. What he wants to see in the garden is something not there at all: the past. "'Fifteen years ago I came here with Lily,' he thought. 'We sat somewhere over there by a lake and I begged her to marry me all through the hot afternoon'" (29). When Eleanor hears his musings, she replies, "Doesn't one always think of the past, in a garden with men and women lying under the trees? Aren't they one's past, all that remains of it, those men and women, those ghosts lying under the trees,…one's happiness, one's reality?" (29–30). Eleanor emphasizes that the garden, providing imaginative release, functions as a liminal place for these worlds of past and present to meet. Woolf seems explicitly to use the flower name "Lily" to illustrate that, while surrounded by gardens, Simon is thinking of a different kind of flower altogether. In a strange echo of Simon's language, Eleanor remembers painting water-lilies as a child, "the first red water-lilies I'd ever seen. And suddenly a kiss, there on the back of my neck. [...] the kiss of an old grey-haired woman" (30). The lilies Simon and Eleanor see in the garden are not really there; the garden functions like a shadow catcher, a light-sensitive surface showing the photographic figment of what was once present. Eleanor's word "ghosts" suggests the spiritual side of life Woolf wants to catch for her reader: much of what we may experience in any given setting is not currently present, yet this does not make it any less "one's reality." Simon and Eleanor share a moment where they tap into their respective pasts; here, the past intrudes into the present as a visualized shade of being. We feel the lingering beauty of these memories until Eleanor snaps back to the present with a no-nonsense statement to the children: "Come, Caroline, come, Hubert" (30). One cannot live in the past; one must reject it for the present to survive. Nonetheless, Woolf's implications about the conjunction of the present moment and memory linger in the ghostly bodies of her characters, for they soon "diminished in size among the trees and looked half transparent" (30).

The theme of tapping into what is ordinarily unseen continues with the second pair of strollers, announced from the snail's perspective as "the feet of other human beings" (31). As two men emerge, the elder refers to "spirits of the dead" who appear to be talking to him "even now" (31). The idea of pleasant memories existing alongside the present moment quickly evolves into something darker for this war-drenched society as the dead are imagined to inhabit a space alongside the living. The elderly man explains to his son or caretaker: "with this war, the spirit matter is rolling between the hills like thunder" (31). The description suggests ghost sound waves that can only be picked up at the right frequency, and the man describes a device to capture them: "You have a small electric battery and a piece of rubber to insulate the wire. [...] and in short the little machine stands in any convenient position by the head of the bed. [...] [T]he widow applies her ear and summons the spirit" (31).

Spiritualism found widespread popularity during the war era.[6] Arthur Conan Doyle wrote of its resurgence: "The deaths occurring in almost every family in the land brought a sudden and concentrated interest in the life after death. People...eagerly sought to know if communication was possible with the dear ones they had lost" (102). Of course, those expecting miracles were easily deceived, and the device described here by the elder man may sound like a bit of chicanery—except that he appears to believe in the voices himself.[7] Woolf further emphasizes extra-sensory communication when the relative or caretaker "touched a flower with the tip of his walking-stick in order to divert the old man's attention" (AHH 32). The elderly man suddenly uses the flower as a kind of communication device, for he "bent his ear to it and seemed to answer a voice speaking from it" (32). While the man's response is clearly on the far side of sanity, Woolf continues the theme of the gardens allowing a moment of perception beyond the ordinary, for the man does not need a machine to tap into something unseen, unheard.[8]

The spirit world seems related to the microcosm of the snail's world in the flower bed: something that we do not readily perceive but with which we might connect. Many contemporary spiritualists believed that the realm of the spirit was a separate plane of existence, yet tangential to our own and somewhat porous, subsisting from elemental matter common to us all. Some philosophers linked this to realms of thought and language; in 1904 Rudolf Steiner described "The Spirit Land" as "woven out of the material of which human thought consists. But thought, as it lives in man, is only a shadow picture, a phantom of its true being" (130). He describes how in the spirit world there is no gap between a word and the thought conjured by that word—an idea which leads to the next plane of the unseen that Woolf explores: the world beyond language.

The third couple in Woolf's story consists of two elderly women, one "nimble" and one "ponderous" who "went on energetically piecing together their very complicated dialogue" (32). Very few scholars discuss this exchange in detail, for it appears we are merely eavesdropping on an unimportant conversation. Indeed there is evidence Woolf intended it to be satiric of lower-middle-class women's chatter, since she mentions in her diary her hesitancy to let women from the Co-operative Guild read the scene.[9] Nonetheless, it contains some unusual content worth contemplating. The exchange is:

"Nell, Bert, Lot, Cess, Phil, Pa, he says, I says, she says, I says, I says—"
"My Bert, Sis, Bill, Grandad, the old man, sugar,
        Sugar, flour, kippers, greens,
        Sugar, sugar, sugar." (32)

The women seem to be planning a meal for company, perhaps with some difficulty; volunteer rationing was encouraged mid-war and by January 1918 sugar was rationed.[10] If their talk is really a "dialogue," the women hardly seem to communicate. The first woman focuses on having her ideas heard and on getting the final say. The second woman seems to be clarifying the list of people invited, but her list is different: "Bert" becomes "My Bert," "Cess" becomes "Sis," "Phil" becomes "Bill," "Pa" becomes "Grandad." While it is possible that these are different names for the same people, the aural variations in the second list of names might also suggest a gap in understanding between the women or the difficulty of our narrator to properly "piece together" this exchange without knowing the referents.

Woolf is experimenting with spoken language as mere sound, drawing it away from sense. The "ponderous woman" begins to experience this, too, as she turns to look at the flower-bed. Like the others, this couple is not intent on just seeing the gardens but on talking and suddenly the upraised flowers serve as a trigger for something else: "The ponderous woman looked through the pattern of falling words at the flowers standing cool, firm, and upright in the earth, with a curious expression. She saw them as a sleeper waking from a heavy sleep sees a brass candlestick" (32–33). As Woolf experiments with sound pulling away from meaning, it is fitting that the word "flour" in the list of groceries turns the woman to its homophone, "flowers" in the garden. A flower again acts as an upraised stimulus drawing in the observer and allowing her to tap into a separate space of experience. She "ceased even to pretend to listen to what the other woman was saying. She stood there letting the words fall over her, swaying the top part of her body slowly backwards and forwards, looking at the flowers. Then she suggested that they should find a seat and have their tea" (33). The ponderous woman glimpses an unseen world outside referential language. For a moment she accesses this alternate reality, swaying in the breeze like a flower herself. She then interrupts her own absorption by suggesting they go have tea; like the other couples, she moves away from the experimental realm provided by the garden back to conforming needs of the body and daily life.

The final couple appears to our insect-inspired narrator to be "in that season [...] when the wings of the butterfly, though fully grown, are motionless in the sun" (33). The adolescents are presumably on a romantic outing. The young man begins by remarking, "Lucky it isn't Friday," because the entrance rates are higher on Friday (33).[11] The young woman queries, "Isn't it worth sixpence?" to which the young man demands, "what do you mean by 'it'?" (34). While many critics have enjoyed thinking philosophically about what Woolf might mean by the elusive "it," what is being contested may simply be the status of the young people's relationship. Again, this couple is not just in the garden to see flowers. The young woman wants to know that the time spent with her is worth something and she is embarrassed to put this into words in front of the young man.

Like the other couples, these young people transcend the ordinary world to find another: "The couple stood still on the edge of the flower-bed, and together pressed the end of her parasol deep down into the soft earth. The action and the fact that his hand rested on the top of hers expressed their feelings in a strange way" (34). The young man then sees before them "shapes [...] little white tables, and waitresses who looked first at her and then at him; and there was a bill that he would pay with a real two shilling piece" (34). He is imagining the romantic excursion they will have together and the vision comes before him as a hope and a pleasure, but it is again something not to be perceived with the actual eye.

When you are middle-aged, you may dream about the past in a garden; when you are young, you may dream about the future, but for both romantic couples that bookend this story, the garden serves as a kind of dream-space. As with the other couples, this dream-space is too much to handle in the real world, and the episode ends in interruption: "but it was too exciting to stand and think any longer, and he pulled the parasol out of the earth with a jerk. [...] 'Come along, Trissie; it's time we had our tea'" (34). In this last example, the world of the imaginary is tangible, sliding into the world of the real. The parasol, serving as an antenna, like the flower stalks and walking cane in the previous examples, has connected a couple with the flower bed and a piece of the unseen world, bringing new experience and new inspiration.

In the story's end, the macrocosm of the gardens becomes a microcosm, the people dissolving into vapor. As they appear mottled and colored like the flower-bed and snail described in the story's opening section, we perceive Kew Gardens as a very small entity indeed, a small "oval-shaped flower-bed" itself. The perspective lifts into an aerial shot of the gardens until we see only the "vast nest of Chinese boxes" of the city below (36). Woolf ends by showing us how "on the top" of the city "the petals of myriads of flowers flashed their colours into the air" (36), as if the city, like the crawling snail, is located on the floor of a very large flower garden and we must adjust our way of seeing to really experience it. The people are reduced to only sound, "[w]ordless voices," as if we are tuning into a frequency we can't quite hear (35). "Kew Gardens" emerges right before the beginnings of radio, when the air would be filled with voices on invisible waves that could only be heard with proper receptors. As if already attuned with their own antennae, the couples in the garden achieve a moment of enriched perception by discovering a world beyond what is commonly seen; as they do so, Woolf encourages us to be more perceptive of the world(s) we inhabit.

Notes

1. Several critics imagine the story narrated by a person seated by the flower-bed; I agree more with Frank Stevenson who compares the snail to a "hidden microphone" catching the voices around it (137). Swanson mentions the difficulty of writing from a non-human perspective, noting perceptively that Woolf "refrains from comparing the nonhuman to the human" (68); what interests me is that our narrator, quite the other way around, cannot refrain from comparing the human to the animal.
2. Only recently have scholars given much importance to the story's people. Edward Bishop, Alice Staveley, and Stef Craps particularly note that since Harold Child first praised the story in *The Times Literary Supplement*, it traditionally has been analyzed for its formal qualities.
3. Bishop notes the couples "constitute a cross-section of social class (middle, upper, and lower), age (maturity, old age, and youth) and relation (husband and wife, male companions, female friends, lovers)" (271). McVicker adds, "These couples represent...ideological binary oppositions: male/female, age/youth, wealth/poverty, sanity/madness" (41).
4. Stef Craps rightly remarks that Kew "became a place of respite for the author after the Woolfs' move to Richmond in 1915" (194). However, most critical discussions neglect Woolf's reflections on the gardens in her diary.
5. The only critic I have found noting this pattern of interruptions is Oliver Taylor; he makes a different point that one member of each couple is redirected by the other (127).
6. Woolf was aware of this; her father had been a member of The Society for Psychical Research. See Wisker, 8.
7. A nineteenth-century oration on spiritualism describes a similar device: "In order to obtain a few simple taps on a table he had an electric battery communicating by wires with the table, and an arrangement of small hammers" (Sexton 11). While a professor did this to show the "humbug of Spiritualism," these devices may have been common and many people fooled.
8. For Woolf, Kew served as a respite from war. In January 1918, she notes "squills or crocuses coming through the grass & dead leaves" as the garden brings life out of death (*D1* 114).
9. In June 1919, Woolf writes, "Mrs. Whitty & another [Co-operative Guild member] pressed me for copies of Kew Gardens. But I don't want them to read the scene of the two women" (*D1* 284).
10. Woolf's sister Vanessa called this the "sugar conversation" (Staveley 61). I am not the first to consider here the influence of food rationed in WWI. Julia Briggs notes the two women show "the economic consequences of the war" (171). In November 1917, Woolf mentions walking to Kew Gardens and then returning home to count "my lumps of sugar" (*D1* 81).
11. A 1917 diary entry echoes this view: when Woolf found herself at the gardens on a Friday (Nov. 23), she decided to turn around and not go in. As a note explains, "Admission...was 6d on Tuesdays and Fridays, 1d on other days" (*D1* 81n).

Works Cited

Bishop, Edward L. "Pursuing 'it' though 'Kew Gardens.'" *Studies in Short Fiction* 19.3 (1982): 269–275.

Briggs, Julia. "Writing By Numbers: An Aspect of Virginia Woolf's Revisionary Practice." *Variants 4: The Book as Artefact, Text, and Border*. Ed. Anne Mette Hansen, Roger Lüdeke, Wolfgang Streit, Cristina Urchueguía and Peter Shillingsburg. Amsterdam: Rodopi, 2005. 165–182.

Craps, Stef. "Virginia Woolf: 'Kew Gardens' and 'The Legacy.'" *A Companion to the British and Irish Short Story*. Ed. Cheryl Alexander Malcolm and David Malcolm. Malden, MA: Wiley-Blackwell, 2008. 193–201.

Doyle, Arthur Conan. *The History of Spiritualism*. Vol. 2. London: Cassell & Company Ltd., 1926.

Kew Royal Botanic Gardens (kew.org). Web. 30 May 2014.

McVicker, Jeanette. "Vast Nests of Chinese Boxes, or Getting from Q to R: Critiquing Empire in 'Kew Gardens' and *To The Lighthouse*." *Virginia Woolf Miscellanies*. Ed. Mark Hussey and Vara Neverow. NY: Pace UP, 1991: 40–42.

Sexton, George. "Spirit-Mediums and Conjurers: An Oration Delivered in the Cavendish Rooms, London, on Sunday Evening, June 15, 1873." London: J. Burns, 1873.

Staveley, Alice. "Kew Will Do: Cultivating Fictions of Kew Gardens." *Virginia Woolf and the Arts: Selected Papers From the Sixth Annual Conference on Virginia Woolf*. Ed. Diane F. Gillespie and Leslie K. Hankins. Clemson, SC: Clemson U Digital P, 1997: 57–66.

Steiner, Rudolf. *Theosophy*. Trans. E.D.S. Chicago: Rand McNally & Company, 1910.

Stevenson, Frank. "Enclosing the Whole: Woolf's 'Kew Gardens' as Autopoeitic Narrative." *Journal of the Short Story in English* 50 (2008): 137–152.

Swanson, Diana L. "Woolf's Copernican Shift: Nonhuman Nature in Virginia Woolf's Short Fiction." *Woolf Studies Annual* 18 (2012): 53–74.

Taylor, Oliver. "'What's "it"—What Do You Mean by "it"?': Lost Readings and Getting Lost in 'Kew Gardens.'" *Journal of the Short Story in English* 50 (2008): 121–135.

Wisker, Gina. "Places, People and Time Passing: Virginia Woolf's Haunted Houses." *Hecate* 37.1 (2011): 4–26.

Woolf, Virginia. *The Diary of Virginia Woolf*. Vol 1. Ed. Anne Olivier Bell. New York: Harcourt Brace Jovanovich, 1979.

———. "Kew Gardens." 1919. *A Haunted House and Other Short Stories*. New York: Harcourt, Brace, 1944. 28–36.

———. "Modern Fiction." 1925. *Collected Essays*. Vol. 2. London: Hogarth Press, 1972: 103–110.

———. *The Waves*. 1931. San Diego: Harcourt, Brace, 1959.

———. *To the Lighthouse*. 1927. San Diego: Harcourt, Brace, 1981.

"THE PROBLEM OF SPACE": EMBODIED LANGUAGE AND THE BODY IN NATURE IN *TO THE LIGHTHOUSE*

by Kim Sigouin

In her novel *To the Lighthouse* (1927), Woolf articulates an ecological consciousness and champions an experimental language that is constantly changing as the sentient body interacts with the volatile forces inherent to the natural environment. Situating the human body within the vast natural landscape, Woolf erodes sharp distinctions between human and nonhuman nature by demonstrating how irregular natural forces compel the individual to contemplate his or her place within a schema of shifting geographies. In doing so, Woolf grapples with similar concerns that later ecocritics, such as Heather Sullivan and Christina Alt, articulate in order to stress the complex matrix that consists of human beings and natural environments. In her strategic deformation of linguistic codes that would promote homogeneity and communicative ease, Woolf advances the subversive plasticity of a protolanguage rooted in the body. I argue that Woolf moves beyond commonplace understandings of language as a system of representation as she examines the interplay between ecstatic motile forms of "embodied language" and transformative natural processes. Her interest in investigating the ecological implications of an embodied language is especially apparent in "On Being Ill" (1926), and later in "Craftsmanship" (1937), her contribution to a radio broadcast titled "Words Fail Me." By placing these essays in dialogue with *To the Lighthouse*, we can see the development of an experimental language that frustrates denotative meaning in favor of evoking the sensorial apparatus of the body as it interacts with, affects, and is affected by volatile forces in the natural environment.

In her essay, "On Being Ill," Woolf advocates "a new hierarchy of the passions" (34) that the human recognizes in illness, suggesting illness compels the individual to acknowledge his or her vulnerability in relation to the ongoing natural processes that stimulate the sensorial body, but remain indifferent to the preservation of the human species. By dismissing an anthropocentric notion of an ordered world in which the chaotic natural forces have been cultivated by human exploits, and the vastness of the natural realm is reduced to clearly demarcated boundaries, Woolf reconceptualizes the human. She criticizes established ideological frameworks that impose stability and, by extension, critiques the notion of an established linguistic order that perpetuates social norms, and subsequently, homogenizes a collective unit. Instead, she demonstrates how the interplay between the rapid transformation of industrial societies and the fluctuating natural environment subjects the individual to a perpetual process of becoming.

The individual does not exercise mastery over natural forces, but is subordinated to and threatened by the natural environment. Woolf deliberately frustrates any romantic notion of the natural environment that severs the relationship between the mind and body, extoling the mind and dismissing the body. Literary tradition, argues Woolf, perpetuates this dualism and maintains that "[p]eople write always about the doings of the mind" and "its noble plans; how it has civilised the universe" (33). The body is depicted simply as a mass that the mind kicks "like an old leather football, across leagues of snow and desert in the pursuit of conquest or discovery" (33). Woolf uses images of invasion to illustrate the militant endeavors that delimit the environment. She, however, rejects these pursuits of human conquest which reduce the natural world to systems of classification, and instead proposes a reconceptualization of the environment that derives from "a reason rooted in the bowels of the earth" (33). The mind cannot order the natural world by harnessing the chaotic forces of the environment. In addition, Woolf stresses that the natural world is not a projection of the mind, and consequently, the mind cannot translate the chaotic natural realm into a knowable entity. Although the sensorial body is receptive to the volatile organic processes of the environment, it is unable to fully register the immensity of the natural world. Woolf then proposes that the human body is not separate from nature and so debunks the notion of the body as divided between disembodied consciousness and the corporeality of the body. This dualism elevates the human being and perpetuates romantic notions of the human seeking communion with god in nature. By contrast, Woolf "shows humans and nature in a contiguous community of interaction—a world occupied by a variety of pulsing life forms that collide, interact, and sustain each other on a daily basis" (Sultzbach 73–74).

Woolf's articulation of the relation between evolutionary and linguistic processes compares to Elizabeth Grosz's theories of "becoming." By drawing on Darwinian evolutionary theories, Grosz suggests that the human being is not distinct from other animal species (Grosz 16–21). She advocates the notion of a perpetual process of becoming, displaying how environmental transformations debunk fixed notions of selfhood. In their investigation of the developmental processes of the human and other organisms, both Woolf and Grosz reject the notion of a linear trajectory of progression which will inevitably culminate in an evolutionary goal. Instead, they indicate that the interrelationship between the organism and the environment is constantly altered by the erratic laws of the universe. As such, they advance the notion of an ecological holism that recognizes the interplay between social and natural spaces, dismissing the notion of a return to a primordial natural environment in lieu of understanding the human and the environment as a process.

Woolf contemplates the possibility of the extinction of the human species, imagining a futurity in which nature "in the end will conquer; [...] stiff with frost we shall cease to drag our feet about the fields; ice will lie thick upon factory and engine; the sun will go out" ("On Being" 39). Yet, she conjectures that "some undulation, some irregularity of surface will mark the boundary of an ancient garden, and there, thrusting its head up undaunted in the starlight, the rose will flower, the crocus will burn" (39). In her depiction of an imagined ancient garden, Woolf does not present a harmonious natural landscape in which the rose and the crocus achieve an ideal fixed state. The rose and the crocus do not exist in a stable, clearly delimited environment, but reveal the dynamic energies of the natural world as the rose blossoms and the crocus burns. Woolf then calls attention to a possible future in which the natural environment extinguishes the human species, but wherein the vibrancy of natural processes establishes a sense of continuity. Moreover, she calls attention to this imagined landscape in order to dismiss it, and focuses instead on the human species, suggesting that "with the hook of life still in us still we must wriggle" (39).

According to Kelly Sultzbach, Woolf "values humans not as a superior species, but instead as a single component jostling in a matrix of larger natural forces" (Sultzbach 75). Woolf stresses the complex matrix of urban space and natural landscape in which cultural norms and organic processes intermesh and develop different formations of selfhood. The interplay between the rhythms of the human body that are regulated by social obligations, and the "endless activity" ("On Being" 37) of the natural environment create new forms of expression. The "incessant making up of shapes and casting them down, this buffeting of clouds together, and drawing vast trains of ships and waggons from North to South" and the "incessant ringing up and down of curtains of light and shade, this interminable experiment with gold shafts and blue shadows, with veiling the sun and unveiling it" (37) demonstrate how the continuous routinized actions of the quotidian experience are interwoven with the endless rhythms of the landscape. The human body thus resists conforming to rigid cultural frameworks that attempt to regiment the body in order to foster the "illusion of a world so shaped that it echoes every groan, of human beings so tied together by common needs and fears that a twitch at one wrist jerks another" (36).

In "Craftsmanship," Woolf elaborates on this dialectical relationship between cultural and natural geographies that disrupts the habitual rhythms of the body and consequently, generates new forms of expression. She highlights the limitations of formulaic linguistic models, suggesting that a systematic linguistic order fosters the "illusion" ("On Being" 36) of an ordered environment. Woolf argues that "words do not live in dictionaries; they live in the mind" ("Craftsmanship" 130), insisting that their meaning is multi-faceted and subject to change. She "describes [language] as a living, organic process that is not entirely owned or controlled by the conscious will of her own mind" (Sultzbach 75). In "On Being Ill," Woolf posits that the unconscious space of the mind resembles "a virgin forest, tangled, pathless" ("On Being" 36). The mind then reflects the vast expanses of the natural world uncultivated by cultural norms. In "Craftsmanship," she further develops this image and contends that words "are the wildest, freest, most irresponsible, most unteachable of all things" ("Craftsmanship" 130). Language, like nature and the human body, is subject to continuous alterations.

Words do not exist outside of the body, and the human body does not enter into an abstracted linguistic order that regulates the body in order to comply with social norms. Instead, Woolf stresses the materiality of language altered by the processes of the corporeal body, a notion explained more fully in "On Being Ill." Woolf suggests that in illness, the individual is better able "to coin words" (34) since the body is no longer attuned to social obligations, but one can then "[take] his pain in one hand, and a lump of pure sound in the other [...] so to crush them together that a brand new word in the end drops out" ("On Being" 34). The emergence of new words results from bodily processes and her study of language reveals how "she frequently draws upon evolutionary concepts for their imaginative power" (Alt 107). Similarly, in "Craftsmanship," the rhythms affecting the body alter established linguistic orders since words imitate the biological processes of the human body by "mating together" ("Craftsmanship" 131). That is, "[r]oyal words mate with commoners" and "English words marry French words" (131), and so the materiality of the words debunks systematic frameworks by collapsing the boundaries between various linguistic orders.

The evolutionary and linguistic theories which Woolf proposes in both essays are at play in her work, *To the Lighthouse*. In this text, Woolf explores the complexity of the human being which resists a finite, systematized expression of self. The characters in the novel oscillate between the domestic interior of the house, which imposes a strict regime of conventionality, and the fluidity of the natural environment, which alters the characters' sense perceptions, and by extension, a sense of self. The volatile natural forces disrupt the individual's sense of stability and, consequently, prevent the individual from reducing the natural environment to geographical coordinates. The characters then are immersed in the immense natural landscape, their sensorial bodies attuned to the shifting configurations of the landscape. Woolf demonstrates the limitations of human perception, shifting between moments of enlightenment that allow one to observe and classify the environment, and moments of confusion in which the individual is unable to decipher the minute details of the landscape. To illustrate, in the scene in which Nancy observes the various organisms that inhabit a pond, Woolf juxtaposes two modes of perception, shifting from a reductive, scientific analysis of the environment to the dynamic energies inherent to the landscape which stimulate the bodily senses and, subsequently, obscure vision. Paul's understanding of the islands derives from a "guide-book" (*TTL* 62). This guide-book infuses the islands with a sense of value that is artificially constructed.

Whereas Paul is at a remove from the environment, relying on and repeating pre-conceived knowledge of the islands, Nancy situates herself in direct proximity to the organisms that inhabit the landscape, and understands the environment through the reciprocal relation between her sensorial body and the tactile elements of the pond. Her initial response is to understand the creatures in the pond as subordinate to the human will, and so, "[b]rooding, she changed the pool into the sea [...] and cast vast clouds over this tiny world by holding her hand against the sun, and so brought darkness and desolation, like God himself, to millions of ignorant and innocent creatures" (63). Woolf then marks a shift in emphasis from a depiction of a microcosm oriented by the centrality of the human will to a depiction of a world in which Nancy is unable to exert her will on the landscape. She becomes "hypnotized, and the two senses of that vastness and this tininess [...] made her feel that she was bound hand and foot and unable to move by the intensity of feelings which reduced her own body, her own life, and the lives of all the people in the world, for ever, to nothingness" (63). This revelatory moment in which Nancy acknowledges the immensity of the landscape marks the character's shift in focus from an anthropocentric view of the world to a biocentric understanding of the world, which, in Bonnie Kime Scott's words, "[decenters] human consciousness as the source of knowledge, leaving humans with the feeling of being transcended by something beyond their control, yet also feeling 'nourished and sustained by it'" (Scott 210).

By opposing an anthropocentric understanding of the natural environment with the organic rhythms of the landscape that decenter the human, Woolf does not suggest that the human will relinquish all ties to the cultural realm. Moreover, the cultural rhythms of the quotidian experience will never be fully assimilated into the natural rhythms of the environment in order to obtain a single harmonious union. Instead, she stresses the dialectical relation between cultural and natural movements, indicating that the human being does not belong exclusively to the natural or cultural realm, but oscillates between the two. The dinner party scene depicts the tension between the fluid natural world and the stasis of the cultural realm exemplified by the encroaching darkness that collapses the boundaries between the natural world and the domestic interior. Woolf highlights the fragile barrier that separates the menacing exterior realm of motion from the sterile conventional acts of the guests, suggesting "that here, inside the room, seemed to be order and dry land; there, outside, a reflection in which things wavered and vanished, waterily"

(*TTL* 79–80). Although the natural world threatens the participants of the dinner party, it does not annihilate the human components, but evokes a momentary stillness in which the characters' sense perceptions are heightened. The characters are not defined simply by strict social structures that regulate their disposition, but the characters see beyond "the bright mask-like look of faces" (80).

The fluidity of the natural world alters systems of classification exemplified by the transformative effect of the invading natural forces on language. Mrs. Ramsay compares words to "the movement of a trout" (87). In doing so, she stresses the multiplicity of meaning associated with words, fragmenting the linearity of sentence structures. Furthermore, she emphasizes the materiality of language, suggesting that "it was as if she had antennae trembling out from her, which, intercepting certain sentences, forced them upon her attention" (87). Woolf thus reveals the interconnectedness between the members at the dinner table by underlining the emotive quality of words. Mrs. Ramsay becomes receptive to the emotional states of her guests which remain ineffable, and so evinces a sense of communion that transcends the rational understanding of the human being which categorizes and subsequently dismantles interpersonal relationships. Woolf denies the complete erasure of the scene. Instead, she indicates that "it changed, it shaped itself differently" (90) and rather than reveal that the darkness extinguishes this social unit, Woolf suggests that Mrs. Ramsay returns to her social role. The intermingling of natural and cultural spaces generates a revelatory moment which disrupts the habituated body and compels the individual to reflect on her place within a larger schema of shifting forces.

Woolf revisits this tension between culture and nature in the "Time Passes" section of the novel, displaying the near elimination of the house. Woolf examines the shifting natural forces that reorient the landscape and refashion the structure of the home, suggesting that the natural landscape and the domestic space are not two severely demarcated domains. She notes that "the empty room, wove into itself the falling cries of birds" (106) and further indicates how "the empty rooms seemed to murmur with the echoes of the fields and the hum of flies" (109). Mrs. McNab's attempts to maintain the proper interior of the home are rendered futile as the invasive natural elements continue to dismantle the structure of the home. The damaging natural forces stress the vulnerability of the human being as "Woolf decentres the human through her description of the slow action upon the Ramsay house, in the midst of which human events are relegated to brief parenthetical asides" (Alt 9). However, Woolf, again, resists the complete expulsion of culture, preserving the cultural artifact of the home, and indicating that "slowly and painfully […] Mrs. McNab, Mrs. Bast stayed the corruption and the rot; rescued from the pool of Time that was fast closing over them now a basin, now a cupboard" (*TTL* 114). The women preserve cultural artifacts and the upkeep of the house compares to "some rusty laborious birth" (114). The generative body of the female then does not simply produce the continuity of the species, but ensures the renewal of cultural artifacts as well, and so represents the intermingling of cultural and organic creative processes.

Natural and cultural rhythms are "always on the verge of harmonising" (115), but never fully achieve unity. Instead, the natural landscape, and by extension the organisms that populate it, remain outside the limits of human perception. The interplay between the destructive natural forces and the restoration of the cultural artifacts marks a moment of revelation in which Lily recognizes the complexity of human nature and is able to complete her artistic reproduction of Mrs. Ramsay. Initially, Lily's interaction with the volatile natural forces translate into a work of art: "her hand [which] quivered with life" dissuades the impeding "habitual currents in which after a certain time experience forms in the mind, so that one repeats words without being aware any longer who originally spoke them" (131). Lily then marks the interplay between habitual rhythms of the body and the sporadic rhythms of the landscape that produce the "flickering" (130) of her gestures. The intercourse between these variant rhythms results in a painting that does not display a reductive representation of Mrs. Ramsay, but reveals the human subject in relation to "the problem of space" (141), which is further exemplified by the oscillation between Lily's perspective from the land and the Ramsay family's perspective from the boat at sea as they attempt to identify themselves in relation to a particular place. Woolf stresses the oscillation between clearly outlined geographical spaces and the blurring of boundaries, and further emphasizes that the dialectical relation between the two provides the individual with moments of revelation within a chaotic environment. The painting reflects this intermingling as Lily "[draws] a line there, in the centre" of the "blurred" canvas (170).

Thus, through her use of an embodied language, Woolf stresses the variable nature of the human body in relation to the dynamic natural forces. She then marks the transition from an established language of abstractions that regulates the body, to the materiality of language that is perpetually in the process of evolving, much like the human organism in which it originates. In doing so, Woolf displays a biocentric worldview in which the human is immersed in the natural landscape. As such, she dismisses a systematic linguistic order that determines the disposition of the human body, and resists reductive representations of the environment. The immensity of the natural environment exceeds systems of classification and therefore cannot be mediated by existing ideological frameworks that preserve social values. Woolf, however, does not simply advocate a return to a primordial nature, but negotiates between cultural and natural geographies. This dialectic between culture and nature prevents the individual from settling within habitual rhythms, and, by extension, a totalized expression of selfhood.

Works Cited

Alt, Christina. *Virginia Woolf and the Study of Nature*. Cambridge: Cambridge UP, 2010.

Grosz, Elizabeth. *Becoming Undone: Darwinian Reflections on Life, Politics, and Art*. Durham, NC: Duke UP, 2011.

Scott, Bonnie Kime. *In the Hollow of the Wave: Virginia Woolf and Modernist Uses of Nature*. Charlottesville: U of Virginia P, 2012.

Sultzbach, Kelly. "The Fertile Potential of Virginia Woolf's Environmental Ethic." *Woolf and the Art of Exploration: Selected Papers from the Fifteenth International Conference on Virginia Woolf*. Ed. Helen Southworth and Elisa Kay Sparks. Clemson, SC: Clemson U Digital P, 2006. 71–77.

Woolf, Virginia. "Craftsmanship." *The Death of the Moth and Other Essays*. London: Hogarth Press, 1942. 126–132.

——. "On Being Ill." 1926. *Woolf Online*. (2011–2014): 33–45. Web. 27 November 2014.

——. *To the Lighthouse*. 1927. Ed. David Bradshaw. Oxford: Oxford UP, 1998.

"Whose Woods These Are":
Virginia Woolf and the Primeval Forests of the Mind

by Elisa Kay Sparks

Judith Allen's interrogation of the multiple meanings of "wildness" in Woolf's work concentrates mostly on grasses and turf and only glancingly mentions forests, which she categorizes with other wild elements as being "outside" the pale of civilization's pavements (69). The impenetrable forest has long been an archetype for human be*wilder*ment: from Dante's dark wood and Spenser's Red Cross Knight in the Wood of Error to Luke Skywalker on Dagobah. John Berger suggests that for Heidegger the forest was "a metaphor for all reality—and the task of the philosopher was to find the *weg*, the woodcutter's path through it" (126). For Berger the forest is a place *in between*, where the difference in *scale* between the lives of insects and those of ancient trees creates a kind of comparable suspension in *time*, a place where we seek protective shelter but which obliges us "to recognize how much is hidden" (127).

In many ways the environmental antithesis of gardens—wild instead of cultivated, seemingly infinite rather than contained, places of mystery and loneliness as opposed to sites of conventional courtship—forests, and their constituent parts, trees and leaves, have some complex metaphorical valences in Virginia Woolf's work. While a few basic patterns for forest associations can be mapped, in many cases forests are endowed with a variety of meanings so diverse as to seem to purposefully dissolve preconceived generalities, a practice of complicating and undercutting dichotomies brilliantly articulated by Derek Ryan in his new book, *Virginia Woolf and the Materiality of Theory*. This paper examines the multifarious uses of the term "forest" in Woolf's published prose in a counter-phenomenological movement: from exterior extension to inner consciousness, collating glimpses of associations without attempting to impose any nefarious allegorical system.

Forests are often a trope for spatial extension in Woolf. We see this from the first in *The Voyage Out* (1915) where references to the immensity of the South American forest bracket the text; it is part of the "immense space" and the "infinite distances" seen by the party walking to the top of Mt. Rosa (131), a perspective given global reach in Terence Hewett's thoughts after Rachel's death: "he thought of the immense river and the immense forest, the vast stretches of dry earth and the plains of the sea that encircled the earth" (345). But references to the forest's immensity are countered by a careful domestication of it as a scene of courtship. Despite the penchant of various critics for referring to the tropical forest in *The Voyage Out* as a "jungle," the term actually only appears once in the novel, in association with an imaginary vision of India. (Terence is described as "'plunging along, like an elephant in the jungle" [188].) In fact, Woolf consistently refers to the area through which Rachel and Terence walk as a "forest," and interestingly it is one that is more redolent with associations to England and Europe than South America. On the voyage up the river, the British travelers seem largely unable to see the tropical forest in the full strangeness of its difference; instead they repeatedly describe it in terms of known and familiar environments, almost as if they can never quite get out of the artistic image of a tropical forest embroidered by Helen Ambrose during the actual sea voyage (*VO* 33). The silence of the forest is compared to a cathedral (*VO* 268); the river party arrange themselves upon fallen logs so complacently that Terence exclaims "You might be sitting on green chairs in Hyde Park" (*VO* 269), and a wide pathway into the forest is twice described as resembling "a drive in an English forest" (*VO* 270, 272).

In later works, as Woolf becomes more interested in the layered densities implied by archeology, forests also often serve as temporal extensions into the deep and primitive past as well as into the unchartered future. *Mrs. Dalloway* (1925) looks both forward to a time when London is once again "a grass-grown path" (16) and "the country reverts to its ancient shape" (23) and backwards to the age "of tusk and mammoth" "when the pavement was grass, when it was swamp" (79). But the first evidence of a specific archeological motif associated with *forests* is in the manuscript version of *A Room of One's Own* (1929) where the speaker's stroll down the pavements of Whitehall is interrupted by the vision of "the primeval woman in a tree" whose task it was to people "every jungle, every forest every swamp" (*WF* 144), but who would prefer to repudiate the resulting civilization and instead go swinging off into the sunshine (*WF* 143). A similar juxtaposition of present and distant future takes place in "I Am Christina Rossetti" (1930) when Woolf imagines how long Rossetti's poetry will last: until "the proud pinnacles of the Albert memorial are dust [...] when Torrington Square is a reef of coral [...] or perhaps the forest will have reclaimed those pavements and the wombat and ratel will be shuffling on soft sagacious feet among the green undergrowth that will then tangle the area railings" (*E5* 213).

These moments of temporal transparency also occur in the 1934 essay "Walter Sickert" and in Woolf's last novel, *Between the Acts* (1941). In the Sickert essay, the reversion to primeval forest is part of long simile comparing the human eye to that of insects, capable of soaking up worlds of color: "On first entering a picture gallery, whose stillness, warmth and seclusion from the perils of the street reproduce the conditions of the primeval forest, it often seems as if we reverted to the insect stage of our long life" (*E6* 37). *Between the Acts* intensifies such moments of transparent time boundaries, also casting them proleptically forward to the devolved future of a wild England both before and after London. Like the essay "Anon" which Woolf was writing simultaneously, *Between the Acts* stretches back to a time when "the untamed forest was king" ("Anon" 382). References to the forest and temporal immensity bracket and are interspersed in the text. Reading an *Outline of History*, Lucy Swithin repeatedly experiences the present moment bumping up against a time when there were rhododendron forests in Piccadilly (*BTA* 6) or the Strand (*BTA* 21) and mammoths walked what would become the streets of the city. When the maid, Grace, enters the room, it takes Lucy a moment to untangle the temporal moments of being: "It took her five seconds in actual time, in mind time ever so much longer, to separate Grace herself, with blue china on a tray, from the leather-covered grunting monster who was about, as the door opened, to demolish a whole tree in the green steaming undergrowth of the primeval forest" (7). The return of the swallows similarly evokes interpenetrating times: "when the earth, upon which the Windsor chair was planted, was a riot of rhododendrons" (75). At the end of the book, Lucy returns to her historical reverie and experiences another moment of doubled glance, but this time the "[t]hick forests [which] covered the land" point forward. The description of "Prehistoric man [...] half-human, half-ape" comments on Bartholomew's departure from the room (148), and sets the stage for the "heart of darkness" in which Isa and Giles will fight and embrace and possibly create another life (148).

Aligned to these transparent temporal overlays of the forest as a heart of darkness are Woolf's many passing mentions of forests as places in which one can be lost and/or chased by wild beasts, often stand-ins for the rapacity of other human beings. In the 1925 short story "Happiness," Mr. Elton's tranquility is threatened by demands for social interaction which make him feel as if he were "being pursued through a forest by wolves" and must "tear off little bits of clothing and break off biscuits" in order to placate them (*CSF* 179). Two years later the essay "Street Haunting" asks, "what greater delight and wonder can there be than to leave the straight lines of personality and deviate into those footpaths that lead beneath brambles and thick tree trunks into the heart of the forest where live those wild beasts, our fellow men?" (*E4* 490–91). And in 1929's *A Room of One's Own,* in another concatenation of forest mazes with visions of the future, the narrator decides to leave the "difficult questions which lie in the twilight of the future" (about why "the poetry [...] is still denied outlet") because such proleptic musings will "stimulate me to wander from my subject into trackless forests where I shall be lost and, very likely, devoured by wild beasts" (76).

The hunting motif appears most insistently and erotically in *The Waves*, particularly in the imagination of Jinny, social butterfly and dancing queen: "He has broken from the wall. He follows. I am pursued through the forest. [...] Now I hear crash and rending of boughs and the crack of antlers as if the beasts of the forest were all hunting, all rearing high and plunging down among the thorns. One has pierced me" (128–29). It is important to note that Woolf's conventional use of the forest as location for predation is matched by fairy tale associations of the forest with the world of Elizabethan romance. Like Woolf's later essay "An Elizabethan Play," *The Voyage Out* associates the plenitude of forests with the exuberance and creativity of Elizabethan language. The vista from Mt. Rosa takes place near "the stump of an Elizabethan watch-tower" (*VO* 131), the first of several references that emphasize Elizabethan connections to the colony of Santa Maria. The botany of desire in *Night and Day* (1919) seems to be similarly situated in a dream landscape the furniture of which is drawn from the lumber room of "the England of the Elizabethan age" (*ND* 141). The vision of "some magnanimous hero, riding a great horse" through the forest and "by the shore of the sea" (107) reappears at least four times explicitly in the novel, the knight—a clear allusion to the King Arthur of Spenser's *Faerie Queene*, the exemplar of magnanimity—eventually becoming identified with Ralph Denham who (at least in contrast to William Rodney) embodies the same virtue of generous open-mindedness.

This forest fantasy is, however, something of an ambivalent feature in the novel, associated with both the past—Katharine's mother comments that she "used to dream of white horses and palanquins too" (212), and Katharine wonders if her poet grandfather also was looking for "heroes riding through the leaf-hung forests" (320)—and with a world of idealization whose rough magic Katharine sometimes wants to abjure. At one point she declares that "the existence of passion is only a traveller's story brought from the heart of deep forests" (216), and frequently she seems to think that the knight in shining armor is yet another sentimental literary myth. But it is while walking the "forest drives" of Kew that she begins to fall in love with Denham (330).

This sense of the romance of forests seem crucially connected with Woolf's own autobiographical resonances—especially her memories of hunting moths in the woods as
a child which segue into her ultimate internalization of the forest as an image of the
complexity and mystery of the human mind. In *Jacob's Room* (1922), Woolf makes a
metaphorical connection between the leaves of a book and the many-layered scenes of
memory which covertly pivots on a comparison between the pages of paper and the leaves
in a forest; the narrator comments on people's isolation from each other on a London
street, saying "Each had his past shut in him like the leaves of a book, known to him by
heart" (65). One of the leaves shut up in Jacob—as in Woolf herself—is the memory of
night-time hunts for moths in the forest. The haunting scene of a lantern standing on
the ground in the forest, lighting up the surrounding leaves and attracting circling moths
is one of the many *memento mori* which mark Jacob's childhood (21). The death of the
swarming insects is accented by the aural memory of a tree falling in the forest, sending
out "a volley of pistol-shots suddenly in the depth of the wood" (21). This scene is reca-
pitulated at Cambridge where King's College Chapel is similarly described as a lantern,
with white robed figures crossing from side to side in its interior and the black-robed
students arriving like so many forest insects: a "curious assembly" which seems "to have
no purpose" (30) but which is suddenly startled by a "volley of pistol-shots," the sound of
a falling tree, "a sort of death in the forest" (31).

As if to accentuate this tree, whose falling (unlike Jacob's death) *does* make a sound,
we see the arboreal carcass again in the London chapters of *Jacob's Room* where "a lorry
[appears] with great forest trees chained to it" among the traffic crossing Waterloo Bridge
(117). The insects which congregated around the fallen tree also make a reappearance
as the crowds of people in London who are part of the "indescribable agitation of life"
caught in "the webs of the forest [which] are schemes evolved for the smooth conduct of
business" (172).

The key forest passage in *Mrs. Dalloway* is the early extension of the metaphor of the
mind as a drift of leaves when Clarissa/the narrator refers to "that leaf-encumbered forest, the soul" (12)—a phrase which resonates with her contemporaneous description of
Conrad's breadth of vision: "The human heart is more intricate than the forest" (E4 231).
David Bradshaw has convincingly argued that Mrs. Dalloway uses "the ancient *topos* of
falling or fallen leaves [as] an age-old simile for the numberless dead" (107), allowing us
to connect Septimus's reiterated assertions that "leaves were alive" (*MD* 22), that "trees
were alive" (22, 66), and that "[m]en must not cut down trees" (24) to an attempt to call a
halt to the senseless slaughter of wartime. Here the ignorant armies of purposeless insects
converging on the lanterns of the night in *Jacob's Room* become the numberless swirls of
autumn leaves.

A number of works written in the late '20s and '30s evoke this tangled bank of associations between childhood memories, forests, and the mysteries of the human mind,
contradicting or adumbrating Douglas Mao's assertion that "trees and other plants make
especially useful synecdoches for the non-sentient world" (48). In *To The Lighthouse*,
James searches for a way to describe the damage done by his father's selfishness using an
image of the forest which echoes lines from Charles Elton's poem: "And all the lives we
ever lived/And all the lives to be,/Are full of trees and changing leaves" (*TTL* 121): "Turning back among the many leaves which the past had folded in him, peering into the heart

of that forest where light and shade so chequer each other that all shape is distorted, and one blunders, now with the sun in one's eyes, now with a dark shadow" (188). The culminating vision of temporal unity with which the original Hogarth Press edition of *Orlando* (1928) ends, similarly evokes the metaphor of the mind as a chequered forest of chiaroscuro impressions: "everything was partly something else, as if her mind had become a forest with glades branching here and there; things came nearer, and further, and mingled and separated and made the strangest alliances and combinations in an incessant chequer of light and shade" (290).[1] And in *The Waves*, Bernard describes the part of himself kept inviolate as "the margin of unknown territory, the forests of the unknown world" (104), while introspective Louis wishes "to follow the dark paths of the mind and enter the past, to visit books, to brush aside their branches and break off some fruit" (130).

In her fascinating on-line photo-essay about trees in Woolf's writing, Susan Trangmar suggests that the tree often stands as "a metaphor for the organic patterning [of] perception, memory and embodied experience" (1). As an intricate collocation of trees, Woolf's forests serve as spatial and temporal extensions of the mind's phenomenological reach in which "[t]he future shadowed their present, like the sun coming through the many-veined transparent vine leaf; a criss-cross of lines making no pattern" (*BTA* 79).

Note

1.　In the American Harcourt editions the wording was changed to read "everything was partly something else, and each gained an odd moving power from this union of itself and something not itself so that with this mixture of truth and falsehood her mind became like a forest in which things moved; lights and shadows changed, and one thing became another" (237).

Works Cited

Allen, Judith. "Interrogating 'Wildness'." *Virginia Woolf and the Politics of Language*. Edinburgh: Edinburgh UP, 2010. 65–84.

Berger, John. "Into the Woods." *Le Monde Diplomatique* (February 2006). Rpt. in *The Sublime* [Documents of Contemporary Art]. Ed. Simon Morley. London: Whitechapel Gallery and Cambridge, MA: MIT Press, 2010. 125–7.

Bradshaw, David. "'Vanished, Like Leaves': The Military, Elegy and Italy in *Mrs Dalloway*." *Woolf Studies Annual* 8 (2002): 107–125.

Mao, Douglas. *Solid Objects: Modernism and the Test of Production*. Princeton, NJ: Princeton UP, 1998.

Ryan, Derek. *Virginia Woolf and the Materiality of Theory*. Edinburgh: Edinburgh UP, 2013.

Trangmar, Susan. "'A Divided Glance': A Dialogue between the Photographic Project 'A Forest of Signs' and the Figure of the Tree in Virginia Woolf's Writing." *Literary London: Interdisciplinary Studies in the Representation of London* 10.1 (2013): 1–13. *Literarylondon.org*. Web.

Woolf, Virginia. "Anon." In "'Anon' and 'The Reader': Virginia Woolf's Last Essays. A Textual Edition, with Introduction and Commentary." Brenda Silver. *Twentieth Century Literature* 25.3/4 (1979/80): 356–441.

——. *Between the Acts*. 1941. Annot. and intro. Melba Cuddy- Keane. Orlando, FL: Harcourt, 2008.

——. *The Complete Shorter Fiction of Virginia Woolf*. Ed. Susan Dick. 2nd ed. New York: Harcourt Brace Jovanovich, 1989.

——. *The Essays of Virginia Woolf*. 6 vols. Ed. Andrew McNeillie and Stuart N. Clarke. New York: Harcourt, 1987–2011.

——. *Jacob's Room*. 1922. Annot. and intro. Vara Neverow. Orlando, FL: Harcourt, 2008.

——. *Moments of Being: Unpublished Autobiographical Writings*. Ed. Jeanne Schulkind. New York: Harcourt, 1976.

——. *Mrs. Dalloway*. 1925. Annot. and intro. Bonnie Kime Scott. Orlando, FL: Harcourt 2005.

——. *Night and Day*. 1920. New York: Harcourt Brace, 1948.

——. *Orlando: A Biography*. London: Hogarth Press, 1928.

——. *Orlando: A Biography*. 1928. Annot. and intro. Maria DiBattista. Orlando, FL: Harcourt, 2006.

——. *A Passionate Apprentice: The Early Journals 1897–1909*. Ed. Mitchell A. Leaska. New York: Harcourt Brace Jovanovich, 1990.

——. *A Room of One's Own*. 1929. Annot. and intro. Susan Gubar. Orlando, FL: Harcourt, 2005.

——. *To the Lighthouse*. 1927. Annot. and intro. Mark Hussey. Orlando, FL: Harcourt, 2005.

——. *The Voyage Out*. 1915. San Diego: Harcourt Brace Jovanovich, 1968.

——. *The Waves*. 1931. Annot. and intro. Molly Hite. Orlando, FL: Harcourt, 2006.

——. *Women and Fiction: The Manuscript Versions of* A Room of One's Own *by Virginia Woolf*. Transcribed and ed. S.P. Rosenbaum. Oxford, UK: Shakespeare Head/Blackwell, 1992.

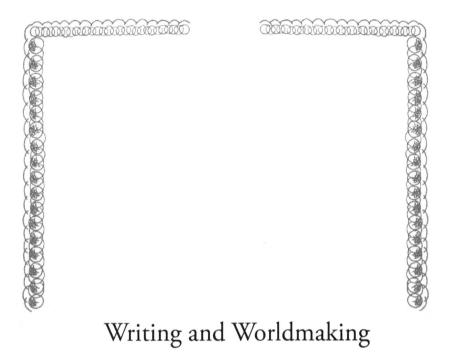

Writing and Worldmaking

NEGATIVE FEMINISM AND ANTI-DEVELOPMENT IN VIRGINIA WOOLF'S *THE VOYAGE OUT*

by Anne Cunningham

Virginia Woolf toiled over her first novel *The Voyage Out* for years before finally publishing it in 1915. While lacking in the formal experimentation and innovation representative of her middle and late period work, *The Voyage Out* is more radical than most critics give it credit for. The novel raises the question of whether a woman can be "a self-determining individual within the conventions and institutions of patriarchal society and, through Rachel Vinrace's failure, seems to answer with a resounding 'no'" (Pease 100). *The Voyage Out* complicates the genre of the *Bildüngsroman* through failure. The young protagonist is unable to inhabit the (usually male) space of maturation and earn her place in the world. Rachel does not achieve significant moral or psychological development through the course of the novel nor does she go on to live a life of purpose after putting her disappointments and mistakes behind her.

I briefly consider here how Woolf's feminist critique in her first novel is linked to a negative feminism and a modernist aesthetic of failure. I am currently working on a larger project on women writers and a modernist feminine aesthetic of failure in the novels of Jean Rhys, Nella Larsen, Djuna Barnes, and Virginia Woolf in which I illuminate how a failure-based aesthetics evinces a commitment to negativity that extends to a feminist practice, and I argue that by rejecting restrictive codes of femininity, these authors' negative female protagonists enact an alternative model of feminine subjectivity based on failure that critiques normative prescriptive codes.

Woolf's Rachel Vinrace enacts a form of shadow feminism—J. Halberstam's concept used to describe an "anti-social, or negative feminism" grounded in refusal, failing and passivity (4).[1] Because readings of Woolf's corpus overlook shadow feminism and tend to explain away the non-triumphant Rachel Vinrace by turning to Woolf's later successful female characters, I discuss *The Voyage Out* here in its own right, to highlight how reading Woolf through a positivist feminist lens obscures shadow feminism. Such readings, I argue, narrow the scope of feminist inquiry.

The novel begins as the widowed Willoughby Vinrace ships off his socially awkward daughter Rachel to South America with her Uncle Ridley and Aunt Helen, in hopes of improving her social graces. At the hotel in South America, Rachel meets a suitor, Terence Hewitt, becomes engaged to him, and, after a brief courtship, dies. *The Voyage Out* refuses to imagine a life for women outside of domestic Victorian middle-class social convention. Rachel's death functions both to critique these values and to advance the form of the novel; the novel "simultaneously narrates a failed *Bildung* for its protagonist and inscribes a successful *Bildung* for its author" (Friedman 109). Woolf, like many of her modernist counterparts put failure to use for aesthetic purposes, but, in *The Voyage Out*, failure serves an ethical purpose too. Failure and a rejection of futurity function as a critique of the choices available to women during Woolf's historical moment. But the novel also anticipates the recent queer theory critique of a patriarchal heteronormative investment in futurity, particularly a rejection of what Lee Edelman refers to as "the cult of the child."[2] Rachel's death occurs after she accepts marriage as her fate. While Rachel is far from heroic, she is disruptive and her absence/death illuminates the necessity for alternative subjectivities beyond the confines of prescribed white patriarchal femininity. Both Rachel's refusal to adhere to prescribed forms of femininity and her ultimate inability to transcend those codes by dying offer a critique grounded in negation; it is in this sense that Woolf evinces a negative modernist turn in her first novel. Rebecca Walkowitz's contention that modernism often proposes that "one must risk being bad—uncertain, inconsistent, and unsuccessful—in order to keep being good" is pertinent here (121). Woolf's writing was purposefully "bad" in the sense that she did not replace "euphemisms of British patriotism with explicitness, transparency, or heroic action," but rather expressed her commitment to critical thinking by developing "narrative strategies that are evasive more than *descriptive* or *Utopian*" (123, emphasis original).

Since conventional understanding of what constitutes "good" literature broadly includes delivering a sense of pleasure to the reader, narrative clarity, direct representation, character development and so on, the lack of these qualities in Woolf's fiction coupled with her canonicity is, on the surface, perplexing. As E. M. Forster wrote of Woolf's writing, there is "no moral, no philosophy, nor has it what is usually understood as Form. It aims deliberately at aimlessness, at long loose sentences that sway and meander" (69). Woolf's "bad" modernist writing here serves more than an aesthetic purpose; it resists literal and unequivocal readings, thereby resisting hegemonic knowledge formations. Moreover, Woolf's evasive modernism "entails a heroic unwillingness to rest in the consolidation of previously existing attitudes" (Walkowitz 121). In this sense, Woolf indeed risked being "bad" in order to be "good." She offers readers not simply a formal use of "failure" but shows us how aesthetic and formal failure in the novel serves an ethical function by refusing to consolidate the social norms embedded in traditional literary form. It is this aesthetic of failure, its formal and thematic innovation in *The Voyage Out*, that makes a more nuanced feminist critique than the direct didacticism found in sentimental or turn-of-the-century feminist protest novels.

One characteristic of a modernist aesthetic of failure is that that it entails female subjectivities that disintegrate rather than develop, refusing a narrative of redemption or progress: Woolf's *The Voyage Out* does not precisely fit this mold.[3] Rachel Vinrace doesn't disintegrate or slowly become undone. Instead, she is unformed from the outset: she is described as "silent, vague, and more of an absence than a presence"; she "knows nothing; she thinks and feels, but she is an outsider to a system that produces knowing individuals" (Pease 102). Yet this outsider quality of Rachel's assumes a stubborn social passivity that disrupts the coming of age plot and is therefore subversive (Esty 129).

Woolf disrupts the coming of age plot by placing Rachel's death so soon after she accepts her engagement proposal. While her death prevents Rachel maturing, the novel suggests her death thwarts an otherwise inevitable life of confinement to female domesticity expected from women of Rachel's classed and raced status; it serves as a bleak reminder of the narrow alternatives available to such women. Throughout the novel, Rachel repeatedly expresses a desire for alternatives but she clearly lacks knowledge of what those alternatives might be. Early on Rachel says, "No. I shall never marry" (62) to Mrs. Dalloway. She later says men and women in general "should live separate; we cannot understand each other; we only bring out what's worst" (174). And, after Rachel and Terence are engaged, Terence says to Rachel "I sometimes think you're not in love with me and never will be. [...] You don't want me as I want you—you're always wanting something else" (352). Rachel thinks "she wanted many more things than the love of one human being—the sea, the sky. [...] [S]he could not possibly want only one human being" (352). After this, she replies to Terence, "[l]et's break it off then"; yet the "words did more to unite them than any amount of argument. [...] They knew that they could not separate; painful and terrible it might be, but they were joined forever" (353). Curiously, Rachel is certain she does not want marriage and romantic love as her sole aim in life, but has no idea of what else to do, and so accepts being "painfully and terribly" joined to him "forever." Moreover, the things Rachel wants—the sea, the sky—cannot be concretely possessed. Death then, accidental or not, is the alternative Woolf constructs.

Critics tend to (rightly) read Rachel's death as a feminist critique. Christine Froula argues that Rachel's death signifies the difficulties Woolf confronted in trying to imagine an alternative to the female initiation plot, but her "more powerful representations of female artists" in her later work enables us to interpret "Woolf's representation of female initiation and authority in *The Voyage Out* not as an ultimate failure but…as an allegorical measure of the very great odds that Woolf herself conquered in forging her own powerful artistic authority" (63). Froula's focus on later "powerful" representations of female artists who manage to triumph over their circumstances underscores how feminism is bound up with notions of progress and positivity and also highlights the success/failure dichotomy so prevalent in feminism. Incidentally, this binary is reiterated by the fact Woolf's subsequent novels are considered more successful as works of literature. That Woolf would only in her later work represent a third, alternative feminine subjectivity represented as the successful woman artist who doesn't perish is telling of how feminism has long been framed in liberal terms as freedom and equality or death. The tendency in feminism to affirm a success/failure dichotomy that is not necessarily achievable also ignores the neoliberal logic of the dichotomy. Furthermore, it elides the position of a historical and, in many ways, ongoing negative feminine subjectivity that was and is for some women an available and alternative position outside of a Eurocentric patriarchally defined femininity.

But by *not* turning to Woolf's later representations of successful female artists in an effort to redeem Rachel, we more clearly understand how a success/failure feminist dichotomy is constructed and normalized. We might also recognize how the critical tendency to privilege positivist, liberal feminism(s) obscures shadow feminism. Although understandable, the success/failure binary obscures how negativity and failure were—and undoubtedly remain—fundamental aspects of women's experience. In a broader, more general sense, the critical tendency to privilege narratives that affirm liberal notions of women's inclusion in or triumph over patriarchal power structures detracts from how negativity and failure may be reframed as a powerful critique of patriarchy.

I have argued elsewhere that negativity and failure are crucial to the formulation of an alternative modernist feminist response that is neither totalizing in its negation of the protagonist nor mired in a redemptive plot complete with a triumphant protagonist.[4] The narratives of disintegration penned by "minor" women modernists employ a shadow feminism that few critics have recognized. Woolf is far from occupying a marginal or "minor" status—she is acknowledged as one of the most important canonical modernist novelists—but it is striking how much her first novel of anti-development shares with minor women writers.

Although perceived by many characters in the novel as naïve and unformed, Rachel's "stubborn passivity" functions as a nuanced but powerful critique of patriarchal conventions. Her fiancé launches a diatribe against the unfair treatment and neglect of women's lives that in some ways prefigures Woolf's argument in *A Room of One's Own*: "the lives of women of forty, of unmarried women, of working women [...] one knows nothing whatever about them. [...] It's the man's view that's represented you see. [...] Doesn't it make your blood boil? If I were a woman I'd blow someone's brains out" (245). Rachel's response is to launch into a lengthy account of her past "twenty-four years" in a laboriously uneventful paragraph that details the daily domestic chores and dull childhood she led with her two spinster aunts. She concludes by saying "[a] girl is more lonely than a boy. No one cares in the least what she does. Nothing's expected of her. Unless one's very pretty people don't listen to what you say....And that is what I like" (248). Though seemingly a passive response in comparison to Terrence's outrage, Rachel enjoys being liberated from the surveillance and expectations that would follow her if she were conventionally "pretty." Rachel's nascent negative feminism is also evident when the two receive congratulatory notes on their engagement. Rachel exclaims to Terence, "I never fell in love, if falling in love is what people say it is, and it's the world that tells the lies and I tell the truth. Oh what lies—what lies!" (294). By objecting to the uniformly unimaginative, lame congratulatory notes, she also is objecting to inhabiting the role of wife as prescribed by patriarchal bourgeois society. Revolted, she says: "[t]hat any one of these people had felt what she felt [...] or had even the right to pretend for a single second that they were capable of feeling it, appalled her [...] and if they didn't feel a thing why did they pretend to?" (294). Rachel's anger at something as seemingly innocuous as a social nicety is an indication of a deeper rejection of normative values; however, because Rachel dies, she does not voice a fully realized critique of these dominant values that disturb her. Yet all of her rejections of normativity throughout the narrative reflect negative feminism and a queer negativity. When Terence tries to comfort her after the note card episode, he extols the virtues of one of the letter writers, a Mrs. Thornsbury who has had many children, likening her to "an old tree murmuring in the moonlight or an old river going on and on" (294). Rachel angrily repudiates him, "I won't have eleven children. [...] I won't have the eyes of an old woman. She looks at one up and down, as if one were a horse" (294). The rejection of futurity and her questioning of marriage as a woman's sole means of fulfillment here anticipates negative feminism and the queer anti-social thesis. Yet Rachel is unable to develop this anti-social subjectivity and fails to fully embody a negative feminist mode of resistance.

Woolf experiments with women's blocked agency in *The Voyage Out*. By showing Rachel's self-determination begin to emerge only to have her fall ill and die, she refuses to write the dominant feminist corrective to the normative script with a heroine who triumphs over her obstacles and transcends her circumstances. Rather, Woolf's first novel is steeped in formal and thematic uses of failure, invoking a negative feminist critique of patriarchal and enlightenment ideas about women's place in the world as educated citizens and as artists. While the majority of Woolf's writing is representative of a more positivist feminism, her first novel opens us up to negative feminism. It is important to remember that these two forms of feminism don't exist in an either/or binary but are often intertwined. As the term suggests, it is easy to let shadow feminism go undetected, but I've hoped to show here the benefit of reading Woolf through the lens of negative feminism to illuminate how feminine failure can provide us with an affective reorientation. Negative feminism may not construct a "better" feminist paradigm in and of itself, but it does help us ask better questions in the effort to widen the scope of feminist inquiry today.

Notes

1. Halberstam defines shadow feminism as a "feminism grounded in negation, refusal, passivity, absence, silence, [that] offers spaces and modes of unknowing, failing and forgetting as part of an alternative feminist project, a shadow feminism [that has] nestled within more positivist accounts and unraveled their logics from within…[and] speaks in the language of self-destruction, masochism, an anti-social femininity and a refusal of the essential bond of mother and daughter that ensures that the daughter inhabits the legacy of the mother and in doing so, reproduces her relationship to patriarchal forms of power (124).

2. Edelman uses this concept in *No Future* to delineate how heteronormative ideology centers the figure of the child to give shape to a rhetoric and politics of reproductive futurity—for Edelman, the figure of the queer is constructed as its radical negation.

3. Protagonists who directly disintegrate in this mode: Jean Rhys's *The Voyage in The Dark* shows the downward spiral of Anna Morgan; in Nella Larsen's *Quicksand*, Helga Crane makes one poor decision after another, finally ending up on death's door after giving birth to numerous children and marrying a repulsive preacher; Djuna Barnes's *Nightwood* ends with Robin Vote abjectly positioned on all fours, barking at a dog in a secluded woodland church.

4. See my article "'Get on or Get Out': Failure and Negative Femininity in Jean Rhys's *Voyage in the Dark.*"

Works Cited

Cunningham, Anne. "'Get on or Get Out': Failure and Negative Femininity in Jean Rhys's *Voyage in the Dark.*" *Modern Fiction Studies:* Special issue on Women's Writing, New Modernisms, and Feminist Theory. Ed. Anne Fernald. 59.2 (2013): 373–394.

Du Plessis, Rachel. *Writing Beyond the Ending.* Bloomington: Indiana UP, 1985.

Edelman, Lee. *No Future: Queer Theory and the Death Drive.* Durham, NC: Duke UP, 2004.

Esty, Jed. *Unseasonable Youth: Modernism, Colonialism, and the Fiction of Development.* Oxford: Oxford UP, 2012.

Forster, E.M. "Visions." *Virginia Woolf: The Critical Heritage.* Eds. Robin Majumdar and Allen McLaurin. New York: Routledge, 1975. 68–70.

Friedman, Susan Stanford. "Spacialization, Narrative Theory, and Virginia Woolf's *The Voyage Out.*" *Ambiguous Discourse: Feminist Narratology and British Women Writers.* Ed. Kathy Mezei. Chapel Hill: U of North Carolina P, 1996. 109–136.

Froula, Christine. "Out of the Chrysalis: Female Initiation and Female Authority in Virginia Woolf's *The Voyage Out.*" *Tulsa Studies in Women's Literature* 5.1 (1986): 63–90.

Halberstam, Judith. *The Queer Art of Failure.* Durham, NC: Duke UP, 2011.

Hite, Molly. "The Public Woman and the Modernist Turn: Virginia Woolf's *The Voyage Out* and Elizabeth Robin's *My Little Sister.*" *Modernism/Modernity* 17.3 (2010): 523–548.

Marshik, Celia. *British Modernism and Censorship.* Cambridge: Cambridge UP, 2006.

——."Publication and 'Public Women': Prostitution and Censorship in Three Novels by Virginia Woolf." *Modern Fiction Studies* 45.4 (1999): 853–886.

Miller, Tyrus. *Late Modernism: Politics of Fiction and the Arts Between the World Wars.* Berkeley: U of California P, 1999.

Pease, Allison. *Modernism, Feminism, and the Culture of Boredom.* Cambridge: Cambridge UP, 2012.

Walkowitz, Rebecca. "Virginia Woolf's Evasion: Critical Cosmopolitanism and British Modernism." *Bad Modernisms.* Durham, NC: Duke UP, 2006.

Woolf, Virginia. *A Room of One's Own.* 1929. Orlando, FL: Harcourt Brace, 1992.

——. *The Voyage Out.* 1915. New York: Penguin, 1992.

Upheavals of Intimacy in *To the Lighthouse*

by *Maayan P. Dauber*

In a recent issue of *The New Yorker*, James Wood published an article entitled "Why? The Fictions of Life and Death," tracking his early interest in literature: "Fiction doesn't merely replicate the license you have, within your head, to think what you like. It adds the doubleness of all fictional life. To witness that freedom in *someone else* is to have a companion, to be taken into the confidence of otherness. We share and scrutinize at the same time; we are, and are not, Raskolnikov, and Mrs. Ramsay, and Miss Brodie, and the narrator of Hamsun's "Hunger," and Italo Calvino's Mr. Palomar" (36). Wood's observation is apt, but it is too generalizing. It is true that we, as readers, may feel a certain "doubleness" when we locate in a character a behavior or trait with which we identify, when we see in their struggles struggles that we in part share. But not all fictional characters are the same. Raskolnikov and Mrs. Ramsay are both characters we follow, characters whose lives we attempt to track, protagonists, to put it simply, but they are not characters who function novelistically in the same way. And if Wood is blind to the difference, Woolf is not. In her 1925 essay, "The Russian Point of View," Woolf writes that what Russian literature teaches is to "make yourselves akin to people. [...] But let this sympathy be not with the mind— for it is easy with the mind—but with the heart" (174). Sympathy of heart is crucial for Woolf's understanding of the difference between herself and the Russians, between, more generally, realist fiction of the nineteenth century and modernist fiction of the twentieth century, and she goes on to say that "the assumption that in a world bursting with misery the chief call upon us is to understand our fellow-sufferers" (174) is what Russian literature offers over the possibilities she now sees for herself. Woolf understands, in other words, that while one of the primary feats of Dostoevsky's novel is the way in which even an average Joe finds himself in the throes of Raskolnikov's morally tortured soul, one of the triumphs of her Mrs. Ramsay is the way in which she resists such finding altogether. Mrs. Ramsay is not someone whose life we both "share and scrutinize," a character whom we both "are and are not." She is someone to whose mind's wanderings we seem to have endless access and yet someone we can never really know. She is a modernist character and the emblem of one of modernism's greatest paradoxes: the more self-reflective a character is, the deeper her inner life, the further away we seem to move from her.

Woolf meditates on this modernist preoccupation with characters in flight in "Mr. Bennett and Mrs. Brown" (1923) and "Character in Fiction" (1924) in which she compares Georgian characters to Edwardian ones of writers like Arnold Bennett, John Galsworthy, and H.G. Wells. For them, subjects are easily transcribed. They have histories, family trees, and tax receipts. They are characters, as a critic put it of Dickens's characters, who have full biographies. But Woolf's Mrs. Brown—like Mr. and Mrs. Ramsay, too—far from having a biography, does not even have a first name. In her, Woolf discovers a character so elusive that capturing her seems impossible. She is a subject who whispers in Woolf's ear "My name is Brown. Catch me if you can" ("Character" 37). And while Woolf will attempt to catch this character on the run, her primary aim is to capture the run itself, to represent people in flight from the usual categories of character and novelistic form that seem now in the early twentieth century outmoded. So Woolf invents a story or two about this Mrs. Brown sitting across from her on the train: that she is a widow, that she has a son who has become wayward, that she is in financial straits. And yet, like all of Woolf's characters, Mrs. Brown is not someone we ever really know, and that is just the point.

Woolf thematizes the problem of knowledge, intimacy, and emotional connection throughout her career, giving it particular attention in *To the Lighthouse* (1927) in which she not only denies the reader's efforts to learn a character but also the other characters' desires to know each other. Lily Briscoe desperately desires to know Mrs. Ramsay but is rebuffed by her closed mind, which is sealed like a beehive. This is a poignant image. The critic Blakey Vermeule, echoing Melville, uses the same metaphor to talk about the problem of "knowledge of others' minds" in literature more generally: "The mind of man, says the narrator of Melville's *Benito Cereno*, is a subtle hive. Writers are always coming up with new ways of getting inside" (75). For Vermeule, all novelistic characters, indeed all people, have minds that are sealed and it is the job of the writer to worm her way into them. But Woolf responds differently than other writers and rather than trying to get inside Mrs. Ramsay's sealed mind and present us with someone we can know, follow, identify and sympathize with, Woolf works toward a relation in the condition of the impossibility of knowing itself.

This is more than a philosophical issue. Martha Nussbaum, another writer interested in the problem of other minds, has persuasively explained this Woolfian tactic to preserve the hive as her dramatization of an epistemological impossibility. No one can ever know another and Woolf's great achievement, in Nussbaum's estimation, is that she understands this fundamental truth. Nussbaum (and Vermeule) may be right philosophically but what are the affective qualities of this epistemological impossibility? How does it feel to come close to someone only to realize that it will never be close enough? And if we never can know another, how do we continue to relate to people anyway? What are the qualities of this new relation? And what can it offer? Finally, how can we account for the shift Woolf's elision of other minds marks in the history of the novel? For if when reading *Jane Eyre* we are compelled by an identification with Jane, what happens in *To the Lighthouse* where no such relationship to Mrs. Ramsay exists? Why do we keep reading? And how can we describe the emotional tenor of that reading?

In a word, I call this alternative form of connection without knowledge, relations without intimacy, "pathos," an emotion explicated as early as ancient Greece but recrudescent in a particularly modernist form. Explored especially by Aristotle, who refers to it as a temporary and extrinsic emotional disruption, untethered, unlike ethos, to character, the distinctiveness of the term is elided during the rise of the British novel when pathos is used synonymously with sympathy.[1] But with the introduction of the modernist novel in the early twentieth century, and with Woolf's work in particular, I propose that the specificity of its meaning, different from sympathy, becomes visible again and I offer the term, used explicitly by Woolf at the end of *To the Lighthouse,* as an affective mode uniquely suited to the modernist condition. In part, I use the term "pathos" in its ordinary meaning, where it suggests despair without immediacy, pity without moral judgment, caring without closeness. I use it in the everyday way in which we tend to use it, to describe a desperate news item about someone we've never met or to chronicle the emotional effect of a film we've seen on screen. In fact, we tend to use it most frequently about a work of art. The top hits for "pathos" on Google when I wrote this, for example, all turned up reviews of various art performances: a review of an opera about Milli Vanilli, the Coen brothers' film *Inside Llewyn Davis*, and ice skating at the Sochi Winter Olympics. In this colloquial usage, we almost never mean to describe a situation of a close relative or friend and if we do, as with the term "pity," we do so only to suggest a certain remove from them. Pathos would never be a term used to describe what a husband and wife feel for each other, or what family members feel for each other, for pathos is a reaction not to someone "we are and are not" but to someone who is neither, to whom the binary no longer applies—a feeling about a Mrs. Ramsay or Mrs. Brown rather than a Raskolnikov or Jane Eyre.

This marks a departure from realist novels of the eighteenth and nineteenth centuries, which are structured around the sympathy and identification of readers for characters. Once thought, in its early stages in England, to be a tool of idleness and distraction, the novel regroups to become, at its most extreme, a tool meant for instruction in moral living. In the preface to *The Adventures of Roderick Random* (1748), for example, Tobias Smollett describes the mechanics of this new, not yet named, form: "The reader gratifies his curiosity, in pursuing the adventures of a person in whose favour he is prepossessed; he espouses his cause, he *sympathizes* with him in distress, his indignation is heated against the authors of his calamity; the humane passions are inflamed" (89, emphasis added). Smollett is describing a form of literature whose primary function is sympathy and identification. This is a trend that continues well into the nineteenth century with novelists like Jane Austen, Charles Dickens, and Elizabeth Gaskell.[2] And it coincides with theories of sentiment and sympathy propounded by eighteenth-century thinkers like Adam Smith and David Hume who argued that man's moral worth is measured by his ability and willingness to identify and sympathize with others.[3]

This begins to change in the late nineteenth and early twentieth centuries, however, and novels of the period seem to dismiss the readerly sympathy and identification that was so crucial to the workings of the realist novel. In part, this shift from sympathy to what I call pathos is the result of ruptures of subjectivity that mark modernist subjects as people without secure grounds, "wandering I's," as Michael Levenson describes them.[4] Woolf herself comically chronicles just such a shift in her memorable comment that "On or about December 1910 human character changed" ("Character in Fiction" 38). And the philosopher Charles Taylor describes something similar. In *Sources of the Self: The Making of Modern Identity*, Taylor explains that modern man gets his first full philosophical elaboration from Descartes, when the self, for the first time, exhibits "inwardness," the realization that he is a unique entity. No longer constituted in advance by some externally imposed structure, he is already himself, whatever his relation to that structure will enable him to become—a sentient, thinking, reasoning agent who makes choices, creates connections to the world, acts on and reacts to the world from the inside of himself. Descartes's famous axiom, "I think therefore I am," succinctly describes just this—a subject constituted by his own, internal capabilities. Of course, this picture of the subject is complicated throughout the development of the realist novel and J. Hillis Miller rightly argues that Victorian novelistic characters come into self-knowledge not through Descartes's "I think, therefore I am" but through something like "'I know myself through my relations to others,' or, 'I am conscious of myself as conscious of others'" (5). Yet even Miller's self can be summarized by what Taylor goes on to call "punctual," or what Michael Levenson calls "justified," "composed of intelligible motives, susceptible to moral analysis" (106). Modernist subjects, however, are neither punctual nor justified but diffuse, fractured, and decentered to the end. Reasoning, feeling, and acting may still have import of sorts. After all, modernist subjects are still people. But these activities no longer seem to be organized as functions of the subjects who do the reasoning, feeling, and acting. And trying to locate in novels of the period anyone whole enough to identify with, a task once natural and inherent to novel reading, is no longer possible. Accordingly, if, as readers of modernist characters, we continue to experience an affective relation to them, it is an affect of a different sort. I return to *To the Lighthouse* to explain the way in which the alternative feeling of pathos emerges in the absence of whole people with whom readers can identify and sympathize.

In the final section of the novel, the Ramsay family—Lily Briscoe and Mr. Carmichael among them—return to their beach house. Ten years have passed since the beginning of the novel and Mrs. Ramsay is dead. Her children Prue and Andrew are dead too and Mr. Ramsay is understandably distraught. The reader is also distraught, only, since the death of Mrs. Ramsay and her children is relayed in parentheses rather than in a fully dramatized deathbed scene, once the centerpiece of sympathetic response in Victorian literature,[5] our distress is tempered. "[Mr. Ramsay, stumbling along a passage one dark morning, stretched his arms out, but Mrs. Ramsay having died rather suddenly the night before, his arms, though stretched out, remained empty]" (128). Here, instead of a frail Mrs. Ramsay dying slowly, we get the stoic terms of parentheses that bracket her death.[6] Worse yet, she is not even the subject of the sentence. Her empty-armed, widower husband Mr. Ramsay dominates, leaving her as the nothingness that fails to fill his outstretched arms. Certainly Mrs. Ramsay's death is a shock but it is a shock that refuses to send the reader into throes of emotional turmoil. Mrs. Ramsay's death does not ask the reader to sympathize. For there is hardly a character there—squashed, as she is, between these parentheses—to sympathize with. Her death rather asks the reader to experience it as pathos, which is to say that it should be acknowledged, witnessed, felt in all of its sadness, and then moved on from.

This tempered emotional state is precisely the condition in which Lily finds herself. Thus feeling, all the more, the inappropriateness of Mr. Ramsay's demand for sympathy, she turns cold: His "immense self-pity, his demand for sympathy poured and spread itself in pools at her feet, and all she did, miserable sinner that she was, was to draw her skirts a little closer round her ankles, lest she should get wet" (152). From a certain, nineteenth-century angle, the problem here is one of degree: Mr. Ramsay requires too much sympathy and Lily gives too little. Or Mr. Ramsay is self-consumed and Lily is socially detached. Here, the solution would lie in both willing themselves closer to each other, willing themselves into what Adam Smith called a "harmony of society," in which the spectator must feel the sufferer's pain and the sufferer, in turn, must align himself with the spectator's relative comfort. In part, this is true. Mr. Ramsay is self-consumed and Lily is detached but an even temper and a more generous heart will not solve anything because it is sympathy itself—rather than the refusal of characters to be sympathetic enough— that's really at issue. And Lily's decision to "draw her skirts a little closer" is not the result of personal preference but of her confrontation with a modernist world that Mr. Ramsay, Victorian that he is, refuses to recognize.

Woolf does not stop there. The outmodedness of sympathy does not yield emotional drought. As the novel marches on, Woolf offers an alternative. Still overwhelmed by his emotional demands, Lily describes Mr. Ramsay like this: "Look at him, he seemed to be saying, look at me; and indeed, all the time he was feeling, Think of me, think of me" (153). Lily is repelled by Mr. Ramsay. His demand for sympathy is not just unreasonable but unethical, a form of narcissism rather than a form of intimacy, and Woolf is keen to critique this aspect of sympathetic relations.[7] In her exasperation, Lily bursts out: "'What beautiful boots!' she exclaimed. She was ashamed of herself. To praise his boots when he asked her to solace his soul; when he had shown her his bleeding hands, his lacerated heart, and asked her to pity them, then to say, cheerfully, 'Ah, but what beautiful boots you wear!' deserved, she knew, and she looked up expecting to get it, in one of his sudden roars of ill temper, complete annihilation. Instead, Mr. Ramsay smiled" (153). Lily's solution, which she is confident will end in "complete annihilation," is to remark on something as inane as Mr. Ramsay's boots. Rather than getting her feet wet, she marvels at the beauty of that which protects feet from getting wet. This is, as Lily knows, a rejection of sympathy. She will not put herself in Mr. Ramsay's shoes, as sympathy demands, but compliments their beauty instead, praising, in other words, their utility in protecting against such an invasion. But that this protective accouterment is what's beautiful to Lily, rather than ugly, unnecessary, or frivolous, is a sign not so much of her rejection of sympathy and all other forms of relating as well, but rather a sign that she is merely turning the wheel of emotion towards pathos. For the discovery of the beautiful in that which keeps people out, in that which protects the distance between people, is precisely the connection that pathos captures.

Ultimately, this is even the language with which Lily understands the connection: "She could see them [Mr. Ramsay's boots] walking to his room of their own accord, expressive in his absence of *pathos*" (153, my emphasis). The boots express pathos without him because pathos is an emotional response to the absence of whole, traditional subjects. It is the emotion, as I've already described, of one who feels far from another and, indeed, of a feeling *for* that farness. It signals an emotional relationship without the intimacy of subject-to-subject contact, a relationship that lacks whole subjects to begin with. But it signals, too, a feeling precisely *for* that lack, offering it as a relation instead. For by acknowledging the pathos in Mr. Ramsay's boots, Lily and Woolf organize feeling around just the loss of sympathy and the loss of traditional forms of intimacy that once required such a person-to-person connection. Mr. Ramsay, self-centered narcissist though he is, accepts Lily's offer—and, surely, the reader is invited to accept Woolf's offer, too.

Notes

1.   See Oksenberg Rorty.
2.   See Lee for counter arguments to the idea that the realist novel is founded fundamentally on sympathy.
3.   For eighteenth-century criticism of sympathetic relations, see, for example, Fielding's *Shamela* and Mary Wollstonecraft. Still, it is precisely because the novel in its greater form assumes this relationship between reader and character in the first place that critics are anxious about its dangers.
4.   For alternative accounts on what produced changes in character, see, for example, Trotter, Boone, and Freedman.
5.   See Wheeler.

6.   E.M. Forster uses a similar technique in *A Passage to India*. For a more thorough account of death in the modernist novel, see Friedman.
7.   Nussbaum, in a more redemptive reading of Mr. Ramsay, points to Mr. and Mrs. Ramsay's marriage as a model of ethical relations.

Works Cited

Aristotle. *The Rhetoric and the Poetics of Aristotle*. Trans. W. Rhys Roberts and Ingram Bywater. New York: Random House, 1984.

Boone, Joseph Allen. *Libidinal Currents: Sexuality and the Shaping of Modernism*. Chicago: U of Chicago P, 1998.

Freedman, Ariela. *Death, Men, and Modernism: Trauma and Narrative in British Fiction from Hardy to Woolf.* New York: Routledge, 2003.

Friedman, Alan Warren. *Fictional Death and the Modernist Enterprise*. Cambridge: Cambridge UP, 1995.

Gallagher, Catherine. "The Rise of Fictionality." *The Novel, Volume 1: History, Geography, Culture*. Ed. Franco Moretti. Princeton, NJ: Princeton UP, 2006.

Lee, Wendy Anne. "Failures of Feeling in the British Novel From Richardson to Eliot." Diss. Princeton University, 2010.

Levenson, Michael. *Modernism and the Fate of Individuality: Character & Novelistic Form from Conrad to Woolf.* Cambridge: Cambridge UP, 1991.

Miller, J. Hillis. *The Form of Victorian Fiction: Thackeray, Dickens, Trollope, George Eliot, Meredith, and Hardy*. Notre Dame, IN: U of Notre Dame P, 1968.

Nussbaum, Martha. "The Window: Knowledge of Other Minds in Virginia Woolf's *To the Lighthouse*." *New Literary History* 26.4 (1995): 731–53.

Oksenberg Rorty, Amélie. "Aristotle on the Metaphysical Status of 'Pathe.'" *The Review of Metaphysics* 37.3 (1984): 521–46.

Smith, Adam. *The Theory of Moral Sentiments*. 1759. New York: Barnes and Noble, 2004.

Smollett, Tobias. "Preface to *The Adventures of Roderick Random* (1748)." *Novel Definitions: An Anthology of Commentary on the Novel, 1688–1815*. Ed. Cheryl Nixon. Toronto, Ontario: Broadview, 2009.

Taylor, Charles. *Sources of the Self: The Making of the Modern Identity*. Cambridge: Harvard UP, 1992.

Trotter, David. "E-Modernism: Telephony in British Fiction 1925–1940." *Critical Quarterly* 51.1 (2009): 1–32.

Vermeule, Blakey. *Why Do We Care About Literary Characters?* Baltimore, MD: Johns Hopkins UP, 2010.

Wheeler, Michael. *Death and the Future Life in Victorian Literature and Theology*. Cambridge: Cambridge UP, 1990.

Wood, James. "Why? The Fictions of Life and Death." *The New Yorker*. 9 Dec. 2013: 34–39.

Woolf, Virginia. "Character in Fiction." 1924. *Selected Essays*. Ed. David Bradshaw. Oxford: Oxford UP, 2008. 37–54.

———. "Mr. Bennett and Mrs. Brown." 1923. *Selected Essays*. Ed. David Bradshaw. Oxford: Oxford UP, 2008. 32–36.

———. "The Russian Point of View." 1925. *The Common Reader*. New York: Harcourt, 2002. 173–82.

———. *To the Lighthouse*. 1927. New York: Harcourt, 1989.

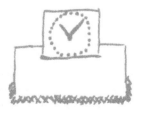

THE RECONCILIATIONS OF POETRY IN VIRGINIA WOOLF'S *BETWEEN THE ACTS*; OR, WHY IT'S "PERFECTLY RIDICULOUS TO CALL IT A NOVEL"

by Amy Kahrmann Huseby

In this paper, I focus on Virginia Woolf's developing attitude toward the relationship between poetry and prose. I say developing because one of the grand narratives that scholars of many time periods cling to is that a text or texts by an author equates to a static representation universalizable across that author's oeuvre. One thing this conference has made clear is that Woolf's work cannot be approached in that way. She was a life-long learner, and her corpus was developing along with her thinking. As a result, my work attempts to demonstrate one of the ways that we can trace the development of an author's generic project, here through identifying a moment of intellectual genesis in which Woolf began to formulate how poetry would inflect her work. Of course, Woolf scholars from time to time raise the question of Woolf's approach to poetry. Jane Goldman has identified a "growing poetic tendency" in Woolf's writing (49); Gillian Beer points out that the "melding" of language is crucial to reading *Between the Acts* (1941); and Kathleen McCluskey has offered us an extensive structuralist reading of the internal coherence produced by phonemic repetitions, and specifically forms of alliteration, in *The Waves* (1931) and *To the Lighthouse* (1927) (49). In fact, McCluskey locates the "saturation" of Woolf's language partly in "the poetry of her prose" (126). Too, at this conference over the past two days, I have heard work by Tony Brinkley whose *Nachleben* methods trace the textual afterlife of Miltonic and Wordsworthian poetry into Woolf's *A Room of One's Own* (1929), while Lindsay Vreeland has pointed out the orality and generic blending extant in *The Waves*. So let us agree that Woolf was "doing something poetic" in her work and that scholars are aware of this fact. It is at least on our radar. However, despite the critical attention to poetic language in Woolf's work, scholars consistently stop short of suggesting that Woolf's prose transformed into something different, something which no longer was purely the "novel."

Consequently, this paper rethinks the genre of Woolf's texts in light of her conscious articulation of the relationship between the worlds of prose and poetry, an articulation which suggests an underexplored relationship between these modes beyond mere binary opposition. Indeed, I suggest that Woolf's insight about Thomas De Quincey in her essay "Impassioned Prose" (1927), that we read De Quincey "for his poetry," may well apply to Woolf herself (*E4* 361).[1] While Emily Kopley claims "Woolf's rivalry with poetry" (8) and Sara Sullam has recently asserted Woolf had a "low estimation of poetry" (1), Woolf's own essays and reviews suggest that her attitudes toward poetry were far less antagonistic, and that she, in fact, understood poetry as an innovative way to "re-form the novel" (*L1* 356).[2] Taking Woolf's essay "Impassioned Prose" and *Between the Acts* as case studies, this essay considers poetry's impact on the development of Woolf's style. More broadly, the implication of Woolf's hybrid poetic prose method is that the modern novel was not only born of an appreciation for the possibilities afforded by poetic forms but that the reconciliation of prose and poetry reached fruition in Woolf's texts.

Put differently, my project is attempting to answer two questions raised by Jane Goldman's exploration of Woolf's elegiac and lyrical experimentalism. Goldman asks whether Woolf's words are "best understood as poetry or prose?" and whether we should "follow Woolf in reaching for a new name to supplant 'novel'?" (67). My answer is yes, we should follow Woolf into those experimental reaches for something to supplant the term novel. But my answer is also no, her words are not poetry *or* prose. Rather, her words are simultaneously poetry and prose, or what I've termed "euphonic prose." In searching for a new name for Woolf's texts to supplant 'novel,' I sought to retain the prosaic as that which structures the visual space of the page, while I also wanted to suggest a term that embodied the conflation of the poetry and the prose without privileging one over the other. Since terms such as "poetry," "verse," "meter," and "rhythm" are highly unstable, and were especially so in the late-nineteenth and early-twentieth century as Meredith Martin's recent monograph *The Rise and Fall of Meter* demonstrates, I felt that privileging one of these terms and merely hyphenating it with prose was imprecise. We have, after all, already got verse novels, prose poetry, prosimetric novels, and many other hybrid genres.[3] But Woolf was doing something different, something which scholars like McCluskey identify at the level of sound. Euphony is the quality of being pleasing to the ear, which in *Between the Acts* takes the form of Anglo-Saxon alliterative meter, and so I chose euphonic prose as the name for Woolf's project and offer it here as a replacement for what she infamously called that "potent bogey," the novel ("What is a Novel?" *E4* 415).

Since alliteration comprised a basic structure of Anglo-Saxon prosody, the use of heavy alliteration in prose suggests something more at work than mere authorial word play, especially on the part of an author as well-read as Woolf. In fact, it points to her recognition of how the tonal qualities of language create meter. Woolf's attention to the sounds of words is evident in any of her texts, though it is fair to say her attentiveness has not been rewarded with equivalent scholarly treatment of the ongoing development of her poetic language. *To the Lighthouse* tends to receive the lion's share of critical attention related to language. In *To the Lighthouse*, some of my favorite alliterative examples include, "vast flapping sheet," "smell of salt," and "like the leathern eyelid of a lizard" (15, 12, 37). Such phrases have the equivalent of what cooks call "good mouth feel." Note, too, that the latter phrase—"like the leathern eyelid of a lizard"—is pentameter. You can also hear that such phrases are not necessarily easy to say, and I feel this difficulty as I read them aloud: "like the leathern eyelid of a lizard" is an awkward half-trochaic, half-iambic tongue twister. Yet, alliterative phrases want to be read aloud, as Anglo-Saxon meters were often performed orally, thereby pulling the language from the silent space of the page into an embodied readerly reality. Since *Between the Acts* is a text structured by performance, it seems especially appropriate to highlight Woolf's awareness of Anglo-Saxon meter as audible text.

The longer version of my project delves into multiple close readings of Anglo-Saxon alliterative meter in *Between the Acts*, but for time considerations, I offer only one example here. I quote at length Woolf's description of a fish pond in order to illustrate her virtuosic use of Anglo-Saxon alliterative meters in her euphonic prose. For your ease of reference, I've highlighted the consonance in bold and underlined the assonance.

Under the **thick pl**a**te** of **gr**ee**n** water, gl**azed** in **th**ei**r** s**e**lf-c**e**ntre*d* world, **fish** sw**a**m—**gold**, spl**a**shed with wh**i**te, str**ea**ked with **bl**a**ck** or silver. S**i**lently, they m**a**noeuvred in their w**a**ter world, poised in the **blue** patch made by the sky, or **sh**ot silently to the **e**dge where the **grass**, tr**e**mbling, m**a**de a fringe of n**o**dding **sh**a**d**ow. On the water-pavement **sp**iders printed their delicate feet. A **grain** f**e**ll and **sp**ir**a**lled **down**; a p**e**t**a**l f**e**ll, **filled** and sank. At that the **fl**ee**t** of boat-sh**a**ped bodies **paused**; **poised**; equi**pp**ed; m**a**iled; then with a w**a**ver of undul**a**tion off they **fl**a**shed**. (BTA 30)

This interlineated reading of the dense alliterative language in *Between the Acts* reveals the extent to which Woolf's language reverberates even within the space of a single paragraph. Sometimes the consonance takes only the initial letter (self-centered, swam, splashed, streaked, silver) or links an initial sound with a final sound (grass, sky), while at other times it includes a paired sound, such as GR or SH (green, grass, grain; shot, shadow, shaped, fish). Note, too, the way that internal consonant sounds, such as the S or the P in "paused; poised; equipped," redound upon initial or terminal consonant sounds. While it might seem like I am making over much of Woolf's clever language in this one passage, Kathleen McCluskey's structuralist methods produce multiple fascinating charts, which arrive at a related conclusion about the sound of Woolf's language. She writes: "In the Woolf texts, vowel patterns are generally much more than decorative; rather they are of central import in the communication. The passage from *To the Lighthouse* which describes Mrs. Ramsay's response to her husband's silent but insistent demand for sympathy provides an illustration. Mrs. Ramsay gathers herself together and pours forth her understanding. In James' eyes, she: "seemed to r**ai**se h**er**s**e**lf with **an** **e**ffort, **an**d **a**t once to p**ou**r **e**rect into the **air** **a** r**ai**n of **e**n**er**gy, a column of spr**ay**" (emphasis the author's; McCluskey 19). To illustrate the internal coherence between phonemes, or sound quantities, and the larger structure of *To the Lighthouse*, McCluskey provides an accompanying schematic of the vowel patterns in the sentence she quotes. Below is my re-drawing of that schematic.

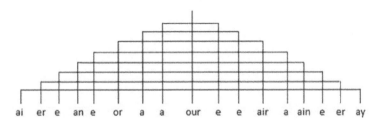

ai er e an e   or   a   a   our e   e   air a ain e er ay

Figure 1: Vowel patterns; adapted from McCluskey, *Reverberations: Sound and Structure in the Novels of Virginia Woolf*, p.19.

We know that Woolf was actively puzzling through the differences between poetry and prose when she wrote *To the Lighthouse* and "Impassioned Prose" contemporaneously during the summer of 1926. Woolf wrote to Vita Sackville-West in March that the style of *To the Lighthouse* was "all rhythm," a comment suggesting that the text was something more than the non-elaborative everyday speech of prose and instead attuned to a certain metrical quality (*L*3 247). And Vita's subsequent reaction to the completed text was that it was "perfectly ridiculous to call it a novel" (Sackville-West 197). Once Woolf began working on "Impassioned Prose" that summer, she expressed frustration at the essay's time demands, writing that she was "slogging through a cursed article" while she could see her "novel glowing like the Island of the Blessed far far away over dismal wastes" (*L3* 276). So why take the time to work on an essay about De Quincey when she clearly wanted to be working on *To the Lighthouse*? Because "Impassioned Prose" was a thought experiment for Woolf in which she began to explore the possibilities of what would become euphonic prose. I argue that the hybrid poetry-prose project Woolf began while composing *To the Lighthouse* and "Impassioned Prose" ripened over the course of her career and reached fruition in *Between the Acts*. The summer of 1926 was a moment of genesis for her methods, and, though frustrating from a time commitment standpoint, the essay on De Quincey was also necessary to her future creative process. In a July 1926 letter to Vita Sackville-West, Woolf famously wrote that she was "in the middle of writing about [De Quincey], and my God Vita, if you happen to know do wire whats the essential difference between prose and poetry—it cracks my brain to consider" (*E4* 368n1). That De Quincey provided a model for Woolf of how she might conflate poetry and prose becomes evident from a close reading of "Impassioned Prose."

Woolf asks with no small irony in "Impassioned Prose" what "could be more damaging" than to assert that one reads a prose writer for his or her poetry, "[f]or if the critics agree on any point it is on this, that nothing is more reprehensible than for a prose writer to write like a poet. Poetry is poetry and prose is prose—how often have we heard that!" (*E4* 361). Yet, the entire point of Woolf's essay is to argue the contrary: that poetry and prose can and do mix; that poetry improves prose; and that prose writers attain heightened levels of skill when they allow something of the "impassioned" possibilities of poetry into their work. One of Woolf's major claims in "Impassioned Prose" is that the novel is hegemonic and no longer the appropriate vehicle for contributing to knowledge: "But unfortunately for those who would wish to see a great many more things said in prose than are now thought proper, we live under the rule of the novelists. If we talk of prose we mean in fact prose fiction. And of all writers the novelist has his hands fullest of facts" (*E4* 362). The conventional novelist's job, according to Woolf, is to detail the quotidian, how a character "gets up, shaves, has his breakfast, taps his egg, reads *The Times*," and poetry allegedly undermines this regimentation. Woolf says, in fact, that such a novel's method "is the antithesis of prose poetry" and that the "whole tendency therefore of fiction is against prose poetry" (*E4* 362). And, so, those seeking to do something new with literature are subjugated to the "rule of the novelists." Poetry muddies the waters too much; it complicates what should be an orderly succession of details. Conventional novelists, Woolf claims, ignore "that side of the mind which is exposed in solitude. [...] They ignore its thoughts, its rhapsodies, its dreams, with the result that the people of fiction bursting with energy on one side are atrophied on the other. [...] But happily there are in every age some writers who puzzle the critics, who refuse to go in with the herd. They stand obstinately across the boundary lines" (*E4* 362). In this group of writers who "stand obstinately across the boundary lines," Woolf includes Robert Browning, Samuel Butler, and De Quincey. Poets all. And, obviously, I would that we include Woolf herself in this lot. She was among those "who would wish to see a great many more things said in prose than are now thought proper" and "who refuse to go in with the herd," like Browning, Butler, and De Quincey.

Woolf seems to have recognized some affinity with De Quincey's odd ways, possessing an "extraordinary gift for the dead languages, and a passion for acquiring knowledge of all kinds" (*E4* 363). De Quincey had to find a mode for expressing his thoughts and neither prose nor poetry independently satisfied. Woolf continues,

> The truth was that he dreamed—he was always dreaming. [...] But in what form was he to express this that was the most real part of his own existence? There was none ready made to hand. He invented, as he claimed, 'modes of impassioned prose'. With immense elaboration and art he formed a style in which to express these 'visionary scenes derived from the world of dreams'. For such prose there were no precedents, he believed; and he begged the reader to remember [...] [that] 'a single false note, a single word in a wrong key, ruins the whole music'. (*E4* 363)

In other words, what form of writing will honor both the world of dreams and the world of the everyday? Woolf's reference here to the relationship of the particulate "single false note" or "single word" to "the whole music," reinforces my belief that theorizing the novel without considering the language level is problematic, while also gesturing back to the musicality of Anglo-Saxon meter that I've identified elsewhere in her work. De Quincey offered a model for Woolf of prose without precedent, of impassioned prose that, through "elaboration and art," married poetry and prose in a hybrid form deftly executed by an author conscious of the relationship between the euphony of words and the whole composition (*E4* 363).

That Woolf's understanding of the possibilities afforded by a combined verse-prose form developed in the mid-1920s while she was working on her essay "Impassioned Prose" suggests not only a clear genesis for her formal innovation but a recovery of poetry's centrality to the construction of the modern novel. Examples of Woolf's euphonic prose in *Between the Acts*, taking the form of Anglo-Saxon alliterative meter, discloses poetry's subversive potential to forestall the cementation of the novel's form and, indeed, to enhance the novel's already acknowledged malleability. In conclusion, Woolf's response to the question of why novels are in prose might well have come from her essay "Modern Novels" (1922): "Let the historian of literature decide. It is for him, too, to ascertain whether we are now at the beginning, or middle, or end, of a great period of prose fiction; all that we ourselves can know is that, whatever stage we have reached, we are still in the thick of the battle" (*E3* 31). Woolf herself was historically immersed in the "thick of the battle," the ongoing conflict over prose and poetry, hacking and slashing her way across conventions. In trying to craft a space for something new to breathe in her work, to "capture" the flag of "fuller and finer truths" through poetry, Woolf succeeded in carving an unconventional path for herself with the fine edge of her euphonic prose, and in so doing she made short work of the "bogey" that had become the novel.

Notes

1.   Though many authors have written about the lyrical mode in Woolf's work, the extent to which the euphony of verse at the language level constructed her novels has been overlooked and undertheorized. While the integral relationship between verse and prose in the modern novel as I will detail it in this paper has not been adequately explored, some attempts to address Virginia Woolf's use of poetry include Justicia, Pellan, Richter, Harvena, and Sutton. For excellent feminist and psychological inquiries into the lyrical mode in Woolf's work, see Friedman. For the foundational work on the lyrical novel, see Freedman.
2.   It is worth pointing out that Kopley's work positions Woolf against the members of the Auden circle, such as Julian Bell, Cecil Day-Lewis, and W. H. Auden himself, as well as other modern male poets. Given that narrow focus, asserting a general antagonism between Woolf's writing and poetry as a genre, or poetic language, is overbroad. When Woolf is positioned historically in continuity with late-nineteenth- and early-twentieth century poetry and prosodic debates about meter, as Meredith Martin suggests we do, her work suggests something quite different.
3.   Prosimetric novels as defined by Catherine Robson are those which contain both prose and verse, such as Lewis Carroll's Alice books.

Works Cited

Beer, Gillian. *Virginia Woolf: The Common Ground*. Ann Arbor: U of Michigan P, 1997.

Freedman, Ralph. *The Lyrical Novel: Studies in Hermann Hesse, Andre Gide, and Virginia Woolf*. Princeton, NJ: Princeton UP, 1963.

Friedman, Susan Stanford. "Lyric Subversion of Narrative in Women's Writing: Virginia Woolf and the Tyranny of Plot." *Reading Narrative: Form, Ethics, Ideology*. Ed. James Phelan. Columbus: Ohio UP, 1989. 162–185.

Goldman, Jane. "From *Mrs. Dalloway* to *The Waves*: New Elegy and Lyric Experimentalism." *The Cambridge Companion to Virginia Woolf*. 2nd ed. Ed. Susan Sellers. Cambridge: Cambridge UP, 2010. 49–69.

Justicia, Nellie Teresa. "Poetics of *Between the Acts* by Virginia Woolf." Diss. NYU, 1986.

Kopley, Emily and Sara Sullam. "To the Readers: Woolf and Literary Genre." *Virginia Woolf Miscellany* 83 (2013): 1–4.

Kopley, Emily. *Virginia Woolf and the Thirties Poets*. London: Cecil Woolf, 2011.

Martin, Meredith. *The Rise and Fall of Meter: Poetry and National Culture, 1860–1930*. Princeton, NJ: Princeton UP, 2012.

McCluskey, Kathleen. *Reverberations: Sound and Structure in the Novels of Virginia Woolf*. Ann Arbor: U of Michigan P, 1996.

Pellan, Françoise. "Virginia Woolf's Posthumous Poem." *Modern Fiction Studies* 29.4 (1983): 695–700.

Richter, Harvena. "The Hidden Poetry of Virginia Woolf." *Virginia Woolf Miscellany* 57 (2001): 3–4.

Robson, Catherine. "Reciting Alice: What Is the Use of a Book Without Poems?" *The Feeling of Reading: Affective Experience & Victorian Literature*. Ed. Rachel Ablow. Ann Arbor: U of Michigan P, 2010. 93–113.

Sackville-West, Vita. *The Letters of Vita Sackville-West and Virginia Woolf*. Eds. Louise DeSalvo and Mitchell Leaska. San Francisco: Cleis Press, 1984.

Sutton, Emma. "'Putting Words on the Backs of Rhythm': Woolf, 'Street Music,' and *The Voyage Out*." *Paragraph* 33.2 (2010): 176–96.

Woolf, Virginia. *Between the Acts*. 1941. Annot. and intro. Melba Cuddy-Keane. Orlando, FL: Harcourt, 2008.

——. *The Essays of Virginia Woolf*. Ed. Andrew McNeillie and Stuart N. Clarke. 6 vols. San Diego: Harcourt Brace Jovanovich, 1986–2011.

——. *The Letters of Virginia Woolf*. Ed. Nigel Nicolson and Joanne Trautmann. 6 vols. London: Chatto and Windus, 1975–80.

——. *To the Lighthouse*. 1927. Annot. and intro. Mark Hussey. Orlando, FL: Harcourt, 2005.

Virginia Woolf, Composition Theorist: How Imagined Audiences Can Wreck a Writer

by *Kelle Sills Mullineaux*

In 1987, Peter Elbow published an article that generated a buzz among composition scholars due to his argument that writers should, at least in the beginning stages of drafting, ignore their audience. "An audience is a field of force," he explained. "The closer we come—the more we think about these readers—the stronger the pull they exert on the contents of our minds" (94). In Elbow's conception, although some audiences are "enabling" and some "inhibiting," most audiences are simply distracting. The effects of these audiences could be devastating to the writing process, as Elbow wrote: "Sometimes we get so tied in knots that we cannot even figure out what we *think*" (97).

Elbow's claims, by his own admission, are ambitious; they go against a common mantra repeated by teachers of writing: *Keep your audience in mind.* Some scholars responded to Elbow with shock and concern, but a fan of Virginia Woolf might read Elbow's work and express no surprise at all. The trials of writing are a familiar subject in Woolf's works, and she was an author who spent an unusual amount of time describing her drafting and revision processes to others. One of her most discussed topics was the relationship between writer and audience. Over fifty years before Elbow's work made waves among compositionists, Woolf published "Professions for Women" (1942), which included a passage describing how her own imaginary audience member, "The Angel in the House," haunted her early writing.

> Had I not killed her she would have killed me. [...] For, as I found, directly I put pen to paper, you cannot review even a novel without having a mind of your own, without expressing what you think to be the truth about human relations, morality, sex. And all these questions, according to the Angel in the House, cannot be dealt with freely and openly by women; they must charm, they must conciliate, they must—to put it bluntly—tell lies if they are to succeed. Thus, whenever I felt the shadow of her wing or the radiance of her halo upon my page, I took up the inkpot and flung it at her. (59–60)

In Woolf's case, certain audiences (represented by the poetic ideal of The Angel in the House) proved to have the ability to influence her writing the same way they influenced her behavior.

Woolf's and Elbow's criticisms of audience are a dissenting opinion in a field that places a great deal of importance on audience awareness. Audience has traditionally been considered necessary to understanding the rhetorical situation as described by dozens of theorists, notably Lloyd Bitzer and Richard Vatz, who remind us of how central the writer/audience relationship is to a quality final product. However, Woolf and Elbow argue that certain kinds of audience do more harm than good.

To better make sense of Woolf's and Elbow's claims, we must acknowledge how many kinds of audiences exist for a writer. Usually, we are picturing the readers of a given work. However, while "readers" implies a literal group of people, "audience" is broader and carries a range of meanings: the physical audience who reads a work, the audience called for by the rhetorical situation that inspired the work, the audience as the reader conceptualizes it, and the audience as the writer conceptualizes it (Park 184). Of these audiences, the one that Woolf and Elbow are concerned with is the audience a writer imagines while creating his/her work.

Imagined audience is often the result of the experiences the writer has had with others, so discussion of the imagined audience requires consideration of the range of social issues that could affect writers: a host of insecurities, societal expectations, and pressure to conform to imagined or real ideals. These pressures take shape as the imaginary audience's responses in a writer's imagination. Once present, they haunt writers more than real audiences ever could. As Woolf wrote, "[i]t is far harder to kill a phantom than a reality" ("Professions" 60).

In regard to Woolf's merit as a composition theorist and her conception of imagined audiences, I offer three arguments. First, Woolf foresaw many of the concerns about imagined audience that would eventually interest modern composition theorists. Second, Woolf's conceptualization of the writer's relationship to audience is revealed through study of both her fiction and nonfiction. Finally, the writer/audience relationship that Woolf illuminates is helpful for teaching students and complements the goals of composition as a field.

WOOLF AS COMPOSITIONIST

One of Woolf's strengths as a writing theorist is her willingness to look at writers as individuals, "suffering human beings," and imagine the problems that could cause them to struggle with their craft (*AROO* 41). She does not place the blame for writers' audience-based anxieties solely on their gender, education, or economic statuses, but instead imagines the problem of audience over-awareness as a combination of these factors and more, stressing that every individual struggles with a unique set of anxieties. The benefit of this way of thinking is that Woolf does not exclude certain writers or minimize the pressures they face. All writers, in Woolf's conception, are pressured by the systems they live in. Because Woolf explored such a wide variety of audience insecurities, her theories on the subject are comparable to those of modern composition scholars.

For example, one source of insecurity for writers is academic—the language and methods used by the university can be difficult for new students and outsiders to emulate. In *A Room of One's Own* (1929), as Woolf struggles in the library, she observes a nearby Oxbridge student who, with "grunts of satisfaction," guides his question toward its answer (28). Woolf suspects that an Oxbridge education makes the difference between her lack of ability and the ease of the capable stranger. However, Woolf does not resent the student and is empathetic toward how advantageous positions can prove limiting. Just as Woolf suffers from the knowledge of being "locked out" of the university, she wonders whether the Oxbridge student carries the physical knowledge of being "locked in" (24). According to Woolf, both tradition and lack of tradition can negatively affect a writer. Half a century after Woolf made this suggestion, David Bartholomae confirmed her suspicions, writing about the frustration felt by teachers whose students, hoping to sound scholarly, try on well-intentioned yet stilted and awkward voices in their academic writing ("Inventing the University"). Both Woolf and Bartholomae highlight the sense of unworthiness writers may feel in the face of university authority, demonstrating through their examples the desire students may feel to act and write in emulation of The Powers that Be.

That said, some writers are challenged to a greater degree than others due to their disadvantageous placement within society. In *A Room of One's Own*, Woolf often describes women's difficulties with writing as "infinitely more formidable" than men's due to the constant influx of opinions from influential men who treat the artistic endeavors of women "not [with] indifference, but [with] hostility" (52). Because writing is dependent on material and social freedom (106), writers without these freedoms will be severely hindered in their efforts (49).

Woolf's arguments about the effect of social position on writers are not restricted to her nonfiction. In a number of her novels, her artistic characters struggle to convey their message to an intimidating, unaccepting audience. Their successes and failures further illustrate Woolf's theories.

Conveying Theory through Fiction

Though Woolf often wrote of the distress readers feel when authors use their characters as a "mouthpiece" for their discontents ("Women and Fiction" 47), the artistic characters in her fictional works often reflect Woolf's views on the writing process and her theories about the writer/audience relationship. For instance, it is possible to see Woolf's statements about the plight of female authors reflected in *To the Lighthouse*'s painter-in-training, Lily Briscoe. Lily starts the novel as a terrified beginner, worried about the critiques that will surely come should others see what she is working on. The chauvinist critics and social commentators Woolf constantly quotes in *A Room of One's Own* are given voices in *To the Lighthouse* through the art teacher, Mr. Paunceforte; the patriarch, Mr. Ramsay; and the aspiring young scholar, Charles Tansley. Tansley's mocking taunt, "Women can't paint, women can't write" (51), constantly echoes through Lily's head as she works. Both the taunt and Lily are referenced almost blatantly by Woolf in *A Room of One's Own*, where she remarks, "[t]here would always have been that assertion—you cannot do this, you are incapable of doing that—to protest, to overcome. Probably for a novelist this germ is no longer of much effect; for there have been women novelists of merit. But for painters it must still have some sting in it" (54). This sting is acutely recognized by Lily, who "often felt herself—struggling against terrific odds to maintain her courage; to say: 'But this is what I see; this is what I see'" (*TTL* 23).

However, in accordance with Woolf's belief that dominant writers still face writing blocks due to imaginary audiences, she depicts both Mr. Ramsay and Tansley as insecure in their place as scholars. Mr. Ramsay, a brilliant academic, struggles with a difficult philosophical problem. Woolf describes it using only letters and focuses on the process of reaching R from Q. "Few people in the whole of England" can attain Q, but Mr. Ramsay is dissatisfied and wishes to reach the next letter, R (*TTL* 37). Though he draws from the manliest qualities he possesses, the imagined audience still comes to distract him. In his head, he hears people say that he is "a failure," and that he will never reach R. In the end, he never does (37). Mr. Tansley faces similar insecurities about manhood, but his are largely tied to social status—he does not have the money, prestige, or background necessary to feel comfortable among the Ramsays. He desperately parrots the authoritative declarations Mr. Ramsay gives, but his listeners disrespect him all the more for it.

At first, Lily is one of these listeners, hating and fearing his words, but Lily becomes a successful example of the artistic process Woolf would eventually articulate in *A Room of One's Own*. According to Woolf, a novel shows integrity if it can convince a reader it shows the truth, "whole and entire" (*AROO* 73). She argues that many novels fail for a number of reasons, including the heavy endurance required to sustain imagination for the length of a novel, or outside factors influencing the authors' thoughts and preventing them from clearly representing their visions (72). These factors are often caused by the writer's adverse relationship to an imagined audience (73, 80, 92). Woolf encouraged writers to stop being distracted by their imaginary audiences, arguing that personal agendas and fear disturbed the prose.

Pressure is a constant presence in Lily's life, and her anxieties usually manifest themselves as abuses heaped on Mr. Tansley. At dinner, she feels that he is "the most uncharming human being she had ever met" (88). She cannot function naturally around him: her wish to see him suffer as she suffers clashes with her desire to stop thinking about him so she can focus on her painting. However, when Lily returns to her picture in the final scenes of *To the Lighthouse*, Tansley appears in her head once more. This time, she is ready to confront him rationally: "Her own idea of him was grotesque, Lily knew well, stirring the plantains with her brush. Half one's notions of other people were, after all, grotesque. They served private purposes of one's own. He did for her instead of a whipping-boy. [...] If she wanted to be serious about him she had to help herself to Mrs. Ramsay's sayings, to look at him through her eyes" (200). Mrs. Ramsay serves as the lens through which Lily learns to observe patriarchs without hate, similar to how 500 pounds freed Woolf's narrator in *A Room of One's Own*. A neutral thought is also a focused one, so her dislike of Tansley's opinions does not distract her from her artistic vision.

Both the men and women Woolf depicts in *A Room of One's Own* and *To the Lighthouse* are adversely distracted by their imagined audiences. Both sides are distracted by gender roles and self-conscious about their masculinity or femininity. Woolf encouraged writers to write androgynously, independent of the limitations placed upon them by gender roles, and for Lily this means confronting her feelings towards both Mr. and Mrs. Ramsay. In her analysis of androgyny in Woolf's works, Nancy Topping Bazin describes Lily's painting as "the androgynous work of art" and argues that Lily manages to establish an equilibrium between Mr. and Mrs. Ramsay through her painting (124). Lily comes to terms with both characters, accepting them even as she refuses to be bound by the gender roles they endorse. Once the pressures of gender no longer appear as a distracting imaginary audience, Lily achieves her vision.

Lily's success story is one of the few in Woolf's fiction. All of her writers and artists struggle with imaginary audiences, and some fail spectacularly. In *Jacob's Room*, Julia Hedge mirrors the library scenario in *A Room of One's Own*, and Clara Durrant is thwarted by the format conventions of her own diary (*JR* 111, 71). *Between the Acts'* Miss La Trobe literally hides from her audience, convinced that her vision has not been conveyed. The most conventional example of a failed writer is *The Waves'* Bernard, which seems surprising given his background; he is educated, rich, male, and well-connected. However, his unwillingness to be himself in front of others, as well as his dependence on approval, prevent him from completing even a letter.

The diversity of these would-be writers serves to illustrate how Woolf's advice to write independently of societal roles is applicable to a variety of individuals and situations. Any of these characters convey important observations about the writing process, but a question remains: what can we do with these representations, and how can any of these characters' struggles prove relatable to those of composition students?

THE FUTURE OF WOOLF AND COMPOSITION

In 1981, while discussing issues of audience in *Writing With Power*, Elbow quoted a passage from a novel whose author, he felt, understood how to stop worrying about audience and "pour all her attention" into what she was saying. The passage was the first paragraph of *Mrs. Dalloway*, and in Elbow's analysis of Woolf's process, he wrote:

> She couldn't have been saying to herself, "Let's see, how can I begin this novel so that the poor reader is not lost or perplexed?" *If* she was thinking consciously about the needs of her audience during this opening paragraph she must have been saying something more like, "How can I start this novel with words so real that readers don't care a hoot about their own needs and are happy to be disoriented."
>
> "Beware of Virginia Woolf," you may say. "Only people who are already experts should ever dream of taking her for a model." Perhaps. But probably not. (177)

Out of all the authors in the world, Elbow chose Woolf—whose complex and inaccessible prose has often been deemed "expert" level—as a model for how writers at any level might create something great by letting go of audience. Elbow's depiction of Woolf's process is similar to the practices she recommended for herself and others. Alex Zwerdling writes that Woolf came to see writing for a general audience as "a form of pandering and self-censorship," and explains that over time, Woolf learned to write for a small circle of friends and intimates—"ideal readers" (8). Restricting her audience to a group of open-minded friends enabled Woolf to create increasingly radical works. When she worried that her experiments had become too radical for even a small audience, she began writing for an "audience of one": either herself or a close friend (9). As Woolf explained in her own diary, she considered it "good practice" to write for herself, believing that the practice loosened her writing and made professional work easier (*Writer's Diary* 13).

Teachers of writing often encourage students to practice audience-less writing, telling them to journal, or freewrite, but advice from a famous writer is always taken a little more seriously. Instructors may find that students can connect to Woolf's views about writing even if her writing is difficult to understand. In her Autobiographical Writing class, Stephanie Oppenheim found that students were able to connect to Woolf's experiences, finding "autobiographical resonance" even when Woolf's experiences were situationally and linguistically much different from their own (175). Danell Jones turned writing advice excerpts from Woolf's essays and publications into an imagined conversation between Woolf and creative writing students in a workshop setting. In these conversations, Woolf answers their questions and "encourages them to embrace their particular vision" (33). When teachers find a way to bridge language and time gaps, Woolf becomes a writer to whom even beginning writers can relate.

Woolf also has a place within the annals of composition theory, as her observations complement several epistemologies within the field. Cognitivists relate to Woolf's openness about the drafting process as well as her candid descriptions of her own writing failures. Expressivists strongly identify with Woolf's audience frustrations and accept her journaling practices as wise. Woolf's works have already found some popularity in the classrooms of social constructionists, who value her groundbreaking observations about the relationship between gender and writing. However, Woolf's depictions of audience anxiety go beyond the boundaries of gender and suggest that every individual struggles with unique anxieties due to the multiple roles he/she must play in society. Scholars who write about the pressures writers face—especially scholars who examine how culture, race, and sex can marginalize writers—continue Woolf's arguments.

Woolf is a challenging, but worthwhile, addition to the composition field and the writing classroom. Not only do her arguments match the current trajectory of composition research, but she offers extensive analysis of writers' emotional processes. Both Woolf and the composition theorists provide hope for the writers they study, looking ahead to a time when writers are no longer blocked by constraint. Although the pressures writers face may never disappear, this does not mean writers have to be bound by their internal critics. In Woolf's novels, although characters feel pressured by the world around them and worry about what their audiences would think, the ones who overcome that pressure achieve peace with their works. Woolf suggested that "there may be some state of mind in which one could continue without effort because nothing is required to be held back" (*AROO* 97). Present day theorists expand on her suggestion pedagogically, finding ways of encouraging students to write without fear.

Works Cited

Bartholomae, David. "Inventing the University." *Cross-Talk in Comp Theory: A Reader.* 2nd ed. Ed. Victor Villanueva. Urbana, IL: NCTE, 2003. 523–553.

Bazin, Nancy Topping. *Virginia Woolf and the Androgynous Vision.* New Brunswick, NJ: Rutgers UP, 1973.

Bitzer, Lloyd. "The Rhetorical Situation." *Philosophy and Rhetoric* 1 (1968): 1–14.

Elbow, Peter. "Closing My Eyes as I Speak: An Argument for Ignoring Audience." *Everyone Can Write: Essays Towards a Hopeful Theory of Writing and Teaching Writing.* New York: Oxford UP, 2000. 93–112.

——. *Writing With Power: Techniques for Mastering the Writing Process.* New York: Oxford UP, 1981.

Hite, Molly. Introduction. *The Waves.* By Virginia Woolf. Annot. and intro. Molly Hite. Orlando, FL: Harcourt, 2006. xxxv–lxvii.

Jones, Danell. *The Virginia Woolf Writers' Workshop: Seven Lessons to Inspire Great Writing.* New York: Bantam, 2007.

Oppenheim, Stephanie. "I Couldn't Relate to It: Virginia Woolf and the Limits of Autobiographical Reading in the Community College Classroom." *Who Speaks for Writing: Stewardship in Writing Studies in the 21st Century.* Ed. Jennifer Rich and Ethna Lay. New York: Peter Lang, 2012. 167–176.

Park, Douglas. "The Meanings of 'Audience'." *Landmark Essays on Rhetorical Invention in Writing.* Ed. Richard E. Young and Yameng Liu. Davis, CA: Hermagoras Press, 1994. 310–319.

Vatz, Richard. "The Myth of the Rhetorical Situation." *Philosophy and Rhetoric* 6.3 (1973): 154–161.

Woolf, Virginia. *Between the Acts*. 1941. Annot. and intro. Melba Cuddy-Keane. Orlando, FL: Harcourt, 2008.

——. *Jacob's Room*. 1922. Annot. and intro. Vara Neverow. Orlando, FL: Harcourt, 2008.

——. "Professions for Women." 1942. *Women and Writing*. Ed. and intro. Michèle Barrett. New York: Harcourt Brace Jovanovich, 1979. 57–63.

——. *A Room of One's Own*. 1929. Annot. and intro. Susan Gibar. Orlando, FL: Harcourt, 2005.

——. *To the Lighthouse*. 1927. Annot. and intro. Mark Hussey. Orlando, FL: Harcourt, 2005.

——. *The Waves*. 1931. Annot. and intro. Molly Hite. Orlando, FL: Harcourt, 2006.

——. "Women and Fiction." 1929. *Women and Writing*. Ed. and intro. Michèle Barrett. New York: Harcourt Brace Jovanovich, 1979. 43–52.

——. *A Writer's Diary: Being Extracts from the Diary of Virginia Woolf*. Ed. Leonard Woolf. London: Hogarth, 1953.

Zwerdling, Alex. "The Common Reader, the Coterie, and the Audience of One." *Virginia Woolf Miscellanies: Proceedings of the First Annual Conference on Virginia Woolf*. Ed. Mark Hussey and Vara Neverow-Turk. New York: Pace UP, 1992. 8–9.

THE PRECARITY OF "CIVILIZATION" IN WOOLF'S CREATIVE WORLDMAKING

by Madelyn Detloff

Let us never cease from thinking—what is this "civilization" in which we find ourselves? What are these ceremonies and why should we take part in them? What are these professions and why should we make money out of them? Where in short is it leading us, the procession of the sons of educated men?

Virginia Woolf, *Three Guineas* (63)

L et me begin by crossing my fingers as a sign of my ambivalence about what I am about to undertake here. I fear that I may be walking a little too close to the edge of apologetics for dominant cultural (white, Western, US-based, educated, middle-class) privilege than is comfortable or safe for my soul—but I am willing to risk that damnation in order to reassert the value of the imaginative, the well-wrought, the beautiful, to the common weal—the public good. This may sound a bit too much like David Brooks, who wrote a moving, but ultimately mistaken, lament for the state of the humanities last year in *The New York Times*:

> Back when the humanities were thriving, the leading figures had a clear defini-
> tion of their mission and a fervent passion for it. The job of the humanities was
> to cultivate the human core, the part of a person we might call the spirit, the
> soul, or, in D.H. Lawrence's phrase, "the dark vast forest."…The humanist's job
> was to cultivate this ground—imposing intellectual order upon it, educating
> the emotions with art in order to refine it, offering inspiring exemplars to get
> it properly oriented. Somewhere along the way, many people in the humanities
> lost faith in this uplifting mission.

The culprits in this sad story of lost faith are those who allegedly abandoned notions of "truth, beauty, and goodness" in order to espouse ideas about "political and social catego-ries like race, class and gender" (Brooks). In other words, according to Brooks, you can have your truth and beauty or you can have your social justice but you can't have both because that will just confuse the youth of America and drive them away from our inspir-ing exemplars to more prosaic pursuits like accounting or engineering.

But *who says* the two concerns (truth and beauty/social justice) are mutually exclu-sive? One could ask Brooks: For *whom* are questions of race, class, gender, merely external matters? (Ought I not ask this question for fear of being accused of sending yet another generation of bright-eyed young people skittering across campus to the business or en-gineering school?) Instead, I will ask: Can a serious examination of the beautiful and the good coexist with advocacy for social justice—with feminist, antiracist, anti-imperialist, critically engaged consciousness? Or are the beautiful and the good abstractions to be contemplated only when one has the luxury to get away from "real world" concerns like earning one's bread or demonstrating at the barricades?

These are "willful" questions insofar as they keep resurfacing whenever we think that the question has been safely put it to rest.[1] In 1940, Woolf noted the discomfort of the 1930s generation of "leaning tower" writers who found the relative insulation from political concerns that their education and economic privilege should have afforded them eroded by the political upheavals of fascism, communism, and Nazism (*M* 139–40). Fast forward to 1993 when Edward Said critiqued the presumed separation of cultural and political spheres in *Culture and Imperialism*: "we have on the one hand an isolated cultural sphere, believed to be freely and unconditionally available to weightless theoretical speculation and investigation, and, on the other, a debased political sphere, where the real struggle between interests is supposed to occur. To the professional student of culture— the humanist, the critic, the scholar—only one sphere is relevant, and, more to the point, it is accepted that the two spheres are separated, whereas the two are not only connected but ultimately the same" (56–57). Or, for a more personal example, let me fast forward again to the year 2000, my second year of teaching at a state university with a student demographic drawn largely from the working poor families of East and Central Los Angeles. Picture a graduate seminar on literary and cultural theory populated by a dozen-or-so LA Unified School District high school teachers taking the course for professional development reasons and another handful of students enrolled in the course in order to cultivate their self-professed appreciation for literature. On the syllabus were two theories of culture that elicited strong responses from both sets of students. The first was John Guillory's *Cultural Capital* and the second was Raymond Williams's "Culture is Ordinary." Guillory argues that literature has served as a marker of "cultural capital" disseminated by institutions (schools) that reproduce and perpetuate unequal class relations.[2] This argument resonated strongly with many of the high school teachers, who were often exhausted and frustrated by unequal, inadequately funded, sometimes outright corrupt working conditions in which they labored to teach those for whom the reproduction of class often meant the perpetuation of poverty and inequality. Although good students, many in the class were nevertheless mistrustful and often angry at the university, which while no Harvard or Princeton, still credentialed and served as gatekeeper over what counted as mastery of knowledge about literature and language. And that mistrust and anger extended to the less tangible institution I represented—the institution of literary studies—widely suspected by these front-line teachers to be the refuge of privileged aesthetes with little knowledge of life on the outskirts of power.

Meanwhile, the other handful of students (many of whom hailed from the same neighborhoods where my high-school-teaching students worked) gravitated strongly to Williams's defense of culture as a common birthright. They found in literature a means of expanding their horizons and enriching their experiences of the world. This group felt validated by Williams's viewpoint that "culture is ordinary," shaped and reshaped by ordinary individuals, like themselves, who possess deep, situated knowledge deriving from their place of origin and from their relations with others in that place: "Every human society has its own shape, its own purposes, its own meanings. Every human society expresses these, in institutions, and in arts and learning. The making of a society is the finding of common meanings and directions, and its growth is an active debate and amendment under the pressures of experience, contact, and discovery, writing themselves into the land. The growing society is there, yet it is also made and remade in every individual mind" (93). For these students, who were not unaware of the cultural imperialism and unequal distribution of cultural capital that my more skeptical high-school-teaching students deftly critiqued, literature also provided for them the opportunity to study the contours of "ordinary common meanings" and to engage in what Williams calls "the special processes of discovery and creative effort" (93). Literature was not, for these students, a dead product of an alien culture to be valorized and then regurgitated on tests (formal and informal) that would open doors for a select few. Literature was, rather, a means of expanding one's thought, of taking place in the "active debate and amendment" characteristic of any cultural formation, whether in the hills of East LA or Williams's Welsh pastureland.

Now picture me, the newly-minted PhD struck with the near paralyzing realization that both viewpoints—that of the savvy and cynical high school teachers and literature-loving locals—were simultaneously true.

Woolf herself expressed ambivalence about the complicity of "traditional" or "high" culture in systems of dominance and power—notably (but not exclusively) in *Three Guineas,* where she wonders publicly whether she ought to send a guinea to "rebuild the college on the old lines," to build a new, "adventurous," and idealistic college, or use the guinea to "buy rags and petrol and Bryant & Mays matches and burn the college to the ground?" (33). The fantasy of burning the old edifices of higher education and starting from scratch receives serious play in Woolf's hypothetical address, but ultimately she errs on the side of pragmatism because she considered material self-sufficiency necessary (but not sufficient) for intellectual liberty or "freedom from unreal loyalties" (*TG* 36, 78). This freedom, or "disinterestedness," was for her key to cultivating the habits of critical thinking that counter the negative impact of "memory and tradition," whether in the form of cultural imperialism or the dominant educational system's reproduction of class relations (*TG* 18). But material self-sufficiency, for those who are not born into money, depends upon employment which in most cases depends upon education. Graduates of the women's college would need to obtain employment in order to earn their livings and, for Woolf, the modicum of financial self-sufficiency derived from earning one's own living freed women from dependence upon patriarchal forces (in the form of financial dependence on fathers and husbands or brothers). Intellectual freedom depends upon material conditions that may render one complicit with cultural formations that compromise intellectual freedom. This is a *persistent* circle for Woolf but not necessarily a *vicious* one. Despite her ambivalence about the reproduction of problematic ideologies through culture, Woolf maintains a belief in its capacity to humanize us, to make us less power-hungry and more capable of rational coexistence and what Paul Gilroy would call "conviviality" (xv).

For Woolf, this belief resolved into what we might call a generative paradox—dominant culture influences literary and artistic culture which, when taught, tends to reinforce dominant cultural values. Noting, if not naming, Woolf's generative paradox, Melba Cuddy-Keane calls Woolf a "democratic highbrow," unpacking the etymology of the term "highbrow" (and its corollaries "lowbrow" and "middlebrow") and disarticulating it from earlier concepts of the "elite" and the "masses" (loc 211–216). For me, the generative paradox is something like a hermeneutic circle that requires, if one is to ante into the circle, interacting with institutions and practices that tend to support dominant ideology.

How does one change that dynamic?, *Three Guineas* asks in its broadest sense. "Dialectically" would be too simple of an answer, but perhaps in the recursive fashion that Barbara Herrnstein Smith describes in *Contingencies of Value* or in a pattern similar to what Judith Butler calls the chain of citation.[3] I hope to find a simpler way to express this.

Let's get back, therefore, to the beautiful and the good: to contemplate how and why an aesthetically complex and intellectually challenging artist such as Woolf still matters today *for her artistry* is to open up a more fundamental conversation about why and how the life of the mind matters. This pursuit is no less trivial today than it was seventy-three years ago when Woolf, in her last novel, *Between the Acts* (written between 1938 and 1941—some very dark years in European history), depicted a community coming together to rebuild "[c]ivilization [...] in ruins [...] by human effort" in the course of an ordinary village pageant (181). The notion of "civilization" carries with it so much baggage of ethnocentric hubris, colonialist exploitation, cultural elitism, and plain old snobbery that one hesitates to recuperate the term for use in a more expansive sense, to describe the development of *civitas*—responsibility to a community or, more colloquially, civics. As Christine Froula notes in *Virginia Woolf and the Bloomsbury Avant-garde*, Bloomsbury thinkers—perhaps most especially Leonard Woolf—were preoccupied with the cultivation and maintenance of civilization in the face of pressure from "barbarians" both inside and outside of British culture (1). Even so, Woolf was intensely aware of the propensity of dominant powers (especially colonialist ones) to commit acts of atrocity in the name of civilization. She points this out frankly in *A Room of One's Own* and expands on this insight with special poignancy in *Mrs. Dalloway*, in which the death of Septimus Smith and the Amritsar massacre as well as the Armenian genocide are not simply afterthoughts but collateral effects of British imperial "civilization." With this critique still present, Woolf nevertheless develops her own concept of civilization described in *Three Guineas* as "the arts that can be taught cheaply and practiced by poor people; such as medicine, mathematics, music, painting and literature. [...] the arts of human intercourse; the art of understanding other people's lives and minds, and the little arts of talk, of dress, of cookery that are allied with them" (34). At her hypothetical experimental college, civilization would be fostered by providing the means to "explore the ways in which the mind and body can be made to co-operate; discover what new combinations make good wholes in human life" (34). Woolf provides glimpses into this concept of civilization in the air raid scene as well as the final gathering of *The Years* and develops this as a necessary survival strategy in *Between the Acts, A Sketch of the Past*, and "Thoughts on Peace in an Air Raid," the latter of which I'll analyze briefly here.

Woolf grappled with value-laden concepts in insightful and often unexpected ways, refashioning the "master's tools" (to quote Audre Lorde) in the service of "mak[ing] happiness"—what the ancient Greeks called *eudemonia*—rather than conquest (*DM* 248). Describing the moment of frozen dread one feels when bombers are directly overhead during an air raid, Woolf contends that:

[d]irectly that fear passes, the mind reaches out and instinctively revives itself by trying to create. Since the room is dark it can create only from memory. It reaches out to the memory of other Augusts—in Bayreuth, listening to Wagner; in Rome, walking over the Campagna; in London. Friends' voices come back.

Scraps of poetry return. Each of those thoughts, even in memory, was far more positive, reviving, healing and creative than the dull dread made of fear and hate. Therefore if we are to compensate the young man for the loss of his glory and of his gun, we must give him access to the creative feelings. We must make happiness. We must free him from the machine. We must bring him out of his prison into the open air. (247–48)

"Creative feelings," in this scenario, are civilizing, connective ("friends' voices come back"), restorative, and liberating. The "open air" (a persistent motif in Woolf's work) signifies liberation from the constraints of parochial thinking, acquisitive materialism, and moribund allegiance to tradition for tradition's sake. For Woolf, the poet or artist teases open (and in some cases cracks open) the fissures in the hard shell of *habitus* (what we might call norms or ideologies) that deadens our perceptions and makes us susceptible to lockstep thinking. Given the perilous consequences of lockstep thinking—the dehumanization of others, the uncritical valorization of conquest, sacrifice, and violence, the insatiable desire to convert others to one's preferred way of life, the premium on acquisitive rather than communal good—it is not too hyperbolic to suggest that creative thinking is essential to the survival of human civilization, if we think of civilization as the cultivation of the conditions necessary for human flourishing, for happiness in its non-utilitarian guise.

In her later work critiquing fascism especially, Woolf outlines the necessity of thinking for one's self, what we might call today the capacity for critical thinking. Echoing her contemporary Gramsci, who also grappled with the question of why so many of us consent to our own oppression as he developed his theory of hegemony, Woolf associates the inability to think for one's self with a form of mental slavery. I can think of no better retort to those who decry the value of the humanities than Woolf's insistence that critical thinking is fostered by creative thinking and that creative thinking is necessary to counter lockstep thinking that leads to an abdication of one's responsibility to others in the world.

Woolf's work, when read as a whole, shows us why and how the generative life of the mind matters. This task is not a straightforward one, because as Woolf herself noted in her 1937 BBC broadcast on "Craftsmanship," when we insist upon the utility of words we strip them of their power. The power of words lies in their complexity, their polyvalence, and their simultaneous historicity and mutability (*DM* 203–05). Words are powerful, Woolf argues in "Craftsmanship," because they refuse to be pinned down but rather insist upon their contextuality and historicity. "In short," Woolf explains, "they hate anything that stamps them with one meaning or confines them to one attitude, for it is their nature to change" (*DM* 206). Woolf's fiction is similarly adverse to being "stamp[ed] with one meaning or confine[d] to one attitude" because its complexity is a hallmark of its artistic virtuosity and its continuing appeal to readers whose contexts may have evolved and whose attitudes may have changed over the decades since Woolf first wrote and published. To say that the endurance of Woolf's work is due in part to its complexity is perhaps not surprising to those with a scientific inclination, given that complexity often allows for the possibility of evolutionary adaptation (to use a biological analogy) or that creative phase changes take place at the "edge of chaos" (to use a complexity theory or physics analogy). But such a claim would miss an important, arguably immeasurable intangible that complements the complexity of Woolf's work—its beauty. The only way to honestly describe or appreciate the beauty of Woolf's work—or any work of art, if we take Woolf's literary and cultural criticism seriously—is to experience it, in this case through reading and discussing it.

Hence, we cannot cede contemplation of the beautiful and the good to conservatives like David Brooks (or Allan Bloom or Matthew Arnold). Woolf's creative and critical work foregrounds the very process of illumination that powerful art engenders. To experience that illumination, we must read her work without asking for it to conform to our critical desires, but rather to be open to the openness (even vulnerability) that it asks of us as readers. If we approach Woolf's work with this openness, then, like all powerful art, it has the capacity to change us—not because of what it says or means but because of the habits of mind that it cultivates as we experience it. While it is no doubt possible to approach any work of literature with such openness (a possibility that Woolf insists upon in "How Should One Read a Book?"), the "value" of Woolf's *oeuvre* is especially enduring because of how compellingly she invites her readers to enter into that experience of openness and transformation.

Notes

1. Sara Ahmed uses the term "willful" to describe the quality of tenacity that a non-dominant perspective may have in disrupting the presumptive calm of normative culture: "[w]illfulness involves persistence in the face of having been brought down, where simply to 'keep going' or to 'keep coming up' is to be stubborn and obstinate" (loc. 174–76).
2. Guillory writes, "I will assume, following Bourdieu, that the distribution of cultural capital in such an institution as the school reproduces the structure of social relations, a structure of complex and ramifying inequality" (loc. 277–79).
3. Herrnstein Smith argues that a work of art that is deemed valuable enough to become canonical "begins increasingly not merely to survive within but to shape and create the culture in which its value is produced and transmitted, and for that very reason, to perpetuate the conditions of its own flourishing" (50). In a similarly circular dynamic, the force of law (or of a norm), for Butler, comes from the citation of that law or norm. That is, the act of citation gives the law force, rather than the law providing force to the citation of it (17).

Works Cited

Ahmed, Sara. *Willful Subjects*. Kindle Edition. Durham, NC: Duke UP, 2014.

Brooks, David. "The Humanist Vocation." *The New York Times*, 20 June 2013. Web. 15 February 2015.

Butler, Judith. "Critically Queer." *GLQ: A Journal of Lesbian and Gay Studies* 1.1 (1993): 17–32.

Cuddy-Keane, Melba. *Virginia Woolf, the Intellectual, and the Public Sphere*. Kindle Edition. New York: Cambridge UP, 2003.

Froula, Christine. *Virginia Woolf and the Bloomsbury Avant-garde: War, Civilization, Modernity*. New York: Columbia UP, 2004.

Gilroy, Paul. *Postcolonial Melancholia*. New York: Columbia UP, 2005.

Guillory, John. *Cultural Capital: The Problem of Literary Canon Formation*. Kindle Edition. Chicago: U of Chicago P, 2013.

Said, Edward. *Culture and Imperialism*. 1993. Kindle Edition. New York: Vintage, 2012.

Smith, Barbara Herrnstein. *Contingencies of Value: Alternative Perspectives for Critical Theory*. Cambridge: Harvard UP, 1988.

Woolf, Virginia. *Between the Acts*. 1941. New York: Harcourt Brace Jovanovich, 1969.

——. "Craftsmanship." 1937. *The Death of the Moth and Other Essays*. Ed. Leonard Woolf. New York: Harcourt Brace Jovanovich, 1970. 198–207.

———. "How Should One Read a Book?" 1932. *The Second Common Reader*. Ed. Andrew McNeillie. New York: Harcourt Brace Jovanovich, 1986. 258–70.

———. "The Leaning Tower." 1940. *The Moment and Other Essays*. Ed. Leonard Woolf. New York: Harcourt Brace Jovanovich, 1948. 128–154.

———. *A Room of One's Own*. 1929. New York: Harcourt Brace Jovanovich, 1981.

———. "Thoughts on Peace in an Air Raid." 1940. *The Death of the Moth and Other Essays*. Ed. Leonard Woolf. New York: Harcourt Brace Jovanovich, 1970. 243–48.

———. *Three Guineas*. 1938. NY: Harcourt Brace, 1966.

Notes on Contributors

Judith Allen leads the Virginia Woolf Reading Group at Kelly Writers House, University of Pennsylvania. She is the author of *Virginia Woolf and the Politics of Language* (2010), *Virginia Woolf: Walking in the Footsteps of Michel de Montaigne* (2012), and "Feminist Politics" in *Virginia Woolf in Context* (2012). Allen is currently co-editing, with Jane Goldman, a new edition of *A Room of One's Own* (forthcoming Cambridge UP).

Charles Andrews is an associate professor of English at Whitworth University in Spokane, WA. He has published articles on Aldous Huxley, T. S. Eliot, David Jones, and Virginia Woolf. His current research examines British novelists active in the interwar peace movement.

Matthew Beeber completed his MA at the University of Colorado at Boulder in 2014 with an emphasis on British and global modernisms. His work has focused predominantly on Virginia Woolf, transnationalism, and material culture. He currently lives in Madrid, Spain, where he is conducting research on Hispanic and Latin American modernisms during the Spanish Civil War. He anticipates entering a PhD program in English in the fall of 2015.

Pamela L. Caughie is Professor of English at Loyola University Chicago and past president of the Modernist Studies Association. Among other works, she is author of *Virginia Woolf and Postmodernism* (1991) and editor of *Virginia Woolf in the Age of Mechanical Reproduction* (2000). She is co-editor of *Woolf Online*, a digital archive of *To the Lighthouse*, and co-Director of Modernist Networks, a federation of digital projects in modernist literature and culture.

Sarah Cole is Professor of English and Comparative Literature at Columbia University, where she teaches courses on British literature of the twentieth century. She is the author of two books, *At the Violet Hour: Modernism and Violence in England and Ireland* (2012) and *Modernism, Male Friendship, and the First World War* (2003), and is currently at work on a book that reassesses one of the twentieth century's most unrecognized geniuses, H. G. Wells.

Anne Cunningham lives in Taos, New Mexico where she teaches English at the University of New Mexico—Taos. She has a PhD in Comparative Literature from SUNY Stony Brook. Her interests are women modernist writers, the novel, and feminist, queer, and affect theory. She has published in *Mfs: Modern Fiction Studies*. She is currently writing a manuscript on feminist failure in the life and work of Jean Rhys, Djuna Barnes, Nella Larsen, and Virginia Woolf.

Maayan Paula Dauber received her PhD in English from Princeton University in February 2015. Her dissertation, *The Pathos of Modernism: Henry James, Virginia Woolf, and Gertrude Stein,* explores the waning hold of the economy of sympathy in twentieth-century fiction and its replacement with an economy of pathos. Her article on Gertrude Stein's troubling Nazi associations is forthcoming in *Texas Studies in Language and Literature.*

Erica Gene Delsandro's research focuses on the 1930s novel and scholarly constructions of modernism vis-à-vis the Great War and its lasting impact on non-combatants, both aging modernists and twentieth-century born writers too young to fight in World War I. She teaches courses in modern literature, gender studies, and queer theory at Bucknell University in Pennsylvania where she is a Visiting Assistant Professor.

Madelyn Detloff is Associate Professor of English and Women's, Gender, and Sexuality Studies at Miami University in Ohio. She is the author of *The Persistence of Modernism: Loss and Mourning in the 20th Century* (2009) and essays in venues such as *Hypatia, Women's Studies: An Interdisciplinary Journal, ELN, Literature Compass, The Journal of the Midwest Modern Language Association,* and *Modernism/modernity.*

David Deutsch is an Assistant Professor in the Department of English at the University of Alabama. He is the author of *British Literature and Classical Music: Cultural Contexts, 1870–1945,* forthcoming from Bloomsbury Academic, and articles on music, early twentieth-century British literature, and culture.

Maud Ellmann is the Randy L. and Melvin R. Professor of the Development of the Novel in English at the University of Chicago. She has written widely on modernism, feminism, and psychoanalysis. Her books include *The Poetics of Impersonality: T.S. Eliot and Ezra Pound* (1987; rpt. 2013), *The Hunger Artists: Starving, Writing, and Imprisonment* (1993), *Elizabeth Bowen: The Shadow Across the Page* (2003), and *The Nets of Modernism: James, Woolf, Joyce, and Freud* (2010).

David J. Fine serves as the assistant director of the Global Citizenship Program at Lehigh University in Pennsylvania and is a doctoral candidate in English literature. His research investigates late modernism and religion. He is particularly interested in the mid-twentieth-century British novel's engagement with mysticism and ethics. With the Global Citizenship Program, he has traveled to China, India, and Cambodia and has taught a wide variety of experiential, community-engaged courses.

J. Ashley Foster is Visiting Assistant Professor of Writing and Fellow in the Writing Program at Haverford College in Philadelphia. Her articles have been published in *Virginia Woolf & 20th Century Women Writers, Virginia Woolf Miscellany, Virginia Woolf Bulletin,* and *Interdisciplinary/Multidisciplinary Woolf: Selected Papers from the Twenty-Second International Conference on Virginia Woolf.* Her work examines the interrelationship between pacifism, modernism, and war, and tries to recuperate the lost threads of modernism's pacifist history.

Susan Stanford Friedman is the Virginia Woolf Professor at the University of Wisconsin-Madison, where she directs the Institute for Research in the Humanities. She has published a number of articles on Woolf, along with books on H.D. and Joyce. *Mappings: Feminism and the Cultural Geographies of Encounter* (1998) has just appeared in Chinese translation. She co-edited *Comparison: Theories, Approaches, Uses* (2013), and her *Planetary Modernisms: Provocations on Modernity Across Time* is forthcoming in 2015.

Christine Froula teaches at Northwestern University. Her publications include *A Guide to Ezra Pound's Selected Poems; To Write Paradise: Style and Error in Pound's Cantos; Modernism's Body: Sex, Culture and Joyce; Virginia Woolf and the Bloomsbury Avant-Garde;* "War, Empire, and Modernist Poetry" (*Cambridge Companion to WWI Poetry*), "War, Peace, Internationalism" (*Cambridge Companion to Bloomsbury*), "Orlando Lives: Virginia Woolf's *Orlando* in Global Adaptation and Performance" (*Contemporary Woolf*), "Leonard Woolf and the Subject of Empire" and "Unwriting *The Waves*" (forthcoming).

Elizabeth Hanna Hanson is a writer and editor in the Chicago area. She earned her PhD in English at Loyola University Chicago in 2013, where her dissertation, *Making Something Out of Nothing: Asexuality and Narrative,* was named Dissertation of the Year in the humanities. Her essay "Toward an Asexual Narrative Structure" appears in *Asexualities: Feminist and Queer Perspectives,* edited by Karli June Cerankowski and Megan Milks (2014).

Christine Haskill teaches Gender and Women's Studies at Western Michigan University and English at Grand Valley State University. She is currently revising her dissertation, "Battling the Separate Spheres: New Woman Writers and British Women Writers of World War I," which examines the continuities between the Victorian and modernist periods through the themes of gender, war, and feminist pacifism.

Elsa Högberg is a postdoctoral fellow at Uppsala University in Sweden and the University of Glasgow. Her current research project focuses on texts by Katherine Mansfield, Rebecca West and Virginia Woolf, and illuminates the relevance of recent developments in contemporary theory as a framework for understanding the convergence of interiority, aesthetics and politics in literary modernism. She is also assisting with the editing of Woolf's *Orlando* for Cambridge University Press.

Erin Holliday-Karre is an Assistant Professor of Literary Criticism and Theory in the Department of English Literature and Linguistics at Qatar University. She is the author of several articles, in such journals as *Feminist Theory* and *Women's Studies: An Interdisciplinary Journal*, that argue for a revaluation of feminist epistemology, literature, and history in light of French theorist Jean Baudrillard's theory of seduction.

Alan Chih-chien Hsieh is a graduate student in the Department of Foreign Languages and Literatures at National Taiwan University. His research interests include transnational modernisms, affect studies, critical theory, and the philosophy of Gilles Deleuze. He is currently working on Woolf with a focus on novelistic objects for his thesis.

Amy Kahrmann Huseby is a doctoral candidate at the University of Wisconsin-Madison. Her dissertation, "Quantified Lives: Victorian Women's Poetry, Biopolitics, and the Nineteenth-century Statistical Imaginary," explores how Victorian women's poetry responded to the institutionalization of vital statistics. She has an essay on Ezra Pound's *Cantos* forthcoming in *South Atlantic Review* and is currently serving as guest editor for a special issue of *Victoriographies* entitled "Longevity Networks," which is scheduled for publication November 2015.

Mark Hussey is Distinguished Professor of English at Pace University in New York. He edits *Woolf Studies Annual*, is General Editor of the Harcourt Annotated Edition of the Works of Virginia Woolf, is on the editorial board of the Cambridge Edition of the Works of Virginia Woolf, for which he recently edited *Between the Acts,* and is a co-editor of *Virginia Woolf Miscellany*. He organized the first annual conference on Woolf at Pace in 1991.

Joyce E. Kelley is an associate professor of English at Auburn University at Montgomery, Alabama. She has published articles in the *Journal of Narrative Theory*, *Victorians*, *The Edinburgh Companion to Virginia Woolf and the Arts*, *Children's Literature*, *Virginia Woolf Miscellany*, and several collected essay volumes from previous Woolf conferences. Her monograph on women modernists and travel is forthcoming from Ashgate.

Paula Maggio has taught as an adjunct and visiting professor in Northeast Ohio. She is the creator and editor of *Blogging Woolf*. Her work includes three monographs in Cecil Woolf Publishers Bloomsbury Heritage Series: *Reading the Skies in Virginia Woolf* (2009), *The Best of Blogging Woolf, Five Years On* (2012), and *Virginia Woolf's Likes and Dislikes* (2012), as well as essays in the *Selected Papers* from the 19th and 23rd Annual Conferences on Virginia Woolf.

Ann Martin is tenured faculty in the Department of English at the University of Saskatchewan. As well as articles on Anglo-American and Canadian modernisms, she is the author of *Red Riding Hood and the Wolf in Bed: Modernism's Fairy Tales* (2006) and, with

Kathryn Holland, co-editor of *Interdisciplinary / Multidisciplinary Woolf: Selected Papers from the Twenty-Second Annual International Conference on Virginia Woolf* (2013). She is currently researching the motif of the motor-car in interwar British fiction.

Eleanor McNees is Professor of English at the University of Denver where she has served in various administrative roles including associate dean of faculty and chair of the English Department. She is the author of *Eucharistic Poetry* (1991) and editor of collections of essays on the Brontë sisters, Virginia Woolf, and the novel. She annotated the Harcourt paperback edition of *The Years*. Her current research is on the influence of James Fitzjames and Leslie Stephen's literary criticism on Virginia Woolf's essays.

Jean Mills is author of *Virginia Woolf, Jane Ellen Harrison, and the Spirit of Modernist Classicism* (2014). She specializes in Woolf Studies, Peace Studies, and feminist theory, and has published essays on Woolf, Gertrude Stein, and issues of gender, class, modernism, and war. An Associate Professor of English at John Jay College (The City University of New York), she is currently at work on her second book, *1924: A Year in the Life of Virginia Woolf.*

Kelle Sills Mullineaux is a PhD student at Northern Illinois University, where she teaches Composition and Writing Across the Curriculum (WAC) and tutors at the University Writing Center. Her research interests center on writing studies, in particular writing centers, WAC, creative writing, composition, and rhetoric. One of her favorite topics is the relationship students have with their writing, making Woolf's thoughts on the subject a fascinating opportunity for scholarship.

Steven Putzel is Professor of English and Comparative Literature at Penn State University, Wilkes-Barre Campus. He is author of *Reconstructing Yeats: The Secret Rose and the Wind Among the Reeds* (1986), and *Virginia Woolf and the Theater* (2013), as well as numerous articles on Virginia Woolf, Leonard Woolf, W. B. Yeats, James Stephens, James Joyce, Sheila Watson, Paul Muldoon, and Sam Shepard.

Kim Sigouin is a third-year PhD student in the Production of Literature program at Carleton University in Canada. Her dissertation investigates the relationship between experimental writing, bodies, and ecology in the work of modernist women writers. In particular, she examines how Virginia Woolf, H.D., and Gertrude Stein anticipated the pertinence of embodied language to contemporary theorizations of ecological consciousness.

Elisa Kay Sparks retired after 35 years of teaching English and women's studies at Clemson University in South Carolina and has published a series of articles on parks, gardens, and flowers in Virginia Woolf's life and work as well as a number of pieces exploring connections between the works of Woolf and the American Modernist painter Georgia O'Keeffe. With Helen Southworth she is co-editor of *Woolf and the Art of Exploration: Selected Papers from the Fifteenth International Conference on Virginia Woolf* (2006).

Diana L. Swanson is associate professor of Women's, Gender, and Sexuality Studies and English at Northern Illinois University. She has published essays on Virginia Woolf, Leonard Woolf, and Jeanette Winterson, focusing on various topics including incest, lesbianism, feminism, imperialism, and, most recently, ecofeminism and nature.

Michael Tratner is a professor at Bryn Mawr College who has written two books about the relationship of modernism to politics and economics: *Modernism and Mass Politics: Joyce, Woolf, Eliot, Yeats* (1995) and *Deficits and Desires: Economics, Sexuality and Literature in the Twentieth Century* (2002). Recently he has been expanding his interests to earlier eras and exploring how biological theories intersect with those other discourses.

Vicki Tromanhauser is Associate Professor of English at the State University of New York, New Paltz. Her articles have appeared in *Journal of Modern Literature, Twentieth-Century Literature, Woolf Studies Annual, Virginia Woolf Miscellany*, and various collections. She received the Andrew J. Kappel Prize in Literary Criticism for 2012. She is currently working on modernism's relationship to human-animal studies, food studies, and the life sciences.

Shao-Hua Aimée Wang is currently reading a DPhil in Medieval and Modern Languages at the University of Oxford. She has received an MA in Comparative Literature from King's College London and a BA in Foreign Languages and Literatures from National Taiwan University. Her research focuses on modernity and city literature in Virginia Woolf and Charles Baudelaire. Her broader research interest includes phenomenology, comparative literature, and the relationship between modernism and modernity.

Conference Program

9:00–10:30 a.m. Concurrent Sessions A

A-1 The Greeks
Chair: Jacqueline Long (Loyola University Chicago)
Linda Jane Cofield (University of Tennessee–Chattanooga): "Becoming a Woman: The Illusion of Choice in *Mrs. Dalloway*"
Manya Lempert (University of California–Berkeley): "Woolf's Tragic Worlds"
Joshua Logan Wall (University of Michigan–Ann Arbor): "Refusing Mastery: The Politics of Not Knowing Greek"

A-2 Ecology and Creation
Chair: Melissa Bradshaw (Loyola University Chicago)
Ashley Heiberger (Northern Illinois University): "The 'Nature' of Women: Trees in the Creative Process of Women Artists in the Works of Virginia Woolf"
Karina Jakubowicz (University College London): "Eden's Evolution: Rewriting the World through Gardens in the Work of Virginia Woolf"
Elisa Kay Sparks (Clemson University): "'Whose Woods These Are': Virginia Woolf and the Primeval Forests of the Mind"

A-3 Ghosts and Hauntings
Chair: Linda Camarasana (SUNY-College at Old Westbury)
Julia Hunter (University of Tennessee–Chattanooga): "Victorian Ghosts Haunting a Room of Her Own: Virginia Woolf's Nostalgia in 'The London Scene'"
Elizabeth Hedrick-Moser (St. Louis University): "Virginia Woolf's 'Sketch of the Past': Giving Voice to the Dead"
Joyce Kelley (Auburn University at Montgomery): "'Stretching our 'Antennae': The Converging Worlds of the Seen and the Unseen in 'Kew Gardens'"

A-4 "A New and Better World": Forms of Ethical Belief
Chair: Pamela L. Caughie (Loyola University Chicago)
Charles Andrews (Whitworth University): "'beauty, simplicity and peace': Faithful Pacifism, Activist Writing, and *The Years*"
Andrew Bingham (Queen's University): "Transcendence, Loss, Ethical Presence: How Revelation in Time Structures Character in *Mrs. Dalloway*"
Cynthia Wallace (St. Thomas More College): "'(No Longer) Shaped by Belief': Mary Gordon's Utopia, After Woolf"

11:00 a.m.–12:30 p.m. Concurrent Sessions B

B-1 Sick at Heart: "Resilient Writing" in the Face of War
Chair: Sarah Polen (Loyola University Chicago)
Lolly Ockerstrom (Park University): "Virginia Woolf, Illness, and World War I"
Karolyn Steffens (University of Wisconsin–Madison): "Wartime Affirmation: *Between the Acts* and Heidegger's Ontology of Death"
Kathleen Wall (University of Regina): "'Torn to ribbons': World War I and Woolf's Aesthetic Practice"

B-2 Reading (in) Woolf
Chair: Eleanor McNees (University of Denver)
Jill Monroe (Eastern Illinois University): "Woolf's Women Readers"
Heather Fielding (Purdue University–North Central): "On Not Reading in Woolf's Novel Theory: Who Makes Fiction's World?"
Erica Stacey Decker (University of Minnesota): "*Three Guineas*, Medicine, and Marginalia"

B-3 Propaganda, Codebreakers, and Spies
Chair: Judith Allen (University of Pennsylvania)
Judith Allen (University of Pennsylvania): "Intersections: Surveillance, Propaganda, and Just War"

Patrizia Muscogiuri (Independent Scholar): "(Un)known Warriors, Bloody Seas, and the Visual Politics of WWI"
Suzanne Bellamy (University of Sydney): "The Code Breaker"

B-4 Horses, Donkeys, and Dogs, Oh My!
Chair: Suzanne Bost (Loyola University Chicago)
Hannah Biggs (Rice University): "The 'long-legged colt[s]' of *Mrs. Dalloway*: Power, Class, Identity, and the Space of the Nonverbal"
Elizabeth Hanson (Independent Scholar): "'And the donkey brays': The Many Donkeys of Virginia Woolf's World"
Vicki Tromanhauser (State University of New York–New Paltz): "Companion Creatures: 'Dogmanity' in *Three Guineas*"

1:00–2:15 p.m. "Using Digital Editions: A Workshop on WoolfOnline"
Pamela L. Caughie (Loyola University Chicago) and
Mark Hussey (Pace University)
Sr. Jean Delores Schmidt Ballroom, Damen Center (second floor)

2:30–4:00 p.m. Concurrent Sessions C
C-1 Woolf's Natural Worlds
Chair: Elaine Wood (University of Illinois-Champaign)
Elaine Wood (University of Illinois-Champaign): "Inheriting the Land: Vita's Knole House and 'The Oak Tree, a poem,' in *Orlando*"
Heather McLeer (University of Illinois-Champaign): "Perceiving Percival: Subjective
Perception and Residual Reality in *The Waves*"
Christin Mulligan (University of North Carolina-Chapel Hill): "Beach Bum Aesthetics: Vacation Rituals, Nature, and Sense-Memory in *To the Lighthouse*"

C-2 Place, Space, and British Imperialism
Chair: Brenda Silver (Dartmouth College)
Lauren Benke (University of Denver): "Woolf's Peripheral Ireland in *The Years*"
Xiaoqin Cao (North University of China): "Virginia Woolf's Chinese Narrative and the Chinese Vogue in Victorian Britain"
Brandon Truett (University of Colorado–Boulder): "Domestic Cosmopolitanism and Worldedness in Virginia Woolf's *The Waves*"

C-3 Material Objects and Consumer Culture
Chair: Barbara Green (University of Notre Dame)
Lois Gilmore (Bucks County Community College): "Global Objects: Woolf, Material Culture, and Living Display"
Alexandria Newsom (University of Colorado–Boulder): "Hats in *Mrs. Dalloway*: The Importance of Being on Top"
Tanya Turneaure (Independent Scholar): "Written in Smoke: Linguistic Agency and the Consumer Narrative"

C-4 The Anxiety of Ownership: Literary Property and Publishing
Chair: Sean O'Brien (Loyola University Chicago)
Deanna Wendel (Indiana University): "Between Orlando and 'The Oak Tree': Self-Annihilating Art as a Form of Textual Materialism"
Irina Rasmussen Goloubeva (Stockholm University): "Virginia Woolf's World-Making Pen"
Christine Reynier (Université Montpellier III): "Woolf, the Monk, and the World: Property, Illegitimacy, and Poverty"

C-5 Woolf, War, and Genre
Chair: Katherine Keenan (Immaculata University)
Lisa Dooley (Bradley University): "*Mrs. Dalloway*: Mapping the Post-WWI World"
Rachel Brunner (Bradley University): "The Duality of Mrs. Dalloway and Septimus Smith: An Illustration of Modernism"
Danielle Glassmeyer (Bradley University): "'The serious consequences of paper flowers to swim in bowls': Trauma and Existence in *Jacob's Room*"

C-6 Seminar: "This Ecstasy": Affect, Woolf, Modernity
Seminar Leader: Jaime Hovey (DePaul University)
Participants: Erik-John Fuhrer, Nell Wasserstrom, David Fine, Elsa Högberg, Lisa Coleman, Sarah Eilefson, Anne Manuel, Elisa Kay Sparks, Karina Jakubowicz, Yaron Aronowicz, Paula Maggio, Prudence Moylan, Linda Jane Cofield, Shao-Hua Wang, Tony Brinkley, Alex Christie, Katie Dyson

C-7 Seminar: Virginia Woolf and Bloomsbury Homosexuality
Seminar Leader: Patricia Morgne Cramer (University of Connecticut-Stamford)
Participants: Benjamin Bagocius, Ann Marshall, Richard Cappucio, David Eberly, Sarah Payne, Kelly Neal, Natalie Kalich, Marissa Grippo, Laura Forman, Sara Fruner, Jessica Mason-McFadden, Andrew Bingham, Lolly Ockerstrom, Catherine Hollis, Ann Gibaldi Campbell, Nina Berman, Michaela Jandacek

4:30–6:00 p.m. Opening Keynote
Dr. Mark Hussey (Pace University)
Roundtable on **Woolf and Violence**
  Roundtable participants:
  Sarah Cole (Columbia University)
  Ashley Foster (Graduate Center of CUNY)
  Christine Froula (Northwestern University)
  Jean Mills (John Jay College)

6:00–7:30 p.m. Welcoming Reception
Former Dean Frank Fennell: Opening Remarks
Dr. Prudence Moylan: "A Woman's College from the Inside: A Brief History of Mundelein College for Women"
Music by Glottal Attack

7:30 p.m. Sarah Ruhl's Orlando
Newhart Family Theatre, Mundelein Center
A concert performance directed by Ann M. Shanahan, Associate Professor of Theatre, Loyola University Chicago
Talkback after the show with Dr. Shanahan and Dr. Jaime Hovey (DePaul University)

FRIDAY—JUNE 6

9:00–10:30 a.m. Concurrent Sessions D
D-1 Queer Fear and Desire
Chair: Jaime Hovey (DePaul University)
Stephanie Brown (University of Arizona): "Negotiating Queer Desire in *The Voyage Out*"
Shawna Lipton (University of Wisconsin–Milwaukee): "Are Queers Afraid of Virginia Woolf?"
Alexandra DeLuise (Southern Connecticut State University): "Outside the Closet: Spaces, Places and Homosexuality in *Jacob's Room* and *Maurice*"
Erik Fuhrer (St. John's University): "The Transgressions of Miss La Trobe, Or: How to Free the Slave Within and Disarm Future Bombs"

D-2 Woolf's Feminism, Feminisms Today
Chair: Urmila Seshagiri (University of Tennessee)
Anne Cunningham (State University of New York–Stony Brook): "Shadow Feminism and Anti-Development in *The Voyage Out*"
Audrey Johnson (University of North Dakota): "Virginia Woolf, Suffrage Politics, and Pacifism: Rhizomatic Feminism in *Three Guineas*"
Anne Manuel (University of Michigan–Ann Arbor): "Would Woolf Lean In? How *Three Guineas* Complicates Current Ideas on Women's Labor"
Emma Slotterback (Bloomsburg University): "Woolf's Contradiction through Pessimism"

D-3 Woolf and World Cultures
Chair: Diana Royer (Miami University)
Maria Aparecida de Oliveira (Universidade Federal do Acre/Capes): "Transamerican, Transatlantic, and Trans-amazonian Woolf. A Meeting of Waters: Woolf, Bishop, and the Amazon Writers"
Emily Burns Morgan (Fordham College at Lincoln Center and Marymount College): "Virginia Woolf, Reluctant Buddhist: *Orlando* as Exploration of Reincarnation"
Benjamin Hagen (University of Rhode Island): "Inseparably Connected: Virginia Woolf's Late Philosophy of Worlds and the Anthropology of Saba Mahmood"

D-4 Writing through Trauma, the Trauma of Writing
Chair: Suzette Henke (University of Louisville)
Nell Wasserstrom (Boston College): "*Durcharbeitung* and *Mrs. Dalloway*: The Process of Fiction as Working-Through"
Cheryl Hindrichs (Boise State University): "On or About 1918, Aesthetics Changed: Woolf as Guide to Post-Pandemic Modernism"
Shannon Rathod (University of Colorado–Boulder): "Uncanny Vertigo: Cosmopolitanism and Trauma in Woolf's *Mrs. Dalloway*"

D-5 Animal Studies
Chair: Michael Tratner (Bryn Mawr College)
Angelica Krajewski (University of Illinois–Chicago): "Flushing Out the Inequalities: The Economic Implications of Virginia Woolf's *Flush*"
Derek Ryan (University of Kent): "'Was it Flush, or was it Pan?' Woolf, Ethel Smyth, and a World of Canine Allusions in *Flush: A Biography*"
Laci Mattison (Florida State University): "'A Little Language': Virginia Woolf and Robert Duncan Write Animality"

D-6 Mythology and Religion
Chair: Cynthia Wallace (St. Thomas More College)
Garry Leonard (University of Toronto): "Thinking of a Kitchen Table When One Is Not There: The Mythic and the Modern in *To the Lighthouse*"
Tony Brinkley (University of Maine): "Othering—Eve, Narcissus—Woolf's Creation of Worlds"
Amy Smith (Lamar University): "'With these fragments I have reimagined community': Re-envisioning the World through Fragmented Allusions to Greek Literature in *Between the Acts*"

D-7 Seminar: Perspectives on Virginia Woolf's Sense of Place
Seminar Leader: Bonnie Kime Scott (San Diego State University)
Particpants: Heather Fielding, Elizabeth Goetz, Alina Oboza, Susan Stanford Friedman, Tabatha Hibbs, Gretchen Gerzina, Charles Andrews, Nathaniel Underland, Linda Camarasana, Katherine Keenan, Candis Bond, Vicki Tromanhauser, Adrianne Krstansky, Abigail Killeen, Irina Rasmussen Goloubeva, Casey Jergenson, Emily Schmidt, Katherine Schneider

11:00 a.m.–12:30 p.m. Concurrent Sessions E

E-1 Woolf as World Writer
Chair: Susan Stanford Friedman (University of Wisconsin-Madison)
Adriana Varga (Butler University): "Virginia Woolf and the Resistance to World Literature"
Pilar Cabrera (Augustana College): "Who Is Afraid of Virgilio Pinera? A Comparative Study"
Shao-Hua Wang (University of Oxford): "From London to Taipei: Writing the Past in *Youyuan jingmeng* (*Wandering in the Garden, Waking from a Dream*)(1968) and *Mrs. Dalloway*"

E-2 Storytelling, Doodling, and Literary Invention
Chair: Julie Vandivere (Bloomsberg University)
Lindsay Vreeland (Northern Illinois University): "Reclaiming Oral Traditions: Orality in Virginia Woolf's *The Waves*"
Emily James (University of St. Thomas): "Scrawling, Scribbling, and Literary Invention"
Sayaka Okumura (Kobe University): "'A dot with strokes raying out round it': Doodles, Eyes, and the World in *The Years*"

E-3 Periodicals and Print Culture
Chair: Denise Ayo (University of Notre Dame)
Barbara Green (University of Notre Dame): "'This is not a book': Woolf, Serial Life-Writing, and Socialist-Feminist Periodicals"
Natalie Kalich (Loyola University Chicago): "The 'Heavy, Horsey Head' vs. 'Sweet Bird-Like Quickness': Virginia Woolf in a Commercial Context"
Illya Nokhrin (University of Toronto): "Examining Woolf's Clothing: Reviews and Advertisements in the Dust Jackets of *The Voyage Out* and *Night and Day*"

E-4 Inner Worlds, Water Worlds
Chair: Diane Gillespie (Washington State University)
Katharine Keenan (Immaculata University): "'And The Sea that Bangs in My Throat': Sea Imagery and Mental Illness in the Works of Virginia Woolf, Anne Sexton, and Sylvia Plath"
Annika Lindskog (Lund University): "Writing the Inner World: Painting with Words in *Night and Day* and *The Waves*"
Diana Royer (Miami University–Hamilton): "Underwater Worlds in Woolf's Fiction"

E-5 Animality and Humanity
Chair: Melba Cuddy-Keane (University of Toronto)
Rebecah Pulsifer (University of Illinois–Urbana-Champaign): "Forgetting All Humankind: Woolf's Nonhuman Imagination"
Nathaniel Underland (University of Maryland): "Posthumanist Woolf and Modernist Heuristics"
Aleksandra Hernandez (University of Notre Dame): "Virginia Woolf's Tiny Moth and the Limits of Narrative 'Worlding'"

E-6 The Woolfs and the Wars
Chair: Prudence Moylan (Loyola University Chicago)
Vara Neverow (Southern Connecticut State University): "Septimus Warren Smith, War Poet: A Close Reading"
Eleanor McNees (University of Denver): "The 1914 'Expurgated Chunk': The Great War in and out of *The Years*"
Wayne Chapman (Clemson University): "War for Peace (1940): Leonard Woolf Writing the International Federation of Peace"
Paula Maggio (Kent State University): "Taking Up Her Pen for Peace: Virginia Woolf, Pacifist"

1:00–2:15 p.m. "The Glass Inward," Multi-media performance workshop inspired by Orlando.
Anna Hensen, Artist
Sr. Jean Delores Schmidt Ballroom, Damen Center

2:30–4:00 p.m. Concurrent Sessions F
F-1 Woolf as a European Writer
Chair: Nina Berman (Loyola University Chicago)
Maggie Humm (University of East London): "Realms of Resemblance: Virginia Woolf, Simone de Beauvoir, and Maï Zetterling"
Patricia Laurence (Brooklyn College-CUNY): "Narrating History: A Comparison of Virginia Woolf and Elizabeth Bowen"
Kathleen Williams Renk (Northern Illinois University): "Blackberrying in the Sun? The Aging Woman in Woolf's *Mrs. Dalloway*, Sackville-West's *All Passion Spent*, and Rhys' *Good Morning, Midnight*"

F-2 Woolf Writing in the Intellectual World of Queer Bloomsbury
Chair: Madelyn Detloff (Miami University)
Melanie Micir (Washington University): "Woolf Queering Lives, Queering Genre"
Kimberly Coates (Bowling Green State University): "Virginia Woolf's Queer Time and Place: Wartime London and a World Aslant"
Brenda Helt (Independent Scholar): "Axiom Bashing: Queer Bloomsbury and Woolf's Opposition to Theories of Androgyny"

F-3 *Mrs. Dalloway*, *The Hours*, and World Making
Chair: Sarah Eilefson (Loyola University Chicago)
Sarah Schaefer (Virginia Tech): "Colonizing Woolf: Fiction, Celebrity, and Politics in Michael Cunningham's *The Hours*"
Sara Fruner (Independent Scholar): "Writing *Laura* before *Brown, Mrs.*: Woolf-in-progress"
Amy Smith (Lamar University): "Peter Walsh's Colonial Desire as Hegemonic Discourse"

F-4 Challenges of Writing the Modern Self
Chair: Catherine Hollis (University of California-Berkeley)
Amanda Styron (Chapman University): "Floating Unattached: Suspension and Liminality in *To the Lighthouse* and *The Waves*"
Caitriona Terry (Northern Illinois University): "Damaged Poets and Angry Intellectuals: The Triumphs and Failures of Woolf's Ungendered Male Characters"
Dave Coodin (York University): "'Beautiful Caves': The Politics of Fragmented Selves in *The Waves*"

F-5 Vita, Pepita, and Orlando
Chair: Vara Neverow (Southern Connecticut State University)
Ann Marshall (Independent Scholar): "Orlando Herself: Time Travel in the Works of Vita Sackville-West""
Julie Vandivere (Bloomsburg University): "Pepita: Woolf's and Sackville-West's"

F-6 Woolf's Intimate World
Chair: Jane de Gay (Leeds Trinity University)
Yaron Aronowicz (Princeton University): "*The Waves'* Captivating World"
Maayan Dauber (Princeton University): "Upheavals of Intimacy in *To the Lighthouse*"
Jacquelin Shin (Towson University): "Voyages Out: *Between the Acts* and Vanishing Points"

F-7 Seminar: Woolf and Cognition's Outward Turn
Seminar Leader: Melba Cuddy-Keane (University of Toronto)
Participants: Derek Ryan, Garry Leonard, Annika Lindskog, George Derk, Alexandria Newsom, Illya Nokhrin, Yike He, Alan Chih-chien Hsieh, Brendan Kavanagh, Zan Cammack, Tanya Turneaure, Deirdre Flynn, Jean Ashley Foster, Emily Burns Morgan, Naomi Gades, Chris Corlew

4:30–6:00 p.m. Keynote
Dr. Maud Ellmann (University of Chicago)
"Sylvia Townsend Warner and Virginia Woolf"
Mundelein Center Auditorium (first floor)

6:00–7:30 p.m. Reception
Palm Court, Mundelein Center (fourth floor)

8:00 p.m. Sarah Ruhl's Orlando
Newhart Family Theatre, Mundelein Center (fourth floor)
Concert performance directed by Ann M. Shanahan, Associate Professor of Theatre, Loyola University Chicago

Saturday—June 7

8:00 a.m. Breakfast, Mundelein Lounge

9:00–10:30 a.m. Concurrent Sessions G
G-1 Woolf in the Near East
Chair: Patricia Laurence (Brooklyn College-CUNY)
Sule Akdogan (Middle East Technical University): "How Do We Read Virginia Woolf in the 21st Century?"
Matthew Beeber (University of Colorado-Boulder): "Fashionable Misconceptions: The Creation of the East in Virginia Woolf's *Orlando*"
Jane de Gay (Leeds Trinity University): "Virginia Stephen and Constantinople: Writing the Other/Writing the Self"

G-2 Masculinity, Femininity, and War
Chair: Maggie Humm (University of East London)
Erin Douglas (Miami University-Hamilton): "Femininity at War in Virginia Woolf's *Three Guineas* and *Between the Acts* and Sarah Waters' *The Night Watch*"
Erica Delsandro (Bucknell University): "Modernism, Memorials, and Masculinity: Virginia Woolf and Christopher Isherwood"
Christine Haskill (Western Michigan University): "The Sex War and the Great War: Woolf's Late-Victorian Inheritance in *Three Guineas*"

G-3 At the Edges of Narrative
Chair: Rebecca Cameron (DePaul University)
Justin Ness (Northern Illinois University): "The Interlude Narrative: Subversive Structure in *The Waves*"
Amy Huseby (University of Wisconsin-Madison): "The Reconciliations of Verse in Virginia Woolf's *Between the Acts*, or Why 'it's perfectly ridiculous to call it a novel'"
Emma Young (University of Lincoln): "Bursting Brevity with Saturated Words: Virginia Woolf and the Short Story's Moment"
Alina Oboza (University of Toronto): "Writing the World to Its Limit and Beyond: The Poetics Threshold Spaces in Virginia Woolf's *Between the Acts*"

G-4 Subject, Object, and the Nature of Reality
Chair: Kathleen Renk (Northern Illinois University)
Archana Kaku (Independent Scholar): "Creating the Subject: Percival as the Ultimate Object in *The Waves*"
Erica Waters Orzechowski (Belmont University): "The Poet and the World: Objectivity/Subjectivity in Woolf's *The Waves*"
Michael Tratner (Bryn Mawr College): "The Bodies in/are *The Waves*."

G-5 Teaching Woolf: New Classrooms, New Contexts
Chair: Beth Rigel Daugherty (Otterbein University)
Kaylee Baucom (College of Southern Nevada): "Who's Afraid of Virginia Woolf in the Community College Classroom?"
Banuta Rubess (University of Toronto): "You're Invited: Performing *Mrs. Dalloway*"
Kelle Mullineaux (Northern Illinois University): "Virginia Woolf, Composition Theorist: How Imagined Audiences Can Wreck a Writer"
Erin Holliday-Karre (Qatar University): "Teaching Woolf in the Middle-East"

G-6 Being, Desire, and Empire
Chair: Harveen Mann (Loyola University Chicago)
Phil Bandy (University of Wisconsin–Milwaukee): "*Between the Acts* and the Moment of Being at the End of Empire"
Alan Chih-chien Hsieh (National Taiwan University): "An Estranged Intimacy with the World: The Post-Colonial Woolf's Ethical Refrain of Planetary Love in *The Voyage Out*"
Sarah Payne (Northeastern University): "Embodiments of Empire in Virginia Woolf's *The Waves*"

G-7 The Sound of the Gramophone, the Sound of War
Chair: Meg Albrinck (Lakeland College)
Zan Cammack (Southern Illinois University–Carbondale): "Gramophones and Trauma in Virginia Woolf's *Between the Acts*"
Tabatha Hibbs (Connors State College): "'They Were Neither One Thing nor the Other': Virginia Woolf and Sound Technology's Challenge to the Subject"
Courtney King (Independent Scholar): "The Sound of War in *Between the Acts*"

11:00 a.m.–12:30 p.m. Concurrent Sessions H
H-1 "Essay Forth! Texting, Contexting, Defining"
Chair: Danielle Glassmeyer (Bradley University)
Leslie Hankins (Cornell College): "Virginia Woolf and Texting in the Twenties: Typography and Title Cards— Moving Pictures/Moving Words"
Diane Gillespie (Washington State University): "Essaying to Publish on the Brink of WWII: The Woolfs and *The Refugees*"
Beth Rigel Daugherty (Otterbein University): "Virginia Woolf: On Essaying the Essay"

H-2 Rethinking Orlando
Chair: Brenda Helt (Independent Scholar)
Todd Nordgren (Northwestern University): "Orlando's Legs: Virginia Woolf's Textual Play between Private and (Inter)national Affairs"
Nina Berman (Loyola University Chicago): "(Re)Thinking Back through *Orlando*'s Reception History"
Georgia Johnston (Saint Louis University): "Storytelling Gender in *Orlando*"

H-3 Philosophical Readings
Chair: Steven J. Venturino (Independent Scholar)
Lisa Coleman (Southeastern Oklahoma State University): "The World(s) Written by 'The Mark on the Wall': Snail Shell as Magic Chrysalis"
Katie Dyson (Loyola University Chicago): "Modernist Intimacy: Ethical Encounters in *Mrs. Dalloway*"
Josh Pfleegor (Bloomsburg University): "Of Woolf, Marx, and Man"

H-4 Woolf's Political Circles
Chair: Ann Martin (University of Saskatchewan)
Deborah Gerrard (De Montfort University): "'Discussed the Universe!' The influence of Edward Carpenter's Immanentist Evolutionary Socialism on the Early Writing of Virginia Stephen (1899–1907)"
Alice Keane (University of Michigan–Ann Arbor): "'A Revision of the Treaty': Bloomsbury's Print Culture, *The Nation and Athenaeum*, and the Problem of German Reparations"
Steven Putzel (Penn State University–Wilkes-Barre): "Leonard Woolf: Writing the World of Palestine, Zionism, and the State of Israel"
Susan Wegener (Southern Connecticut State University): "Processing Prejudice: Writing Woolf's Jewish World"

H-5 The Family and Ways of Knowing
Chair: Shawna Lipton (University of Wisconsin-Milwaukee)
Ann Gibaldi Campbell (Independent Scholar): "Tunneling into the Past: Remembering Mothers in *To the Lighthouse* and Alison Bechdel's *Are You My Mother?*"
Catherine Hollis (University of California–Berkeley): "Walking the World: A Stephen Family Ramble"
Rachel Gaubinger (Princeton University): "Synecdoche, the Family, and *The Years*"

H-6 Woolf Among the "Buggers": Whitman, Pater, Carpenter, Strachey, and Forster
Chair: David Eberly (Independent Scholar)
Patricia Morgne Cramer (University of Connecticut-Stamford): "Neville and Percival: Hellenist Homosexuality in *The Waves*"
David Eberly (Independent Scholar): "What Passes: The Unseen Influence of Edward Carpenter on the Work of Virginia Woolf"
Diana L. Swanson (Northern Illinois University): "Woolf and Forster with Whitman: Homosexuality, Nature, and Democracy"

H-7 Seminar: Bloomsbury Worlds
Seminar Leaders: Urmila Seshagiri (University of Tennessee) and Rishona Zimring (Lewis and Clark College)
Participants: Maggie Humm, Philip Bandy, Helen Harrison, Brandon Truett, Jill Monroe, Adriana Varga, Erica Waters Orzechowski, Kimberley Androlowicz, Matthew Beeber, Erica Delsandro, Justin Ness, Angelica Krajewski, Shannon Rathod, Christine Reynier, Nell Toemen, Judith Allen, Stephanie Kucsera, Mary Harmon

1:00–2:15 p.m. "Performing Woolf: 'A Mark on the Wall'"
Adrianne Krstansky (Brandeis University) and Abigail Killeen (Bowdoin College)
Damen Center Theater (the main level, west side by PNC Bank)

2:30–4:00 p.m. Concurrent Sessions I
I-1 "Civilization" and Empire
Chair: Rishona Zimring (Lewis and Clark College)
Madelyn Detloff (Miami University): "The Precarity of 'Civilization' in Woolf's Creative Worldmaking"
Gretchen Gerzina (Dartmouth College): "Bloomsbury and Empire"
Raghov Kaul (Georgia Institute of Technology): "The Subject-Object Relationship: Using Woolf to Understand Colonial Dichotomies and Postcolonial Critique"
David Fine (Lehigh University): "Teaching Privileges: *Three Guineas* and the Cost of Global Citizenship"

I-2 The Home Front: Socks, Cars, and Civilians
Chair: Evelyn Haller (Doane College)
Jen Holland (Northern Illinois University): "The Power of Socks: Virginia Woolf and the World of War-Craft in *Three Guineas*"

Sarah Eilefson (Loyola University Chicago): "A World Apart: Civilians and War in Virginia Woolf"

Ann Martin (University of Saskatchewan): "Sky Haunting: The British Motor-Car Industry and the World Wars"

I-3 Politics, Aesthetics, and the Disruption of Genre

Chair: Mary Jean Corbett (Miami University)

Meg Albrinck (Lakeland College): "'All kinds of forms in one book': Generic Disruption as Political Act in Virginia Woolf's *Three Guineas*"

Robyn Byrd (Northern Illinois University): "Discourse of the Undivided Mind: The Rhetoric of Woolf's Cultural Critiques"

Aileen Waters (Washington University St. Louis): "Virginia Woolf and the Power of Pretense: The Mass Audience and the Novel Form"

I-4 Natural Worlds, Natural Connections

Chair: Derek Ryan (University of Kent)

Benjamin Bagocius (Indiana University): "Queer Entomology: Virginia Woolf's Butterflies"

Mary McCarthy (Independent Scholar): "The Natural Worlds of Female Initiation in Virginia Woolf's *The Voyage Out* and D. H. Lawrence's *The Lost Girl*"

Kelly Neal (Georgia State University): "'The Little Coloured Ball of Earth': Land, Identity, and Character in *Between the Acts*"

Bonnie Kime Scott (San Diego State University): "Natural Connections: Virginia Woolf and Katherine Mansfield"

I-5 Philosophical Inquiry in/and *To the Lighthouse*

Chair: Wayne Chapman (Clemson University)

Kim Sigouin (Carleton University): "'The Problem of Space': Embodied Language and the Body in Nature in *To the Lighthouse*"

Harriet Calver (Princeton University): "'The emerging monster to whom we are attached': The Style of Woolf's Hybrid World in 'Time Passes'"

Debrah Raschke (Southeast Missouri State University): "'It will be fine tomorrow' Eighty-Six Years Later: Atwood's Dialogue with Woolf"

I-6 Cinematics

Chair: Garry Leonard, University of Toronto

Ting-Ting Chan (Northern Illinois University): "*Mrs. Dalloway* and *Mrs. Dalloway*: A Cross-form Reading of Virginia Woolf's Novel and Its Film Adaptation"

George Derk (University of Virginia): "Cinematic Woolf: Distance, Recording, and Projection in *To the Lighthouse*"

Deirdre Flynn (University of Toronto): "Woolf's Cin-Ethics: Moving through Words to an Other's Time and Space"

I-7 Media and the Public

Chair: Natalie Kalich (Loyola University Chicago)

Brendan Kavanagh (University of Cambridge): "Beyond the Fabrication of 'a rice pudding world, a white counterpane world': Media Ecology as Political Ecology in Woolf's 'Craftsmanship,' *Between the Acts*, and the BBC Broadcast of the 1937 Coronation of George VI"

David Deutsch (University of Alabama): "'They crashed; solved; united': Virginia Woolf and Britain's Cosmopolitan Musical Culture"

Denise Ayo (University of Notre Dame): "Staging (Self-) Censorship: Virginia Woolf's 'Women Must Weep'"

4:30–6:00 p.m. Keynote

Dr. Tuzyline Allan (Baruch College–CUNY)

"The Voyage In, Out, and Beyond: Virginia Woolf After Post colonialism"

Sunday, June 8

9:00–10:30 a.m. Concurrent Sessions J

J-1 Flânerie and City Spaces

Chair: Patricia Morgne Cramer (University of Connecticut–Stamford)

Elizabeth Goetz (City University of New York Graduate Center): "Gendered Flânerie in Virginia Woolf's *Mrs. Dalloway*"

Candis Bond (St. Louis University): "A Model Subject: Fanny Elmer's Transgressive Spatial Practices, Female Identity, and Mapping a New London in *Jacob's Room*"

Yike He (University of Toronto): "Interaction Between Body and City in *Night and Day*"

J-2 Life Writing

Chair: Sherrie Weller (Loyola University Chicago)

Gill Lowe (University Campus Suffolk): "'I am fast locked up': Virginia Woolf's 1897 Journal as Threshold Text"

Jeremy Lakoff (State University of New York–Buffalo): "'She Never Writes Her Own Life': Historiography and Maintenance Labor in Woolf's Writing"

Alice Lowe (Independent Scholar): "Woolf as Memoirist 'I am made and remade continually'"

J-3 Where One Stands: Place and Perspective

Chair: Bonnie Kime Scott (San Diego State University)

Katie Starliper (Bloomsburg University): "Isolation, Ephemerality, and Fear of Place in 'Kew Gardens'"

John McIntyre (University of Prince Edward Island): "'Poor little universe': The Contested Island Setting in *To the Lighthouse*"

Catherine Rush (Independent Scholar): "Portrait and Porpoise: Subject, Standpoint, and Agency in *Freshwater*"

J-4 Ecological Humanism

Chair: Katie Dyson (Loyola University Chicago)

Sarah Dunlap (Ohio State University): "Bound Together: The Global Ecosystem of *The Waves*"

Kevin MacDonnell (St. John's University): "Mesh-with-Self: Language of the In-Between in *The Waves*"

Elsa Högberg (Uppsala University): "Virginia Woolf's Object-Oriented Ontology"

J-5 Seminar: Queering/Cripping Modernism

Seminar Leader: Madelyn Detloff (Miami University)

Participants: Elaine Wood, Dave Coodin, Manya Lempert, Melanie Micir, Courtney King, Sarah Schaefer, Georgia Johnston, Rebecah Pulsifer, Benjamin Hagen, Michael Tratner, Steph Brown, Alexandra DeLuise, Christine Iwanecki, Archana Kaku, Lauren Benke, Maren Linnett, Nathalie Duthroy, Nancy Goldberger

11:00 a.m.–12:30 p.m. Concurrent Sessions K

K-1 Shakespeare's Sisters?

Chair: Georgia Johnston (St. Louis University)

Mary Lamb Shelden (Virginia Commonwealth University): "A Regular Shakespeare's Sister: Alcott and Woolf on the Subject of Women's Genius"

Susan Stanford Friedman (University of Wisconsin-Madison): "Before and After *A Room of One's Own*: Shakespeare's Sister in India"

K-2 Opposing War by Other Means

Chair: Christine Froula (Northwestern University)

Arturo Chang (DePaul University): "*Orlando* as Critique of Realist International Politics and Domestic Patriarchy"

Mary Jean Corbett (Miami University): "Opposing War by Other Means: Vernon Lee and Virginia Woolf in Dialogue"

Charlotte Taylor-Suppe (King's College London): "Raising an Army: Mothering and the Great War in *Jacob's Room* and 'A Society'"

K-3 Connectivity, Cosmology, Cognition

Chair: Naomi Gades (Loyola University Chicago)

Melba Cuddy-Keane (University of Toronto): "Mind-Wandering and Mindfulness: Neural Connectivity in *Mrs. Dalloway* and *To the Lighthouse*"

Gerald Maki (Ivy Tech Community College): "An Eclipsed Consciousness: Virginia Woolf and Sir Arthur Eddington's Cosmological Idealism"

Jessica Mason McFadden (Western Illinois University): "Woolf's Alternative Medicine: Queer Cognition, Narrative Defiance, and the Undoing of Diagnosis"

Appendix

VIRGINIA WOOLF CONFERENCE EXHIBIT ITEMS
NEWBERRY LIBRARY
Wednesday June 4, 3:00–4:30, Liesl Olson and Mark Hussey
Thursday, June 5, 10:00–11:30, Liesl Olson

Group I: Bloomsbury and the Visual Arts in Chicago

1. Arts Club Papers, Catalog of An Exhibition of Original Drawings by Pablo Picasso with an Introduction by Clive Bell, 1923
Arts Club Papers, Series 1, Box 1, Folder 21
In folder with the correspondence about this exhibit among Harshe, Roullier, Prince Argotinsky, etc.

2. Arts Club Papers, Letter from Clive Bell to Alice Roullier, 1930
Arts Club Papers, Series 5, Box 2, Folder 29
"The fact is I have asked that little German paintress, whom I was to pilot—and who has ceased suddenly to be a fuzzy little art-student and become an elegant and entourée cinema-actress—to lunch on Monday. She is amiable and simple, nowise remarkable, shall I bring her? I shan't be in the least surprised if you say no: only in that case I can't come—for I never let women down. Please make a note of that."

3. Arts Club Papers, Letter from Clive Bell to Bobsy Goodspeed, 1939
Arts Club Papers, Series 1, Box 24, Folder 394
Regarding an exhibit of Vanessa Bell's and Duncan Grant's work (which didn't take place). Rishona Zimring makes the point that the Arts Club was advocating British modernism before the Second World War alongside the European avant-garde. The club exhibited Fry's work, for instance, in 1933.

4. Catalog of the International Exhibition of Modern Art (Armory Show) at the Art Institute of Chicago
Case N5015. A8 1913
Owned by Alice Roullier. Inside front cover: "Went with Alice & Will Henderson & Roland Young of Welch players.—"Hindle Wake's"= After all had dinner at Tip Top Inn then back to WPH studio. (Alice Roullier) Per R.W.S."

Group II: Print cultures in Chicago

5. *Recent Paintings By Vanessa Bell* with a Foreword by Virginia Woolf (The London Artists Association, 1930).
Case VV 1145 .087
Plain binding, slim book, interest is that it was owned by Morton Dauwen Zabel.

6. Virginia Woolf, *The Captain's Death Bed* (New York: Harcourt Brace and Company, 1950)
Case PR 6045. 072 C3 1950b
Vanessa Bell designed cover; published posthumously; price tag from Carson Pirie Scott & Co. $3 (Chicago department store with a book department with new literature); gift of Palmer Dawson. The book would have been owned by Dawson family—important Chicago family that included poet Mitchell Dawson and painter Manierre Dawson.

7. Fanny Butcher Papers, Guestbook
Box 36, Folder 1565
Begins Feb 9, 1920. Signed by such figures as Padraic Column, Eunice Tietjens (Feb 28, 1920); W.B. Yeats (March 1); Carl Sandburg (March 8), who writes: "Next to a real restaurant what is more holy

than a real bookshop? May the spiders be a long while getting this one of Fanny Butcher—"; Alfred Kreymbourg (March 9) who writes "Nice to follow Carl, though I'm a day late"; Harriet Monroe "St. Patrick's Day!" Menken and Edna Ferber both visit on June 7, 1920. Mencken writes: "Your prayers, ladies and gents, are laughable/horrible! I practice the worst of trades in the worst of cities in the worst of countries at the worst time in the history of the worst of possible worlds." Ferber writes: "I like my job. I like Chicago. I like 1920 A.D. I even like Mencken, the misanthrope. Pollyanna." Edgar Lee Masters (July 2, 1920); W.S. Maughn (October 19); Sherwood Anderson (sometime in 1920, when he first met Hemingway); Sinclair Lewis (Feb 17); Floyd Dell (who writes that his residence is Croton on Hudson); Willa Cather (Aug. 31, 1921); Aldous Huxley (May 15, 1925). Ends in 1927. Peters out—only a few names each year after 1920/21.

8. Will Ransom Papers, Correspondence with Hogarth Press
Box 36, Folders 1240, 1241
F 1240 Correspondence with Hogarth Press, including booklet "Complete Catalogue of the Hogarth Press," cover designed by V. Bell: includes all books of first 12 years, 1917–1928. In "Forward," notes that the press's second publication was Mansfield's *Prelude*.
F 1241 Catalogs of books to be published by Hogarth Press, as well as advertisements for particular books and series ("Hogarth Living Poets Series"; "Virginia Woolf New Uniform Edition"), 1929–1931. Having all of these catalogs collected together is a rarity. The New Uniform Edition of VW includes *The Voyage Out, Jacob's Room, Mrs. Dalloway, The Common Reader* and says "Of these books *Jacob's Room* and *Mrs. Dalloway* have been out of print for some time."

Group III: Woolf First Editions

9. Virginia Woolf, *The Voyage Out* (London: Duckworth & Co., 1915)
Case oPR 6045 . 072 V68 1915
Green binding; interesting in that this first novel was published by Gerald Duckworth, VW's half-brother. The title page has name of publisher (Duckworth & Co.) and woodcut design of flower with the word "Desormais" (translation from French would mean 'henceforth')—very arts and crafts.

10. Virginia Woolf, *A Room of One's Own* (New York: The Fountain Press; London: The Hogarth Press, 1929)
Case Y 0895. 978
Not particularly interesting in terms of binding, no dust jacket, but signed by Virginia Woolf in purple ink. #164 of 492 copies printed by Robert S. Josephy in October 1929—all signed (see note in back of book). Josephy was a New York designer; Fountain Press was his fine press (beautiful paper); colophon says book was printed for both FP and Hogarth. 100 copies were probably for Hogarth; the rest for Random House.

11. Virginia Woolf, *A Haunted House* (London: Hogarth Press, 1943).
Case PR 6045.072 H3 1943
Vanessa Bell designed cover; book printed during the war and after VW's death, collects stories from *Monday or Tuesday* with new stories; dustjacket back flap advertisement for BBC, which brings people "the truth from London."

12. Virginia Woolf, *Street Haunting* (San Francisco: The Westgate Press, 1930)
Wing ZP 983 .G7565
Limited Edition of 500 copies printed in San Francisco; Signed in purple by Woolf.
The printer—Grabhorn (noted inside)—is the biggest, most important West Coast fine press printer; they are treating Woolf as a canonical writer. They were also printing Chaucer, Verlaine, etc. This book was bought at auction in 1947 under Stanley Pargellis in a purchase that included *A Room of One's Own* (item 10) and books by Aldington, Beerom, e. e. cummings, Dawson, Gissing, Huxley, Rebecca West, and more.

Group IV: Katherine Mansfield Papers

13. Photograph of Katherine Mansfield, undated
Mansfield Papers, Box 3, Folder 13
On back: "I took this when K.M. was convalescent at Rottingham—L.M" "LM" are the initials of Mansfield's girlhood friend from school who always steps in when Mansfield needs help. Her name was Ida Baker; they had made up names for one another and "Lesley Moore" is what she made up. Photo shows Mansfield standing outside in white blouse and long skirt, looking askance—very beautiful; less stylized.

14. Photograph of Katherine Mansfield, undated
Mansfield Papers, Box 3, Folder 14
Inscribed: "Dear Sullivan / I am / your long friend / Katherine Mansfield"; studio portrait shows her in modern dress with bobbed hair. This is the photo that went on her collected stories and other publications.

15. Katherine Mansfield Papers, June 1917 letter describing party
Mansfield Papers, Box 6, Folder 43
June 1917, typed letter describing a party held by Mary Hutchinson. "Greaves" is Robert Graves. "Mary, of course, went all out for Roger Fry and Robby Ross, with an eye on Greaves and an eyebrow on T. Eliot....." Also describes how she liked T.S. Eliot. (Most of her letters to Ottoline Morrell are handwritten—this is more rare). (At this point, KM is refashioning *The Aloe* into *Prelude*; *Prufrock* has been circulated.) This letter is published. Not all of them are. (One of the Mansfield scholars guessed that this was Middleton Murray's typing of Mansfield's letters because there are blanks that he left, and then filled in with pencil—figuring out what he couldn't read.)

16. Katherine Mansfield Papers, Notebook
Mansfield Papers, Box I, Folder 43
Notebook #1: There are many other notebooks in the collection, most not as nice as this one, in which Mansfield has transcribed her poems (not drafts) and what looks like a play. She marked which poems appeared in which journals. Interesting in how she collects them together.

17. Katherine Mansfield Papers, Desk Blotter
Mansfield Papers, Box 3, Folder 21
Desk Blotter—with ribbon and embroidered cover

Not on display (fragile):

Manuscript of Mansfield's *The Aloe*
Box 1, Folder 1

Manuscript of Mansfield's *Bliss*
Box 1, Folder 3

*Prelude is a reworking of *The Aloe*—*Prelude* was published by the Hogarth Press (their second publication, in 1917). Newberry has first editions of *Prelude* but in very fragile condition.

*Mansfield Papers were a gift from Jane Warner Dick, a collector and friend of the Newberry, in 1959. She started collecting Mansfield's work when she first read it—in the 1920s—because she was so moved by Mansfield's stories. Mansfield's manuscripts and correspondence went on the market pretty soon after Mansfield's death—Middleton Murray wanted it to go to the British Museum or to New Zealand. (Some of it did). But much went to American dealers too. James Wells, who was then a curator at the Newberry, had a particular interest in Bloomsbury. Another big collection of Mansfield material is in New Zealand (Alexander Turnbull Library) but it is largely correspondence while Newberry's collection has much manuscript material.